SpringBoard®
English
Language Arts

STUDENT EDITION   GRADE 8

ABOUT THE COLLEGE BOARD

The College Board is a mission-driven not-for-profit organization that connects students to college success and opportunity. Founded in 1900, the College Board was created to expand access to higher education. Today, the membership association is made up of more than 6,000 of the world's leading educational institutions and is dedicated to promoting excellence and equity in education. Each year, the College Board helps more than seven million students prepare for a successful transition to college through programs and services in college readiness and college success—including the SAT® and the Advanced Placement Program®. The organization also serves the education community through research and advocacy on behalf of students, educators and schools. For further information, visit www.collegeboard.org.

ISBN: 978-1-4573-0837-6

1 2 3 4 5 6 7 8   18 19 20 21 22 23 24
Printed in the United States of America

ACKNOWLEDGMENTS

The College Board gratefully acknowledges the outstanding work of the classroom teachers and writers who have been integral to the development of this revised program. The end product is testimony to their expertise, understanding of student learning needs, and dedication to rigorous and accessible English Language Arts instruction.

Colleen Ancrile
English Teacher
Los Angeles Unified School District
Sun Valley, California

Leia Bell
English Teacher
Hillsborough County Public Schools
Tampa, Florida

Alli Bennett
Assistant Principal
Bethel School District 403
Spanaway, Washington

Jessica Brockman
English Teacher
Hillsborough County Public Schools
Tampa, Florida

Kirstin A. Daniels
English Teacher
Sunnyside Unified School District
Tucson, Arizona

Paul DeMaret
SpringBoard/AP English Teacher
Poudre School District
Fort Collins, Colorado

Allison Fonseca
English Teacher
Hillsborough County Public Schools
Tampa, Florida

Karen Fullam
Advanced Academics Coordinator
Hillsborough County Public Schools
Tampa, Florida

Ron Lybarger
English Teacher/Department Head
Decatur Public School District #61
Decatur, Illinois

Glenn Morgan
English Teacher
San Diego Unified School District
San Diego, California

Michelle Nellon
English Teacher
Los Angeles Unified School District
Sun Valley, California

Carmen P. Padilla, M.Ed.
English Teacher
Los Angeles Unified School District
Los Angeles, California

Bryan Craig Sandala
6–12 ELA Specialist
School District of Palm Beach County
West Palm Beach, Florida

Stephanie Sharpe
English Teacher
Hillsborough County Public Schools
Tampa, Florida

Holly Talley
Writing Coach
Hillsborough County Public Schools
Ruskin, Florida

Susan Van Doren
English/AP English Language/AP
Computer Science Teacher
Douglas County School District
Zephyr Cove, Nevada

Rebecca Wenrich
English Teacher
Peninsula School District 401
Gig Harbor, Washington

Tom Wilkins
English Teacher
Fayette County Public Schools
Lexington, Kentucky

SPRINGBOARD ENGLISH LANGUAGE ARTS

Lori O'Dea
Executive Director
Content Development

Doug Waugh
Executive Director
Product Management

Joely Negedly
Senior Director
Humanities Curriculum and Instruction

JoEllen Victoreen
Senior Product Manager
English Language Arts

Julie Manley
Senior Director
Professional Learning

Sarah Balistreri
Director
ELA Content Development

Eden Orlando
SpringBoard District Coach

Jacquelyn Gomez
District Instructional Coach

Jennifer Duva
English Language Arts Editor

Rebecca Grudzina
English Language Arts Editor

Spencer Gonçalves
Associate Director
SpringBoard Content Development

RESEARCH AND PLANNING ADVISORS

We also wish to thank the members of our SpringBoard Advisory Council and the many educators who gave generously of their time and their ideas as we conducted research for both the print and online programs. Your suggestions and reactions to ideas helped immeasurably as we planned the revisions. We gratefully acknowledge the teachers and administrators in the following districts.

Bellevue School District 405
Bellevue, Washington

Fresno Unified School District
Fresno, California

Hawaii State Department of Education
Honolulu, Hawaii

Hillsborough County Public Schools
Tampa, Florida

Kenton County School District
Fort Wright, Kentucky

Los Angeles Unified School District
Los Angeles, California

Milwaukee Public Schools
Milwaukee, Wisconsin

Newton County Schools
Covington, Georgia

Noblesville Schools
Noblesville, Indiana

Orange County Public Schools
Orlando, Florida

Quakertown Community School District
Quakertown, Pennsylvania

St. Vrain School District
Longmont, Colorado

San José Unified School District
San José, California

Scottsdale Public Schools
Phoenix, Arizona

Seminole County Public Schools
Sanford, Florida

Spokane Public Schools
Spokane, Washington

Sunnyside Unified School District
Tucson, Arizona

Contents

Unit 1 | The Challenge of Heroism

Activities

Unit 2   The Challenge of Utopia

Activities

Unit 3 | The Challenge to Make a Difference

Activities

Unit 4 The Challenge of Comedy

Activities

Resources

Texts not included in these materials.

To the Student

WELCOME TO SPRINGBOARD!

Dear Student,

Welcome to the SpringBoard program! This program has been created with you in mind: it contains the English Language Arts content you need to learn, the tools to help you learn, and tasks to strengthen the critical thinking skills that prepare you for high school and beyond.

In SpringBoard, you will explore compelling themes through reading, writing, discussions, performances, and research. You will closely read short stories, novels, poems, historical texts, and articles. You'll also view and interpret films, plays, and audio texts while comparing them to their related print versions. With frequent opportunities to write creatively and analytically throughout the program, you will develop fluency, research skills, and an understanding of how to craft your writing based on audience and purpose. Through collaborative discussions, presentations, performances, and debates with your peers, you will deepen your understanding of the texts you've read and viewed and learn how to convey your ideas with clarity and voice.

Tools to help you learn are built into every lesson. At the beginning of each activity, you will see suggested learning strategies, each of which is explained in full in the Resources section of your book. These strategies will help you deeply analyze text, collect evidence for your writing, and critically think about and discuss issues and ideas. Within the activities, you'll also notice explanations about essential vocabulary and grammar concepts that will enrich your ability to read and write effectively.

With high school right around the corner, now is the time to challenge yourself to develop skills and habits you need to be successful throughout your academic career. The SpringBoard program provides you with meaningful and engaging activities built on the rigorous standards that lead to high school, college, and career success. Your participation in SpringBoard will help you advance your reading, writing, language, and speaking and listening skills, all while helping you build confidence in your ability to succeed academically.

We hope you enjoy learning with the SpringBoard program. It will give you many opportunities to explore ideas and issues collaboratively and independently and to cultivate new skills as you prepare for your future.

Sincerely,

SpringBoard

AP CONNECTIONS

When you reach high school, you may have an opportunity to take Advanced Placement (AP) classes or other rigorous courses. When the time comes to make that decision, we want you to be equipped with the kind of higher-order thinking skills, knowledge, and behaviors necessary to be successful in AP classes and beyond. You will see connections to AP in the texts that you read, the strategies you use, and the writing tasks you encounter throughout the course.

Connections to AP Language and Literature will help you

- Read closely and analyze both literary and nonfiction texts

- Analyze relationships among author's purpose, literary/stylistic devices, rhetorical appeals, and desired effects for intended audiences

- Write with attention to selecting textual evidence and organizational patterns according to purpose and audience

- Write to interpret and evaluate multiple perspectives in literature

- Develop the control of language and command of conventions required for academic writing

PSAT/SAT CONNECTIONS

Sometime during the course of your academic career, you will likely be expected to take a college readiness test like the PSAT or SAT. Many colleges require applicants to submit SAT scores along with their school transcripts and essays, and a good PSAT score can lead to scholarships and other awards. The SAT suite is designed to predict which students are on track to leave secondary school and enter college or a career. Your SpringBoard ELA coursework will help you succeed on the Reading, Writing and Language, and Essay tests.

The PSAT/SAT will require you to:

- Read, analyze, and use reasoning to comprehend challenging literary and informational texts to demonstrate and expand your knowledge and understanding.

- Revise and edit texts for expression of ideas and to show facility with a core set of grammar, usage, and punctuation conventions.

- Make careful and considered use of evidence as you read and write.

- Reveal an understanding of relevant words in context and of how word choice helps shape meaning and tone.

THE SPRINGBOARD DIFFERENCE

SpringBoard is different because it provides instruction with hands-on participation that involves you and your classmates in daily discussions and analysis of what you're reading and learning. You will have an opportunity to

- Discuss and collaborate with your peers to explore and express your ideas

- Explore multiple perspectives by reading a variety of texts—both fiction and nonfiction—that introduce you to different ways of thinking, writing, and communicating

- Examine writing from the perspective of a reader and writer and learn techniques that good writers use to communicate their message effectively

- Gain a deep understanding of topics, enabling you to apply your learning to new and varied situations

- Take ownership of your learning by practicing and selecting strategies that work for you

- Reflect on your growth and showcase your best work as a reader, writer, speaker, and listener in a working Portfolio

MIDDLE SCHOOL AT A GLANCE
Grade 6

SpringBoard grade 6 is developed around the thematic concept of **change**. During the year, you will learn how writers use that theme to tell stories in poetry, short stories, and nonfiction texts. Among the many authors whose work you will read is Langston Hughes, a famous writer who was part of the Harlem Renaissance. Sharon Creech explores change resulting from the loss of a parent in her novel *Walk Two Moons*. Gary Soto and Sandra Cisneros tell vivid stories about the awkward changes that can be part of growing up. John Steinbeck takes you on a trip around the country with his dog, Charley. Scenes from one of William Shakespeare's plays take you into the world of drama. As you read these texts and make connections to experiences in your own life, you will begin to see how writers use the details of everyday life to create stories that we all enjoy.

Reading and writing go hand in hand, and SpringBoard grade 6 gives you opportunities to write your own stories (narrative writing), explain information (explanatory writing), and create an argument to persuade an audience (argumentative writing). Specific strategies for writing and revising support your writing efforts from planning to drafting, revising, and editing. You will be writing a personal narrative and a short story, essays in which you share your ideas about a fictional story and a real-life story, and an argumentative letter to persuade others to support your position on an issue.

You will also be asked to deepen your understanding by analyzing how film presents a topic and by conducting research on topics of interest. In this grade you will view a video biography of Temple Grandin while also reading about her life and how she has coped with autism.

Grade 7

In SpringBoard grade 7, you will investigate the thematic concept of **choice**. All of us make choices every day. Some of those choices have a short-term impact (like what to have for lunch), while others have a greater impact (like whether to study in school or to goof off!). By reading from his autobiography, you will learn about Nelson Mandela's choice to fight segregation in South Africa—even though it meant going to jail. A famous poem by Robert Frost, the novel *Tangerine*, Sojourner Truth's historic speech on slavery, and a drama by Shakespeare all show you the choices that real and imaginary characters make and how those choices affect their lives. Close reading strategies will help you to determine what each text says explicitly and to make logical inferences from what it does not say explicitly. Writing and speaking will focus on text-based evidence. For example, you and your peers will write a literary analysis of a novel and include findings from research to

produce a multimedia biographical presentation. Much like in 6th grade, you will be asked to write in narrative, explanatory, and argumentative modes.

You will also look at print texts and then examine how those same texts are portrayed in performances. You will get to star in a performance of a scene from another of Shakespeare's plays.

Grade 8

In SpringBoard grade 8, units of study focus on the theme of **challenge**. Among the many texts that you will read are an essay about Civil War heroes, narratives about the Holocaust, a novel and short story by Ray Bradbury, Elie Wiesel's Nobel Prize acceptance speech, poetry by Walt Whitman, and a play by Shakespeare.

These texts take you into the world of heroes—both everyday heroes and extraordinary ones—who face challenges and take actions to overcome them. You will learn about the archetype of "hero," which is a model that writers follow in creating stories about heroes. Writing and speaking opportunities are varied and engaging. For example, you will write a hero's journey narrative about a hero of your choice, along with essays and an argument that presents your position on an issue in a compelling way. Using research on an issue of national or global significance, you will create an informative multimedia presentation. Viewing film is also a part of researching and analyzing what authors are communicating. As part of studying comedy and Shakespeare, you will analyze scenes from the play *A Midsummer Night's Dream* and then view those scenes in film to determine how and why a film director may have changed the scenes.

CLASSROOM TOOLS

As you move through each SpringBoard unit, your teacher will guide you to use tools that will help you develop strong study habits, keep your work organized, and track your learning progress.

Reader/Writer Notebook

Your **Reader/Writer Notebook** is a place to record and keep track of vocabulary words, grammar practice, notes and reflections on readings, some writing assignments, brainstorms, and other items as determined by your teacher. You will use your Reader/Writer Notebook often, so think of it as an extension of the main SpringBoard book.

Word Wall

Your teacher will regularly add new vocabulary words to the class **Word Wall**. The Word Wall gives you and your classmates a visual reminder of the words you are learning throughout the unit of study. Also, you can use the Word Wall to easily check the spelling of new words.

Performance Portfolio

Your **Performance Portfolio** is a place to keep your assignments organized so that you can see your growth and learning across the school year. Keeping a portfolio will make it easier to share your work with others, reflect on what you are learning, revise certain pieces of work, and set goals for future learning.

Your teacher will guide you to include items in your portfolio that illustrate a wide range of work, such as first drafts, final drafts, quickwrites, notes, reading logs, graphic organizers, audio and video examples, and graphics that represent a variety of genres, forms, and media created for a multitude of purposes. As you progress through the course, you will have opportunities to revisit prior work, revise it based on new learning, and reflect on the learning strategies and activities that help you be successful.

Independent Reading

Based on your personal interests and preferences, you will be encouraged to select books, articles, and other texts to read independently. Reading independently not only reinforces the learning you're doing in class, but it also gives you a chance to expand your knowledge about topics that fascinate you.

You can find **Independent Reading Lists** in the Resources section at the back of your book. The lists provide ideas for texts that complement the reading you're doing in each SpringBoard unit. These are suggestions to get you started, but you may also choose other readings with input from your teacher, family, and peers.

While you work your way through each SpringBoard unit, your teacher will give you time to read independently. You can record general thoughts or reactions to your independent reading in the **Independent Reading Log** in the Resources section of your book. You may also use the Independent Reading Log to respond to the occasional **Independent Reading Links** that you'll encounter in each SpringBoard unit. These links prompt you to think about your independent reading by responding to questions, doing research, making connections between texts and themes, discussing ideas in book groups, and recommending titles to your classmates.

We hope you enjoy exploring the texts, topics, and themes in SpringBoard and that you feel inspired to deepen your reading, writing, speaking, and analytic skills through the program.

College and Career Readiness Standards

Reading Standards for Literature

Key Ideas and Details	RL.8.1	Cite the textual evidence that most strongly supports an analysis of what the text says explicitly as well as inferences drawn from the text.
	RL.8.2	Determine a theme or central idea of a text and analyze its development over the course of the text, including its relationship to the characters, setting, and plot; provide an objective summary of the text.
	RL.8.3	Analyze how particular lines of dialogue or incidents in a story or drama propel the action, reveal aspects of a character, or provoke a decision.
Craft and Structure	RL.8.4	Determine the meaning of words and phrases as they are used in a text, including figurative and connotative meanings; analyze the impact of specific word choices on meaning and tone, including analogies or allusions to other texts.
	RL.8.5	Compare and contrast the structure of two or more texts and analyze how the differing structure of each text contributes to its meaning and style.
	RL.8.6	Analyze how differences in the points of view of the characters and the audience or reader (e.g., created through the use of dramatic irony) create such effects as suspense or humor.
Integration of Knowledge and Ideas	RL.8.7	Analyze the extent to which a filmed or live production of a story or drama stays faithful to or departs from the text or script, evaluating the choices made by the director or actors.
	RL.8.8	(Not applicable to literature)
	RL.8.9	Analyze how a modern work of fiction draws on themes, patterns of events, or character types from myths, traditional stories, or religious works such as the Bible, including describing how the material is rendered new.
Range of Reading and Text Complexity	RL.8.10	By the end of the year, read and comprehend literature, including stories, dramas, and poems, at the high end of grades 6–8 text complexity band independently and proficiently.

Reading Standards for Informational Text

Key Ideas and Details	RI.8.1	Cite the textual evidence that most strongly supports an analysis of what the text says explicitly as well as inferences drawn from the text.
	RI.8.2	Determine a central idea of a text and analyze its development over the course of the text, including its relationship to supporting ideas; provide an objective summary of the text.
	RI.8.3	Analyze how a text makes connections among and distinctions between individuals, ideas, or events (e.g., through comparisons, analogies, or categories).
Craft and Structure	RI.8.4	Determine the meaning of words and phrases as they are used in a text, including figurative, connotative, and technical meanings; analyze the impact of specific word choices on meaning and tone, including analogies or allusions to other texts.
	RI.8.5	Analyze in detail the structure of a specific paragraph in a text, including the role of particular sentences in developing and refining a key concept.
	RI.8.6	Determine an author's point of view or purpose in a text and analyze how the author acknowledges and responds to conflicting evidence or viewpoints.
Integration of Knowledge and Ideas	RI.8.7	Evaluate the advantages and disadvantages of using different mediums (e.g., print or digital text, video, multimedia) to present a particular topic or idea.
	RI.8.8	Delineate and evaluate the argument and specific claims in a text, assessing whether the reasoning is sound and the evidence is relevant and sufficient; recognize when irrelevant evidence is introduced.
	RI.8.9	Analyze a case in which two or more texts provide conflicting information on the same topic and identify where the texts disagree on matters of fact or interpretation.
Range of Reading and Text Complexity	RI.8.10	By the end of the year, read and comprehend literary nonfiction at the high end of the grades 6–8 text complexity band independently and proficiently.

Writing Standards

Text Types and Purposes	W.8.1	Write arguments to support claims with clear reasons and relevant evidence.
	W.8.1a	Introduce claim(s), acknowledge and distinguish the claim(s) from alternate or opposing claims, and organize the reasons and evidence logically.
	W.8.1b	Support claim(s) with logical reasoning and relevant evidence, using accurate, credible sources and demonstrating an understanding of the topic or text.
	W.8.1c	Use words, phrases, and clauses to create cohesion and clarify the relationships among claim(s), counterclaims, reasons, and evidence.
	W.8.1d	Establish and maintain a formal style.
	W.8.1e	Provide a concluding statement or section that follows from and supports the argument presented.
	W.8.2	Write informative/explanatory texts, to examine a topic and convey ideas, concepts, and information through the selection, organization, and analysis of relevant content.
	W.8.2a	Introduce a topic clearly, previewing what is to follow; organize ideas, concepts, and information into broader categories; include formatting (e.g., headings), graphics (e.g., charts, tables), and multimedia when useful to aiding comprehension.
	W.8.2b	Develop the topic with relevant, well-chosen facts, definitions, concrete details, quotations, or other information and examples.
	W.8.2c	Use appropriate and varied transitions to create cohesion and clarify the relationships among ideas and concepts.
	W.8.2d	Use precise language and domain-specific vocabulary to inform about or explain the topic.
	W.8.2e	Establish and maintain a formal style.
	W.8.2f	Provide a concluding statement or section that follows from and supports the information or explanation presented.
	W.8.3	Write narratives to develop real or imagined experiences or events using effective technique, relevant descriptive details, and well-structured event sequences.
	W.8.3a	Engage and orient the reader by establishing a context and point of view and introducing a narrator and/or characters; organize an event sequence that unfolds naturally and logically.

Writing Standards

Text Types and Purposes	W.8.3b	Use narrative techniques, such as dialogue, pacing, description, and reflection, to develop experiences, events, and/or characters.
	W.8.3c	Use a variety of transition words, phrases, and clauses to convey sequence, signal shifts from one time frame or setting to another, and show the relationships among experiences and events.
	W.8.3d	Use precise words and phrases, relevant descriptive details, and sensory language to capture the action and convey experiences and events.
	W.8.3e	Provide a conclusion that follows from and reflects on the narrated experiences or events.
Production and Distribution of Writing	W.8.4	Produce clear and coherent writing in which the development, organization, and style are appropriate to task, purpose, and audience. (Grade-specific expectations for writing types are defined in standards 1–3 above.)
	W.8.5	With some guidance and support from peers and adults, develop and strengthen writing as needed by planning, revising, editing, rewriting, or trying a new approach, focusing on how well purpose and audience have been addressed. (Editing for conventions should demonstrate command of Language standards 1–3 up to and including grade 8.)
	W.8.6	Use technology, including the Internet, to produce and publish writing and present the relationships between information and ideas efficiently as well as to interact and collaborate with others.
Research to Build and Present Knowledge	W.8.7	Conduct short research projects to answer a question (including a self-generated question), drawing on several sources and generating additional related, focused questions that allow for multiple avenues of exploration.
	W.8.8	Gather relevant information from multiple print and digital sources, using search terms effectively; assess the credibility and accuracy of each source; and quote or paraphrase the data and conclusions of others while avoiding plagiarism and following a standard format for citation.
	W.8.9	Draw evidence from literary or informational texts to support analysis, reflection, and research.
	W.8.9a	Apply grade 8 Reading standards to literature (e.g., "Analyze how a modern work of fiction draws on themes, patterns of events, or character types from myths, traditional stories, or religious works such as the Bible, including describing how the material is rendered new").
	W.8.9b	Apply grade 8 Reading standards to literary nonfiction (e.g., "Delineate and evaluate the argument and specific claims in a text, assessing whether the reasoning is sound and the evidence is relevant and sufficient; recognize when irrelevant evidence is introduced").
Range of Writing	W.8.10	Write routinely over extended time frames (time for research, reflection, and revision) and shorter time frames (a single sitting or a day or two) for a range of discipline-specific tasks, purposes, and audiences.

Speaking and Listening Standards

Comprehension and Collaboration	SL.8.1	Engage effectively in a range of collaborative discussions (one-on-one, in groups, and teacher-led) with diverse partners on grade 8 topics, texts, and issues, building on others' ideas and expressing their own clearly.
	SL.8.1a	Come to discussions prepared, having read or researched material under study; explicitly draw on that preparation by referring to evidence on the topic, text, or issue to probe and reflect on ideas under discussion.
	SL.8.1b	Follow rules for collegial discussions and decision-making, track progress toward specific goals and deadlines, and define individual roles as needed.
	SL.8.1c	Pose questions that connect the ideas of several speakers and respond to others' questions and comments with relevant evidence, observations, and ideas.
	SL.8.1d	Acknowledge new information expressed by others, and, when warranted, qualify or justify their own views in light of the evidence presented.
	SL.8.2	Analyze the purpose of information presented in diverse media and formats (e.g., visually, quantitatively, orally) and evaluate the motives (e.g., social, commercial, political) behind its presentation.
	SL.8.3	Delineate a speaker's argument and specific claims, evaluating the soundness of the reasoning and relevance and sufficiency of the evidence and identifying when irrelevant evidence is introduced.
Presentation of Knowledge and Ideas	SL.8.4	Present claims and findings emphasizing salient points in a focused, coherent manner with relevant evidence, sound valid reasoning, and well-chosen details; use appropriate eye contact, adequate volume, and clear pronunciation.
	SL.8.5	Integrate multimedia and visual displays into presentations to clarify information, strengthen claims and evidence, and add interest.
	SL.8.6	Adapt speech to a variety of contexts and tasks, demonstrating command of formal English when indicated or appropriate. (See grade 8 Language standards 1 and 3 for specific expectations.)

Language Standards

Conventions of Standard English	L.8.1	Demonstrate command of the conventions of standard English grammar and usage when writing or speaking.
	L.8.1a	Explain the function of verbals (gerunds, participles, infinitives) in general and their function in particular sentences.
	L.8.1b	Form and use verbs in the active and passive voice.
	L.8.1c	Form and use verbs in the indicative, imperative, interrogative, conditional, and subjunctive mood.
	L.8.1d	Recognize and correct inappropriate shifts in verb voice and mood.
	L.8.2	Demonstrate command of the conventions of standard English capitalization, punctuation, and spelling when writing.
	L.8.2a	Use punctuation (comma, ellipsis, dash) to indicate a pause or break.
	L.8.2b	Use an ellipsis to indicate an omission.
	L.8.2c	Spell correctly.
Knowledge of Language	L.8.3	Use knowledge of language and its conventions when writing, speaking, reading, or listening.
	L.8.3a	Use verbs in the active and passive voice and in the conditional and subjunctive mood to achieve particular effects (e.g., emphasizing the actor or the action; expressing uncertainty or describing a state contrary to fact).
Vocabulary Acquisition and Use	L.8.4	Determine or clarify the meaning of unknown and multiple-meaning words or phrases based on grade 8 reading and content, choosing flexibly from a range of strategies.
	L.8.4a	Use context (e.g., the overall meaning of a sentence or paragraph; a word's position or function in a sentence) as a clue to the meaning of a word or phrase.
	L.8.4b	Use common, grade-appropriate Greek or Latin affixes and roots as clues to the meaning of a word (e.g., precede, recede, secede).
	L.8.4c	Consult general and specialized reference materials (e.g., dictionaries, glossaries, thesauruses), both print and digital, to find the pronunciation of a word or determine or clarify its precise meaning or its part of speech.
	L.8.4d	Verify the preliminary determination of the meaning of a word or phrase (e.g., by checking the inferred meaning in context or in a dictionary).

Language Standards

Vocabulary Acquisition and Use	L.8.5	Demonstrate understanding of figurative language, word relationships, and nuances in word meanings.
	L.8.5a	Interpret figures of speech (e.g. verbal irony, puns) in context.
	L.8.5b	Use the relationship between particular words to better understand each of the words.
	L.8.5c	Distinguish among the connotations (associations) of words with similar denotations (definitions) (e.g., bullheaded, willful, firm, persistent, resolute).
	L.8.6	Acquire and use accurately grade-appropriate general academic and domain-specific words and phrases; gather vocabulary knowledge when considering a word or phrase important to comprehension or expression.

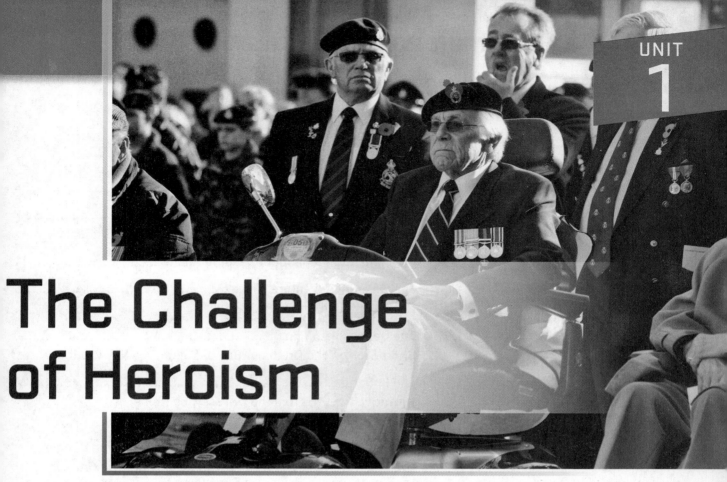

The Challenge of Heroism

Visual Prompt: What do you picture when you hear the word *hero*? What words and images immediately come to mind?

Unit Overview

This unit focuses on the challenges of *heroism*. Because this word is used every day—in television shows, movies, video games, books, the news, school, and conversations—we rarely take time to actually think about what it means. In this unit, you will research, read, and write to develop a more complex understanding of this important societal and cultural concept.

The Challenge of Heroism

GOALS:

- To create and present an original illustrated narrative based on the Hero's Journey archetype
- To analyze and synthesize a variety of texts to develop an original definition of *hero*
- To analyze and evaluate explanatory texts for ideas, structure, and language
- To develop explanatory texts using strategies of definition

ACADEMIC VOCABULARY

context
concise
nuance
function
negation
coherence

Literary Terms

archetype
imagery
setting
point of view
conflict
mood
plot
pacing
epic
tone
diction
denotation
connotation
allegory

Contents

Activities

Sermon: Excerpt from White House Funeral Sermon
for Abraham Lincoln, by Dr. Phineas D. Gurley
Poetry: "O Captain! My Captain!" by Walt Whitman
Poetry: "Frederick Douglass," by Robert Hayden
Autobiography: Excerpt from *The Narrative of the Life of
Frederick Douglass, an American Slave,* by Frederick Douglass

Essay: "A Definition of a Gentleman," by John Henry Newman

Texts not included in these materials.

Language and Writer's Craft
• Verbs and Mood (1.7)

MY INDEPENDENT READING LIST

Previewing the Unit: Understanding Challenges

Literary Terms
An **archetype** is a character, symbol, story pattern, or other element that is common to human experience across cultures and that occurs frequently in literature, myth, and folklore.

My Notes

Learning Targets

- Discuss the big ideas and vocabulary for the unit.
- Demonstrate an understanding of the skills and knowledge needed to complete Embedded Assessment 1 successfully.
- Analyze and collaborate to discuss quotes and identify connections between the concepts of *challenges* and *heroism*.

Making Connections

This unit introduces the challenge theme by examining how we define heroes. You will be introduced to the **archetype** of the hero's journey and will study various examples of heroes and how their journeys fit the archetype. You will also have the opportunity to practice explanatory writing and write a definition essay about heroism.

Essential Questions

Based on your current thinking, how would you answer these questions?

1. What defines a hero?

2. How does the Hero's Journey archetype appear in stories throughout time?

Developing Vocabulary

Create a chart to use the **QHT** strategy to sort the Academic Vocabulary and the Literary Terms from the Contents page.

Unpacking Embedded Assessment 1

Closely read the assignment for Embedded Assessment 1: Writing a Hero's Journey Narrative.

> Think about all the heroes you have encountered in fiction and in real life. What type of hero appeals to you? Write and create an illustrated narrative about an original hero. Use the Hero's Journey archetype to develop and structure your ideas. Orally present your narrative to your classmates.

Find the Scoring Guide and work with your class to paraphrase the expectations for the assignment. Create a graphic organizer to use as a visual reminder of the required skills and concepts. Copy the graphic organizer into your Reader/Writer Notebook.

After each activity in the first half of this unit, use this graphic organizer to guide reflection about what you have learned and what you still need to learn in order to be successful in the Embedded Assessment.

The Concept of Challenge

3. When you hear the word *challenges,* what comes to mind? Is the word positive or negative? How can challenges be helpful to an individual? How can they be harmful?

4. Using the graphic organizer below, analyze the quote you are assigned. Begin by diffusing the text by identifying and defining unfamiliar words. Then paraphrase the quote and brainstorm examples from life or literature that support the speaker's idea about challenges. Lastly, categorize the quote based on how the speaker defines *challenge*: as an obstacle, a difficult task, or an opportunity. Be prepared to discuss your analysis and explain how the speaker's definition of *challenge* connects to the concept of *heroism*.

Quotes

A. "The true measure of a man is not how he behaves in moments of comfort and convenience, but how he stands at times of controversy and challenges."—Rev. Dr. Martin Luther King, Jr. (clergyman, activist)

B. "Accept the challenges so that you can feel the exhilaration of victory." — George S. Patton (U.S. Army officer)

C. "The block of granite which was an obstacle in the pathway of the weak became a stepping-stone in the pathway of the strong." —Thomas Carlyle (writer, essayist, historian)

D. "Life's challenges are not supposed to paralyze you; they're supposed to help you discover who you are." —Bernice Johnson Reagon (singer, composer, scholar, activist)

My Notes

Which Quote Are You Analyzing?

Paraphrase	Examples	Challenge Category

Previewing the Unit: Understanding Challenges

5. Assign speaking parts for the presentation.

Element of Presentation	Speaker
(a) Fluently read the quote and explain the meaning.	
(b) Provide specific examples from life or literature.	
(c) Explain the group's categorization of the quote.	
(d) Explain how the quote connects to the concept of heroism.	

6. Present using appropriate eye contact, adequate volume, and clear pronunciation.

7. As other groups present, listen to them, try to comprehend their main points, and take notes in your Reader/Writer Notebook.

Check Your Understanding

Think about the content of all four quotes. How does the concept of *challenge* connect to the concept of *heroism*?

Understanding the Hero's Journey Archetype

Learning Targets
- Analyze how a film uses the Hero's Journey to structure its plot.
- Identify the stages of the Hero's Journey within a film.

The Archetype of the Hero's Journey

In literature, an **archetype** is a character, symbol, story pattern, or other element that is common to human experience across cultures. It refers to a common **plot** pattern or to a character type, such as the Innocent, the Mother Figure, or the Hero, or to images that occur in the literature of all cultures.

The archetype of the **Hero's Journey** describes a plot pattern that shows the development of a hero. The information below describes the structure of a Hero's Journey.

> Joseph Campbell, an American anthropologist, writer, and lecturer, studied the myths and stories of multiple cultures and began to notice common plot patterns. In *The Hero with a Thousand Faces,* Campbell defines common elements of the Hero's Journey. Campbell found that most journey myths had three parts:

- Departure: The hero leaves home to venture into the unknown on some sort of quest.
- Initiation: The hero faces a series of problems.
- Return: With the help of a friend, the hero returns home successfully.

While these elements may be referred to as the stages of the Hero's Journey, these stages may not always be presented in the exact same order, and some stories do not contain every element of the journey.

Preview
In this activity, you will learn the stages of the Hero's Journey. Then you will watch a film and think about how it fits into the archetype of the Hero's Journey.

Setting a Purpose for Viewing
- As you study the stages of the Hero's Journey archetype in the graphic organizer that follows, use metacognitive markers to indicate your level of understanding and to guide future discussion:
  ? = questions, ! = connections, and * = comments.
- Circle unknown words and phrases. Try to determine the meaning of the words by using context clues, word parts, or a dictionary.

After you review the stages of the Hero's Journey archetype as a class, you will use the last column of the graphic organizer to record details from the film that align to each stage. For now, leave it blank.

LEARNING STRATEGIES:
Metacognitive Markers, Close Reading, Graphic Organizer, Note-taking, Collaborative Discussion

Literary Terms
Plot is the sequence of related events that make up a story. There are five main elements of plot: exposition, rising action, climax, falling action, and resolution.

WORD CONNECTIONS

Etymology

Etymology is the study of the origin of words. Many English words come from other languages, including Latin, German, and Greek. Knowing a word's etymology can help you determine the meaning of unfamiliar words. The Greek prefix *arch-* in **archetype** means "first," and the root *-type-* means "model." When first used in the 14th century, it meant "original pattern from which copies are made." Today it is used to denote a story element common to many people or a perfect example of something.

My Notes

Understanding the Hero's Journey Archetype

Hero's Journey Archetype

Stage 1: Departure

Steps	Explanation	Example
1. **The Call to Adventure** The future hero is first given notice that his or her life is going to change.	The story's **exposition** introduces the hero, and soon the hero's normal life is disrupted. Something changes; the hero faces a problem, obstacle, or challenge.	
2. **Refusal of the Call** The future hero often refuses to accept the call to adventure. The refusal may stem from a sense of duty, an obligation, a fear, or insecurity.	At first the hero is reluctant to accept the change. Usually this reluctance presents itself as second thoughts or personal doubt. Hesitation, whether brief or lengthy, humanizes the hero for the reader.	
3. **The Beginning of the Adventure** The hero begins the adventure, leaving the known limits of his or her world to venture into an unknown and dangerous realm where the rules and limits are unknown.	The hero finally accepts the call and begins a physical, spiritual, and/or emotional journey to achieve a boon, something that is helpful or beneficial.	

Stage 2: Initiation

Steps	Explanation	Example
4. **The Road of Trials** The hero experiences and is transformed by a series of tests, tasks, or challenges. The hero usually fails one or more of these tests, which often occur in threes.	The story develops **rising action** as the hero faces a series of challenges that become increasingly difficult as the story unfolds.	
5. **The Experience with Unconditional Love** During the Road of Trials, the hero experiences support (physical and/or mental) from a friend, family member, mentor, etc.	This love often drives the hero to continue on the journey, even when the hero doubts him/herself.	

Hero's Journey Archetype

6. The Ultimate Boon

The goal of the quest is achieved. The boon can be a physical object or an intangible item such as knowledge, courage, or love. The Road of Trials makes the hero strong enough to achieve this goal.

The story reaches the **climax** as the hero gains what he or she set out to achieve.

The Call to Adventure (what the hero is asked to do), the Beginning of the Adventure (what the hero sets out to do), and the Ultimate Boon (what the hero achieves) must connect.

Stage 3: Return

7. Refusal of the Return

When the goal of the adventure is accomplished, the hero may refuse to return with the boon or gift, either because the hero doubts the return will bring change or because the hero prefers to stay in a better place rather than return to a normal life of pain and trouble.

The **falling action** begins as the hero begins to think about the Return. Sometimes the hero does not want to look back after achieving the boon. Sometimes the hero likes the "new world" better.

This step is similar to the Refusal of the Call (in both cases, the hero does not take action right away).

8. The Magic Flight

The hero experiences adventure and perhaps danger as he or she **returns** to life as it was before the Call to Adventure.

For some heroes, the journey "home" (psychological or physical) can be just as dangerous as the journey out. Forces (sometimes magical or supernatural) may keep the hero from returning.

This step is similar to the Road of Trials.

9. Rescue from Without

Just as the hero may need guides and assistance on the quest, oftentimes he or she must have powerful guides and rescuers to bring him or her back to everyday life. Sometimes the hero does not realize that it is time to return, that he or she can return, or that others are relying on him or her to return.

Just as it looks as if the hero will not make it home with the boon, the hero is "rescued." The rescuer is sometimes the same person who provided love or support throughout the journey.

10. The Crossing or Return Threshold

At this final point in the adventure, the hero must retain the wisdom gained on the quest, integrate that wisdom into his or her previous life, and perhaps decide how to share the wisdom with the rest of the world.

The final step is the story's **resolution,** when the hero returns with the boon. The theme is typically revealed at this point.

To determine theme, think about the hero's struggles, transformation, and achievement. The reader is expected to learn a lesson about life though the hero's experience.

Understanding the Hero's Journey Archetype

Literary Terms

Setting is the time and place in which a narrative occurs.

Conflict is a struggle between opposing forces, either internal or external. Common conflicts are man vs. self, man vs. man, man vs. society, and man vs. nature.

My Notes

Working from the Film

Embedded Assessment 2 requires you to use the Hero's Journey to sequence and structure events in your narrative. You already know the basic elements of **plot** development. All plot development includes:

Exposition: Events that set the context for the story: the **setting** (time and place), characters, and central **conflict** are introduced.

Rising Action: Events that develop the plot and lead to the climax.

Climax: The main event; the turning point, or highest point of tension in the story.

Falling Action: The events that lead to the resolution.

Resolution: Conflict is completely resolved, and the lesson has been learned.

1. Label each step in the plot diagram. Then, provide examples of each step from the film you just watched. Use your notes from the film for guidance.

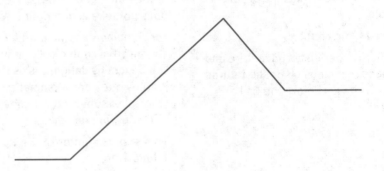

2. Return to your Hero's Journey Archetype graphic organizer. Label each stage of the Hero's Journey based on where on the plot diagram it would fall.

3. **Discussion:** One narrative technique that writers use is **pacing**. Read the Literary Terms box to learn about this technique. Notice how the plot diagram gives an idea of how rising action is paced in contrast to falling action. How does a writer effectively pace plot events?

Check Your Understanding

In your Reader/Writer Notebook, write about a movie you have seen recently that has a Hero's Journey archetype plot pattern. Include the title of the movie and information about how the plot pattern follows the Hero's Journey structure.

Literary Terms

Pacing is a narrative technique that refers to the amount of time a writer gives to describing each event and the amount of time a writer takes to develop each stage in the plot. Some events and stages are shorter or longer than others.

Planning for Independent Reading

Learning Targets
- Examine ways to choose a literary text for independent reading.
- Set goals in an independent reading plan.

Planning Independent Reading

The focus of this unit is the Hero's Journey archetype. For Embedded Assessment 1, you will be writing your own Hero's Journey narrative with accompanying visuals. In the previous activity, you were able to preview the stages of the Hero's Journey using a film. Now, in your Independent Reading, you have the opportunity to read a full-length Hero's Journey story. Reading a full-length story will help you with creating your Embedded Assessment, and it will you expose you to how authors create a Hero's Journey narrative. In the back of your SpringBoard book, you'll find a list of suggested Hero's Journey narratives. To help you choose the right book, use the following questions as a guide.

1. What have you enjoyed reading in the past? What is your favorite book or favorite type of book? Who is your favorite author?

2. Preview the book you have selected: What do the front and back covers show you? What type of visual is shown? What types of fonts and colors are used? Are there awards or brags that tell you about the book?

3. Read the first few pages. Are they interesting? How does the author try to hook you to keep reading? What can you tell about the characters and setting (location and time) so far? Does this seem too hard, too easy, or just right?

Reading Discussion Groups

Your teacher will guide you in a book pass. Practice previewing each book, looking at the covers and reading the first few pages.

4. In your Reader/Writer Notebook, record each book's title and author, something from your previewing that stands out to you, and your rating of the book.

5. After previewing each book and thinking about the goals of this unit, do you want to continue reading the book you brought to the group or choose something else?

6. Create an Independent Reading Plan to help you set personal reading goals. Keep this plan in your Reader/Writer Notebook.

I have chosen to read _____

by (author) _____

because (reason from previewing) _____

_____

I will set aside time to read at (time, place) _____

I should finish this text by (date) _____

7. Record your daily reading pace in your Independent Reading Log. Write a brief daily report in your log responding to what you have read.

8. As you identify new titles to read for your independent reading, add them to the My Independent Reading List on the Table of Contents pages of this unit.

LEARNING STRATEGIES:
Collaborative Discussion

INDEPENDENT READING LINK

In this unit, you will be reading excerpts from many hero stories. Select a full-length work that follows the hero's journey. Book lists are available in the back of this textbook, and you can use book discussions and recommendations from classmates to help you choose. Use your Reader/Writer Notebook and your Independent Reading Log to keep notes on what you are reading and answer questions that come up.

My Notes

Planning for Independent Reading

9. Use this graphic organizer to record each stage of the Hero's Journey from your Independent Reading book.

Text: _____

Stage 1: Departure

1. **The Call to Adventure:**

2. **Refusal of the Call:**

3. **The Beginning of the Adventure:**

Stage 2: Initiation

4. **The Road of Trials:**
   (a)
   (b)
   (c)

5. **The Experience with Unconditional Love:**

6. **The Ultimate Boon:**

Stage 3: Return

7. **Refusal of the Return:**

8. **The Magic Flight:**

9. **Rescue from Without:**

10. **The Crossing or Return Threshold:**
    (Theme Statement)

Learning Targets

- Analyze the imagery in a poem to understand how it reveals an idea or theme.
- Revise writing by substituting a different point of view and adding imagery for effect.

Preview

In this activity, you will read a poem and think about how the author uses **imagery** to express an idea or theme about adventure.

Setting a Purpose for Reading

- As you read, use metacognitive markers to indicate your level of understanding and to guide future discussion:
  ? = questions, ! = connections, and * = comments.
- Circle unknown words and phrases. Try to determine the meaning of the words by using context clues, word parts, or a dictionary.

ABOUT THE AUTHOR

Constantine P. Cavafy (1863–1933) was a Greek poet. Cavafy wrote "Ithaka," which was inspired by the Homeric return journey of Odysseus to his home island, as described in the *Odyssey*. Cavafy lived much of his life as an obscure poet sharing his poetry amongst a few close friends. Many of his poems were personal, and most were not published until after his death.

> **LEARNING STRATEGIES:**
> Marking the Text, Discussion Groups, Rereading, Summarizing, Predicting, Substituting, Adding

> **Literary Terms**
> **Imagery** is descriptive or figurative language used to create word pictures in a reader's mind.

My Notes

Poem

Ithaka

by C. P. Cavafy
translated by Edmund Keeley and Philip Sherrard

As you set out for Ithaka
hope your road is a long one,
full of adventure, full of discovery.
Laistrygonians, Cyclops,
5 angry Poseidon—don't be afraid of them;
you'll never find things like that on your way
as long as you keep your thoughts raised high,
as long as a rare excitement
stirs your spirit and your body.
10 Laistrygonians, Cyclops,
wild Poseidon—you won't encounter them
unless you bring them along inside your soul.
unless your soul sets them up in front of you.

Hope your road is a long one.
15 May there be many summer mornings when,
with what pleasure, what joy,
you enter harbors you're seeing for the first time;
may you stop at Phoenician trading stations
to buy fine things,
20 mother of pearl and coral, amber and ebony,

My Notes

sensual perfume of every kind—
as many sensual perfumes as you can;
and may you visit many Egyptian cities
to learn and go on learning from their scholars.

25 Keep Ithaka always in your mind.
Arriving there is what you're destined for.
But don't hurry the journey at all.
Better if it lasts for years,
so you're old by the time you reach the island,
30 wealthy with all you've gained on the way,
not expecting Ithaka to make you rich.

Ithaka gave you the marvelous journey.
Without her you wouldn't have set out.
She has nothing left to give you now.

35 And if you find her poor, Ithaka won't have fooled you.
Wise as you will have become, so full of experience,
you'll have understood by then what these Ithakas mean.

Second Read

- Reread the poem to answer these text-dependent questions.
- Write any additional questions you have about the text in your Reader/Writer Notebook.

1. **Craft and Structure:** Look at stanza 3. What are some synonyms for the word *destined*? Why did Cavafy choose *destined*?

Literary Terms
Mood is the overall emotion, which is created by the author's language and tone and the subject matter.

2. **Craft and Structure:** What is the **mood** of this poem? How do you feel after reading this poem? Explain.

3. **Key Ideas and Details:** Make an inference about what this part of the poem means:
"Ithaka gave you the marvelous journey. / Without her you wouldn't have set out. / She has nothing left to give you now."

4. **Craft and Structure:** What do you think Cavafy is using the journey to Ithaka as a metaphor for? Why do you think that?

Working from the Text

5. As you hear the poem read aloud, make mental visualizations of the words you hear.

6. Make a list of images you pictured while you listened to the poem in the My Notes alongside the poem.

7. Return to the poem. Highlight the parts of the text that inspired the images you pictured.

8. Form small groups. Look at the words you highlighted in the poem. Then, look at the **context** of those words. What is the author saying in that part of the poem? Draw a visual in the margin to help illustrate your meaning.

Check Your Understanding

Focus on the words you highlighted in "Ithaka," and think about the underlying message the poet is trying to convey. Write a theme statement for the poem in your Reader/Writer Notebook.

Writing to Sources: Explanatory Text

Write a short summary explaining what you think Cavafy means by the first three lines in the opening stanza in "Ithaka."

"As you set out for Ithaka / hope your road is a long one, / full of adventure, full of discovery."

Use other stanzas from the poem to support your ideas. Be sure to:

- Include a clear topic sentence that explains what you think the first three lines mean.
- Provide details to support your claim.
- Explain how the imagery in this poem helps create the mood and reveal the theme.
- Use transition words to flow your ideas logically.

My Notes

ACADEMIC VOCABULARY
You know the word **context** from context clues to define words. **Context** also refers to the circumstances or facts that surround a particular event or situation. In a story or novel, **contextual** information can help you understand the time and place as well as the situation in the story.

INDEPENDENT READING LINK
Read and Connect
Examine the opening chapter of your independent reading book and write about how it sets the context for the hero's challenges. What mood does the author set in the opening of your book? How is it similar to or different from the mood that is set in the poem in this activity?

The Departure

My Notes

Learning Targets
- Analyze a story for archetypal structure and narrative techniques.
- Draft the opening of an original Hero's Journey narrative.

The Departure
Joseph Campbell describes the first stage of the Hero's Journey as the hero's departure or separation. The Departure Stage consists of three steps: the Call to Adventure, Refusal of the Call, and the Beginning of the Adventure.

Preview
In this activity, you will read a story about a hero's departure and begin creating a hero of your own.

Setting a Purpose for Reading
- As you read, think about the stages of a hero's journey. Put a star next to parts of this story that show the stages of Joby's journey.
- Circle unknown words and phrases. Try to determine the meaning of the words by using context clues, word parts, or a dictionary.

ABOUT THE AUTHOR
Ray Bradbury (1920–2012) authored the novel *Fahrenheit 451*, which was first published in 1953. Bradbury called his books fantasy rather than science fiction because he wrote stories that could not happen in real life. Other well-known works by Bradbury include *The Martian Chronicles* and *Something Wicked This Way Comes*. Bradbury also authored hundreds of short stories and even wrote and published his own fan magazine.

Short Story

"The Drummer Boy of Shiloh"

by Ray Bradbury

1 In the April night, more than once, blossoms fell from the orchard trees and lit with rustling taps on the drumskin. At midnight a peach stone left miraculously on a branch through winter flicked by a bird fell swift and unseen struck once like panic, which jerked the boy upright. In silence he listened to his own heart **ruffle** away away—at last gone from his ears and back in his chest again.

2 After that, he turned the drum on its side, where its great lunar face peered at him whenever he opened his eyes.

3 His face, alert or at rest, was solemn. It was indeed a solemn night for a boy just turned fourteen in the peach field near the Owl Creek not far from the church at Shiloh.[1]

ruffle: to flutter or move in a slow, wavy pattern

---

[1] **Shiloh** (n.): site of a Civil War battle in 1862; now a national military park in southwest Tennessee

4 "…thirty-one, thirty-two, thirty-three…"

5 Unable to see, he stopped counting.

6 Beyond the thirty-three familiar shadows, forty thousand men, exhausted by nervous expectation, unable to sleep for **romantic** dreams of battles yet unfought, lay crazily askew in their uniforms. A mile yet farther on, another army was strewn **helter-skelter**, turning slow, basting themselves with the thought of what they would do when the time came: a leap, a yell, a blind plunge their strategy, raw youth their protection and **benediction**.

romantic: fondly imaginary
helter-skelter: in a confused or disorderly way
benediction: a prayer or blessing

7 Now and again the boy heard a vast wind come up, that gently stirred the air. But he knew what it was—the army here, the army there, whispering to itself in the dark. Some men talking to others, others murmuring to themselves, and all so quiet it was like a natural element arisen from South or North with the motion of the earth toward dawn.

8 What the men whispered the boy could only guess, and he guessed that it was: "Me, I'm the one, I'm the one of all the rest who won't die. I'll live through it. I'll go home. The band will play. And I'll be there to hear it."

9 Yes, thought the boy, that's all very well for them, they can give as good as they get!

10 For with the careless bones of the young men harvested by the night and **bindled** around campfires were the similarly strewn steel bones of their rifles, with bayonets fixed like eternal lightning lost in the orchard grass.

bindled: held together in a sack

11 Me, thought the boy, I got only a drum, two sticks to beat it and no shield.

12 There wasn't a man-boy on the ground tonight who did not have a shield he cast, riveted or carved himself on his way to his first attack, compounded of remote but nonetheless firm and fiery family devotion, flag-blown patriotism and cocksure **immortality** strengthened by the touchstone of very real gunpowder; ramrod, Minié ball[2] and flint. But without these last the boy felt his family move yet farther off away in the dark, as if one of those great prairie-burning trains had chanted them away never to return—leaving him with this drum which was worse than a toy in the game to be played tomorrow or some day much too soon.

immortality: the ability to live forever

13 The boy turned on his side. A moth brushed his face, but it was peach blossom. A peach blossom flicked him, but it was a moth. Nothing stayed put. Nothing had a name. Nothing was as it once was.

14 If he lay very still when the dawn came up and the soldiers put on their bravery with their caps, perhaps they might go away, the war with them, and not notice him lying small here, no more than a toy himself.

15 "Well … now," said a voice.

16 The boy shut up his eyes to hide inside himself, but it was too late. Someone, walking by in the night, stood over him.

17 "Well," said the voice quietly, "here's a soldier crying before the fight. Good. Get it over. Won't be time once it all starts."

18 And the voice was about to move on when the boy, startled, touched the drum at his elbow. The man above, hearing this, stopped. The boy could feel his eyes, sense him slowly bending near. A hand must have come down out of the night, for there was a little rat-tat as the fingernails brushed and the man's breath fanned his face.

---

[2] **Minié ball:** a type of rifle bullet that became prominent during the Civil War

My Notes

WORD CONNECTIONS

Etymology

In the past, people would test the quality of gold or silver by rubbing a stone across it and analyzing the color of the streak it left. The 15th-century Middle English word *touch* meant "to test," so this stone became known as a *touchstone*. This term is now a metaphor for any method used to test the quality or effectiveness of something else.

My Notes

19 "Why, it's the drummer boy, isn't it?"

20 The boy nodded not knowing if his nod was seen. "Sir, is that you?" he said.

21 "I assume it is." The man's knees cracked as he bent still closer.

22 He smelled as all fathers should smell, of salt sweat, ginger, tobacco, horse, and boot leather, and the earth he walked upon. He had many eyes. No, not eyes—brass buttons that watched the boy.

23 He could only be, and was, the general.

24 "What's your name, boy?" he asked.

25 "Joby," whispered the boy, starting to sit up.

26 "All right Joby, don't stir." A hand pressed his chest gently and the boy relaxed. "How long you been with us, Joby?"

27 "Three weeks, sir."

28 "Run off from home or joined legitimately, boy?"

29 Silence.

30 ". . . Fool question," said the general. "Do you shave yet, boy? Even more of a … fool. There's your cheek, fell right off the tree overhead. And the others here not much older. Raw, raw, the lot of you. You ready for tomorrow or the next day, Joby?"

31 "I think so, sir."

32 "You want to cry some more, go on ahead. I did the same last night."

33 "You, sir?"

34 "It's the truth. Thinking of everything ahead. Both sides figuring the other side will just give up, and soon, and the war done in weeks, and us all home. Well, that's not how it's going to be. And maybe that's why I cried."

35 "Yes, sir," said Joby.

36 The general must have taken out a cigar now, for the dark was suddenly filled with the smell of tobacco unlit as yet, but chewed as the man thought what next to say.

37 "It's going to be a crazy time," said the general. "Counting both sides, there's a hundred thousand men, give or take a few thousand out there tonight, not one as can spit a sparrow off a tree, or knows a horse clod from a Minié ball. Stand up, bare the breast, ask to be a target, thank them and sit down, that's us, that's them. We should turn tail and train four months, they should do the same. But here we are, taken with spring fever and thinking it blood lust, taking our sulfur with cannons instead of with molasses, as it should be, going to be a hero, going to live forever. And I can see all of them over there nodding agreement, save the other way around. It's wrong, boy, it's wrong as a head put on hindside front and a man marching backward through life… More innocents will get shot out of pure … enthusiasm than ever got shot before. Owl Creek was full of boys splashing around in the noonday sun just a few hours ago. I fear it will be full of boys again, just floating, at sundown tomorrow, not caring where the tide takes them."

38 The general stopped and made a little pile of winter leaves and twigs in the darkness, as if he might at any moment strike fire to them to see his way through the coming days when the sun might not show its face because of what was happening here and just beyond.

39 The boy watched the hand stirring the leaves and opened his lips to say something, but did not say it. The general heard the boy's breath and spoke himself.

40 "Why am I telling you this? That's what you wanted to ask, eh? Well, when you got a bunch of wild horses on a loose rein somewhere somehow you got to bring order, rein them in. These lads, fresh out of the milkshed, don't know what I know, and I can't tell them: men actually die in war. So each is his own army. I got to make one army of them. And for that, boy, I need you.

41 "Me!" The boy's lips barely twitched.

42 "Now, boy," said the general quietly, "you are the heart of the army. Think of that. You're the heart of the army. Listen, now."

43 And, lying there, Joby listened. And the general spoke on.

44 If he, Joby, beat slow tomorrow, the heart would beat slow in the men. They would lag by the wayside. They would drowse in the fields on their muskets. They would sleep for ever, after that, in those same fields—their hearts slowed by a drummer boy and stopped by enemy lead.

45 But if he beat a sure, steady, ever faster rhythm, then, then their knees would come up in a long line down over that hill, one knee after the other, like a wave on the ocean shore! Had he seen the ocean ever? Seen the waves rolling in like a well-ordered cavalry charge to the sand? Well, that was it that's what he wanted, that's what was needed! Joby was his right hand and his left. He gave the orders, but Joby set the pace!

46 So bring the right knee up and the right foot out and the left knee up and the left foot out. One following the other in good time, in brisk time. Move the blood up the body and made the head proud and the spine stiff and the jaw **resolute**. Focus the eye and set the teeth, flare the nostrils and tighten the hands, put steel armor all over the men, for blood moving fast in them does indeed make men feel as if they'd put on steel. He must keep at it, at it! Long and steady, steady and long! The men, even though shot or torn, those wounds got in hot blood—in blood he'd helped stir—would feel less pain. If their blood was cold, it would be more than slaughter, it would be murderous nightmare and pain best not told and no one to guess.

47 The general spoke and stopped, letting his breath **slack** off. Then after a moment, he said, "So there you are, that's it. Will you do that, boy? Do you know now you're general of the army when the general's left behind?"

48 The boy nodded mutely.

49 "You'll run them through for me then boy?"

50 "Yes, sir."

51 "Good. And maybe, many nights from tonight, many years from now, when you're as old or far much older than me, when they ask you what you did in this awful time, you will tell them—one part humble and one part proud—'I was the drummer boy at the battle of Owl Creek,' or the Tennessee River, or maybe they'll just name it after the church there. 'I was the drummer boy at Shiloh.' Who will ever hear those words and not know you, boy, or what you thought this night, or what you'll think tomorrow or the next day when we must get up on our legs and move!"

52 The general stood up. "Well then … Bless you, boy. Good night."

53 "Good night, sir." And tobacco, brass, boot polish, salt sweat and leather, the man moved away through the grass.

My Notes

resolute: determined

slack: to diminish or fade away

The Departure

54 Joby lay for a moment, staring but unable to see where the man had gone. He swallowed. He wiped his eyes. He cleared his throat. He settled himself. Then, at last, very slowly and firmly, he turned the drum so that it faced up toward the sky.

55 He lay next to it, his arm around it, feeling the tremor, the touch, the muted thunder as, all the rest of the April night in the year 1862, near the Tennessee River, not far from the Owl Creek, very close to the church named Shiloh, the peach blossoms fell on the drum.

Second Read

- Reread the excerpt to answer these text-dependent questions.
- Write any additional questions you have about the text in your Reader/Writer Notebook.

1. **Key Ideas and Details:** What textual evidence in the beginning of the story shows that the boy is afraid?

2. **Craft and Structure:** The word "harvested" is used figuratively in paragraph 10. How do you know it is used figuratively, and why did the author choose this word?

3. **Craft and Structure:** Consult reference materials to find the meanings of "ramrod" and "flint." Relate these words to the meaning of the sentence in paragraph 12. How does the sentence convey the boy's mood?

4. **Key Ideas and Details:** How did Joby join the army? What is significant about that?

5. **Craft and Structure:** Consult reference material to find the meaning of the word "drowse." How does that word create a contrast in paragraph 44?

6. **Key Ideas and Details:** What shift happens in paragraphs 44, 45, and 46? Use textual evidence in your answer.

7. **Key Ideas and Details:** How does the general's comment, "Do you know now you're general of the army when the general's left behind?" prove to be a decisive moment in the conversation between him and Joby?

Working from the Text

8. The author establishes a **setting** and **point of view** in the opening of the narrative. Using evidence from the text, summarize the setting and point of view.

9. Summarize the Departure Stage of the Hero's Journey as it relates to Joby in "The Drummer Boy of Shiloh." Which stage is Joby in? Embed at least one direct quotation in your summary to strengthen your response.

My Notes

_____
_____
_____
_____
_____
_____
_____
_____

Literary Terms
Setting is the time and place in which a narrative occurs. Point of view is the perspective from which a story is told. In **first-person point of view,** a character tells the story from his or her own perspective. In **third-person point of view,** a narrator (not a character) tells the story.

_____
_____
_____
_____
_____
_____
_____
_____
_____
_____
_____
_____
_____
_____

The Departure

10. Reread a chunk of the text to identify and evaluate the narrative elements listed in the graphic organizer.

Structure: Exposition	What descriptive detail does the author provide?	How effective is the description?
Setting		
Character		
Conflict		
Point of View		

Techniques	How does the author use each element to develop the story?	How effective is the author's technique?
Description		
Dialogue		
Pacing		

Check Your Understanding

Now that you have identified and evaluated the narrative elements of the story, determine its central idea. Write a summary of the central idea, supporting your interpretation using evidence from the text. Explain how the author communicates the idea that Joby is now ready to start his journey.

11. Use your imagination to create an original hero. In your Reader/Writer Notebook, sketch your image of a hero. Label unique characteristics and give him or her a meaningful name. In the right column, use the prompting questions to brainstorm ideas for a story.

The Hero: _____ (name)	The Story Exposition
Use these questions to spark ideas. Is the hero male or female? Young or old? Beautiful or unattractive? Well liked or misunderstood? Conspicuous (obvious) or nondescript (ordinary)?	**Setting:** (In what kind of place does your hero live? Does he or she live in the past, present, or future?) **Character:** (What are the hero's strengths and weaknesses? Who are the hero's family and friends? What does the hero do every day? What does the hero want in life? What do others want from the hero?) **Conflicts:** (What challenges might the hero experience? How might the hero transform into someone stronger?)

Drafting the Embedded Assessment

Think about the hero you just envisioned. What might the hero experience in the Departure Stage of his or her journey? Draft the beginning of a narrative using the three steps in this stage (The Call, The Refusal, and The Beginning) to guide your structure and development. Be sure to:

- Establish a context (exposition) and point of view (first person or third person).
- Use narrative techniques such as dialogue, pacing, and description to develop experiences, events, and/or characters.
- Use details and imagery to create mood.

INDEPENDENT READING LINK

Read and Connect

What kinds of challenges has the hero of your independent reading text encountered? What do these challenges or obstacles reveal about the character? Write your response in your Reader/ Writer Notebook.

My Notes

The Initiation

WORD CONNECTIONS

Cognates

The English word *initiation* has at its root *-init-*, which comes from the Latin word *initialis*, meaning "beginning." Its Spanish cognate is *iniciación*, which derives from *iniciar*, meaning "to begin."

Literary Terms

An **epic** is a long narrative about the deeds of heroes or gods.

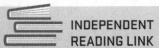

INDEPENDENT READING LINK

Read and Discuss

Think about the hero of the book you are reading outside of class. Meet with a partner and describe the mental and physical strengths your book's hero possesses that will be important when facing challenges and obstacles. Talk to classmates who chose a different independent reading book than you. Discuss how the strengths of your book's hero are similar to those of the heroes in their books.

Learning Targets

- Analyze an excerpt of an epic poem for archetype and narrative techniques.
- Examine visual depictions of an epic poem.
- Demonstrate understanding of these concepts by drafting and illustrating an event in a hero's Road of Trials.

Preview

In this activity, you will read and analyze an excerpt from an **epic** poem and various images of these scenes.

Setting a Purpose for Reading

- Read the excerpt and make observations and inferences about Odysseus's character. Make note of words that describe his appearance, as well as his own words, actions, thoughts, and feelings. Also note how others react to him.
- Circle unknown words and phrases. Try to determine the meaning of the words by using context clues, word parts, or a dictionary.

ABOUT THE AUTHOR

Homer is an ancient Greek poet, thought to have been born sometime between the 12th and 8th centuries BC. While little is known about Homer's life, many scholars believe him to be the author of two famous epic poems, the *Iliad* and the *Odyssey*. These epic poems, written to follow the Hero's Journey archetype, were some of the earliest known works of literature. Homer's epic poems greatly influenced Greek culture and inspired many further works of literature, following in the epic style. His poems continue to be relevant, discussed, and debated today.

Epic

From

the ODYSSEY

by Homer
Translation by Tony Kline

Book IX: 152–192
ODYSSEUS TELLS HIS TALE: THE CYCLOPS'S CAVE

1 Looking across to the land of the neighboring Cyclops,[1] we could see smoke and hear their voices, and the sound of their sheep and goats. Sun set and darkness fell, and we settled to our rest on the shore.

2 As soon as rosy-fingered Dawn appeared, I gathered my men together, saying: "The rest of you loyal friends stay here, while I and my crew take ship and try and find out who these men are, whether they are cruel, savage and lawless, or good to strangers, and in their hearts fear the gods."

---

[1] **Cyclops:** one-eyed giants

3 With this I went aboard and ordered my crew to follow and loose the cables. They boarded swiftly and took their place on the benches then sitting in their rows struck the grey water with their oars. When we had reached the nearby shore, we saw a deep cave overhung with laurels at the cliff's edge close to the sea. Large herds of sheep and goats were penned there at night and round it was a raised yard walled by deep-set stones, tall pines and high-crowned oaks. There a giant spent the night, one that grazed his herds far off, alone, and keeping clear of others, lived in lawless solitude. He was born a monster and a wonder, not like any ordinary human, but like some wooded peak of the high mountains, that stands there isolated to our gaze.

Book IX: 193–255
ODYSSEUS TELLS HIS TALE: POLYPHEMUS RETURNS

4 Then I ordered the rest of my loyal friends to stay there and guard the ship, while I selected the twelve best men and went forward. I took with me a goatskin filled with dark sweet wine that Maron, son of Euanthes, priest of Apollo, guardian god of Ismarus, had given me, because out of respect we protected him, his wife and child. He offered me splendid gifts, seven **talents** of well-wrought gold, and a silver mixing-bowl: and wine, twelve jars in all, sweet unmixed wine, a divine **draught**. None of his serving-men and maids knew of this store, only he and his loyal wife, and one housekeeper. When they drank that honeyed red wine, he would pour a full cup into twenty of water, and the bouquet that rose from the mixing bowl was wonderfully sweet: in truth no one could hold back. I filled a large goatskin with the wine, and took it along, with some food in a bag, since my instincts told me the giant would come at us quickly, a savage being with huge strength, knowing nothing of right or law.

5 Soon we came to the cave, and found him absent; he was grazing his well-fed flocks in the fields. So we went inside and marveled at its contents. There were baskets full of cheeses, and pens crowded with lambs and kids, each flock with its firstlings, later ones, and newborn separated. The pails and bowls for milking, all solidly made, were swimming with **whey**. At first my men begged me to take some cheeses and go, then to drive the lambs and kids from the pens down to the swift ship and set sail. But I would not listen, though it would have been best, wishing to see the giant himself, and test his hospitality. When he did appear he proved no joy to my men.

6 So we lit a fire and made an offering, and helped ourselves to the cheese, and sat in the cave eating, waiting for him to return, shepherding his flocks. He arrived bearing a huge weight of dry wood to burn at suppertime, and he flung it down inside the cave with a crash. Gripped by terror we shrank back into a deep corner. He drove his well-fed flocks into the wide cave, the ones he milked, leaving the rams and he-goats outside in the broad courtyard. Then he lifted his door, a huge stone, and set it in place. Twenty-two four-wheeled wagons could not have carried it, yet such was the great rocky mass he used for a door. Then he sat and milked the ewes, and bleating goats in order, putting her young to each. Next he **curdled** half of the white milk, and stored the whey in wicker baskets, leaving the rest in pails for him to drink for his supper. When he had busied himself at his tasks, and kindled a fire, he suddenly saw us, and said: "Strangers, who are you? Where do you sail from over the sea-roads? Are you on business, or do you roam at random, like pirates who chance their lives to bring evil to others?"

My Notes

talent: an ancient coin
draught: a liquid that one drinks

WORD CONNECTIONS

Etymology

The English word *bouquet* comes from a French word of the same spelling meaning "little wood." The term derives from the Medieval Latin word *boscus*, which means "grove."

whey: the watery part of milk

curdled: separated the solid parts out of milk

The Initiation

sacked: attacked a city and stole from it

slew: killed

suppliants: people who beg

devoid: absent

revere: to regard with devotion and awe

aegis: protection

whelp: a young child or animal

Book IX: 256–306
ODYSSEUS TELLS HIS TALE: TRAPPED

7 Our spirits fell at his words, in terror at his loud voice and monstrous size. Nevertheless I answered him, saying: "We are Achaeans, returning from Troy, driven over the ocean depths by every wind that blows. Heading for home we were forced to take another route, a different course, as Zeus,[1] I suppose, intended. We are followers of Agamemnon, Atreus' son, whose fame spreads widest on earth, so great was that city he **sacked** and host he **slew**. But we, for our part, come as suppliants to your knees, hoping for hospitality, and the kindness that is due to strangers. Good sir, do not refuse us: respect the gods. We are **suppliants** and Zeus protects visitors and suppliants, Zeus the god of guests, who follows the steps of sacred travelers."

8 His answer was **devoid** of pity. "Stranger, you are a foreigner or a fool, telling me to fear and **revere** the gods, since the Cyclopes care nothing for **aegis**-bearing Zeus: we are greater than they. I would spare neither you nor your friends, to evade Zeus' anger, but only as my own heart prompted. But tell me, now, where you moored your fine ship, when you landed. Was it somewhere nearby, or further off? I'd like to know."

9 His words were designed to fool me, but failed. I was too wise for that, and answered him with cunning words: "Poseidon,[2] Earth-Shaker, smashed my ship to pieces, wrecking her on the rocks that edge your island, driving her close to the headland so the wind threw her onshore. But I and my men here escaped destruction."

10 Devoid of pity, he was silent in response, but leaping up laid hands on my crew. Two he seized and dashed to the ground like **whelps**, and their brains ran out and stained the earth. He tore them limb from limb for his supper, eating the flesh and entrails, bone and marrow, like a mountain lion, leaving nothing. Helplessly we watched these cruel acts, raising our hands to heaven and weeping. When the Cyclops had filled his huge stomach with human flesh, and had drunk pure milk, he lay down in the cave, stretched out among his flocks. Then I formed a courageous plan to steal up to him, draw my sharp sword, and feeling for the place where the midriff supports the liver, stab him there. But the next thought checked me. Trapped in the cave we would certainly die, since we'd have no way to move the great stone from the wide entrance. So, sighing, we waited for bright day.

Book IX: 307–359
ODYSSEUS TELLS HIS TALE: OFFERING THE CYCLOPS WINE

11 As soon as rosy-fingered Dawn appeared, Cyclops relit the fire. Then he milked the ewes, and bleating goats in order, putting her young to each. When he had busied himself at his tasks, he again seized two of my men and began to eat them. When he had finished he drove his well-fed flocks from the cave, effortlessly lifting the huge door stone, and replacing it again like the cap on a quiver. Then whistling loudly he turned his flocks out on to the mountain slopes, leaving me with murder in my heart searching for a way to take vengeance on him, if Athene[3] would grant me inspiration. The best plan seemed to be this:

---

[1] **Zeus:** the king of the gods
[2] **Poseidon:** god of the sea and of earthquakes
[3] **Athene:** goddess of wisdom, the arts, and war

My Notes

12 The Cyclops' huge club, a trunk of green olive wood he had cut to take with him as soon as it was seasoned, lay next to a sheep pen. It was so large and thick that it looked to us like the mast of a twenty-oared black ship, a broad-beamed merchant vessel that sails the deep ocean. Approaching it, I cut off a six-foot length, gave it to my men and told them to smooth the wood. Then standing by it I sharpened the end to a point, and hardened the point in the blazing fire, after which I hid it carefully in a one of the heaps of dung that lay around the cave. I ordered the men to **cast lots** as to which of them should dare to help me raise the stake and twist it into the Cyclops' eye when sweet sleep took him. The lot fell on the very ones I would have chosen, four of them, with myself making a fifth.

cast lots: to throw a set of objects in order to impartially decide something

13 He returned at evening, shepherding his well-fed flocks. He herded them swiftly, every one, into the deep cave, leaving none in the broad yard, commanded to do so by a god, or because of some **premonition**. Then he lifted the huge door stone and set it in place, and sat down to milk the ewes and bleating goats in order, putting her young to each. But when he had busied himself at his tasks, he again seized two of my men and began to eat them. That was when I went up to him, holding an ivy-wood bowl full of dark wine, and said: "Here, Cyclops, have some wine to follow your meal of human flesh, so you can taste the sort of drink we carried in our ship. I was bringing the drink to you as a gift, hoping you might pity me and help me on my homeward path: but your savagery is past bearing. Cruel man, why would anyone on earth ever visit you again, when you behave so badly?"

premonition: a vision of the future

14 At this, he took the cup and drained it, and found the sweet drink so delightful he asked for another draught: "Give me more, freely, then quickly tell me your name so I may give you a guest gift, one that will please you. Among us Cyclopes the fertile earth produces rich grape clusters, and Zeus' rain swells them: but this is a taste from a stream of **ambrosia and nectar**."

ambrosia and nectar: the food and drink of the gods

Book IX: 360–412
ODYSSEUS TELLS HIS TALE: BLINDING THE CYCLOPS

15 As he finished speaking I handed him the bright wine. Three times I poured and gave it to him, and three times, foolishly, he drained it. When the wine had **fuddled** his wits I tried him with **subtle** words: "Cyclops, you asked my name, and I will tell it: give me afterwards a guest gift as you promised. My name is Nobody. Nobody, my father, mother, and friends call me."

fuddled: made confusing
subtle: not obvious

16 Those were my words, and this his cruel answer: "Then, my gift is this. I will eat Nobody last of all his company, and all the others before him."

17 As he spoke, he reeled and toppled over on his back, his thick neck twisted to one side, and all-conquering sleep overpowered him. In his drunken slumber he vomited wine and pieces of human flesh. Then I thrust the stake into the depth of the ashes to heat it, and inspired my men with encouraging words, so none would hang back from fear. When the olivewood stake was glowing hot, and ready to catch fire despite its greenness, I drew it from the coals, then my men stood round me, and a god breathed courage into us. They held the sharpened olivewood stake, and thrust it into his eye, while I threw my weight on the end, and twisted it round and round, as a man bores the timbers of a ship with a drill that others twirl lower down with a strap held at both ends, and so keep the drill continuously moving. We took the red-hot stake and twisted it round and round like that in his eye, and the blood poured out despite the heat. His lids and brows were scorched by flame from the burning eyeball, and its

My Notes

treachery: a betrayal of trust

fleece: the coat of wool on a ram

roots crackled with fire. As a great axe or adze causes a vast hissing when the smith dips it in cool water to temper it, strengthening the iron, so his eye hissed against the olivewood stake. Then he screamed, terribly, and the rock echoed. Seized by terror we shrank back, as he wrenched the stake, wet with blood, from his eye. He flung it away in frenzy, and called to the Cyclops, his neighbors who lived in caves on the windy heights. They heard his cry, and crowding in from every side they stood by the cave mouth and asked what was wrong: "Polyphemus, what terrible pain is this that makes you call through deathless night, and wake us? Is a mortal stealing your flocks, or trying to kill you by violence or **treachery**?"

18 Out of the cave came mighty Polyphemus' voice: "Nobody, my friends, is trying to kill me by violence or treachery."

19 To this they replied with winged words: "If you are alone, and nobody does you violence, it's an inescapable sickness that comes from Zeus: pray to the Lord Poseidon, our father."

Book IX: 413–479
ODYSSEUS TELLS HIS TALE: ESCAPE

20 Off they went, while I laughed to myself at how the name and the clever scheme had deceived him. Meanwhile the Cyclops, groaning and in pain, groped around and labored to lift the stone from the door. Then he sat in the entrance, arms outstretched, to catch anyone stealing past among his sheep. That was how foolish he must have thought I was. I considered the best way of escaping, and saving myself, and my men from death. I dreamed up all sorts of tricks and schemes, as a man will in a life or death matter: it was an evil situation. This was the plan that seemed best. The rams were fat with thick **fleeces**, fine large beasts with deep black wool. These I silently tied together in threes, with twists of willow on which that lawless monster, Polyphemus, slept. The middle one was to carry one of my men, with the other two on either side to protect him. So there was a man to every three sheep. As for me I took the pick of the flock, and curled below his shaggy belly, gripped his back and lay there face upwards, patiently gripping his fine fleece tight in my hands. Then, sighing, we waited for the light.

21 As soon as rosy-fingered Dawn appeared, the males rushed out to graze, while the un-milked females udders bursting bleated in the pens. Their master, tormented by agonies of pain, felt the backs of the sheep as they passed him, but foolishly failed to see my men tied under the rams' bellies. My ram went last, burdened by the weight of his fleece, and me and my teeming thoughts. And as he felt its back, mighty Polyphemus spoke to him:

22 "My fine ram, why leave the cave like this last of the flock? You have never lagged behind before, always the first to step out proudly and graze on the tender grass shoots, always first to reach the flowing river, and first to show your wish to return at evening to the fold. Today you are last of all. You must surely be grieving over your master's eye, blinded by an evil man and his wicked friends, when my wits were fuddled with wine: Nobody, I say, has not yet escaped death. If you only had senses like me, and the power of speech to tell me where he hides himself from my anger, then I'd strike him down, his brains would be sprinkled all over the floor of the cave, and my heart would be eased of the pain that nothing, Nobody, has brought me."

23 With this he drove the ram away from him out of doors, and I loosed myself when the ram was a little way from the cave, then untied my men. Swiftly, keeping an eye behind us, we shepherded those long-limbed sheep, rich and fat, down to the ship. And a welcome

sight, indeed, to our dear friends were we, escapees from death, though they wept and sighed for the others we lost. I would not let them weep though, but stopped them all with a nod and a frown. I told them to haul the host of fine-fleeced sheep on board and put to sea. They boarded swiftly and took their place on the benches then sitting in their rows struck the grey water with their oars. When we were almost out of earshot, I shouted to the Cyclops, mocking him: "It seems he was not such a weakling, then, Cyclops, that man whose friends you meant to tear apart and eat in your echoing cave. Stubborn brute not shrinking from murdering your guests in your own house, your evil deeds were bound for sure to fall on your own head. Zeus and the other gods have had their revenge on you."

Book IX: 480-525
ODYSSEUS TELLS HIS TALE: TELEMUS' PROPHECY

24   He was enraged all the more by my words, and shattering the crest of a tall cliff, he hurled it at us, so that it fell seaward of our blue-prowed vessel, and almost struck the steering oar. The water surged beneath the stone as it fell, and the backwash like a tidal swell from the open sea, carried the ship landward and drove it onto the shore. But seizing a long pole in my hands, I pushed the boat off, and rousing my men ordered them with urgent signs to bend to the oars and save us from disaster. They bent to their oars and rowed, but as soon as we had put water behind us and doubled our distance I began shouting to the Cyclops, though the men round me called out on every side, trying to deter me with their appeals: "Why provoke the savage to anger in this stubborn way? The rock he threw into the sea just now drove the ship back on shore, and we thought we were done for. If he had been able to hear us speak but a word, he would have hurled another jagged stone, and crushed our heads and the ship's timbers with the power of his throw."

25   So they argued, but could not daunt my ardent spirit, and I shouted to him again in anger: "Cyclops, if any man asks how you came by your blindness, say that Odysseus, sacker of cities, Laertes' son, a native of Ithaca, maimed you."

As Odysseus and his men escape on their ship, Polyphemus reveals that long ago he heard prophecy that one day Odysseus would blind him. He tries to coerce Odysseus and his men to return, promising that Poseidon will safely see Odysseus home, but Odysseus rebukes Polyphemus and continues on his way.

Second Read
- Reread the excerpt to answer these text-dependent questions.
- Write any additional questions you have about the text in your Reader/Writer Notebook.

1. **Key Ideas and Details:** Why does Odysseus go to the land of the Cyclops? What evidence in the first two paragraphs tells you this?

2. **Key Ideas and Details:** What does the following quote from paragraph 5 reveal about Odysseus's character? "But I would not listen, though it would have been best, wishing to see the giant himself, and test his hospitality. When he did appear he proved no joy to my men."

My Notes

The Initiation

My Notes

3. **Key Ideas and Details:** Based on the words and actions of the Cyclops, how would you describe his character and his perspective?

4. **Key Ideas and Details:** What does the following reflection reveal about Odysseus's character? "His words were designed to fool me, but failed. I was too wise for that, and answered him with cunning words."

5. **Craft and Structure:** List the verbs used in the blinding of the Cyclops. What effect do these verbs have on the pacing of this event?

6. **Key Ideas and Details:** Why does Odysseus give the Cyclops a false name? How does it help him?

7. **Key Ideas and Details:** Summarize paragraphs 21 and 22. How do Odysseus and his men escape? What makes paragraph 22 dramatic?

8. **Key Ideas and Details:** The adventure on the Road of Trials concludes with Odysseus having the last word of dialogue. Is this an effective way to end? Why or why not?

Working from the Text

9. Use the following chart to organize your notes about Odysseus. Fill in the description column with your notes, and then analyze what this information means about Odysseus. Fill in the analysis column with descriptive words.

Character Analysis of Odysseus		
Element of Character Development	Description	Analysis
Appearance (Adjectives)		
Actions (Verbs)		
Words (Verbs)		
Thoughts/Feelings		
Others' Reactions		

Check Your Understanding

Write a statement to describe Odysseus's character, based on what you've read. Include at least two examples of text evidence to support your statement.

The Initiation

My Notes

10. Which step in the Initiation Stage would best describe these chapters from the *Odyssey*?

11. Analyze the structure of the narrative: map out the sequence of events on a plot diagram. What is the turning point for Odysseus and his men?

12. Return to the passage and skim the text for transition words. Underline any transitional words or phrases you find. What words were used to identify transitions in the passage? How does the author use transitions to convey sequence and signal shifts?

13. What is the mood of this adventure? How does the author create the mood?

Illustrating the Journey

In preparation for the illustrated Hero's Journey Narrative that you will create for the Embedded Assessment, you will analyze a variety of visuals that are used to illustrate text in the activities that follow. In this activity, you will use the graphic organizer that follows to analyze three different images by three different artists, each depicting a scene from the excerpt you just read. First, locate and summarize the text evidence used to illustrate the scene depicted in the image. Then, analyze the language used. What mood is communicated? Lastly, think about the choices the artist made. Does the image accurately reflect the text? Did the artist take any liberties? Is the image effective?

Visual Depictions of the *Odyssey*			
Visuals	**Text Evidence**	**Mood**	**Artist Interpretation**
 As the Cyclops lay sleeping, Odysseus and his men blinded him.			
 Odysseus and his men sneak out of the cave past the Cyclops by hiding among the sheep.			
 Polyphemus tosses rocks at the fleeing Odysseus and his crew.			

The Initiation

14. Discussion Group: Choose an image. Why would the artist choose to illustrate this scene in particular?

15. How is this event related to the Hero's Journey?

16. How does this depiction of Odysseus align with your character analysis?

Drafting the Embedded Assessment

Think about the hero you created in the previous activity. What might the hero experience in the Initiation Stage of his or her journey? Draft an event using your understanding of the Road of Trials to guide your structure and development. Be sure to:

- Use narrative techniques such as dialogue, pacing, and description and develop experiences, events, and/or characters.
- Use diction, detail, and imagery to create tone and mood.
- Sequence the event logically and naturally and use transitions to connect ideas.

Think about the shapes, shading, and expressions used in the visual depictions of the *Odyssey* and how the artist uses these devices to evoke a certain mood. What scene from your narrative would make a good visual?

The Return

Learning Targets
- Analyze a narrative for archetype and narrative techniques.
- Draft and illustrate the final event in a narrative.

The Return
While some stories end once the hero has achieved the Ultimate Boon (the goal he or she set out to achieve), most stories continue into the final stage: The Return.

Preview
In this activity, you will read an excerpt from *A Wrinkle in Time* and think about the archetype of the Hero's Return.

Setting a Purpose for Reading
- As you read, identify steps in the Hero's Return. Mark the text to indicate evidence of each step. Highlight transitions that indicate sequencing through time.
- Circle unknown words and phrases. Try to determine the meaning of the words by using context clues, word parts, or a dictionary.
- In paragraph 3, Meg is posed with a riddle that she must try to solve. When you read the riddle, make a prediction about the answer and write it in the My Notes section. Revise it as you get more information. You will eventually confirm your prediction later in the passage.

LEARNING STRATEGIES:
Marking the Text, Shared Reading, Close Reading, Rereading, Diffusing, Skimming/Scanning, Drafting, Visualizing

WORD CONNECTIONS
Roots and Affixes

The prefix *re-*, as in *return*, is a very common and useful Latin prefix that means "again" or "back." You can see it in many English words, such as *replay*, *rewrite*, *replace*, *regenerate*, *reproduce*, *recall*, *recreate*, and so on.

My Notes

ABOUT THE AUTHOR
Madeleine L'Engle (1918–2007) authored numerous books for children and adults. Her best-known work, *A Wrinkle in Time*, won the 1963 Newbery Medal for best children's book of the year. Oddly enough, L'Engle submitted her manuscript for this book to 26 different publishers—all of whom rejected it. The 27th agreed to its publication. L'Engle's work also included plays and poetry, as well as her autobiography. *A Wrinkle in Time* is part of a series. Other books in the series are *A Wind in the Door*, *A Swiftly Tilting Planet*, *Many Waters*, and *An Acceptable Time*.

Novel

from A Wrinkle in Time

by Madeleine L'Engle
Excerpt from Chapter 12, "The Foolish and the Weak"

This excerpt comes near the end of Meg Murry's journey. She has found her father and they have escaped Camazotz, but they were forced to leave behind her younger brother Charles Wallace in the grip of the "Black Thing." Now Meg must return to Camazotz to get her brother.

1   Immediately Meg was swept into darkness, into nothingness, and then into the icy devouring cold of the Black Thing. Mrs Which won't let it get me, she thought over and over while the cold of the Black Thing seemed to crunch at her bones.

The Return

GRAMMAR & USAGE
Prepositional Phrases

Writers use **prepositional phrases** to add details. Prepositional phrases show relationships of time, direction, or location. Prepositional phrases function as adjectives or adverbs. Look at paragraph 1 in the excerpt from *A Wrinkle in Time*. In the first sentence, the author uses three prepositional phrases beginning with the preposition *into*: *into darkness*, *into nothingness*, and *into the icy devouring cold*. These three prepositional phrases function as adverbs, describing where Meg went. In that same sentence, the author uses the prepositional phrase *of the Black Thing* as an adjective, describing the noun *cold*. Notice how the author's use of these prepositional phrases adds vivid details to describe what is happening to Meg.

As you read *A Wrinkle in Time*, pay attention to how the author uses prepositional phrases to paint a more vivid picture for readers.

eerie: spooky; inspiring fear

consequence: importance

imperceptibly: in a manner that is hardly noticeable

2 Then they were through it, and she was standing breathlessly on her feet on the same hill on which they had first landed on Camazotz. She was cold and a little numb, but no worse than she had often been in the winter in the country when she had spent an afternoon skating on the pond. She looked around. She was completely alone. Her heart began to pound.

3 Then, seeming to echo from all around her, came Mrs Which's unforgettable voice, "I hhave nnott ggivenn yyou mmyy ggifftt. *Yyou hhave ssomethinngg thatt ITT hhass nnott. Thiss ssomethinngg iss yyourr onlly wweapponn. Bbutt yyou mmusstt ffinndd itt fforr yyourrssellff.*" Then the voice ceased, and Meg knew that she was alone.

4 She walked slowly down the hill, her heart thumping painfully against her ribs. There below her was the same row of identical houses they had seen before, and beyond these the linear buildings of the city. She walked along the quiet street. It was dark and the street was deserted. No children playing ball or skipping rope. No mother figures at the doors. No father figures returning from work. In the same window of each house was a light, and as Meg walked down the street all the lights were extinguished simultaneously. Was it because of her presence, or was it simply that it was time for lights out?

5 She felt numb, beyond rage or disappointment or even fear. She put one foot ahead of the other with precise regularity, not allowing her pace to lag. She was not thinking; she was not planning; she was simply walking slowly but steadily toward the city and the domed building where IT lay.

6 Now she approached the outlying buildings of the city. In each of them was a vertical line of light, but it was a dim, **eerie** light, not the warm light of stairways in cities at home. And there were no isolated brightly lit windows where someone was working late, or an office was being cleaned. Out of each building came one man, perhaps a watchman, and each man started walking the width of the building. They appeared not to see her, At any rate they paid no attention to her whatsoever, and she went on past them.

7 What have I got that IT hasn't got? she thought suddenly. What have I possibly got?

8 Now she was walking by the tallest of the business buildings. More dim vertical lines of light. The walls glowed slightly to give a faint illumination to the streets. CENTRAL Central Intelligence was ahead of her. Was the man with red eyes still sitting there? Or was he allowed to go to bed? But this was not where she must go, though the man with red eyes seemed the kind old gentleman he claimed to be when compared with IT. But he was no longer of any **consequence** in the search for Charles Wallace. She must go directly to IT.

9 IT isn't used to being resisted. Father said that's how he managed, and how Calvin and I managed as long as we did. Father saved me then. There's nobody here to save me now. I have to do it myself. I have to resist IT by myself. Is that what I have that IT hasn't got? No, I'm sure IT can resist. IT just isn't used to having *other* people resist.

10 CENTRAL Central Intelligence blocked with its huge rectangle the end of the square. She turned to walk around it, and almost **imperceptibly** her steps slowed.

11 It was not far to the great dome which housed IT.

12 I'm going to Charles Wallace. That's what's important. That's what I have to think of. I wish I could feel numb again the way I did at first. Suppose IT has him somewhere else? Suppose he isn't there?

13 I have to go there first, anyhow. That's the only way I can find out.

14   Her steps got slower and slower as she passed the great bronzed doors, the huge slabs of the CENTRAL Central Intelligence building, as she finally saw ahead of her the strange, light, pulsing dome of IT.

15   Father said it was all right for me to be afraid. He said to go ahead and be afraid. And Mrs Who said—I don't understand what she said but I think it was meant to make me not hate being only me, and me being the way I am. And Mrs Whatsit said to remember that she loves me. That's what I have to think about. Not about being afraid. Or not as smart as IT. Mrs Whatsit loves me. That's quite something, to be loved by someone like Mrs Whatsit.

16   She was there.

17   No matter how slowly her feet had taken her at the end, they had taken her there.

18   Directly ahead of her was the circular building, its walls glowing with **violet** flame, its silvery roof pulsing with a light that seemed to Meg to be insane. Again she could feel the light, neither warm nor cold, but reaching out to touch her, pulling her toward IT.

19   There was a sudden sucking, and she was within.

20   It was as though the wind had been knocked out of her. She gasped for breath, for breath in her own rhythm, not the **permeating** pulsing of IT. She could feel the inexorable beat within her body, controlling her heart, her lungs.

21   But not herself. Not Meg. It did not quite have her.

22   She blinked her eyes rapidly and against the rhythm until the redness before them cleared and she could see. There was the brain, there was IT, lying pulsing and quivering on the dais, soft and exposed and **nauseating**. Charles Wallace was crouched beside IT, his eyes still slowly twirling, his jaw still slack, as she had seen him before, with a **tic** in his forehead **reiterating** the revolting rhythm of IT.

23   As she saw him it was again as though she had been punched in the stomach, for she had to realize afresh that she was seeing Charles, and yet it was not Charles at all. Where was Charles Wallace, her own beloved Charles Wallace?

24   What is it I have got that IT hasn't got?

25   "You have nothing that IT hasn't got," Charles Wallace said coldly. "How nice to have you back, dear sister. We have been waiting for you. We knew that Mrs Whatsit would send you. She is our friend, you know."

26   For an appalling moment Meg believed, and in that moment she felt her brain being gathered up into IT.

27   "No!" she screamed at the top of her lungs. "No! You lie!"

28   For a moment she was free from ITs clutches again.

29   As long as I can stay angry enough IT can't get me.

30   Is that what I have that IT doesn't have?

31   "Nonsense," Charles Wallace said. "You have nothing that IT doesn't have."

32   "You're lying," she replied, and she felt only anger toward this boy who was not Charles Wallace at all. No, it was not anger, it was loathing; it was hatred, sheer and unadulterated, and as she became lost in hatred she also began to be lost in IT. The red miasma swam before her eyes; her stomach churned in ITs rhythm. Her body trembled with the strength of her hatred and the strength of IT.

My Notes

violet: a purplish-blue color

permeating: spreading everywhere

nauseating: making feel ill

reiterating: repeating

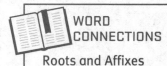

WORD CONNECTIONS

Roots and Affixes

In the word *inexorable*, the prefix *in-* means "not." It has the same meaning in *ineffective* and *inexperienced*. The suffix *-able* means "worthy of," as in *debatable* and *laughable*. The root *-exor-* comes from Latin and means "to plead for." Put together, *inexorable* can be seen to mean "not worthy of pleading for," or in this usage, "unable to be stopped." Use this knowledge to clarify the meaning of the word *extortion* or *insufferable*.

vestige: a bit or trace of
something

WORD CONNECTIONS

Etymology

The word *miasma* appeared
in the 1660s as a Modern
Latin word meaning "noxious
vapors." It derives from the
same Greek word that means
"stain" or "pollution." Now it
is used to mean a poisonous
atmosphere.

My Notes

vulnerable: susceptible to danger

33 With the last **vestige** of consciousness she jerked her mind and body. Hate was nothing that IT didn't have. IT knew all about hate.

34 "You are lying about that, and you were lying about Mrs Whatsit!" she screamed.

35 "Mrs Whatsit hates you," Charles Wallace said.

36 And that was where IT made ITs fatal mistake, for as Meg said, automatically, "Mrs Whatsit loves me; that's what she told me, that she loves me," suddenly she knew.

37 She knew!

38 Love.

39 That was what she had that IT did not have.

40 She had Mrs Whatsit's love, and her father's, and her mother's, and the real Charles Wallace's love, and the twins', and Aunt Beast's.

41 And she had her love for them.

42 But how could she use it? What was she meant to do?

43 If she could give love to IT perhaps it would shrivel up and die, for she was sure that IT could not withstand love. But she, in all her weakness and foolishness and baseness and nothingness, was incapable of loving IT. Perhaps it was not too much to ask of her, but she could not do it.

44 But she could love Charles Wallace.

45 She could stand there and she could love Charles Wallace.

46 Her own Charles Wallace, the real Charles Wallace, the child for whom she had come back to Camazotz, to IT, the baby who was so much more than she was, and who was yet so utterly **vulnerable**.

47 She could love Charles Wallace.

48 Charles. Charles, I love you. My baby brother who always takes care of me. Come back to me, Charles Wallace, come away from IT, come back, come home. I love you, Charles. Oh, Charles Wallace, I love you.

49 Tears were streaming down her cheeks, but she was unaware of them.

50 Now she was even able to look at him, at this animated thing that was not her own Charles Wallace at all. She was able to look and love.

51 I love you. Charles Wallace, you are my darling and my dear and the light of my life and the treasure of my heart, I love you. I love you. I love you.

52 Slowly his mouth closed. Slowly his eyes stopped their twirling. The tic in the forehead ceased its revolting twitch. Slowly he advanced toward her.

53 "I love you!" she cried. "I love you, Charles! I love you!"

54 Then suddenly he was running, pelting, he was in her arms, he was shrieking with sobs. "Meg! Meg! Meg!"

55 "I love you, Charles!" she cried again, her sobs almost as loud as his, her tears mingling with his. "I love you! I love you! I love you!"

56 A whirl of darkness. An icy cold blast. An angry, resentful howl that seemed to tear through her. Darkness again. Through the darkness to save her came a sense of Mrs Whatsit's presence, so that she knew it could not be IT who now had her in its clutches.

57 And then the feel of earth beneath her, of something in her arms, and she was rolling over on the sweet-smelling **autumnal** earth, and Charles Wallace was crying out, "Meg! Oh, Meg!"

autumnal: related to autumn

58 Now she was hugging him close to her, and his little arms were clasped tightly about her neck. "Meg, you saved me! You saved me!" he said over and over.

My Notes

_____

_____

_____

59 "Meg!" came a call, and there were her father and Calvin hurrying through the darkness toward them.

60 Still holding Charles she struggled to stand up and look around. "Father! Cal! Where are we?"

61 Charles Wallace, holding her hand tightly, was looking around, too, and suddenly he laughed, his own, sweet, **contagious** laugh. "In the twins' vegetable garden! And we landed in the broccoli!"

contagious: passed from one person to another

62 Meg began to laugh, too, at the same time that she was trying to hug her father, to hug Calvin, and not to let go of Charles Wallace for one second.

63 "Meg, you did it!" Calvin shouted. "You saved Charles!"

64 "I'm very proud of you, my daughter." Mr. Murry kissed her **gravely**, then turned toward the house. "Now I must go in to Mother." Meg could tell that he was trying to control his anxiety and eagerness.

gravely: seriously

65 "Look!" she pointed to the house, and there were the twins and Mrs. Murry walking toward them through the long, wet grass.

66 "First thing tomorrow I must get some new glasses," Mr. Murry said, squinting in the moonlight, and then starting to run toward his wife.

67 Dennys's voice came crossly over the lawn. "Hey, Meg, it's bedtime."

68 Sandy suddenly yelled, "Father!"

69 Mr. Murry was running across the lawn, Mrs. Murry running toward him, and they were in each other's arms, and then there was a tremendous happy jumble of arms and legs and hugging, the older Murrys and Meg and Charles Wallace and the twins, and Calvin grinning by them until Meg reached out and pulled him in and Mrs. Murry gave him a special hug all of his own. They were talking and laughing all at once, when they were startled by a crash, and Fortinbras, who could bear being left out of the happiness not one second longer, catapulted his sleek black body right through the screened door to the kitchen. He dashed across the lawn to join in the joy, and almost knocked them all over with the exuberance of his greeting.

_____

_____

_____

_____

_____

_____

_____

_____

70 Meg knew all at once that Mrs Whatsit, Mrs Who, and Mrs Which must be near, because all through her she felt a flooding of joy and of love that was even greater and deeper than the joy and love which were already there.

71 She stopped laughing and listened, and Charles listened, too. "Hush."

72 Then there was a whirring, and Mrs Whatsit, Mrs Who, and Mrs Which were standing in front of them, and the joy and love were so tangible that Meg felt that if she only knew where to reach she could touch it with her bare hands.

WORD CONNECTIONS

Cognates

The English word *tangible* is spelled the same as, but pronounced differently than, its Spanish cognate with the same meaning. The Spanish word *catapultar* is a cognate of the English verb *catapult*.

73 Mrs Whatsit said breathlessly, "Oh, my darlings, I'm sorry we don't have time to say good-by to you properly. You see, we have to—"

74 But they never learned what it was that Mrs Whatsit, Mrs Who, and Mrs Which had to do, for there was a gust of wind, and they were gone.

The Return

My Notes

Second Read

- Reread the excerpt to answer these text-dependent questions.
- Write any additional questions you have about the text in your Reader/Writer Notebook.

1. **Craft and Structure:** The word "devouring" is used in paragraph 1. What is the effect of this word choice on the mood of the opening?

2. **Craft and Structure:** Why does the author use mathematical terms such as "linear" and "vertical" to describe the scene?

3. **Key Ideas and Details:** What can you infer about IT as a character in the novel? Provide textual evidence to support your inferences.

4. **Key Ideas and Details:** Throughout the story, how do others assist Meg in her quest to rescue her brother?

5. **Craft and Structure:** Use context clues to determine the meaning of the word "loathing" in paragraph 32. What other word(s) helped you?

6. **Key Ideas and Details:** What is the power of "the Black Thing," of IT, that Meg must battle against? Choose a line that best expresses IT's power and explain your choice.

7. **Knowledge and Ideas:** How does Meg use "the Ultimate Boon" to conquer the power of IT?

8. **Craft and Structure:** What is the meaning of the word "animated" in paragraph 50? Use context clues to help you, and cite textual evidence in your response.

Working from the Text

9. What steps in the Return Stage are illustrated in this section of the novel *A Wrinkle in Time*?

10. Quote examples of Meg's dialogue and internal thoughts (reflections) that show her anxiety and fear about the task she has to do.

11. What does Meg learn during her attempt to conquer the challenge?

Language and Writer's Craft: Verbs and Mood

Writers form and use verbs in the correct mood. The list below shows the moods of English verbs.

Indicative Mood: Verbs that indicate a fact or opinion.
I am too ill to go to school today.

Imperative Mood: Verbs that express a command or request.
Go to school. Please get up and get dressed.

Interrogative Mood: Verbs that ask a question.
Are you going to school? Do you feel ill?

The Return

Conditional Mood: Verbs that express something that hasn't happened or something that can happen if a certain condition is met.

I would have gone to school yesterday if I had felt well.

Your teacher might want you to complete the assignments you missed.

Subjunctive Mood: Verbs that describe a state that is uncertain or contrary to fact. When using the verb "to be" in the subjunctive, always use *were* rather than *was.*

I wish my cold were better today.

If you were to go to school, what would you learn?

PRACTICE Look over the excerpt from *A Wrinkle in Time* again. Find an example of a sentence to illustrate each of the moods above. Write and label these examples in your Reader/Writer Notebook. If you have time, create a few more examples on your own and add those to your Reader/Writer Notebook.

Check Your Understanding

Write 3–4 sentences explaining how Meg represents the Hero in the Hero's Journey archetype. Use text evidence from the excerpt to support your claim.

Reading Graphic Novels

To continue thinking about how to illustrate your narrative, you will take a look at a graphic novel adaptation of the *A Wrinkle in Time* excerpt that you just read. Graphic novels use a combination of images and words to tell real or fictional stories. As you explore the graphic novel, you should note the distinct features that characterize this type of storytelling. Following is a list of features and their uses. These terms can help you speak and write about graphic novels with precision.

Panel—squares or rectangles that contain a single image
Gutter—space between panels
Dialogue Balloon—circular shape that contains communication between/among characters
Thought Bubbles—shape that contains a character's thoughts shared only with the reader
Caption—box that provides background information about the scene or character
Sound Effect—visual clue about sounds in the scene
Long Shot—image that shows a character or object from the distance so you can see its entirety
Extreme Long Shot—image that shows objects or characters in very small scale, often showing a landscape or crowd of characters
Close-up—image that is shown in a large view taking up at least 80 percent of the panel
Extreme Close-up—image that is shown in very large view, often focusing on a small portion of a larger object or character

Setting a Purpose for Reading

As you read the graphic novel adaptation of *A Wrinkle in Time*, identify the step in the Hero's Journey that is illustrated in the excerpt. In addition, think about how the illustrator, Hope Larson, uses graphic novel features to create different effects.

Graphic Novel

from A *Wrinkle* in *Time:* The Graphic Novel

adapted and illustrated by Hope Larsen

My Notes

The Return

The Return

The Return

The Return

The Return

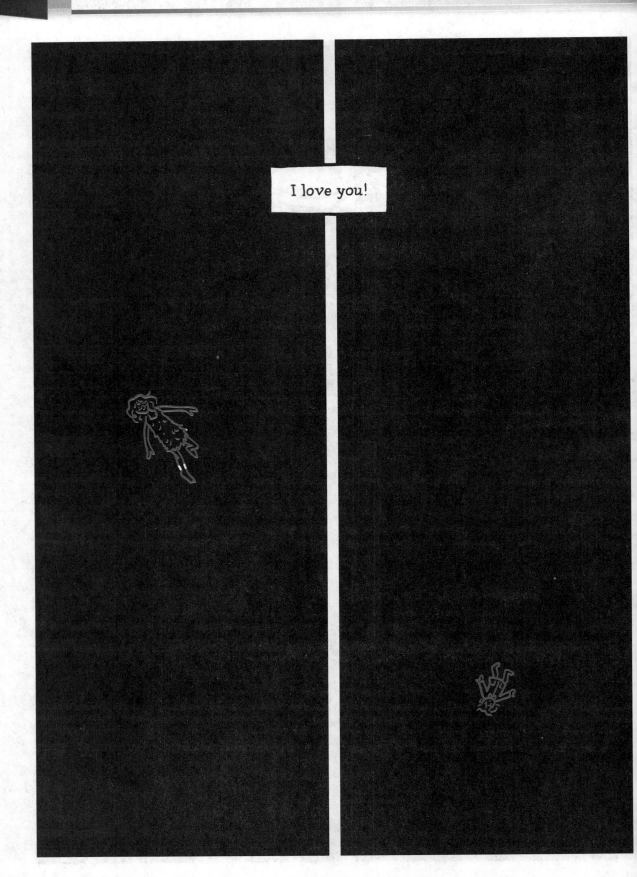

Working from the Text

12. Pick a series of panels (2–3) from the graphic novel to analyze. Once you have made your choice, identify the graphic novel features that were used by the illustrator. Go back to the text and make annotations in the margins where the features are being used.

13. Use the following graphic organizer to record your thoughts about the intended effect of the illustrator's choices.

Feature Identified	Description of Feature	Intended Effect

14. Explain how the illustrator used those features to create a specific mood. Provide supporting detail and commentary for the first feature, using the frame below to guide your response. Then write supporting details for the other two techniques.

Topic Sentence:

The illustrator of *A Wrinkle in Time: The Graphic Novel*, Hope Larson, uses [feature 1], [feature 2], and [feature 3] to create a _____ mood in the ending scene of her graphic novel.

Supporting Detail:

For example, she uses [technique 1] to _____
_____.

Commentary:

[connect the supporting details to the mood]

The Return

Drafting the Embedded Assessment

Revisit your hero narrative. What might your hero learn by the end of the Return Stage in his or her journey? Draft an ending to your narrative using your understanding of the Crossing/Return Threshold to guide your development. Be sure to:

- Use narrative techniques such as dialogue, pacing, and description to communicate ideas.
- Sequence the event logically and naturally (with the beginning and middle).
- Incorporate sentences that use the different verb moods you've learned about in this lesson.

 Independent Reading Checkpoint

What accomplishments did the protagonist in your independent reading text achieve? What vivid language did the author use to describe these accomplishments? Explain why you think these accomplishments do or do not make this character a hero.

Revising and Editing

Learning Targets
- Identify and apply effective techniques and strategies for writing groups.
- Revise and edit a narrative draft through a collaborative writing group.

> **LEARNING STRATEGIES:**
> Collaborative Discussion,
> Sharing and Responding,
> Summarizing, Self-Editing/
> Peer-Editing

Writing Group Roles

For groups to be effective, each member must participate to help achieve the goals of the group. The purpose of writing groups is to:
- Provide an open-minded place to read, respond to, and revise writing.
- Provide meaningful feedback to improve writing based on specific criteria.
- Create specific roles to solicit and manage sharing and responding.
- Focus on posing open-ended questions for the writer to consider.

Writing group members have roles and responsibilities.

Role	Guidelines	Discussion / Response Starters
The Reader: Reads the text silently, then aloud. Begins the conversation after reading.	The Reader's purpose is to share an understanding of the Writer's words. The Reader sees the physical structure of the draft and may comment on that as well. The Reader follows all listeners' guidelines as well.	Reader's and Listeners' **compliments**: • I liked the words you used, such as . . . • I like the way you described . . . • This piece made me feel . . . • This piece reminded me of . . . • I noticed your use of _____ from the Hero's Journey when you . . .
The Listeners: Take notes and prepare open-ended questions for the Writer or make constructive statements.	The Listeners begin with positive statements, using "I" statements to talk about the writing, not the Writer. The Listeners use the **writer's checklist** to produce thoughtful questions that will help strengthen the writing.	Reader's and Listeners' **comments and suggestions**: • I really enjoyed the part where . . . • What parts are you having trouble with? • What do you plan to do next? • I was confused when . . .
The Writer: Listens to the draft, takes notes, responds to questions, and asks questions for clarification.	As his or her work is being read aloud by another, the Writer can get an overall impression of the piece. The Writer takes notes on needed changes. The Writer asks questions to get feedback that will lead to effective revision.	Writer's **questions**: • What do you want to know more about? • Which part does not make sense? • Which section of the text does not work? • How can I improve this part?

1. Summarize the purpose and process of working in a successful writing group.

Revising and Editing

My Notes

The Revision Process

Very few people are able to write a perfect first draft, so revising is a typical part of the writing process—even for famous writers. In an interview done for *The Paris Review* in 1956, the interviewer asked Ernest Hemingway about his writing.

> Interviewer: How much rewriting do you do?
>
> Hemingway: It depends. I rewrote the ending of *Farewell to Arms*, the last page of it, 39 times before I was satisfied.
>
> Interviewer: Was there some technical problem there? What was it that had stumped you?
>
> Hemingway: Getting the words right.
>
> (From Ernest Hemingway, "The Art of Fiction," *The Paris Review* Interview, 1956)

2. Writing groups can help you revise and get your words right. Throughout this unit, you have started a narrative about a hero. As you think about revising your draft, what are some guiding questions you might ask? You might use the Embedded Assessment 1 Scoring Guide to prompt your questions to focus on ideas, organization, and your use of language.

Introducing the Strategy: Self-Editing, Peer-Editing

Editing your writing is a part of the writing process (self-editing). This strategy can be used with a partner (peer-editing) to examine a text closely to identify areas that may need to be corrected for language, grammar, punctuation, capitalization, or spelling.

3. In addition to asking questions, having a writer's checklist can help you revise. Next you will work with members of your writing group to create, on separate paper, a writer's checklist for your Hero's Journey narrative. This checklist should reflect your group's ideas about the following:

   - **Ideas:** Think of the purpose of the writing, the topic, and the details.
   - **Structure:** Think of the writing mode and purpose, as well as organization of the writing.
   - **Use of language:** Think about figurative language, descriptive details, transitions, diction, etc.

4. After completing your writer's checklist, your writing group will read and discuss each member's draft of the Hero's Journey narrative. Group members should trade roles of Reader, Listener, and Writer as they proceed through each draft, following the information in the chart on the previous pages.

Using Resources and References to Revise

How does a writer improve a text through revision? Deep revision takes time and effort. Skilled writers do the following:

- **Add** ideas and language to enhance effect.
- **Delete** irrelevant, unclear, and repetitive ideas and language to improve pacing and effect.
- **Rearrange** ideas to improve sequence.
- **Substitute** ideas and language for effect.

5. Use the writer's checklist you created, the feedback from your peers, and the revision strategies above to guide your revision. Share one of your revisions with the class by explaining specifically what you revised and how it improved your writing.

Editing a Draft

6. New writers sometimes confuse revision with editing or proofreading. Both are extremely important in creating a polished piece of writing, but they are different and separate processes.

- Revision focuses on ideas, organization, and language and involves adding, deleting, rearranging, and substituting words, sentences, and entire paragraphs.
- Editing focuses on conventions of standard English. It involves close proofreading and consulting reference sources to correct errors in grammar and usage, capitalization, punctuation, and spelling.
- After drafting a text, students often either revise *or* edit rather than doing both. Skipping either step in the writing process greatly affects the quality of your final draft.

7. It is essential that writers take the time to edit drafts to correct errors in grammar and usage, capitalization, punctuation, and spelling. Return to your draft and self-edit and peer-edit to strengthen the grammar and language conventions in your draft. Be sure to create a new writer's checklist that contains specific areas of concern.

Check Your Understanding

Exchange your hero narrative draft with a partner. Using the writer's checklist you created in step 3 of this activity, review your partner's draft and make notes about places where the draft can be improved. Provide specific feedback so your partner can make effective revisions.

My Notes

Writing a Hero's Journey Narrative

ASSIGNMENT

Think about all the heroes you have encountered in fiction and real life. What type of hero appeals to you? Write and create an illustrated narrative about an original hero. Use the Hero's Journey archetype to develop and structure your ideas. Orally present your narrative to your classmates.

Planning and Prewriting: Take time to make a plan for your narrative.	▪ What characteristics will your hero possess, and what setting will you choose? ▪ What are the essential elements of a narrative that you will need to include? ▪ What prewriting strategies will you use to plan the organization?
Drafting: Create a draft that includes the elements of an effective narrative.	▪ How will you introduce characters, context, and setting and establish a point of view? ▪ How will you use dialogue, details, and description to create an original, believable hero? ▪ How will you sequence events logically and naturally using steps of the Hero's Journey archetype? ▪ How will you provide a conclusion or resolution that follows from and reflects on the events of the narrative? ▪ How will you find or create illustrations to capture key imagery, emphasize ideas, or add interest?
Evaluating and Revising: Create opportunities to review and revise your work.	▪ When will you share your work with your writing group? ▪ What is your plan to incorporate suggestions and ideas for revisions into your draft? ▪ How can you improve connotative diction and imagery to create tone and mood? ▪ How can the Scoring Guide help you evaluate how well your draft meets the requirements of the assignment?
Checking and Editing: Confirm that your final draft is ready for publication.	▪ How will you proofread and edit your draft to demonstrate command of the conventions of standard English capitalization, punctuation, spelling, grammar, and usage? ▪ How will you create a title and assemble your illustrations in an appealing manner? ▪ How will you prepare a final draft for publication and presentation?

🛜 Technology Tip

Avoid using images in a way that would violate copyright law. You may download or copy an image for personal use and provide the source, but you may not broadcast the image without the owner's permission.

Reflection

After completing this Embedded Assessment, think about how you went about accomplishing this task, and respond to the following:

• How did your understanding of the Hero's Journey archetype help you create an original narrative?

SCORING GUIDE

Scoring Criteria	Exemplary	Proficient	Emerging	Incomplete
Ideas	The narrative • creates a complex, original protagonist • establishes a clear point of view, setting, and conflict • uses precise and engaging details, dialogue, imagery, and description • includes a variety of enhancing visuals.	The narrative • creates a believable, original protagonist • establishes point of view, setting, and conflict • uses adequate details, dialogue, imagery, and description • includes sufficient visuals.	The narrative • creates an unoriginal or undeveloped protagonist • establishes a weak point of view, setting, or conflict • uses inadequate narrative techniques • includes insufficient, unrelated, or inappropriate visuals.	The narrative • lacks a protagonist • does not establish point of view, setting, or conflict • uses minimal narrative techniques • includes few or no visuals.
Structure	The narrative • engages and orients the reader with detailed exposition • sequences events in the plot effectively, including a variety of steps from the Hero's Journey archetype • uses a variety of transitional strategies effectively and purposefully • provides a thoughtful resolution.	The narrative • orients the reader with adequate exposition • sequences events in the plot logically, including some steps of the Hero's Journey archetype • uses transitional words, phrases, and clauses to link events and signal shifts • provides a logical resolution.	The narrative • provides weak or vague exposition • sequences events unevenly, including minimal or unclear steps of the Hero's Journey archetype • uses inconsistent, repetitive, or basic transitional words, phrases, and clauses • provides a weak or disconnected resolution.	The narrative • lacks exposition • has minimal plot with no apparent connection to the Hero's Journey archetype • uses few or no transitional strategies • lacks a resolution.
Use of Language	The narrative • is presented using effective volume, clarity, and eye contact • demonstrates command of the conventions of standard English capitalization, punctuation, spelling, grammar, and usage (including appropriate use of a variety of moods).	The narrative • is presented using appropriate volume, pronunciation, and eye contact • demonstrates adequate command of the conventions of standard English capitalization, punctuation, spelling, grammar, and usage (including appropriate use of moods).	The narrative • is presented with some attention to eye contact, volume, and pace of delivery • demonstrates partial or inconsistent command of the conventions of standard English capitalization, punctuation, spelling, grammar, and usage.	The narrative • is presented with little attention to eye contact, volume, and pacing • lacks command of the conventions of standard English capitalization, punctuation, spelling, grammar, and usage; frequent errors obscure meaning.

LEARNING STRATEGIES:
QHT, Close Reading,
Paraphrasing, Graphic
Organizer

My Notes

_____
_____
_____
_____
_____
_____
_____
_____

ACADEMIC VOCABULARY
It is important to be precise
and **concise** in writing and
speaking. To be **concise** is
to be brief and to the point.
Conciseness is expressing
a great deal in just a few
words.

_____
_____
_____
_____
_____
_____
_____
_____
_____
_____
_____
_____
_____
_____
_____
_____
_____

Learning Targets
- Reflect on previous learning and make connections to new learning.
- Identify and analyze the skills and knowledge necessary to be successful in completing Embedded Assessment 2.

Making Connections
In the first part of this unit, you learned about the archetype of the Hero's Journey, and you wrote your own illustrated narrative depicting a protagonist who makes a heroic journey. In this half of the unit, you will continue thinking about heroism and what makes a hero; your work will culminate in an essay in which you create your definition of a hero.

Essential Questions
Reflect on your understanding of Essential Question 1: How has your understanding of the Hero's Journey changed over the course of this unit? Then, respond to Essential Question 2, which will be the focus of the rest of the unit: How does the Hero's Journey archetype appear in stories throughout time?

Developing Vocabulary
Re-sort the vocabulary from the first half of the unit, using the QHT strategy. Compare the new sort with your original sort. How has your understanding changed? Select one word and write a **concise** statement about how your understanding of the word has changed over the course of this unit.

Unpacking Embedded Assessment 2
Read the assignment for Embedded Assessment 2 closely to identify and analyze the components of the assignment.

> Think about people who deserve status as a hero from the past, from the present, from life, and from literature. What defines a hero? Write a multi-paragraph essay that develops your definition of heroism. Be sure to use strategies of definition (function, example, and negation) to guide your writing.

Using the assignment and the Scoring Guide, work with your class to analyze the prompt and create a graphic organizer to use as a visual reminder of the required concepts (what you need to know) and skills (what you need to do). Copy the graphic organizer in your Reader/Writer Notebook.

After each activity, use this graphic to guide reflection about what you have learned and what you still need to learn in order to be successful on the Embedded Assessment.

Preparing for Explanatory Writing

1. How are explanatory and narrative writing similar? How are they different? List ideas below, and then create a graphic organizer on separate paper to show your thinking.

Similarities	Differences

My Notes

Preparing for Explanatory Writing

2. You are often asked to define vocabulary terms and to explain your understanding of what something means. Abstract concepts, such as heroism, can also be defined. Practice thinking about how to define an abstract concept by working in a small group or with a partner to develop a list of words that describe each of the concepts below.

- freedom
- responsibility
- sacrifice
- friendship

Check Your Understanding

Working with the same partner or group, write a brief paragraph defining one of the abstract concepts listed above. Make sure the paragraph demonstrates your understanding of the concept.

INDEPENDENT READING LINK

Read and Research

Continue your exploration of the *heroes* theme by choosing a fiction or nonfiction text about a historical or modern hero for your independent reading. Research the author of the text to find out why they might have chosen to write about this particular hero.

The Nuance of Tone

LEARNING STRATEGIES:
Note-taking, Graphic Organizer,
Discussion Groups

Literary Terms

Tone is a writer's or speaker's attitude toward a subject.
Diction is a writer's or speaker's choice of words.
Denotation is the direct meaning of a word or expression, as distinguished from the ideas or meanings associated with it or suggested by it.
Connotation is the implied associations, meanings, or emotions associated with a word.

ACADEMIC VOCABULARY

Nuance refers to a subtle difference or distinction in meaning.

My Notes

Learning Target

• Explain how nuances in tone words arise from connotation.

Understanding Tone

In literature, being able to recognize the **tone** of a story or poem or essay is an important skill in understanding the author's purpose. An author who is trying to create a comedy skit needs to choose content and language that communicates humor rather than sadness. Writers purposefully select diction to create an appropriate tone.

1. What is the connection between **tone** and **diction**? Many words have a similar **denotation**, but one must learn to distinguish among the **connotations** of these words in order to accurately identify meaning and tone. Careful readers and writers understand **nuances** (subtle differences) in word meanings. This means that they recognize that words have varying levels of meaning.

   Examples: *house, home, abode, estate, shack, mansion,* and *hut* all describe or **denote** a place to live, but each has a different **connotation** that determines meaning and tone.

2. Create examples like the one above illustrating ranges of words that have the same denotation but different connotations. Independently, write your examples below, and then pair with another student to share your words.

3. Use one of the examples you just created to discuss how connotation connects to tone.

Identifying Nuances in Diction

4. On the following page are some common tone words and their **synonyms**. Use a dictionary to determine or clarify each synonym's precise meaning. After taking notes on the denotation of each word, number the words to indicate the various levels of meaning, from least intense to most intense (1 = least intense). If your group feels that two words have the same connotation and level of meaning, give them the same ranking.

Angry: upset, enraged, irritated, sharp, vexed, livid, infuriated, incensed
Happy: mirthful, joyful, jovial, ecstatic, light-hearted, exultant, jubilant, giddy
Sad: poignant, despondent, sentimental, lugubrious, morose, woeful, mournful, desolate
Honest: sincere, candid, outspoken, forthright, frank, unbiased, blunt
Calm: placid, still, bored, composed, peaceful, tranquil, serene, soothing
Nervous: anxious, apprehensive, hesitant, fretful, agitated, jittery, afraid
Smart: wise, perceptive, quick-witted, clever, sagacious, intellectual, brainy, bright, sharp

5. Prepare to present your findings to the class. Use the outline below to prepare for your presentation.

My Notes

Our group studied words that have the same denotation as _____.

The most intense word is _____, which means _____.

One would feel _____ if / when _____ [specific situation].

The least intense word is _____, which means _____.

One would feel _____ if / when _____ [specific situation].

Our favorite word is _____, which means _____.

One would feel _____ if / when _____ [specific situation].

6. While other groups present, listen to comprehend, and take notes. You will be responsible for applying this vocabulary in future activities.

Check Your Understanding

You've learned how words with the same denotation, or meaning, can have different connotations, or tone. Think about the many different verbs you can use to describe how someone walks from one place to another. Rewrite the sentence below twice, first replacing the underlined verb with a verb that has a connotation of joy and then replacing it with a verb that has a connotation of anger.

Jack walked out of the house.

Physical and Emotional Challenges

LEARNING STRATEGIES:
TP-CASTT, Diffusing,
Rereading, Paraphrasing,
Summarizing, Close Reading,
Marking the Text, Free Writing

Learning Targets

- Analyze and compare the structure of a literary and an informational text on similar subjects.
- Make thematic connections relating to heroism in a written response.

Preview

In this activity, you will read a poem and an informational text on similar subjects and compare them.

Introducing the Strategy: TP-CASTT

This reading strategy is used to analyze a poetic text by identifying and discussing each topic in the acronym: *Title, Paraphrase, Connotation, Attitude, Shift, Title* again, and *Theme*. The strategy is a guide designed to lead you in an analysis of a literary text. It is most effective if you begin at the top and work your way down the elements. However, you will find that as you study one element, you will naturally begin to explore others. For example, a study of *connotation* often leads to a discussion of **tone** and *shifts*. Revisiting the *title* often leads to a discussion of the *theme*.

Setting a Purpose for Reading

- As you read, connect this poem to the ideas of challenge, the Hero's Journey, and heroism. Put an exclamation mark next to phrases, stanzas, or paragraphs that remind you of these ideas.
- Circle unknown words and phrases. Try to determine the meaning of the words by using context clues, word parts, or a dictionary.

ABOUT THE AUTHOR

Nina Cassian (1924–2014) was a prominent writer in Romania until she was exiled for her poems satirizing the Romanian president's regime. She sought refuge in the United States and lived in New York City for many years. Cassian wrote more than 50 volumes of work, including poetry, fiction, and books for children. Cassian was also a journalist, film critic, and composer of classical music.

Poetry

A Man

by Nina Cassian

While fighting for his country, he lost an arm

And was suddenly afraid:

"From now on, I shall only be able to do things by halves.

I shall reap half a harvest.

My Notes

5 I shall be able to play either the tune
  or the accompaniment on the piano,
  but never both parts together.
  I shall be able to bang with only one fist
  on doors, and worst of all
10 I shall only be able to half hold
  my love close to me.
  There will be things I cannot do at all,
  applaud for example,
  at shows where everyone applauds."

15 From that moment on, he set himself to do
  everything with twice as much enthusiasm.
  And where the arm had been torn away
  a wing grew.

Second Read

- Reread the poem to answer these text-dependent questions.
- Write any additional questions you have about the text in your Reader/Writer Notebook.

1. **Key Ideas and Details:** What kinds of things is the man afraid of not being able to do? What do these worries tell you about his character?

2. **Craft and Structure:** Is the last sentence of this poem meant to be understood literally or figuratively? How does the connotation of "wing" help create the mood of the poem?

Working from the Text

3. Use the TP-CASTT strategy to analyze the poem. Record your responses in the graphic organizer that follows. Read the poem several times, each time discussing aspects of the TP-CASTT strategy and recording your responses.

4. After reading the poem several times, return to the TP-CASTT graphic organizer and write a brief paragraph to summarize the poem and state its meaning.

My Notes

Physical and Emotional Challenges

Strategy	Response / Analysis
Title: Think about the title before reading the text to predict what it will be about.	**Prediction:**
Paraphrase: After diffusing the text, translate the most challenging lines of the poem into your own words (you may need to reread the text several times). Then briefly summarize the poem.	**Poem Summary:**
Connotation: Mark the text by highlighting the diction (words and phrases) used for positive effect (color 1) and/or negative effect (color 2). Then, study the diction to determine a pattern (e.g., mostly negative, begins negatively but ends positively) and record your analysis.	**Pattern: (+/−)**
Attitude (Tone): Determine how the writer or speaker feels about the subject of the poem. (There might be more than one tone.) Highlight words that convey tone. Be sure to use precise tone words (e.g., mournful, not sad). Finally, summarize the tone.	**Tone Summary:**
Shift: Identify shifts, such as in the speaker, setting, subject, tone, or images. After **marking the text** with a star and numbering each, study and explain the shifts.	**Shifts:**
Title: Examine the title to determine the deeper meaning. Look beyond the literal, even if the title is simple (e.g. "Choices"). Record ideas.	**Deeper Meaning:**
Theme: Determine the message about life implied in the poem. After you identify a subject (e.g., friendship), write a statement about the subject that sounds like a piece of advice (e.g., For a friendship to survive, one must be selfless, not selfish). Record your theme statement(s).	**Theme Statement(s):**

Setting a Purpose for Reading

- As you read this newspaper article, think about its audience and purpose. Write ideas you have in the My Notes section.
- Circle unknown words and phrases. Try to determine the meaning of the words by using context clues, word parts, or a dictionary.

Article

Soldier home after losing his leg in AFGHANISTAN

by Gale Fiege

1 LAKE STEVENS – It started out as just another day in the Zabul Province of southern Afghanistan.

2 On Sept. 18, 2010, Army Pfc. Tristan Eugene Segers, a 2002 graduate of Lake Stevens High School, was driving his armored patrol vehicle when a homemade bomb exploded in the road underneath Segers' floorboard.

3 One of the vehicle's 800-pound tires was found a half-mile away.

4 Just below his knee, Segers' right leg was gone. He had **shrapnel** sticking out of his eyeballs, face and arms.

5 After nearly two years of surgeries and rehabilitation in Texas, Segers, a handsome 28-year-old, moved back to Snohomish County last week in time to celebrate Independence Day with his folks in the home where he grew up.

6 Segers is married now to his high school girlfriend, Lindsay Blanchard. They are expecting a baby boy in October. He plans to return to culinary arts school this fall and they are about to move into an apartment in the Bothell area.

shrapnel: small fragments of a bomb after it explodes

GRAMMAR &USAGE
Appositives

An appositive is a noun or pronoun that identifies or explains another noun or pronoun near it. If an appositive has modifiers, then it is part of an appositive phrase. A nonrestrictive appositive is not necessary to the meaning of the sentence, so it is set off with commas. See the Grammar Handbook for more about restrictive and nonrestrictive appositives.

In paragraph 2 of the article, the writer uses an appositive phrase to explain who Tristan Eugene Segers is: ". . . Eugene Segers, **a 2002 graduate of Lake Stevens High School,** was driving . . . ." The appositive is the noun *graduate*. The other words in the phrase modify *graduate*. The article contains several more appositives and appositive phrases. Find one or two and note which noun each one identifies or explains.

WORD CONNECTIONS

Etymology

The English word *culinary* appeared in the 1630s, having derived from the Latin word *culinarius,* which means "of the kitchen." About 20 years later, it took on the meaning "of cooking." The English word *kiln*, which is an oven, also comes from the same Latin root.

grueling: physically demanding
elite: made of the best and most able

My Notes

_____

_____

_____

_____

rigorous: full of difficulty

_____

_____

_____

_____

_____

_____

_____

_____

_____

_____

_____

_____

_____

7 Until his official Army retirement date on Aug. 21, he is Cpl. Segers, the owner of a Purple Heart.[1]

8 Segers wears shorts in the warm summer weather, not even pretending to hide his prosthetic leg. He has run a marathon. A specially designed gas pedal is on the left side of his slate-gray Toyota Tacoma truck.

9 Nothing is stopping him.

10 "Everybody's injury is different and everybody handles it in their own way. There is no way to measure it, whether it's physical or mental," Segers said. "I just kept telling the doctors that I didn't want my life to be different than it was before. Of course, the loss of a leg changed me. But it doesn't define me or the rest of my life."

11 Segers was enjoying a promising start to a career as a chef when the economic recession forced him to consider joining the Army. He figured he would serve in the family tradition set by his father and grandfather.

12 After **grueling** training in the hot Georgia sun, he landed a spot in the Army's 101st Airborne Pathfinder Division, an **elite** infantry unit, and was sent to Afghanistan in February 2010 to work on personnel recovery missions.

13 After the explosion, Segers was stabilized and flown to the Army hospital in Landstuhl, Germany.

14 "My eyes were completely bandaged and I was in a lot of pain. The stretchers were on bunks in the airplane, so when I woke up it felt like I was in a coffin," Segers said. "I was so glad to hear the voice of my buddy, Andrew Leonard, a guy from Boston who had been injured earlier."

15 Tristan Segers can't say enough good things about the surgeons, psychiatrists, physical therapists and other staff at the Army hospital, as well as the numerous charitable organizations such as the Fisher House Foundation that help wounded veterans.

16 "I was truly cared for," he said. "The rehabilitation was **rigorous** and I pushed it, building back my muscles and learning to use the prosthetic leg.

17 "But they never told me I was doing a good job for fear that I might get complacent. There were many guys there who had given up on life."

18 "Most of the time when people see my leg, they think I've been in a car accident or something. But sometimes an old veteran will stop me and thank me for my service," Segers said. "I didn't do anything special, but if the progress I have made motivates another wounded veteran to keep going, then that's great."

---

[1] **Purple Heart:** a medal given to U.S. military personnel who are injured in the line of duty

Second Read

- Reread the article to answer these text-dependent questions.
- Write any additional questions you have about the text in your Reader/Writer Notebook.

5. **Key Ideas and Details:** What is the purpose of the first four paragraphs of this article?

6. **Craft and Structure:** The author uses the word "folks" in paragraph 5 to mean family. What effect does this word choice have?

7. **Key Ideas and Details:** Choose a statement made by Segers that expresses the central idea driving Segers's life now. What facts in the story support this idea?

8. **Knowledge and Ideas:** Notice how the language changes as it describes his Army assignment. What is an "elite" infantry unit? What are "personnel recovery missions"?

Working from the Text

9. Consider the audience and purpose of each of the texts you just read. How are they similar and different?

10. How does the structure of each text support its purpose? What language choices does each author make to support his or her purpose?

11. Write a paragraph that compares and contrasts the structure and language of both the poem and the article and analyzes how this contributes to their meaning and style.

12. To determine the theme of both texts, ask yourself, what does each text say about the concept of heroism? Write a theme statement about heroism that connects both texts. Then, write a summary that supports your interpretation using evidence from both the poem and the article.

My Notes

Check Your Understanding

Briefly explain how the character in the poem and Tristan Eugene Segers in the article exemplify the concept of "hero."

Introducing the Strategy: Free Writing

The **free writing** strategy allows writers to write freely without pressure to be correct or complete. A free write gives a writer the freedom to write in an informal style and get ideas on paper in preparation for a more complete and formal writing assignment. This strategy helps writers refine and clarify thoughts, spark new ideas, and/or generate content during drafting or revision.

13. Before you complete the writing prompt, use the free writing strategy to prepare.

Explanatory Writing Prompt

Write an explanatory essay about a challenge you have faced that includes examples of specific things you did to overcome adversity. Be sure to:

* Clearly explain the challenge you faced.
* Cite specific examples and experiences that helped you overcome your challenge.
* Summarize your outcome clearly.

Definition Strategies

Learning Targets
- Identify and apply definition strategies of function, example, and negation.
- Form an initial definition of heroism.

Preview
In this activity, you will learn and use various definition strategies and read an article about how one author defines a hero.

Writing to Define
For Embedded Assessment 2, you will be writing a definition essay to share your personal understanding of the concept of heroism. To write this definition of heroism, you will need various strategies and knowledge to create an expanded definition of the concept. First, you can expand your collection of words that describe heroes and heroism.

1. **Defining heroes:** Generate a list of
   - **Adjectives** that could describe what a hero is:
     A hero is (adjective) brave,
   - **Nouns** that could define what a hero shows:
     A hero shows (noun) courage,

   - **Verbs** that could define what a hero does:
     A hero (verb) fights,

2. After sharing and consulting additional resources such as a thesaurus, group and then sort synonyms to represent the nuances of the words (subtle differences in meanings). Record these terms in your Reader/Writer Notebook for future reference.

Defining a Concept
Part of defining any concept is finding ways to describe the concept to make it clear to others. Writers of a **definition essay** use **strategies of definition** to clarify, develop, and organize ideas. The three **definition** strategies you will learn in this unit are **function**, **example**, and **negation**.
- **Definition by function:** Paragraphs using the **function** strategy explain how the concept functions or operates in the real world.
- **Definition by example:** Paragraphs using the **example** strategy use specific examples of the concept from texts or life.
- **Definition by negation:** Paragraphs using the **negation** strategy explain what something is by showing what it is not. A nonexample should be based on what someone else would say is an example. If no one would disagree with the negation, it is ineffective.

My Notes

Definition Strategies

ACADEMIC VOCABULARY

ACADEMIC VOCABULARY
Describing the **function** of something is telling how something is used. The verb *to function* means "to act as or to operate as."

Just as a **negative** answer would be a no, to **negate** is to deny or make ineffective. The noun *negation* means "showing what something is not in order to prove what it is."

My Notes

3. Read the following passages of definition and decide whether they contain definition by **function**, example, and/or **negation**. Be able to explain why you categorized ideas as you did. First, highlight the topic being defined. Then, decide the type of definition being used.

- "But just for the purposes of this discussion, let us say: one's family are those toward whom one feels loyalty and obligation, and/or from whom one derives identity, and/or to whom one gives identity, and/or with whom one shares habits, tastes, stories, customs, memories." (Marilynn Robinson, "Family." *The Death of Adam: Essays on Modern Thought*. Houghton Mifflin, 1998)

- "It's always seemed odd to me that *nonfiction* is defined, not by what it *is*, but by what it is *not*. It is *not* fiction. But then again, it is also *not* poetry, or technical writing or libretto. It's like defining classical music as *nonjazz*." (Philip Gerard, *Creative Nonfiction*. Story Press, 1996)

- "Love is patient and kind; love does not envy or boast; it is not arrogant or rude. It does not insist on its own way; it is not irritable or resentful; it does not rejoice at wrongdoing, but rejoices with the truth. Love bears all things, believes all things, hopes all things, endures all things. Love never ends." (*The Bible*, I Corinthians 13:4–8a)

- "Let me not to the marriage of true minds
  admit impediments. Love is not love
  which alters when it alteration finds,
  or bends with the remover to remove:

  O no! It is an ever-fixed mark
  that looks on tempests and is never shaken;
  it is the star to every wandering bark,
  whose worth's unknown, although his height be taken.

  Love's not time's fool, though rosy lips and cheeks
  within his bending sickle's compass come:
  love alters not with his brief hours and weeks,
  but bears it out even to the edge of doom.

  If this be error and upon me proved,
  I never writ, nor no man ever loved."

  ("Sonnet 116," by William Shakespeare)

Setting a Purpose for Reading

- As you read, put exclamation marks next to the author's definition of heroism.
- Highlight details the author gives to support his definition.
- Circle unknown words and phrases. Try to determine the meaning of the words by using context clues, word parts, or a dictionary.

ABOUT THE AUTHOR

Oliver Stone became a movie director after serving in the Vietnam War. Stone's films have explored historical subjects, such as the Vietnam War and President Kennedy's assassination. Stone has won two Academy Awards for Best Director for the films *Platoon* and *Born on the Fourth of July*. He also won an Academy Award for Best Screenplay Writing for *Midnight Express*.

Article
Where I Find My Heroes

by Oliver Stone

from McCall's Magazine, November 1992

1   It's not true that there are no heroes anymore—but it is true that my own concept of heroism has changed radically over time. When I was young and I read the Random House biographies, my heroes were always people like George Washington and General Custer and Abraham Lincoln and Teddy Roosevelt. Men, generally, and doers. Women—with the exception of Clara Barton, Florence Nightingale, and Joan of Arc — got **short shrift**. Most history was oriented toward male heroes.

2   But as I've gotten older, and since I've been to war, I've been forced to reexamine the nature of life and of heroism. What is true? Where are the myths?

3   The simple acts of heroism are often overlooked—that's very clear to me not only in war but in peace. I'm not **debunking** all of history: Crossing the Delaware was a magnificent action. But I am saying that I think the meaning of heroism has a lot to do with evolving into a higher human being. I came into contact with it when I worked with Ron Kovic, the **paraplegic** Vietnam vet, on *Born on the Fourth of July*. I was impressed by his life change, from a patriotic and strong-willed athlete to someone who had to deal with the total surrender of his body, who grew into a nonviolent and peaceful advocate of change in the Martin Luther King, Jr., and Gandhi tradition. So heroism is tied to an evolution of consciousness....

4   Since the war, I've had children, and I'm wrestling now with the everyday problems of trying to share my knowledge with them without overwhelming them. It's difficult to be a father, to be a mother, and I think that to be a kind and loving parent is an act of heroism. So there you go—heroes are everyday, common people. Most of what they do goes unheralded, unappreciated. And that, ironically, is heroism: not to be recognized.

My Notes

short shrift: little attention

debunking: proving false

paraplegic: not having movement in the legs

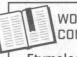

WORD CONNECTIONS

Etymology

The English word *advocate* was first used in the mid-1300s to refer to someone who argues a case in court. It was derived from the French word *avocar*, meaning "spokesman," which was itself derived from the Latin *advocatus*, meaning "one called to aid." The word *advocate* was first used as a verb in the 1640s.

Definition Strategies

My Notes

corruption: fraud

strive: to work hard for
ridiculing: making fun of

5 Who is heroic? Scientists who spend years of their lives trying to find cures for diseases. The teenager who says no to crack. The inner-city kid who works at McDonald's instead of selling drugs. The kid who stands alone instead of joining a gang, which would give him an instant identity. The celebrity who remains modest and treats others with respect, or who uses his position to help society. The student who defers the immediate pleasure of making money and finishes college or high school. People who take risks despite fears. People in wheelchairs who don't give up….

6 We have a lot of **corruption** in our society. But we mustn't assume that everything is always basely motivated. We should allow for the heroic impulse—which is to be greater than oneself, to try to find another version of oneself, to grow. That's where virtue comes from. And we must allow our young generation to **strive** for virtue, instead of **ridiculing** it.

Second Read

• Reread the article to answer these text-dependent questions.
• Write any additional questions you have about the text in your Reader/Writer Notebook.

4. **Key Ideas and Details:** What is the connection among the examples of heroes Stone lists in paragraph 5?

Working from the Text

5. How is Stone's definition of a hero different from the traditional idea of a hero as represented by the examples in paragraph 1?

6. State Stone's definition of heroism in one concise statement.

7. How does Stone use the example strategy to support his definition? Cite textual evidence to support your analysis.

8. How do the final sentences provide a call to action and a final clarification of heroism?

INDEPENDENT READING LINK

Read and Respond

Think about how you could use the protagonist of the book you are reading as part of a definition of a hero. How is he/she an example of a heroic type? Write your response in your Reader/Writer Notebook.

9. The heroes mentioned by Oliver Stone are listed below. Choose one or think of one of your own. Do a quick search to determine what made the person a hero.

- George Washington
- General Custer
- Abraham Lincoln
- Teddy Roosevelt
- Martin Luther King, Jr.

- Clara Barton
- Florence Nightingale
- Joan of Arc
- Ron Kovic
- Mohandas Gandhi

Beginning a Definition of Hero

10. After reading and thinking about definition strategies and heroes, use the graphic organizer that follows to begin organizing your definition of a hero according to the three different strategies for definition: function, example, and negation.

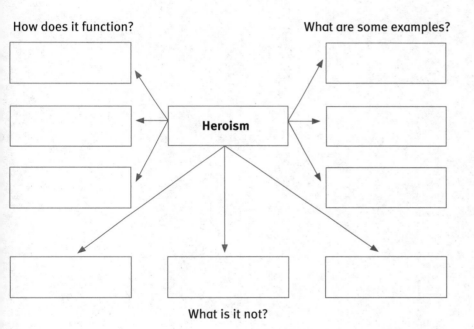

How does it function?

What are some examples?

Heroism

What is it not?

Check Your Understanding

Quickwrite: Describe a person you know or have read about who is a "hero."

My Notes

Definition Strategies

Explanatory Writing Prompt

Think about how to define a hero by how he or she functions or acts. Draft a paragraph that establishes the function of a hero. Cite examples from texts you have read throughout this unit. Remember that the function strategy explains how an idea or concept operates in the world. Be sure to:

- Begin with a topic sentence that states how a hero functions in the world.
- Provide supporting detail (paraphrased and directly quoted) from life and from the texts you have read and provide commentary to develop ideas.
- Use transitions to create coherence.

Revise the language in your draft by creating figurative imagery (a metaphor) to express an idea.

Learning Targets

- Compare two sets of poems to autobiographical excerpts and analyze how structure contributes to meaning.
- Draft a written response using the example definition strategy.

Preview

In this activity, you will read two sets of paired passages. The first pair is about Abraham Lincoln, and the second is about Frederick Douglass.

Setting a Purpose for Reading

- As you read, underline words and phrases that the authors use to portray Lincoln as a heroic figure.
- Circle unknown words and phrases. Try to determine the meaning of the words by using context clues, word parts, or a dictionary.

> **ABOUT THE AUTHOR**
>
> Dr. Phineas D. Gurley (1816–1868) was the pastor of the New York Avenue Presbyterian Church (in Washington, D.C.), which Abraham Lincoln attended during his presidency. Gurley was also Chaplain of the United States Senate. Gurley preached this funeral sermon in the White House East Room on April 19, 1865, four days after Lincoln's assassination.

LEARNING STRATEGIES:
TP-CASTT, Diffusing, Close Reading, Marking the Text, Paraphrasing, Summarizing, Rereading

My Notes

Sermon

from White House Funeral

Sermon

for Abraham Lincoln

by Dr. Phineas D. Gurley

He is dead; but the God in whom he trusted lives, and He can guide and strengthen his successor, as He guided and strengthened him. He is dead; but the memory of his virtues, of his wise and patriotic counsels and labors, of his calm and steady faith in God lives, is precious, and will be a power for good in the country quite down to the end of time. He is dead; but the cause he so **ardently** loved, so ably, patiently, faithfully represented and defended—not for himself only, not for us only, but for all people in all their coming generations, till time shall be no more—that cause survives his fall, and will survive it. The light of its brightening prospects flashes cheeringly to-day athwart[1] the gloom occasioned by his death, and the language of God's united **providences** is telling us that, though the friends of Liberty die, Liberty itself is **immortal**. There is no assassin strong enough and no weapon deadly enough to **quench** its inextinguishable life, or arrest its onward march to the conquest and empire of the world. This is our confidence, and this is our consolation, as we weep and mourn to-day. Though our beloved President is slain, our beloved country is saved. And so we sing of mercy as well as of judgment. Tears of gratitude mingle with those of sorrow. While there is darkness, there is also the dawning of a brighter, happier day upon our stricken and weary land. God be praised that our fallen Chief lived long enough to see the day dawn and the daystar of joy and peace arise upon the nation. He saw it, and he was glad. Alas! alas! He only saw the *dawn*. When the *sun* has risen, full-orbed and glorious, and a happy

ardently: passionately
providences: guardianship exercised by a deity
immortal: living forever
quench: to put an end to

---

[1] **athwart:** across or against

consecrated: blessed
repair: to go often
incentives: reasons to do
something

reunited people are rejoicing in its light—alas! alas! it will shine upon his grave. But that grave will be a precious and a **consecrated** spot. The friends of Liberty and of the Union will **repair** to it in years and ages to come, to pronounce the memory of its occupant blessed, and, gathering from his very ashes, and from the rehearsal of his deeds and virtues, fresh **incentives** to patriotism, they will there renew their vows of fidelity[2] to their country and their God.

My Notes

_____
_____
_____
_____
_____
_____
_____
_____
_____

ABOUT THE AUTHOR

Walt Whitman (1819–1892) is now considered one of America's greatest poets, but his untraditional poetry was not well received during his lifetime. As a young man, he worked as a printer and a journalist while writing free-verse poetry. His collection of poems, *Leaves of Grass*, first came out in 1855, and he revised and added to it several times over the years. During the Civil War, he worked in Washington, first caring for injured soldiers in hospitals and later as a government clerk.

Poetry

O Captain! My Captain!

by Walt Whitman

O Captain! my Captain! our fearful trip is done;
The ship has weather'd every **rack**, the prize we sought is won;
The port is near, the bells I hear, the people all exulting,
While follow eyes the steady keel, the **vessel** grim and daring:
5   But O heart! heart! heart!
      O the bleeding drops of red,
        Where on the deck my Captain lies,
          Fallen cold and dead.

O Captain! my Captain! rise up and hear the bells;
10 Rise up—for you the flag is flung—for you the bugle trills;
For you bouquets and ribbon'd wreaths—for you the shores a-crowding,
For you they call, the swaying mass, their eager faces turning;
    Here Captain! dear father!
      This arm beneath your head;
15   It is some dream that on the deck,
        You've fallen cold and dead.

My Captain does not answer, his lips are pale and still;
My father does not feel my arm, he has no pulse nor will;
The ship is anchored safe and sound, its voyage closed and done;

rack: a windy storm

vessel: a ship

_____
_____
_____
_____
_____
_____
_____
_____
_____
_____

[2] **fidelity:** loyalty, faithfulness to a person, cause, or belief

20 From fearful trip the victor ship comes in with object won:

Exult O shores, and ring O bells!

But I with **mournful** tread,

Walk the deck my Captain lies,

Fallen cold and dead.

mournful: sad

Second Read

- Reread the sermon and the poem to answer these text-dependent questions.
- Write any additional questions you have about the text in your Reader/Writer Notebook.

White House Funeral Sermon for Abraham Lincoln

1. **Key Ideas and Details:** Choose a sentence that shows that Dr. Gurley sees hope within the sorrow of Lincoln's death. Explain how your choice shows this.

2. **Craft and Structure:** What does the word "arrest" mean in this sermon? How do you know?

3. **Knowledge and Ideas:** How do Dr. Gurley's contrasting statements echo the feeling of that moment in history?

O Captain! My Captain!

4. **Key Ideas and Details:** As an **allegory** representing the death of Abraham Lincoln, who does the Captain represent? What does the ship represent? What does the trip or voyage represent?

My Notes

> **Literary Terms**
> An **allegory** is a literary technique of extending a metaphor through an entire poem or story so that objects, persons, and actions in the text are equated with meanings that lie outside the text.

Historical Heroes: Examples

5. **Craft and Structure:** How does Whitman establish the same mood of sorrow and hope in his poem as Dr. Gurley does in his sermon? Explain by choosing a line that represents the mood.

Working from the Text

6. Use the following table to record details about Lincoln's character expressed in each of the texts you just read.

White House Funeral Sermon for Abraham Lincoln	O Captain! My Captain!
Quality: Evidence:	Quality: Evidence:
Quality: Evidence:	Quality: Evidence:
Quality: Evidence:	Quality: Evidence:

Check Your Understanding

In your Reader/Writer Notebook, write a topic sentence that compares these two texts about Abraham Lincoln. How are they similar? How are they different?

Setting a Purpose for Reading

- The next two texts are about Frederick Douglass. One is a poem written as a tribute. The other is an excerpt from Douglass's autobiography. Underline words and phrases that link Douglass to the concept of a hero.

- Circle unknown words and phrases. Try to determine the meaning of the words by using context clues, word parts, or a dictionary.

ABOUT THE AUTHOR

Robert Hayden (1913–1980) was born in Detroit, Michigan. He had a lifelong love of literature and became a teacher and writer. Through his work for the Federal Writers' Project in the 1930s, he studied African American history and folk life, both of which became inspirations for his works of poetry. Slavery and emancipation were recurring themes in his work.

Poetry

Frederick Douglass

by Robert Hayden

When it is finally ours, this freedom, this liberty, this beautiful

and terrible thing, needful to man as air,

usable as earth; when it belongs at last to all,

when it is truly instinct, brain matter, **diastole, systole,**

5   reflex action; when it is finally won; when it is more

than the **gaudy** mumbo jumbo of politicians:

this man, this Douglass, this former slave, this Negro

beaten to his knees, **exiled,** visioning a world

where none is lonely, none hunted, alien,

10 this man, superb in love and logic, this man

shall be remembered. Oh, not with statues' **rhetoric,**

not with legends and poems and wreaths of bronze alone,

but with the lives grown out of his life, the lives

fleshing his dream of the beautiful, needful thing.

diastole: the act of the heart filling with blood
systole: the act of the heart pumping blood
gaudy: showy in a tasteless way
exiled: forced to leave one's native land
rhetoric: language or speech

Second Read

- Reread the excerpt to answer these text-dependent questions.
- Write any additional questions you have about the text in your Reader/Writer Notebook.

7. **Craft and Structure:** In the first six lines, circle all the uses of the word "it" and "thing." What is "it"? How is it described?

My Notes

My Notes

8. **Knowledge and Ideas:** How is the cause of both Lincoln and Douglass the same according to these tributes?

ABOUT THE AUTHOR

Frederick Douglass (1818?–1895) was born into slavery in Maryland. He learned to read as a house servant in Baltimore. In 1838, Douglass escaped from his plantation and settled in Massachusetts. After spending two years abroad, he published an antislavery newspaper and was an advisor to President Lincoln during the Civil War. He was later appointed to positions in the U.S. government never before achieved by an African American.

Autobiography

from The Narrative of the Life of Frederick Douglass, an American Slave

by Frederick Douglass

WORD CONNECTIONS

Prefixes and Suffixes

In the word *subjected*, the Latin prefix *sub-* means "below" or "less than." It has the same meaning in *submarine* and *subset*. The Latin root *-ject-* means "to throw." It appears in words like *trajectory* and *reject*.

mariner: one who works on a ship

damp: lessen
ardor: strong devotion

1   I felt assured that if I failed in this attempt, my case would be a hopeless one—it would seal my fate as a slave forever. I could not hope to get off with anything less than the severest punishment and being placed beyond the means of escape. It required no very vivid imagination to depict the most frightful scenes through which I should have to pass in case I failed. The wretchedness of slavery, and the blessedness of freedom, were perpetually before me. It was life and death with me. But I remained firm, and, according to my resolution, on the third day of September, 1838, I left my chains, and succeeded in reaching New York without the slightest interruption of any kind. How I did so—what means I adopted—what direction I travelled, and by what mode of conveyance—I must leave unexplained, for the reasons before mentioned.

2   I have been frequently asked how I felt when I found myself in a free State. I have never been able to answer the question with any satisfaction to myself. It was a moment of the highest excitement I ever experienced. I suppose I felt as one may imagine the unarmed **mariner** to feel when he is rescued by a friendly man-of-war from the pursuit of a pirate. In writing to a dear friend, immediately after my arrival at New York, I said I felt like one who had escaped a den of hungry lions. This state of mind, however very soon subsided; and I was again seized with a feeling of great insecurity and loneliness. I was yet liable to be taken and subjected to all the tortures of slavery. This in itself was enough to **damp** the **ardor** of my enthusiasm. But the loneliness overcame me. There I was in the midst of thousands, and yet a perfect stranger; without home and without friends, in the midst of thousands of my own brethren—children of a common Father, and yet I dared not to unfold to any one of them my sad condition. I was afraid to speak to any one for fear of speaking to the wrong one, and thereby falling into the hands of money-loving kidnappers, whose business it was to lie in wait for the panting fugitive, as the ferocious beasts of the forest lie in wait for their prey. [I]n the midst of plenty, yet suffering the terrible gnawing of hunger—in the midst of houses, yet having no home— among fellow–men, yet feeling as if in the midst of wild beasts, whose greediness to swallow up the trembling and half-famished **fugitive** is only equalled by that with

fugitive: one who flees

which the monsters of the deep swallow up the trembling and half-famished fish upon which they subsist—I say let him be placed in this most trying situation—the situation in which I was placed—then, and not till then, will he fully appreciate the hardships of, and know how to sympathize with, the toil-worn and whip-scarred fugitive slave.

...

3   In about four months after I went to New Bedford, there came a young man to me, and inquired if I did not wish to take the "Liberator." I told him I did; but just having made my escape from slavery, I remarked that I was unable to pay for it then. I, however, finally became a subscriber to it. The paper came, and I read it from week to week with such feelings as it would be quite idle for me to attempt to describe. The paper became my meat and my drink. My soul was set all on fire. Its sympathy for my **brethren** in **bonds**—its **scathing denunciations** of slaveholders—its faithful exposures of slavery—and its powerful attacks upon the upholders of the institution—sent a thrill of joy through my soul, such as I had never felt before!

4   I had not long been a reader of the "Liberator," before I got a pretty correct idea of the principles, measures and spirit of the anti-slavery reform. I did with a joyful heart, and never felt happier than when in an anti-slavery meeting. I seldom had much to say at the meetings, because what I wanted to say was said so much better by others. But, while attending an anti-slavery convention at Nantucket, on the 11th of August, 1841, I felt strongly moved to speak, and was at the same time much urged to do so by Mr. William C. Collin, a gentleman who had heard me speak in the colored people's meeting at New Bedford. It was a severe cross, and I took it up reluctantly. The truth was, I felt myself a slave, and the idea of speaking to white people weighed me down. I spoke but a few moments, when I felt a degree of freedom, and said what I desired with considerable ease. From that time until now, I have been engaged in pleading the cause of my brethren—with what success, and with what devotion, I leave those acquainted with my labors to decide.

Second Read

- Reread the excerpt to answer these text-dependent questions.
- Write any additional questions you have about the text in your Reader/Writer Notebook.

9. **Key Ideas and Details:** What images in paragraph 2 does Douglass use to describe his first feelings of freedom and his fear of capture?

10. **Key Ideas and Details:** What did the "Liberator" write about? Why did it send "a thrill of joy" through Douglass's soul?

My Notes

brethren: people sharing in a similar situation
bonds: ties used to keep one in place
scathing: harshly critical
denunciations: formal accusations of wrongful activities

Historical Heroes: Examples

My Notes

11. **Key Ideas and Details:** What kind of mental, emotional, and physical courage did Douglass convey in this excerpt from his autobiography?

Working from the Text

12. Compare Hayden's poem to Douglass's autobiographic narrative. What topic of the autobiographic narrative do you see reflected in Robert Hayden's tribute to Douglass?

13. Review the elements of a well-developed explanatory body paragraph before responding to the Writing Prompt.

- **Topic Sentence:** Paragraphs begin with a sentence that includes a subject and an interpretation. The two main functions of a topic sentence are to make a point that supports the thesis of the essay and to indicate the main idea of a paragraph.

- **Supporting Detail:** Specific and relevant facts, details, examples, and quotations are used to support the topic sentence and thesis and to develop ideas.

- **Commentary:** Commentary explains the significance of the supporting detail in relation to the thesis and further develops ideas. It also brings a sense of closure to the paragraph.

Check Your Understanding

In your Reader/Writer Notebook, make a brainstorming web for Abraham Lincoln and a second one for Frederick Douglass. On each web, write 5–10 words that describe the hero.

Writing to Sources: Explanatory Text

Think about the four texts you just read. Explain how Abraham Lincoln and Frederick Douglass were heroic. Draft a definition paragraph using the example strategy. Be sure to:

- Begin with a topic sentence that answers the prompt.
- Provide supporting details and commentary to develop ideas.
- Use formal style and appropriate diction for the purpose and audience.

Transitions and Quotations

Learning Target
- Examine and appropriately apply transitions and embedded quotations to create coherence in writing.

LEARNING STRATEGIES:
Marking the Draft, Adding, Substituting

Reviewing and Extending Transitions

You have learned that transitions connect ideas. Writers use transitional words and phrases to create **coherence** and to help readers move smoothly through the essay. In formal writing, transitions establish relationships between one thought and the next, both within and between body paragraphs.

ACADEMIC VOCABULARY
Coherence is the clear and orderly presentation of ideas in a paragraph or essay.

Transitions are used for different purposes:

To offer evidence:	To introduce an interpretation:	To compare and contrast:
Most important,	Therefore,	Although _____,
For example,	For these reasons,	Even though _____,
For instance,	Consequently,	Instead,
According to _____,	Furthermore,	On the other hand,
To illustrate,	In addition,	On the contrary,
In this case,	Moreover,	Rather,
	Thus,	Yet, / But, / However,
		Still,
		Nevertheless,
		In contrast,
		Similarly,
		Likewise,
		In the same way,

To add information:	To clarify:	To conclude:
Additionally,	In other words,	As a result,
In addition,	For instance,	Therefore,
For example,	That is,	Thus,
For instance,	Put another way,	Finally,
Likewise,		
Finally,		
Equally important,		
Again,		

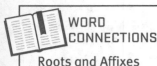

WORD CONNECTIONS

Roots and Affixes

Coherence contains the Latin root *-her-*, meaning "to stick," and the prefix *co-*, meaning "together." Use your knowledge of the root *-her-* to determine the meaning of the words *cohere*, *coherent*, *adhere*, and *inherent*.

My Notes

1. The following sample paragraph is based on a folklore story from China about a girl, Mulan, who chooses to go to war in place of her ill father. Mark the draft to indicate where transitions could be added to create coherence.

Mulan is courageous because she has the ability to disregard fear for a greater good. Mulan takes her father's place in the Chinese army because she knows that he is hurt. It is a crime punishable by death to impersonate a man and a soldier. Mulan has the strength and the nerve to stand up for her father and protect him. She gathers all of her courage and leaves before anyone can stop her, which is what courage is all about. Her pluck allows her to face the impossible and not think about the outcome, the fear or the danger, until she is far enough to be ready for it. The heroes that we look up to are everyday heroes, ordinary, average people who have conquered huge challenges by finding the strength and the courage within themselves to continue on. "A hero is an ordinary individual who finds the strength to persevere and endure in spite of overwhelming obstacles" (Christopher Reeve). Mulan is an ordinary girl who finds courage and strength to continue training and fighting in battles, even though she may be frightened. It is impossible to endure and overcome fearful obstacles when you have fear of them. Courage is what gives heroes the drive to move forward. The heroes that have the courage and the will to move on are the heroes that we all know and admire, the ones that we strive to be like.

Providing Support for a Claim

Supporting details can be paraphrased or directly quoted, depending on the writer's purpose and intended effect. Examine the difference between a paraphrase and an embedded quotation.

Paraphrase: Early in the story, Mulan reveals that she knows she will hurt her family if she is true to herself (*Mulan*).

Embedded Quotation: Early in the story, Mulan reveals her fears when she sings, "Now I see, that if I were truly to be myself, I would break my family's heart" (*Mulan* 5).

Note that an embedded quotation shows a more detailed and precise knowledge of the text.

A direct quotation *should not*:	A direct quotation *should*:
contain a simple idea that a writer could easily paraphrase	contain a complex idea that is thought-provoking
repeat an idea that has already been said	add another layer of depth to the writing
stand alone	be smoothly embedded into the writing; begin with a transition and lead-in
be lengthy	be no more than three lines

Use the acronym TLQC to help you remember how to embed a quotation smoothly. The letters stand for Transition, Lead-in, Quote, Citation.

Element	Definition/Purpose	Example
Transition	Use as a bridge to link ideas and strengthen cohesion and fluency.	**Early in the story,** Mulan reveals her fears when she sings, "Now I see, that if I were truly to be myself, I would break my family's heart."
Lead-in	Use to set the context for the information in the quote (complex sentences work well).	Early in the story, **Mulan reveals her fears when she sings,** "Now I see, that if I were truly to be myself, I would break my family's heart."
Quote	Use ideas from a credible source to strengthen your ideas, illustrate a point, and/or support your controlling idea.	Early in the story, Mulan reveals her fears when she sings, **"Now I see, that if I were truly to be myself, I would break my family's heart."**
Citation	Include author's last name and page number to give credit to the author and to make your writing credible to the reader.	Early in the story, Mulan reveals her fears when she sings, "Now I see, that if I were truly to be myself, I would break my family's heart" (***Mulan* 5**).

My Notes

Transitions and Quotations

Note: If you are citing a different type of source, such as a website, provide the first piece of information listed in a source citation.

2. Return to the sample paragraph and revise the writer's ideas about *Mulan* by smoothly embedding Christopher Reeve's quote (already there but not carefully embedded) and by adding the following quotation from the film:

Mulan: "It's going to take a miracle to get me into the army."

Check Your Understanding

Return to the paragraph you wrote about Lincoln and Douglass as historical heroes. Mark your draft to indicate missing or ineffective transitions. Then, revise the organization by adding or substituting transitional words and phrases to create coherence. Next, find a significant quote in two of the texts you have read and add those ideas into your paragraph by smoothly embedding the quotes.

Reflection: What types of transitions did you add during your revision? Why? How do the direct quotations strengthen your ideas?

Negation Strategy of Definition

Learning Targets
- Examine and analyze examples of the negation strategy of definition.
- Apply the negation strategy to a new topic.

Review of the Negation Strategy

1. Review the negation definition strategy:

Paragraphs using the **negation** strategy explain what something is by showing what it *is not*. Pointing out what the subject *is not* can make what it *is* clearer to the reader. For example, here is an excerpt from a definition of a horse that uses the negation strategy:

> A horse, a zebra, and a mule, though alike in many ways, have significant differences. A horse, unlike a zebra, can be tamed and trained. And unlike a mule, which is a sterile beast of burden, a horse is a valued breeder of future generations of racing champions and hardworking ranch animals.

Preview

In this activity, you will read a definition essay about the concept of a "gentleman" and evaluate how the author used the negation strategy.

Setting a Purpose for Reading
- As you read, underline examples of the negation strategy.
- Circle unknown words and phrases. Try to determine the meaning of the words by using context clues, word parts, or a dictionary.

ABOUT THE AUTHOR

John Henry Newman (1801–1890) was a scholar and clergyman who became an influential figure at Oxford College. Newman was a pioneer of the Oxford Movement, which sought to inject more Catholic dogma into the Protestant-leaning Church of England. Some of his works, including the seminal *Parochial and Plain Sermons*, helped influence the ideals of the Oxford Movement. In 1845 he converted to Roman Catholicism. Pope Benedict XVI beatified Newman in 2010, which means he was officially bestowed as someone in the church to be glorified and exalted.

Essay

"A Definition of a GENTLEMAN"

by John Henry Newman

(1) The true gentleman in like manner carefully avoids whatever may cause a jar or a jolt in the minds of those with whom he is cast;—all clashing of opinion, or collision of feeling, all restraint, or suspicion, or gloom, or resentment; his great concern being to make everyone

My Notes

Negation Strategy of Definition

absurd: something that is ridiculous

wearisome: causing to be tired

slander: spoken lies about someone

insinuates: implies

maxim: truthful adage
sage: wise person

at their ease and at home. (2) He has his eyes on all his company; he is tender towards the bashful, gentle towards the distant, and merciful towards the **absurd**; he can recollect to whom he is speaking; he guards against unseasonable allusions, or topics which may irritate; he is seldom prominent in conversation, and never **wearisome**. (3) He makes light of favours while he does them, and seems to be receiving when he is conferring. (4) He never speaks of himself except when compelled, never defends himself by a mere retort, he has no ears for **slander** or gossip, is scrupulous in imputing motives to those who interfere with him, and interprets everything for the best. (5) He is never mean or little in his disputes, never takes unfair advantage, never mistakes personalities or sharp sayings for arguments, or **insinuates** evil which he dare not say out. (6) From a long-sighted prudence, he observes the **maxim** of the ancient **sage**, that we should ever conduct ourselves towards our enemy as if he were one day to be our friend.

From *The Idea of a University*, by John Henry Newman, originally delivered as a series of lectures in 1852.

My Notes

Second Read

- Reread the excerpt to answer the text-dependent question.
- Write any additional questions you have about the text in your Reader/Writer Notebook.

2. **Craft and Structure:** How does negation make this portrait of a gentleman clearer and more extensive?

Check Your Understanding

In your Reader/Writer Notebook, make a T-chart. Label one side "A Gentleman," and label the other side "NOT a Gentleman." Fill in the T-chart accordingly.

Writing to Sources: Explanatory Text

Write about what heroism is not. Use the negation strategy to distinguish what heroism is from what it is not. Be sure to:

- Begin with a topic sentence that answers the prompt.
- Provide supporting detail and commentary to develop ideas.
- Cite examples from the texts you have read.
- Use transitions to create coherence.

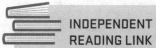

INDEPENDENT READING LINK

Read and Recommend

Your independent reading choice can be used as a source in your definition essay. Write about how the protagonist of your reading faced and overcame obstacles and challenges. Then discuss with a classmate why you think this text will be valuable in writing your definition essay. Be sure to provide clear reasons for your recommendation.

My Notes

Explanatory Writing Focus: Organization

LEARNING STRATEGIES:
Close Reading, Marking
the Text, Note-taking,
Collaborative Discussion

My Notes

Learning Targets
- Identify and evaluate the effectiveness of the structural elements of a definition essay.
- Draft a thesis and outline ideas for a definition essay.

Planning a Definition Essay
1. Review the Scoring Criteria for Embedded Assessment 2. What defines a proficient definition essay? List required skills and concepts for each category.

Ideas	
Organization	
Language and Conventions	

Introduction
The **introduction** to an essay has three main parts (listed in the order in which they should appear):

I. **The Hook:** If the opening lines are dull or confusing, the reader loses interest right away. Therefore, you must write an opening that grabs the reader's attention. Lure your readers into the piece with a *hook*—an anecdote, compelling question, quote, or intriguing statement (AQQS)—to grab them so firmly that they will want to read on.

- **Anecdote:** Begin with a brief anecdote (a story from real life) that relates to the point of your essay.

- **Question:** Ask a thought-provoking universal question relating to the concept of your thesis. You will answer this question in your essay. Don't ask simplistic questions such as "How would you feel if …?" or "What would you do if …?"

- **Quote:** Find a quote to state an ordinary idea in an extraordinary or provocative way or state a provocative idea in an ordinary way. Either will grab the reader's interest. This quote can come from any source: someone you know, someone famous, or a song.
- **Intriguing statement:** Knock down a commonly held assumption or define a word in a new and startling way.

II. **The Bridge:** This writing represents the content between the hook and the thesis (the controlling idea of the essay). The purpose of the bridge is to make a clear and concise connection between these two parts. The bridge is also the place where a writer provides necessary background information to set the context for the ideas in the essay.

III. **The Thesis:** Your thesis is your response to the writing prompt, and it includes information about both the topic and your interpretation of it. The thesis is the single most important part of the essay in establishing focus and coherence; all parts of the essay should work to support this idea. Your thesis should be a clear and precise assertion. It should not be an announcement of your intent, nor should it include the first person (*I*/*my*).

A thesis should show a level of sophistication and complexity of thought. You may want to try to create a complex sentence as your thesis statement. Complex sentences contain a dependent clause that begins with a dependent marker, such as *because, before, since, while, although, if, until, when, after, as,* or *as if.*

Evaluating and Revising Introductions

2. Read the following introductions. For each one, identify, label, and evaluate the three parts of the introduction: hook, bridge, and thesis.

Sample 1

Aristotle said, "The beauty of the soul shines out when a man bears with composure one heavy mischance after another, not because he does not feel them, but because he is a man of high and heroic temper." When someone goes though calamity with poise, it is not because they don't feel anything; it is because they are of a heroic nature. Heroism is being brave and helping other people before yourself, but it does not always have a happy ending.

Sample 2

"A hero is no braver than an ordinary man, but he is braver five minutes longer." When heroes keep on going and keep battling a challenge or problem, it makes them that much more heroic. Anyone could just give up, but heroes keep going. Instead of stressing over satisfying everyone, heroes know that their best is good enough and focus on doing the right thing. Heroism is putting others before yourself and directly facing challenges, but not always saving or satisfying everyone.

WORD CONNECTIONS

Etymology

The Latin root *-voc-* in ***provocative*** comes from a Latin word meaning "to call." This root appears in words related to a calling, such as *vocation* and *advocate*. The Latin prefix *pro-* means "forth," "before," or "forward."

My Notes

My Notes

3. Now reread each introductory paragraph, evaluate its effectiveness, and mark it for revision. Use these questions to aid your evaluation:

- Is the hook engaging?
- If the hook is a quote, is it integrated smoothly?
- Is there a bridge that effectively links the hook to the thesis?
- Is the thesis a clear and precise interpretation of the topic?
- Is the use of language formal or informal?
- Is the language effective? Where can it be made clearer, or where can ideas be stated more smoothly?

Check Your Understanding

Revise one of the two paragraphs above based on your evaluation and discussion of how it could benefit by additional content, reworking sentences, and using more precise or formal diction.

Revising Thesis Statements

Examine the following model thesis statement, and then see how the statement has been revised to have a complex sentence structure with a beginning dependent clause.

- **Model thesis statement:** Heroism involves selflessness and dedication to a challenge. It means helping others without desire for recognition or stardom.
- **Revised model:** *Because* heroism involves selflessness, it requires dedication to a challenge and helping others without desire for recognition or stardom.

4. What is the value of combining the two sentences in this way? How does it improve the communication of ideas in the thesis statement?

5. Now follow the model to revise the remaining thesis statements on the next page. Create a complex sentence structure by using a dependent marker to create a dependent clause at the beginning of the sentence. Revise other elements as needed for smooth expression while still keeping the same ideas.

- **Thesis statement:** Heroism means taking action when you are needed, showing dedication to your quest, and not giving up even when the odds are against you.

  Revised thesis statement:

- **Thesis statement:** Heroism means putting others before oneself and directly facing challenges, but not always saving or satisfying everyone.

  Revised thesis statement:

- **Thesis statement:** Heroism is being brave and helping other people before yourself, but it does not always guarantee a happy ending.

  Revised thesis statement:

Writing a Concluding Paragraph

The **concluding** paragraph in an essay is the last thing your reader takes from your essay. Try to make the reader think in a new way, feel emotional, or feel enlightened. Choose the ending carefully. Avoid clichés or something stale, such as "The end," "That is all I have to say," or "That's my definition of heroism." Make your readers feel that they have arrived somewhere by sharing with them what you have learned, discovered, or realized.

The following are some possible ways to conclude your essay.

- Be genuine. Explain why this topic is important to you and/or important in life.
- If you used a quote as your hook, refer back to it. If you didn't use a quote, use one to guide your conclusion.
- You may finish by reviewing the paper's main point, but with new insight.
- Direct the readers into the future. How does an understanding of this topic relate to future thought or action? What will or should happen in the months or years ahead?

My Notes

WORD
CONNECTIONS

Etymology

The word *cliché* is from the French and means "something that is overused." It derives from the French word *clicher*, meaning "to click," which resembled a sound made when using printing plates. One method of creating printing plates was called *stereotype,* and this method could produce the same image repetitively. The word *stereotype* is now used as a synonym of *cliché*.

My Notes

Evaluating and Revising Conclusions

6. As you read examples of a conclusion, identify which technique the writer used and how effective the conclusion is.

Sample 1

The best heroes out there are those that put others before themselves. How do we know when someone is a hero? When they face challenges with pure determination, but don't save or satisfy everyone in the end. It blows us away every time a hero can fix sticky situations, but it is more important to know that a hero is doing what they're doing for the protection of everyone else. Making mistakes is what makes everything else that they do even more spectacular.

Sample 2

Heroes often look like the normal people we see walking down the street and they might be the plainest form of normal there is. Behind that normal appearance there has been struggle and challenge that has turned into wisdom. Heroes have to not only overcome challenges, but have done it with dignity. Heroes have grown from their experiences and now put a different value on life itself. Heroes are absolutely essential to life, for without heroes we would have no one to admire or set our goals to their standards.

Check Your Understanding

Revise one of the two paragraphs above based on your evaluation and discussion of how it could benefit by additional content, reworking sentences, and using more precise or formal diction.

Writing Body Paragraphs

Body paragraphs are the meat of your essay. Outlined by the thesis, they include the reasons, plus the details and examples, that provide the support for your thesis. Part of the strength of your support is **synthesizing,** or pulling together, examples and details from your experiences and from texts and resources you have read or studied. As you write body paragraphs, be sure to include the following:

- A topic sentence that introduces the focus of the paragraph
- A concluding sentence that follows from the information and explanations presented
- Details and examples relevant and sufficient to make your point
- Commentary that explains why these details and examples are significant
- Paraphrases and embedded quotations conveying important details and examples
- Transitions to show your understanding of the content by showing the connections among ideas

WORD CONNECTIONS

Cognates

The English word *synthesize* has the same meaning as its Spanish cognate *sintetizar*.

Evaluating and Revising Body Paragraphs

7. Read the following body paragraph and evaluate its effectiveness. Look at the transitions, the details and examples, and the commentary, as well as the skill with which paraphrases and embedded quotations are handled.

Heroism is trying your hardest, no matter the obstacles, to go beyond the needs of yourself to help others. A son writes about how his mother, Ana, has an obstacle, but does all that she can to fight it, and does not complain. He says that she fights cancer with a smile and "hasn't let it slow her down, either" (Gandara). This shows that even though she could complain and give up fighting the disease, she tries her hardest, which inspires her loved ones. In addition, in the movie *Mulan*, the main character wants to help her father by enlisting in the army, which is impossible according to Chinese law because she is a girl. Instead of giving up on this, Mulan decides to pretend to be a man and goes to extremes to keep up her charade. This is heroic because her father, being the only male in his family, had to enlist in the army, yet he was too sick to fight and would have undoubtedly died in the conflict. Facing illness or danger with courage for the sake of another is inspiring and heroic.

Check Your Understanding

Return to the texts you have read and studied in this unit. Begin to think about which ones you can use to help support your definition of heroism. Make a list of the texts, the heroes, and the events you may be able to use in your essay. Begin to categorize them as you think of each definition strategy: function, example, and negation.

My Notes

Explanatory Writing Focus: Organization

Explanatory Writing Prompt

Think about people who deserve status as a hero from the past, from the present, from life, and from literature. What defines a hero? Draft an insightful thesis statement using a complex sentence structure. Then, outline ideas for your essay. Remember to return to your work in Activity 1.12 on defining a hero.

Hero Definition Essay Outline

I. **INTRODUCTION**

Hook: (What would make an effective hook?)
Bridge: (background information and connections)
Thesis: (state your original definition)

II. **BODY PARAGRAPH 1** (Function/Example/Negation)

Topic Sentence: (connect to thesis)

Supporting Detail: (list source)

Paraphrase, quotations, examples with commentary

Supporting Detail: (list source)

III. **BODY PARAGRAPH 2** (Function/Example/Negation)

Topic Sentence: (connect to thesis)

Supporting Detail: (list source)

Paraphrase, quotations, examples with commentary

Supporting Detail: (list source)

IV. **BODY PARAGRAPH 3** (Function/Example/Negation)

Topic Sentence: (connect to thesis)

Supporting Detail: (list source)

Paraphrase, quotations, examples with commentary

Supporting Detail: (list source)

V. **CONCLUSION**

(What would make an effective conclusion?)

 Independent Reading Checkpoint

Look back at the article about Tristan Segers on page 67. Compare how his life and the life of the hero in your independent reading text fit into the hero's archetype that you have learned about in this unit.

Writing a Definition Essay

ASSIGNMENT

Think about people who deserve status as heroes—from the past, from the present, from life, and from literature. What defines a hero? Write a multi-paragraph essay that develops your definition of heroism. Be sure to use strategies of definition (function, example, and negation) to guide your writing.

Planning and Prewriting: Take time to make a plan for your essay.	▨ Which activities and texts have you collected that will help you refine and expand your definition of a hero? ▨ What prewriting strategies (such as free writing or graphic organizers) could help you brainstorm ideas and organize your examples?
Drafting: Write a multi-paragraph essay that effectively organizes your ideas.	▨ How will you provide a hook, a bridge, and a thesis in the introduction? ▨ How will you use the strategies of definition (function, example, negation) in your support paragraphs? ▨ How will your conclusion demonstrate the significance of heroism and encourage readers to accept your definition?
Evaluating and Revising: Create opportunities to review and revise your work.	▨ During the process of writing, when can you pause to share and respond with others? ▨ What is your plan to include suggestions and revision ideas in your draft? ▨ How can the Scoring Guide help you evaluate how well your draft meets the requirements of the assignment?
Checking and Editing for Publication: Confirm that your final draft is ready for publication.	▨ How will you proofread and edit your draft to demonstrate command of the conventions of standard English capitalization, punctuation, spelling, grammar, and usage? ▨ What would be an engaging title for your essay?

Reflection

After completing this Embedded Assessment, think about how you went about accomplishing this task, and respond to the following:

- Explain how the activities in this unit helped prepare you for success in the Embedded Assessment.

- Which activities were especially helpful, and why?

Writing a Definition Essay

SCORING GUIDE

Scoring Criteria	Exemplary	Proficient	Emerging	Incomplete
Ideas	The essay • uses all three strategies of definition effectively to define a hero • maintains a precise and original thesis • integrates relevant supporting details and evidence (quotes and paraphrases) with citations and commentary.	The essay • uses strategies of definition (function, example, negation) to define a hero • maintains a clear thesis • includes adequate supporting details and evidence (quotes and paraphrases) with citations and commentary.	The essay • uses insufficient strategies of definition to define a hero • has an unclear or unfocused thesis • includes inadequate supporting details and evidence; may have inconsistent citations and/or weak commentary.	The essay • does not define a hero using strategies of definition • has no discernible thesis • lacks supporting details, citations, and/or commentary.
Structure	The essay • introduces the main idea with an engaging hook, bridge, and thesis • organizes ideas into focused support paragraphs that progress smoothly • creates coherence with the purposeful use of a variety of transitions and topic sentences • provides an insightful conclusion.	The essay • introduces the topic with a hook, bridge, and thesis • organizes ideas into support paragraphs that progress logically • creates coherence with the use of transitions and topic sentences • provides a conclusion that follows from the ideas presented.	The essay • includes an ineffective or partial introduction • has unrelated, undeveloped, or insufficient support paragraphs • uses transitions and topic sentences ineffectively or inconsistently • provides a weak, illogical, or repetitive conclusion.	The essay • lacks an introduction • has minimal, absent, or flawed support paragraphs • uses few or no transitions and topic sentences • lacks a conclusion.
Use of Language	The essay • uses consistent diction and style appropriate for an academic audience • demonstrates command of the conventions of standard English capitalization, punctuation, spelling, grammar, and usage (including complex sentences).	The essay • uses diction and style that is generally appropriate for an academic audience • demonstrates adequate command of the conventions of standard English capitalization, punctuation, spelling, grammar, and usage (including complex sentences).	The essay • uses diction or a style that is basic or inappropriate to an academic audience • demonstrates partial or inconsistent command of the conventions of standard English capitalization, punctuation, spelling, grammar, and usage.	The essay • uses flawed diction • lacks command of the conventions of standard English capitalization, punctuation, spelling, grammar, and usage; frequent errors obscure meaning.

The Challenge of Utopia

Visual Prompt: The perfect society may mean different things to different people. What type of society does each image represent? What does each say about what is important to the people who prefer one over the other?

Unit Overview

We probably all agree that we would like to live in an ideal society where everyone is free and happy, but what does that actually mean, and why do definitions of the ideal society differ so greatly? Some would argue that an ideal life is a life without conflict or problems, but what is a "perfect" life? In this unit, you will read, write, and engage in various types of collaborative discussions to explore these universal questions. Then, you will move from discussion and exposition into debate and effective argumentation as you research and develop a claim about a contemporary issue.

The Challenge of Utopia

GOALS:
- To analyze a novel for archetype and theme
- To analyze and evaluate a variety of explanatory and argumentative texts for ideas, structure, and language
- To develop informative/explanatory texts using the compare/contrast organizational structure
- To understand the use of active voice and passive voice
- To develop effective arguments using logical reasoning, relevant evidence, and persuasive appeals for effect

ACADEMIC VOCABULARY
compare/contrast
perspective
Socratic
seminar
argument
debate
controversy
research
search terms

Literary Terms
antagonist

Contents

Activities

Texts not included in these materials.

Language and Writer's Craft
- Embedding Direct Quotations (2.3)
- Active and Passive Voice (2.3)
- Choosing Mood (2.5)
- Shifts in Voice and Mood (2.17)

MY INDEPENDENT READING LIST

The Challenge of Utopia

LEARNING STRATEGIES:
Think-Pair-Share, QHT, Close Reading, Marking the Text, Paraphrasing, Graphic Organizer

My Notes

Learning Targets
- Preview the big ideas and vocabulary for the unit.
- Identify and analyze the skills and knowledge necessary to be successful in completing Embedded Assessment 1.

Making Connections
In the last unit you studied what it is to be a hero and how heroes test themselves to find their own heroic qualities. In this unit you will read a novel that features a hero who must struggle to combat forces greater than he knows in his quest for an individual sense of freedom and identity.

Essential Questions
The following Essential Questions will be the focus of the unit study. Respond to both questions.

1. To what extent can a perfect or ideal society exist?

2. What makes an argument effective?

Vocabulary Development
Create a QHT chart in your Reader/Writer Notebook and sort the Academic Vocabulary and Literary Terms on the Contents page into the columns Q, H, and T. One academic goal would be to move all words to the "T" column by the end of the unit.

Unpacking Embedded Assessment 1
Read the assignment for Embedded Assessment 1: Writing an Explanatory Essay.

Think about how writers organize and develop ideas in explanatory writing. Use an explanatory structure to communicate your understanding of the concept of dystopia and/or the concept of the Hero's Journey. Select one of the prompts below:

- Write an essay that compares and contrasts life in a dystopian society with modern day society.
- Write an essay that explains how the protagonist (hero) changes as a result of conflict with his dystopian society (Road of Trials), and explain how this change connects to the novel's theme (the Crossing, or Return Threshold).

Work with your class to paraphrase the expectations and create a graphic organizer to use as a visual reminder of the required concepts and skills. Once you have analyzed the assignment, go to the Scoring Guide for a deeper look into the requirements of the assignment. Add additional information to your graphic organizer.

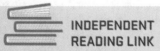

INDEPENDENT READING LINK

Read and Research
During this half of the unit, you will read a science fiction novel together as a class. The protagonist in this novel is a hero fighting against a challenge in society. Think about challenges in your own society that interest you. Research news articles, narrative nonfiction pieces, or contemporary short stories that discuss the challenge, and what people are trying to do to fix it. List the pieces you will read in your My Independent Reading List.

Explanatory Writing: Compare/Contrast

Learning Targets
- Analyze and explain how a writer uses the compare/contrast structure to communicate ideas.
- Write a paragraph that demonstrates an ability to use compare/contrast organizational structure.

LEARNING STRATEGIES:
Graphic Organizer, QHT, Close Reading, Marking the Text, Summarizing, Rereading, Brainstorming, Drafting

Review of Explanatory Writing

You have had many experiences writing in the explanatory mode. Every time you explain something or define a concept or idea, you are writing an explanatory text. One form of explanatory writing is **compare/contrast**. This method of organization is an important model of exposition to master and can be used in many different writing situations.

1. Brainstorm ideas for topics for different school subjects that would require you to write a compare/contrast essay.

> **ACADEMIC VOCABULARY**
> **Compare/contrast** is a rhetorical strategy and method of organization in which a writer examines similarities and differences between two people, places, ideas, or things.

My Notes

2. Writers use planning and prewriting to decide how to organize their ideas. The graphic organizer below shows two methods of organizing a compare/contrast essay, using "reptiles vs. mammals" as a topic.

Subject-by-Subject Organization	Feature-by-Feature Organization
Discuss all the features of one subject and then all the features of the other.	Select a feature common to both subjects and then discuss each subject in light of that feature. Then go on to the next feature.
Subject A: Mammals Habitat Reproduction Physiology **Subject B: Reptiles** Habitat Reproduction Physiology	**Habitat** Subject A: Mammals Subject B: Reptiles **Reproduction** Subject A: Mammals Subject B: Reptiles **Physiology** Subject A: Mammals Subject B: Reptiles

3. Why would a writer select one organizational structure over the other?

Explanatory Writing: Compare/Contrast

My Notes

4. Writers often use a graphic organizer to generate ideas. Explain how the graphic organizer could help you in structuring an essay comparing and contrasting two subjects.

Preview

In this activity, you will read and analyze a text that compares and contrasts two Civil War heroes: Ulysses S. Grant, leader of the Union Army (North), and Robert E. Lee, leader of the Confederate Army (South). You will then think about how these two men connect to your previous study of heroism.

Setting a Purpose for Reading

- As you read, pay attention to the organization of the text. Write the focus of each paragraph in the My Notes section.
- Circle unknown words and phrases. Try to determine the meaning of the words by using context clues, word parts, or a dictionary.
- Underline transitional words and phrases that help you follow the changes in focus.

ABOUT THE AUTHOR

Bruce Catton (1899–1978) was a noted historian and journalist whose books on the Civil War were celebrated for narrative historical style. The third book in a trilogy on the Civil War, *A Stillness at Appomattox,* earned Catton both a Pulitzer Prize and the National Book Award (1954).

Essay

GRANT AND LEE: A STUDY IN CONTRASTS

by Bruce Catton

1   When Ulysses S. Grant and Robert E. Lee met in the parlor of a modest house at Appomattox Court House, Virginia, on April 9, 1865, to work out the terms for the surrender of Lee's Army of Northern Virginia, a great chapter on American life came to a close, and a great new chapter began.

2   These men were bringing the Civil War to its virtual finish. To be sure, other armies had yet to surrender, and for a few days the **fugitive** Confederate government would struggle desperately and **vainly**, trying to find some way to go on living now that its chief support was gone. But in effect it was all over

Ulysses S. Grant

fugitive: fleeting; transient
vainly: futilely; unsuccessfully

when Grant and Lee signed the papers. And the little room where they wrote out the terms was the scene of one of the **poignant**, dramatic contrasts in American History.

poignant: passionate; emotional

3   They were two strong men, these oddly different generals, and they represented the strengths of two conflicting currents that, through them, had come into final collision.

4   Back of Robert E. Lee was the notion that the old aristocratic concept might somehow survive and be dominant in American life.

5   Lee was tidewater Virginia, and in his background were family, culture, and tradition . . . the age of chivalry transplanted to a New World which was making its own legends and its own myths. He embodied a way of life that had come down through the age of knighthood and the English country squire. America was a land that was beginning all over again, dedicated to nothing much more complicated than the rather hazy belief that all men had equal rights and should have an equal chance in the world. In such a land Lee stood for the feeling that it was somehow of advantage to human society to have a pronounced inequality in the social structure. There should be a leisure class, backed by ownership of land; in turn, society itself should be tied to the land as the chief source of wealth and influence. It would bring forth (according to this ideal) a class of men with a strong sense of obligation to the community; men who lived not to gain advantage for themselves, but to meet the solemn obligations which had been laid on them by the very fact that they were privileged. From them the country would get its leadership; to them it could look for higher values—of thought, of conduct, or personal **deportment**—to give it strength and virtue.

deportment: behavior

My Notes

6   Lee embodied the noblest elements of this aristocratic ideal. Through him, the landed nobility justified itself. For four years, the Southern states had fought a desperate war to uphold the ideals for which Lee stood. In the end, it almost seemed as if the Confederacy fought for Lee; as if he himself was the Confederacy . . . the best thing that the way of life for which the Confederacy stood could ever have to offer. He had passed into legend before Appomattox. Thousands of tired, underfed, poorly clothed Confederate soldiers, long since past the simple enthusiasm of the early days of the struggle, somehow considered Lee the symbol of everything for which they had been willing to die. But they could not quite put this feeling into words. If the Lost Cause, sanctified by so much heroism and so many deaths, had a living justification, its justification was General Lee.

Robert E. Lee

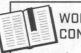 WORD CONNECTIONS

Etymology

Sanctified comes from the Latin words *facere* ("to make") and *sanctus* ("holy").

7   Grant, the son of a **tanner** on the Western frontier, was everything Lee was not. He had come up the hard way and embodied nothing in particular except the eternal toughness and **sinewy** fiber of the men who grew up beyond the mountains. He was one of a body of men who owed **reverence** and **obeisance** to no one, who were self-reliant to a fault, who cared hardly anything for the past but who had a sharp eye for the future.

tanner: leather worker
sinewy: lean and muscular
reverence: deep respect
obeisance: respectful submission or yielding to the judgment, opinion, will, etc., of another

Explanatory Writing: Compare/Contrast

GRAMMAR & USAGE
Conditional Mood

The conditional mood is used to express the conditions under which certain things will happen. Sentences in the conditional will usually read as *if/then* statements. *If this one thing happens, then this other thing will happen.*

Consider this sentence from the passage.

"If the land was settled, with towns and highways and accessible markets, he could better himself."

What idea is this sentence expressing?

As you read, look for other examples of conditional mood and note both parts of the *if/then* statement.

implicit: implied though not directly stated

tenacity: the quality of holding together; remaining persistent

burgeoning: quickly growing or developing; flourishing

fidelity: strict observance of promises, duties, etc.; loyalty; faithfulness

WORD CONNECTIONS

Content Connections

Diametrically, in the context of Grant and Lee being opposed, means "completely or directly." Mathematically speaking, *diametrically opposed* refers to "two points directly opposite of each other on a circle or sphere." The mathematic meaning provides a picture of the complete opposite viewpoints and traits we observe in Grant and Lee.

8   These frontier men were the precise opposites of the tidewater aristocrats. Back of them, in the great surge that had taken people over the Alleghenies and into the opening Western country, there was a deep, **implicit** dissatisfaction with a past that had settled into grooves. They stood for democracy, not from any reasoned conclusion about the proper ordering of human society, but simply because they had grown up in the middle of democracy and knew how it worked. Their society might have privileges, but they would be privileges each man had won for himself. Forms and patterns meant nothing. No man was born to anything, except perhaps to a chance to show how far he could rise. Life was competition.

9   Yet along with this feeling had come a deep sense of belonging to a national community. The Westerner who developed a farm, opened a shop, or set up in business as a trader could hope to prosper only as his own community prospered—and his community ran from the Atlantic to the Pacific and from Canada down to Mexico. If the land was settled, with towns and highways and accessible markets, he could better himself. He saw his fate in terms of the nation's own destiny. As its horizons expanded, so did his. He had, in other words, an acute dollars-and-cents stake in the continued growth and development of his country.

10   And that, perhaps, is where the contrast between Grant and Lee becomes most striking. The Virginia aristocrat, inevitably, saw himself in relation to his own region. He lived in a static society which could endure almost anything except change. Instinctively, his first loyalty would go to the locality in which that society existed. He would fight to the limit of endurance to defend it, because in defending it he was defending everything that gave his own life its deepest meaning.

11   The Westerner, on the other hand, would fight with an equal **tenacity** for the broader concept of society. He fought so because everything he lived by was tied to growth, expansion, and a constantly widening horizon. What he lived by would survive or fall with the nation itself. He could not possibly stand by unmoved in the face of an attempt to destroy the Union. He would combat it with everything he had, because he could only see it as an effort to cut the ground out from under his feet.

12   So Grant and Lee were in complete contrast, representing two diametrically opposed elements in American life. Grant was the modern man emerging; beyond him, ready to come on the stage was the great age of steel and machinery, of crowded cities and a restless **burgeoning** vitality. Lee might have ridden down from the old age of chivalry, lance in hand, silken banner fluttering over his head. Each man was the perfect champion for his cause, drawing both his strengths and his weaknesses from the people he led.

13   Yet it was not all contrast, after all. Different as they were—in background, in personality, in underlying aspiration—these two great soldiers had much in common. Under everything else, they were marvelous fighters. Furthermore, their fighting qualities were really very much alike.

14   Each man had, to begin with, the great virtue of utter tenacity and **fidelity**. Grant fought his way down the Mississippi Valley in spite of acute personal discouragement and profound military handicaps. Lee hung on in the trench at Petersburg after hope born of a fighter's refusal to give up as long as he can still remain on his feet and lift his two fists.

15 Daring and resourcefulness they had, too: the ability to think faster and move faster than the enemy. These were the qualities which gave Lee the dazzling campaigns of Second Manassas and Chancellorsville and won Vicksburg for Grant.

16 Lastly, and perhaps greatest of all, there was the ability, at the end, to turn quickly from the war to peace once the fighting was over. Out of the way these two men behaved at Appomattox came the possibility of peace of reconciliation. It was a possibility not wholly realized, in the year to come, but which did, in the end, help the two sections to become one nation again … after a war whose bitterness might have seemed to make such a reunion wholly impossible. No part of either man's life became him more than the part he played in their brief meeting in the McLean house at Appomattox. Their behavior there put all succeeding generations of Americans in their debt. Two great Americans, Grant and Lee—very different, yet under everything very much alike. Their encounter at Appomattox was one of the great moments of American history.

Second Read

- Reread the passage to answer these text-dependent comprehension questions.
- Write any additional questions you have about the text in your Reader/Writer Notebook.

5. **Craft and Structure:** How does Catton use a metaphor to illustrate conflict in paragraph 3?

6. **Craft and Structure:** Find the words "aristocratic," "chivalry," "knighthood," and "country squire" in the passage. How are these words related? Make an inference about what the author believes Robert E. Lee embodied.

7. **Key Ideas and Details:** Choose a sentence from paragraph 5 or 6 and one from paragraph 7 or 8 showing the greatest contrast between the two generals. Explain your choice.

My Notes

Explanatory Writing: Compare/Contrast

8. **Craft and Structure:** Which paragraph signals a change from a discussion of the generals' differences to a discussion of their similarities? What transition words help you see this?

Working from the Text

9. This essay was very carefully organized. Skim the paragraphs, noting the content of the paragraphs and the text you have noted. Then, create a brief outline of the text's organizational structure.

10. What is the central idea or purpose of the text? Provide textual evidence to support your analysis.

Creating Coherence

In Unit 1, you learned that *coherence* in writing is the clear and orderly presentation of ideas in a paragraph or essay. One way a writer creates coherence is to use transitional words, phrases, and sentences to link ideas within and between paragraphs. The following chart lists some transitional words and phrases that create coherence in compare/contrast essays.

Transitions That Compare	Transitions That Contrast	
Likewise	Although	Nevertheless
Similarly	Instead	Still
In the same way	Even though	However
	On the other hand	Yet/But
	On the contrary	Rather
	In contrast	Conversely

11. Sort the transitions using the QHT strategy. Then, practice using some of the transitions on a subject that you know about such as *short stories versus poetry*. Write a few sentences in the My Notes section of this page.

Check Your Understanding

To prepare for your Writing to Sources activity, create a Venn diagram in your Reader/Writer Notebook to compare and contrast Robert E. Lee and Ulysses S. Grant. Think of ways the two men are alike and ways they are different.

Writing to Sources: Explanatory Text

After reading "Grant and Lee: A Study in Contrasts," write a short compare/contrast paragraph comparing Robert E. Lee and Ulysses S. Grant. Be sure to:

- Explain at least one difference and one similarity of the two subjects.
- Organize ideas logically (subject-by-subject or feature-by-feature). Refer to the chart on page 105 for these organizational structures.
- Create coherence by using transitional words and phrases.
- Support your explanations and ideas with evidence from the text.

My Notes

Utopian Ideals and Dystopian Reality

LEARNING STRATEGIES:
Close Reading, Rereading, Diffusing, Paraphrasing, Marking the Text, Shared Reading, Think Aloud

WORD CONNECTIONS

Roots and Affixes

The word *utopia* is made from the Greek *ou-,* meaning "no" or "not," and *topos,* meaning "place." But it is also similar to *eutopia,* made from the English prefix *eu-,* meaning "good," and *topos.* This implies that the perfectly "good place" is really "no place."

WORD CONNECTIONS

Roots and Affixes

A dystopia is a community or society, usually fictional, that is in some important way undesirable or frightening. The word *dystopia* comes from the Latin prefix *dys-,* meaning "bad, abnormal," and the word *utopia,* which you've already learned means "good place" or "no place."

Learning Targets
- Use direct quotations and correct punctuation for effect.
- Closely read a story and analyze the relationship between character and theme.

The Concept of Utopia

A utopia is an ideal or perfect community or society. It is a real or imagined place considered to be ideal or perfect (politically, socially, economically, technologically, ecologically, religiously, etc.). People in a utopia lead civilized lives filled with peace, fulfillment, and happiness.

The western idea of utopia originates in the ancient world, where legends of an earthly paradise (e.g. Eden in the Old Testament, the mythical Golden Age of Greek mythology), combined with the human desire to create, or re-create, an ideal society, helped form the utopian idea.

The English statesman Sir Thomas More (1478–1535) wrote the book *Utopia* in 1516. Describing a perfect political and social system on an imaginary island named Utopia, the term "utopia" has since entered the English language, meaning any place, state, or situation of ideal perfection.

Both the desire for Eden-like perfection and an attempt to start over in "unspoiled" America led religious and nonreligious groups and societies to set up communities in the United States. These experimental utopian communities were committed to such ideals as simplicity, sincerity, and brotherly love.

Once the idea of a utopia was created, its opposite, the idea of a dystopia, was also created. It is the opposite of a utopia. Such societies appear in many works of fiction, particularly in stories set in a speculative future.

Preview

In this activity, you will read a story and expand your understanding of the concepts of utopia and dystopia.

Setting a Purpose for Reading
- As you read, take note of the setting and the rules of the community. Underline any sentences that give you this information.
- Circle unknown words and phrases. Try to determine the meaning of the words by using context clues, word parts, or a dictionary.

ABOUT THE AUTHOR

Kurt Vonnegut (1922–2007) was one of the most influential American writers of the 20th century. He wrote such works as *Cat's Cradle* (1963), *Slaughterhouse-Five* (1969), and *Breakfast of Champions* (1973), blending satire, black comedy, and science fiction. He was known for his humanist beliefs and was honorary president of the American Humanist Association.

Short Story

Harrison Bergeron

by Kurt Vonnegut

1 THE YEAR WAS 2081, and everybody was finally equal. They weren't only equal before God and the law. They were equal every which way. Nobody was smarter than anybody else. Nobody was better looking than anybody else. Nobody was stronger or quicker than anybody else. All this equality was due to the 211th, 212th, and 213th Amendments to the Constitution, and to the **unceasing vigilance** of agents of the United States Handicapper General.

2 Some things about living still weren't quite right, though. April for instance, still drove people crazy by not being springtime. And it was in that clammy month that the H-G men took George and Hazel Bergeron's fourteen-year-old son, Harrison, away.

3 It was tragic, all right, but George and Hazel couldn't think about it very hard. Hazel had a perfectly average intelligence, which meant she couldn't think about anything except in short bursts. And George, while his intelligence was way above normal, had a little mental handicap radio in his ear. He was required by law to wear it at all times. It was tuned to a government transmitter. Every twenty seconds or so, the transmitter would send out some sharp noise to keep people like George from taking unfair advantage of their brains.

4 George and Hazel were watching television. There were tears on Hazel's cheeks, but she'd forgotten for the moment what they were about, as the ballerinas came to the end of a dance.

5 A buzzer sounded in George's head. His thoughts fled in panic, like bandits from a burglar alarm.

6 "That was a real pretty dance, that dance they just did," said Hazel.

7 "Huh," said George.

8 "That dance—it was nice," said Hazel.

9 "Yup," said George. He tried to think a little about the ballerinas. They weren't really very good—no better than anybody else would have been, anyway. They were burdened with sash weights and bags of birdshot, and their faces were masked, so that no one, seeing a free and graceful gesture or a pretty face, would feel like something the cat drug in. George was toying with the vague notion that maybe dancers shouldn't be handicapped. But he didn't get very far with it before another noise in his ear radio scattered his thoughts.

10 George winced. So did two out of the eight ballerinas.

11 Hazel saw him wince. Having no mental handicap herself, she had to ask George what the latest sound had been.

12 "Sounded like somebody hitting a milk bottle with a **ball peen hammer**," said George.

13 "I'd think it would be real interesting, hearing all the different sounds," said Hazel a little envious. "All the things they think up."

**WORD
CONNECTIONS**

Etymology

The verb *to handicap* is a word taken from sports. In the late 19th century, *handicap* meant the extra weight given to a superior race horse to even the odds of winning for other horses. The sports term became generalized over time and came to mean the practice of assigning disadvantage to certain players to equalize the chances of winning. Vonnegut's "Handicapper General" is in charge of dumbing down and disabling citizens who are above average so that all citizens are equal.

unceasing: relentless; persistent; continuous
vigilance: watchfulness; alertness

My Notes

ball-peen hammer: a hammer used in metalworking, distinguished by a hemispherical head

Utopian Ideals
and Dystopian Reality

My Notes

doozy: something that is
unusually good, bad, severe, etc.

14 "Um," said George.

15 "Only, if I was Handicapper General, you know what I would do?" said Hazel. Hazel, as a matter of fact, bore a strong resemblance to the Handicapper General, a woman named Diana Moon Glampers. "If I was Diana Moon Glampers," said Hazel, "I'd have chimes on Sunday—just chimes. Kind of in honor of religion."

16 "I could think, if it was just chimes," said George.

17 "Well—maybe make 'em real loud," said Hazel. "I think I'd make a good Handicapper General."

18 "Good as anybody else," said George.

19 "Who knows better than I do what normal is?" said Hazel.

20 "Right," said George. He began to think glimmeringly about his abnormal son who was now in jail, about Harrison, but a twenty-one-gun salute in his head stopped that.

21 "Boy!" said Hazel, "that was a **doozy**, wasn't it?"

22 It was such a doozy that George was white and trembling, and tears stood on the rims of his red eyes. Two of the eight ballerinas had collapsed to the studio floor, were holding their temples.

23 "All of a sudden you look so tired," said Hazel. "Why don't you stretch out on the sofa, so's you can rest your handicap bag on the pillows, honeybunch." She was referring to the forty-seven pounds of birdshot in a canvas bag, which was padlocked around George's neck. "Go on and rest the bag for a little while," she said. "I don't care if you're not equal to me for a while."

24 George weighed the bag with his hands. "I don't mind it," he said. "I don't notice it any more. It's just a part of me."

25 "You been so tired lately—kind of wore out," said Hazel. "If there was just some way we could make a little hole in the bottom of the bag, and just take out a few of them lead balls. Just a few."

26 "Two years in prison and two thousand dollars fine for every ball I took out," said George. "I don't call that a bargain."

27 "If you could just take a few out when you came home from work," said Hazel. "I mean—you don't compete with anybody around here. You just sit around."

28 "If I tried to get away with it," said George, "then other people'd get away with it—and pretty soon we'd be right back to the dark ages again, with everybody competing against everybody else. You wouldn't like that, would you?"

29 "I'd hate it," said Hazel.

30 "There you are," said George. The minute people start cheating on laws, what do you think happens to *society*?"

31 If Hazel hadn't been able to come up with an answer to this question, George couldn't have supplied one. A siren was going off in his head.

32 "Reckon it'd fall all apart," said Hazel.

33 "What would?" said George blankly.

34 "Society," said Hazel uncertainly. "Wasn't that what you just said?

35 "Who knows?" said George.

36 The television program was suddenly interrupted for a news bulletin. It wasn't clear at first as to what the bulletin was about, since the announcer, like all announcers, had a serious speech **impediment**. For about half a minute, and in a state of high excitement, the announcer tried to say, "Ladies and Gentlemen."

37 He finally gave up, handed the bulletin to a ballerina to read.

38 "That's all right—" Hazel said of the announcer, "he tried. That's the big thing. He tried to do the best he could with what God gave him. He should get a nice raise for trying so hard."

39 "Ladies and Gentlemen," said the ballerina, reading the bulletin. She must have been extraordinarily beautiful, because the mask she wore was hideous. And it was easy to see that she was the strongest and most graceful of all the dancers, for her handicap bags were as big as those worn by two-hundred pound men.

40 And she had to apologize at once for her voice, which was a very unfair voice for a woman to use. Her voice was a warm, luminous, timeless melody. "Excuse me—" she said, and she began again, making her voice absolutely uncompetitive.

41 "Harrison Bergeron, age fourteen," she said in a **grackle** squawk, "has just escaped from jail, where he was held on suspicion of plotting to overthrow the government. He is a genius and an athlete, is under-handicapped, and should be regarded as extremely dangerous."

42 A police photograph of Harrison Bergeron was flashed on the screen—upside down, then sideways, upside down again, then right side up. The picture showed the full length of Harrison against a background calibrated in feet and inches. He was exactly seven feet tall.

43 The rest of Harrison's appearance was Halloween and hardware. Nobody had ever borne heavier handicaps. He had outgrown **hindrances** faster than the H-G men could think them up. Instead of a little ear radio for a mental handicap, he wore a tremendous pair of earphones, and spectacles with thick wavy lenses. The spectacles were intended to make him not only half blind, but to give him whanging headaches besides.

44 Scrap metal was hung all over him. Ordinarily, there was a certain **symmetry**, a military neatness to the handicaps issued to strong people, but Harrison looked like a walking junkyard. In the race of life, Harrison carried three hundred pounds.

45 And to offset his good looks, the H-G men required that he wear at all times a red rubber ball for a nose, keep his eyebrows shaved off, and cover his even white teeth with black caps at snaggle-tooth random. "If you see this boy," said the ballerina, "do not—I repeat, do not—try to reason with him."

46 There was the shriek of a door being torn from its hinges.

47 Screams and barking cries of **consternation** came from the television set. The photograph of Harrison Bergeron on the screen jumped again and again, as though dancing to the tune of an earthquake.

48 George Bergeron correctly identified the earthquake, and well he might have—for many was the time his own home had danced to the same crashing tune. "My God—" said George, "that must be Harrison!"

49 The realization was blasted from his mind instantly by the sound of an automobile collision in his head.

impediment: a hindrance; a physical defect that prevents normal speech

My Notes

grackle: any of several blackbirds smaller than a crow

hindrances: obstacles; deterrents; impediments

symmetry: balance; arrangement

consternation: alarm; bewilderment

My Notes

50 When George could open his eyes again, the photograph of Harrison was gone. A living, breathing Harrison filled the screen.

51 Clanking, clownish, and huge, Harrison stood—in the center of the studio. The knob of the uprooted studio door was still in his hand. Ballerinas, technicians, musicians, and announcers cowered on their knees before him, expecting to die.

52 "I am the Emperor!" cried Harrison. "Do you hear? I am the Emperor! Everybody must do what I say at once!" He stamped his foot and the studio shook.

53 "Even as I stand here," he bellowed, "crippled, hobbled, sickened—I am a greater ruler than any man who ever lived! Now watch me become what I can become!"

54 Harrison tore the straps of his handicap harness like wet tissue paper, tore straps guaranteed to support five thousand pounds.

55 Harrison's scrap-iron handicaps crashed to the floor.

56 Harrison thrust his thumbs under the bar of the padlock that secured his head harness. The bar snapped like celery. Harrison smashed his headphones and spectacles against the wall.

57 He flung away his rubber-ball nose, revealed a man that would have awed Thor, the god of thunder.

58 "I shall now select my Empress!" he said, looking down on the cowering people. "Let the first woman who dares rise to her feet claim her mate and her throne!"

59 A moment passed, and then a ballerina arose, swaying like a willow.

60 Harrison plucked the mental handicap from her ear, snapped off her physical handicaps with marvelous delicacy. Last of all he removed her mask.

61 She was blindingly beautiful.

62 "Now—" said Harrison, taking her hand, "shall we show the people the meaning of the word dance? Music!" he commanded.

63 The musicians scrambled back into their chairs, and Harrison stripped them of their handicaps, too. "Play your best," he told them, "and I'll make you barons and dukes and earls."

64 The music began. It was normal at first—cheap, silly, false. But Harrison snatched two musicians from their chairs, waved them like batons as he sang the music as he wanted it played. He slammed them back into their chairs.

65 The music began again and was much improved.

66 Harrison and his Empress merely listened to the music for a while—listened gravely, as though synchronizing their heartbeats with it.

67 They shifted their weights to their toes.

68 Harrison placed his big hands on the girl's tiny waist, letting her sense the weightlessness that would soon be hers.

69 And then, in an explosion of joy and grace, into the air they sprang!

70 Not only were the laws of the land abandoned, but the law of gravity and the laws of motion as well.

gamboled: leapt; pranced

71 They reeled, whirled, swiveled, flounced, capered, **gamboled**, and spun.

72 They leaped like deer on the moon.

73 The studio ceiling was thirty feet high, but each leap brought the dancers nearer to it.

74 It became their obvious intention to kiss the ceiling. They kissed it.

75 And then, neutralizing gravity with love and pure will, they remained suspended in air inches below the ceiling, and they kissed each other for a long, long time.

76 It was then that Diana Moon Glampers, the Handicapper General, came into the studio with a double-barreled ten-gauge shotgun. She fired twice, and the Emperor and the Empress were dead before they hit the floor.

77 Diana Moon Glampers loaded the gun again. She aimed it at the musicians and told them they had ten seconds to get their handicaps back on.

78 It was then that the Bergerons' television tube burned out.

79 Hazel turned to comment about the blackout to George. But George had gone out into the kitchen for a can of beer.

80 George came back in with the beer, paused while a handicap signal shook him up. And then he sat down again. "You been crying," he said to Hazel.

81 "Yup," she said.

82 "What about?" he said.

83 "I forget," she said. "Something real sad on television."

84 "What was it?" he said.

85 "It's all kind of mixed up in my mind," said Hazel.

86 "Forget sad things," said George.

87 "I always do," said Hazel.

88 "That's my girl," said George. He winced. There was the sound of a riveting gun in his head.

89 "Gee—I could tell that one was a doozy," said Hazel.

90 "You can say that again," said George.

91 "Gee—" said Hazel, "I could tell that one was a doozy."

Second Read

- Reread the passage to answer these text-dependent comprehension questions.
- Write any additional questions you have about the text in your Reader/Writer Notebook.

1. **Key Ideas and Details:** What is George's "little mental handicap radio" and what is it intended to do?

My Notes

Utopian Ideals
and Dystopian Reality

My Notes

2. **Key Ideas and Details:** Why is the punishment for removing weight from the "handicap bag" so harsh? Find textual evidence to support your answer.

3. **Key Ideas and Details:** According to this society, what are the things that make George and his son and people like the ballerinas so dangerous? Cite textual evidence to support your inference.

4. **Craft and Structure:** How does the author use parallel structure for effect in paragraph 51? In paragraph 53?

5. **Craft and Structure:** Examine the author's choice of verbs to describe the actions of Harrison and the ballerina in motion. What is the intended effect?

6. **Key Ideas and Details:** How is the story's theme reflected in the conversation between Hazel and George that concludes the story?

7. **Key Ideas and Details:** Summarize what happens in this story.

Language and Writer's Craft: Embedding Direct Quotations

Once you have come up with the thesis for a paragraph or essay, you need to provide ideas and evidence that support the thesis. You can do this through paraphrasing and direct quotations. Note that it is important to avoid plagiarism—using another writer's words without giving the writer credit.

When you **paraphrase,** you restate an idea in your own words while still keeping the same meaning.

When you use a direct quote, you use quotation marks to indicate that the text is from another source. It may be easier to paraphrase, but providing direct quotations strengthens your thesis.

Look for examples of paraphrasing and direct quotes in this paragraph explaining how the reader knows the ballerina is beautiful and has a lovely voice. Notice that words and phrases that are quoted directly from the story are enclosed in quotation marks.

In this society, everyone must be exactly equal. As a result, the government forces people to be handicapped so they are not better than anyone else. We know the ballerina must be more beautiful than others because she wears a "hideous" mask and that she must be strong and graceful because "her handicap bags were as big as those worn by two-hundred pound men." The reader can infer that the ballerina does not usually speak, because she doesn't have a handicap for her voice. Instead, when she has to make an announcement, she apologizes for her voice, "which was a very unfair voice for a woman to use" and makes "her voice absolutely uncompetitive."

PRACTICE Read paragraphs 41 and 42. In your Reader/Writer Notebook, write a paragraph explaining why the government believes Harrison Bergeron is a criminal. Correctly use paraphrasing and direct quotes from the story as evidence for your argument.

Working from the Text

8. Complete the following chart, citing evidence by embedding quotes from the text.

(a) What "ideal" is the society based upon?	Interpretation: Evidence:
(b) What did the society sacrifice in order to create this "ideal" life?	Interpretation: Evidence:
(c) How was this **utopian** ideal transformed into a **dystopian** reality?	Interpretation: Evidence:
(d) What new problems were created?	Interpretation: Evidence:

GRAMMAR & USAGE
Conventions

An **ellipsis** is a row of three dots (. . .) that indicates something omitted from within a quoted passage, usually because it doesn't apply to the point the writer is trying to convey. Look at paragraph 42 from the story. If you only want to quote the part of the paragraph that describes Harrison, you could use ellipses to indicate the portion you removed, like so:

> *A police photograph of Harrison Bergeron was flashed on the screen. . . The picture showed the full length of Harrison against a background calibrated in feet and inches. He was exactly seven feet tall.*

When you use ellipses, be sure that your revised quote doesn't change the intent of the original meaning. If your quoted text uses more ellipses than words, consider paraphrasing it rather than using a direct quotation.

Brackets ([ ]) are most often used to clarify the meaning of quoted material. If it isn't clear what your quoted material is about, consider using brackets to clarify it.

For example, if you quote line 21 without providing any context, the reader won't know what "that" refers to. You can add context by using brackets.

> *"Boy!" said Hazel, "that [the noise] was a doozy, wasn't it?"*

As you prepare to write your analysis, look for instances where you can use ellipses and brackets to clarify your text.

Utopian Ideals and Dystopian Reality

Check Your Understanding

Throughout the story, George shows signs that he knows there is something wrong with the handicapping system. Find two direct quotes that support this statement.

Writing to Sources: Explanatory Text

Write a short essay explaining how "Harrison Bergeron" conveys the conflict between the needs or ideals of society and the realities of individuals. Be sure to:

- Provide examples from the text and use at least one direct quotation to support your ideas.
- Include a reference to utopia and dystopia.
- Use active voice unless you choose passive voice for a certain effect.

Language and Writer's Craft: Active and Passive Voice

Writers use **active** and **passive voice** to convey certain effects. As you write, consider which voice you are using and how it affects the impact of your writing.

The active voice puts the emphasis on who or what is performing the action. The passive voice places the emphasis on the thing or person being acted upon. A verb in the passive voice starts with some form of *be* (*is, was, were*) and ends with the past form of the main verb.

Active: Harrison <u>removed</u> their handicaps.

Passive: The handicaps <u>were removed</u> by Harrison.

Note that using the passive voice is not incorrect. It can be useful in many situations, such as when the performer of the action is unknown or unimportant. However, using the active voice usually makes your writing more exciting and vibrant.

PRACTICE Review your response to the Writing to Sources activity. Look for active voice sentences and passive voice sentences. Did you choose the most effective voice for each sentence? Rewrite sentences that you think would have more impact in the other voice.

Language Checkpoint: Using Subject-Verb Agreement

Learning Targets

- Understand how to use verbs that agree with their subjects.
- Revise writing to check for subject-verb agreement.

Subject-Verb Agreement

Complete sentences always have a subject and a verb. In other words, someone or something—the subject—*is* or *does* something. The word that expresses what the subject is or does is called the verb. Making the verb match the subject is called **subject-verb agreement**.

1. Read the following sentences about "Harrison Bergeron" by Kurt Vonnegut. Underline the subjects and circle the verbs.

   a. A buzzer sounds in George's head.

   b. A news bulletin interrupts the television program.

   c. Screams come from the television set.

2. What do you notice about the subjects and verbs in the sentences above? With a partner, look at the subjects and verbs and make an observation about what makes them agree.

3. Read the following excerpt from a student's analysis of "Harrison Bergeron." Find the subjects and verbs in each sentence and write them in the chart below. Then decide whether each subject is singular or plural.

   In Kurt Vonnegut's story, the main character is not allowed to think. Because his intelligence is far above average, as soon as he begins to have a thought, a buzzer sounds in his head. The sounds of bells, sirens, and other awful noises chase away his thoughts. As a result, his intelligence remains at the level of average people. The conflict begins when George sees his missing son on television. Although his memories quickly escape him, they linger and haunt him nonetheless.

Subjects and Verbs	Singular (S) or Plural (P)
character is	S

4. With your partner, look at the subjects and verbs you added to the chart. Then read the observation you wrote earlier about what makes subjects and verbs agree, and decide whether to add anything to your observation.

Language Checkpoint:
Using Subject-Verb Agreement

Subject-Verb Agreement in Long Sentences

Writers have to pay careful attention to subject-verb agreement, especially in longer sentences where the subject and the verb are not next to each other.

5. Read the following sentences from a student's analysis of "Harrison Bergeron." Identify the subjects and verbs by underlining the subject and circling the verb. Then decide whether the subjects and verbs agree or not.

   a. The United States Handicapper General, resembling Hazel Bergeron, applies handicaps to people with positive attributes.

   b. A rubber ball on his perfectly formed nose hides Harrison Bergeron's attractiveness.

   c. The newscaster, a man with a serious speech impediment, was unable to deliver his announcement.

6. Work with a partner to come up with a way to check for subject-verb agreement in long sentences.

Revising

Read the paragraph below from a student's essay about "Harrison Bergeron." Work with a partner to check whether subjects and verbs agree. Mark the text to show how you would correct any mistakes you notice. Remember that sentences may contain more than one subject and verb.

[1] Hazel, who is considered to have too many emotions, are of average intelligence. [2] However, the United States Handicapper General, the person who regulates each citizen's emotions, appearance, intelligence, and skill, always ensure that Hazel's emotions stay in check. [3] She forget her emotions almost instantly. [4] At the same time, Hazel, despite the government's best efforts, seem unable to escape her emotions. [5] Even though she cannot remember why she is upset, she find herself crying frequently. [6] The image of her son on television, for instance, bring her to tears.

Check Your Understanding

Imagine you are editing a classmate's writing, and you notice this sentence:

Intelligence, strength, and good looks, qualities that Harrison Bergeron possesses, is just what the government is trying to control.

In your own words, write an explanation so that your classmate understands how to correct the sentence. Then add an item to your Editor's Checklist to help you remember how to check your writing for subject-verb agreement.

Practice

Return to the summary you wrote in Activity 2.3 and check it for subject-verb agreement. Trade your work with a partner. Be sure to:

• Underline subjects and circle verbs in the summary.

• Check that subjects and verbs agree.

Understanding a Society's Way of Life

Learning Targets

- Collaboratively analyze the opening chapters of a fictional text citing text evidence to support your analysis.
- Analyze the significance of specific passages to interpret the relationship between character and setting.

Levels of Questions

Remember that questioning a text on multiple levels can help you explore its meaning more fully. Read the definitions below and write an example of each type of question, based on texts you have read in this unit.

- A **Level 1** question is **literal** (the answer can be found in the text).

- A **Level 2** question is **interpretive** (the answer can be inferred based on textual evidence).

- A **Level 3** question is **universal** (the answer is about a concept or idea beyond the text).

You will be reading a novel that questions whether a utopian society is possible. Such novels generally fit into the genre of science fiction.

1. Read the following text to gather more information about science fiction (from readwritethink.org). As you read, highlight the characteristics of science fiction.

Science fiction is a genre of fiction in which the stories often tell about science and technology of the future. It is important to note that science fiction has a relationship with the principles of science—these stories involve partially true/partially fictitious laws or theories of science. It should not be completely unbelievable with magic and dragons, because it then ventures into the genre of fantasy. The plot creates situations different from those of both the present day and the known past. Science fiction texts also include a human element, explaining what effect new discoveries, happenings and scientific developments will have on us in the future. Science fiction texts are often set in the future, in space, on a different world, or in a different universe or **dimension**. Early pioneers of the genre of science fiction are H. G. Wells (*The War of the Worlds*) and Jules Verne (*20,000 Leagues Under the Sea*). Some well-known 20th-century science fiction texts include *1984* by George Orwell and *Brave New World* by Aldous Huxley.

> **LEARNING STRATEGIES:**
> Visualizing, Levels of Questions, Predicting, Graphic Organizer, Note-taking, Discussion Groups

My Notes

WORD CONNECTIONS

Etymology

Fantasy comes from the Old French word *fantasie* ("fantasy"), the Latin word *phantasia* ("imagination"), and the Ancient Greek word *phantasia*, meaning "apparition." The literary genre of fantasy is imaginative fiction crafted in a setting other than the real world. It involves creatures and events that are improbable or impossible in the world as we know it.

dimension: a level of existence or consciousness

Understanding a Society's Way of Life

Literary Terms

An **antagonist** is the opposite of a protagonist and is the character who fights against the hero or main character (the protagonist).

My Notes

Reviewing Vocabulary of Literary Analysis

Theme, or the central message of the story, is revealed through an understanding of and the resolution to the conflicts, both internal and external, that the central *character* experiences throughout the story.

Characterization is the method of developing characters through *description* (e.g., appearance, thoughts, feelings), *action*, and *dialogue*. The central character or protagonist is usually pitted against the **antagonist**, his or her enemy, rival, or opponent.

Evidence in analysis includes many different things, such as descriptions of characters and actions, objects, title, dialogue, details of setting, and plot.

Novel Study

Preview the novel you will be reading as a class.

2. The cover art of a novel tries to represent important aspects of the content of the novel. Study the cover of your novel to make predictions about the story. Based on your reading about the genre of science fiction, what might you predict about a science fiction story?

- Setting:

- Characters:

- Plot:

- Theme:

3. Use the graphic organizer to note evidence that reveals important information about the protagonist and setting. Then, make inferences based on the evidence.

Literary Element	Evidence (page #)	Inferences
Protagonist _____ (name)		
Setting (description of the society/the way of life)		

4. In your Reader/Writer Notebook, begin a personal vocabulary list. Identify, record, and define (in context) at least five new words. Plan to do this for every reading assignment.

5. Select and record an interesting quotation—relating to the protagonist or setting—that you think is important to understanding the conflict or theme. Then, analyze the idea and form two thoughtful questions for discussion.

Quotation (page #)

Analysis

Questions

Level 1:

Level 2:

Check Your Understanding

Using the questions you have created for the novel you are reading, participate in a brief discussion about the society the novel presents and the protagonist's role in it.

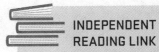

INDEPENDENT READING LINK

Read and Respond

What challenge are you studying? How did this challenge begin? Who does it affect? What are the opposing sides? Write a summary of what you have learned so far, citing information from a few sources. Write your response in you Reader/Writer Notebook.

Contemplating Conflicting Perspectives

LEARNING STRATEGIES:
Shared Reading, Close
Reading, Rereading,
Questioning the Text, Note-
taking, Discussion Groups

My Notes

Learning Targets
- Analyze conflicting perspectives within the novel and explain how the author uses this technique to shape readers' understanding of the story.
- Identify and analyze the importance of specific vocabulary to the story.

Novel Study

In this activity, you will look at the different perspectives in the novel you are reading.

1. Other than the protagonist, who are the most important characters so far in the story? What do we know about each of these characters? Make a list of these characters and provide a brief description of each.

2. Which of these characters usually agree with one another? Which of these characters tend to disagree?

ACADEMIC VOCABULARY
Perspective is a point of view or a specific attitude toward something. Your *perspective* describes how you look at or interpret situations or events.

3. Conflict among people or between people and society is a result of conflicting **perspectives.** Support this idea by identifying a topic that has created the most important conflict so far in the story and contrast two different perspectives about the topic.

Topic:	
Character 1:	Character 2:
Perspective:	Perspective:
Textual Evidence (#):	Textual Evidence (#):

4. Write questions for discussion based on the information you provided in the chart.
   - **Level 1 (literal, factual):**

   - **Level 2 (interpretive):**

5. Which characters are questioning society? How might that tie in to the novel's theme?

6. Continue to add to your personal vocabulary list in your Reader/Writer Notebook. Identify, record, and define (in context) at least five new words. Choose one you think is important to understanding the character, setting, or conflict of the story. Explain why you chose that word.

7. In addition to creating differences in characters' perspectives, authors create differences between the perspectives of the characters and that of the reader. Support this idea by identifying a topic and comparing and contrasting a character's perspective with your own perspective. This time, include the main reason for each perspective and provide evidence from the text for each reason.

Topic:	
Character's Perspective:	**My Perspective:**
Main Reason:	**Main Reason:**
Textual Evidence (page #)	**Textual Evidence (page #)**

Contemplating Conflicting Perspectives

Language and Writer's Craft: Choosing Mood

Recall what you learned in the last unit about verbal mood.

Indicative Mood: Verbs that indicate a fact or opinion.

I am too ill to go to school today.

Imperative Mood: Verbs that express a command or request.

Go to school. Please get up and get dressed.

Interrogative Mood: Verbs that ask a question.

Are you going to school? Do you feel ill?

Conditional Mood: Verbs that express something that has not happened or something that can happen if a certain condition is met.

I would have gone to school yesterday if I had felt well.

Your teacher might want you to complete the assignments you missed.

Subjunctive Mood: Verbs that describe a state that is uncertain or contrary to fact. When using the verb "to be" in the subjunctive, always use *were* rather than *was*.

I wish my cold were better today.

If you were to go to school, what would you learn?

PRACTICE The sentence *Tina will go to the game* is in the indicative mood. In your Reader/Writer Notebook, revise the sentence using each of the other four moods: imperative, interrogative, conditional, and subjunctive.

8. Which verbal mood would be most suitable for a topic sentence? Identify the mood and then choose the most suitable topic sentence below.
   • If Harrison and his mother were put in the same room, they would not be able to communicate.
   • Arrest Harrison Bergeron immediately.
   • Are Harrison and Hazel Bergeron really so different?
   • Harrison and George Bergeron are father and son.
   • If Harrison's father were not handicapped, would he be like his son?
9. Which of the sentences might be a good hook for an introductory paragraph?

Check Your Understanding

Choose a topic from your novel, other than the one you used for step 7, on which your own perspective is different from that of one of the characters. Briefly explain your own perspective and how it contrasts with the character's.

Writing to Sources: Explanatory Text

Identify the perspectives of two characters and show how the contrast between them highlights a conflict in the story. Be sure to:
• Create a topic sentence indicating contrasting perspectives.
• Provide examples from the text and at least one direct quotation.
• Choose the appropriate mood for each of your verbs.
• Use correct subject-verb agreement.

Questioning Society

Learning Targets

- Evaluate specific rules and laws in a fictional society and compare them to present society, referencing the text and notations from additional research and reading materials.
- Contribute analysis and evidence relating to this topic in a Socratic Seminar.

Preview

In this activity, you will read a short article about banned books and make connections to the novel you are reading.

Setting a Purpose for Reading

- As you read this article, underline words and phrases that relate to big concepts you have been thinking about in this unit.
- Circle unknown words and phrases. Try to determine the meaning of the words by using context clues, word parts, or a dictionary.

LEARNING STRATEGIES:
Shared Reading, Marking the Text, Questioning the Text, Socratic Seminar, Fishbowl

WORD CONNECTIONS

Etymology

Censorship comes from the Latin word *censor*. A censor in Rome was responsible for counting citizens and for supervising and regulating their morals. The suffix *-ship* makes the word a noun.

Article

Banned Books Week:
Celebrating the Freedom to Read

1 Banned Books Week (BBW) is an annual event celebrating the freedom to read and the importance of the First Amendment. Held during the last week of September, Banned Books Week highlights the benefits of free and open access to information while drawing attention to the harms of censorship by spotlighting actual or attempted bannings of books across the United States.

2 Intellectual freedom—the freedom to access information and express ideas, even if the information and ideas might be considered unorthodox or unpopular— provides the foundation for Banned Books Week. BBW stresses the importance of ensuring the availability of unorthodox or unpopular viewpoints for all who wish to read and access them.

3 The books featured during Banned Books Week have been targets of attempted bannings. Fortunately, while some books were banned or restricted, in a majority of cases the books were not banned, all thanks to the efforts of librarians, teachers, booksellers, and members of the community to retain the books in the library collections. Imagine how many more books might be challenged—and possibly banned or restricted—if librarians, teachers, and booksellers across the country did not use Banned Books Week each year to teach the importance of our First Amendment rights and the power of literature, and to draw attention to the danger that exists when **restraints** are **imposed** on the availability of information in a free society.

GRAMMAR & USAGE
Mood

In the last activity you learned that the imperative mood is one that expresses a command or request and the interrogative mood asks a question.

> **Imperative Mood:** *Read this book.*

> **Interrogative Mood:** *Have you read this book?*

The sentence beginning "Imagine . . ." in paragraph 3 is in the imperative mood. Notice how the imperative mood strengthens the impact of this sentence. How would it be different if it had been written in the interrogative mood?

Look for imperative and interrogative sentences as you read. Interrogative sentences are easy to notice because of the question mark at the end. Imperative sentences have an understood subject (*you*) that does not actually appear in the sentence.

restraints: confines; controls
imposed: forced

Questioning Society

Second Read

- Reread the passage to answer the text-dependent comprehension question.
- Write any additional questions you have about the text in your Reader/Writer Notebook.

1. **Craft and Structure:** What clues in the text help you understand the meaning of the word *banned*?

Working from the Text

2. **Quickwrite:** Explain why books are an important part of our society. Which values do they symbolize? You may use the informational text to guide your response.

Novel Study

Setting is not simply the time and place in a story. It is also the *social circumstances* that create the world in which characters act and make choices. Readers who are sensitive to this world are better able to understand and judge the behavior of the characters and the significance of the action. The social circumstances of a story will often provide insights into the theme of a literary piece.

3. Using "Harrison Bergeron," show how the setting connects to the character and theme.

4. How are books viewed in the society of your novel's protagonist?

5. Compare and contrast perspectives relating to banned books. How might this connect to the story's theme?

6. Think about the way of life in this society. Which rules and/or laws do you completely disagree with? Take notes in the chart on the next page to prepare for a collaborative discussion based on this topic.

State the rule or law (paraphrase or directly quote).	Analyze: Underlying Value	Evaluate: State why you disagree with the rule or law and then form a thoughtful Level 3 question to spark a meaningful conversation with your peers.
1. page(s): ___		Response: Level 3 Question:
2. page(s): ___		Response: Level 3 Question:
3. page(s): ___		Response: Level 3 Question:

7. Continue to add to your personal vocabulary list. Identify, record, and define (in context) at least five new words.

Check Your Understanding

What do you think our country would be like if the government could ban books? State your thesis and give three examples to back it up. Record your answer in your Reader/Writer Notebook.

Introducing the Strategy: Socratic Seminar

A **Socratic Seminar** is a type of collaborative discussion designed to explore a complex question, topic, or text. Participants engage in meaningful dialogue by asking one another questions and using textual evidence to support responses. The goal is for participants to arrive at a deeper understanding of a concept or idea by the end of the discussion. A Socratic Seminar is not a debate.

ACADEMIC VOCABULARY
The word **Socratic** is an adjective formed from the name of the philosopher Socrates, who was famous for using the question-and-answer method in his search for truth and wisdom. A **seminar** is a term used to describe a small group of students engaged in intensive study.

Questioning Society

My Notes

8. You will next participate in a Socratic Seminar. During the Seminar, follow these rules for collegial discussions:

- Challenge yourself to build on others' ideas by asking questions in response to a statement or question. To do this effectively, you will have to listen to comprehend and evaluate.
- Work to transition between ideas to maintain coherence throughout the discussion.
- Work to achieve a balance between speaking and listening within a group. Make sure everyone has a chance to speak, and allow quiet time during the discussion so people have a chance to formulate a thoughtful response.
- Have you heard the expression: "Be a frog, not a hog or a log"? What do you think that means? Set two specific and attainable goals for the discussion:

Speaking Goal:

Listening Goal:

Oral Discussion sentence starters:

- I agree with your idea relating to . . . , but it is also important to consider . . .
- I disagree with your idea about . . . , and would like to point out . . .
- You made a point about the concept of . . . How are you defining that?
- On page ___, (a specific character) says . . . I agree/disagree with this because . . .
- On page ___, (a specific character) says . . . This is important because . . .
- On page ____, we learn . . . , so would you please explain your last point about . . . ?
- Add your own:

Introducing the Strategy: Fishbowl

Fishbowl is a speaking and listening strategy that divides a large group into an inner and an outer circle. Students in the inner circle model appropriate discussion techniques as they discuss ideas, while students in the outer circle listen to comprehend ideas and evaluate the discussion process. During a discussion, students have the opportunity to experience both circles.

9. Engage in the Socratic Seminar.

- When you are in the *inner* circle, you will need your work relating to rules and laws, a pen or pencil, and the novel.
- When you are in the *outer* circle, you will need a pen or pencil and the note-taking sheet on the next page.

Socratic Seminar Notes

Topic: Rules and Laws in a Utopian/Dystopian Society

Listening to Comprehend

- **Interesting points:**
  1. _____:

  2. _____:

  3. _____:

- **My thoughts:**
  1.

  2.

  3.

Listening to Evaluate

- **Speaking:**
  Strength:

  Challenge:

- **Listening:**
  Strength:

  Challenge:

Reflection

- I did/did not meet my speaking and listening goals.
  Explanation:

- I am most proud of:

- Next time I will:

My Notes

A Shift in Perspective: Beginning the Adventure

My Notes

Learning Targets

- Analyze and explain how the Hero's Journey archetype provides a framework for understanding the actions of a protagonist.
- Develop coherence by using transitions appropriate to the task.

Novel Study

In this activity, you will reflect on the protagonist in your novel and the journey he or she is on.

1. What can you infer about the protagonist in this story? Make an inference based on relevant *descriptions* (e.g., appearance, thoughts, feelings), *actions*, and/or *dialogue*. Support your inference with evidence from the text. Follow this format:

   Topic Sentence: State an important character trait.

   - **Supporting Detail/Evidence**: Provide a transition, lead-in, and specific example that demonstrates the trait.
   - **Commentary/Analysis:** Explain how the evidence supports the trait.
   - **Commentary/Analysis:** Explain why this character trait is important to the story.

2. In Unit 1 you studied the Hero's Journey archetype. What do you remember about the departure? Provide a brief summary of each of the first three steps and their importance.

   Stage 1: The Departure

Stage and Definition	Connection to the Story
Step 1: The Call to Adventure	
Step 2: Refusal of the Call	
Step 3: The Beginning of the Adventure	

3. The protagonist is considered the hero of the story. Readers most often identify with his or her perspective. While you read, use sticky notes to mark text that could reflect the protagonist's Departure. On each note, comment on the connection to the archetype.

4. Continue to add to your personal vocabulary list in your Reader/Writer Notebook. Identify, record, and define (in context) at least five new words.

5. Skim/scan the first half of the story and revisit your sticky notes to determine the beginning of the protagonist's journey, the Departure. It may be easiest to start with Step 3, the Beginning of the Adventure.

- Remember that the Hero's Journey is organized sequentially, in chronological order (although some steps may occur at the same time or not at all). This means that once you connect a step to the story, the next step in the journey must reflect an event that occurs later in the story.

- Because this task is based on interpretation, there is more than one correct answer. To convince an audience of your interpretation, you must be able to provide a convincing explanation.

- Go back to the chart outline above and add connections to the story. Use this information in your response to the prompt below.

Check Your Understanding

In preparation for writing, create an outline of the protagonist's departure in your novel. Use transition words in the outline. For example:

- First, she did this:
- Then this happened:
- As a result:
- Next, she went here:
- Finally this happened:

Writing to Sources: Explanatory Text

Explain the beginning of the protagonist's journey using the first three steps of the Hero's Journey archetype to guide your explanation. Be sure to:

- Establish a clear controlling idea.
- Develop ideas with relevant and convincing evidence from the text (include at least one direct quotation) and analysis.
- Use appropriate and varied transitions to create coherence and clarify the relationships among ideas (e.g., steps in the Hero's Journey).
- Use the active rather than the passive voice in your analysis, unless there is a specific reason to use the passive.

WORD CONNECTIONS

Roots and Affixes

Sequential is the adjective form of the word *sequence*, which comes from the Latin root *sequi*, meaning "to follow."

Chronological order means "time order," reflecting the origin of the word in *chronos*, a Greek word meaning "time."

My Notes

Navigating the Road of Trials

My Notes

Learning Targets

- Analyze conflicts revealed through specific passages of dialogue.
- Contribute analysis and evidence in a small group collaborative discussion.

Novel Study

In this activity, you will continue exploring your protagonist's journey.

1. Review the Initiation stage of the Hero's Journey. What do you remember about:

   Step 4. The Road of Trials

   Step 5. The Experience with Unconditional Love

2. In the previous activity, you interpreted the protagonist's Departure. Now begin your interpretation of the next two steps in the protagonist's journey: the Road of Trials and the Experience with Unconditional Love.

   - List three significant trials (conflicts)—in chronological order—that occur *after* the event you identified as Step 3 of the Hero's Journey.
   - Connect *the experience with unconditional love* to the *trial* (if present).
   - Analyze how the *trial* and the *experience with unconditional love* affect the protagonist.

Trial: (focus on conflicts with other characters and society)	Experience with Unconditional Love:	Effect: (actions; words; thoughts/ feelings)
1.		
2.		
3.		

3. Who is the antagonist in the story? How would you describe this character? What does he or she value or believe?

4. Prepare for a small group discussion by continuing to focus on the *trials* and *unconditional love* experienced by the protagonist. Use sticky notes for the following:

   • Mark conflicts reflected in dialogue spoken by other characters, and analyze how the dialogue affects the protagonist's perspective on his society, encouraging him to reject their way of life.

   • Mark evidence of *unconditional love* reflected in dialogue spoken by other characters, and analyze how the dialogue affects the protagonist's perspective on his society, encouraging him to reject their way of life.

5. In your Reader/Writer Notebook, continue to add to your personal vocabulary list. Identify, record, and define (in context) at least five new words.

6. Using the notes you have prepared about important dialogue, engage in a small group discussion based on the following prompt.

   Discussion Prompt: Analyze how specific lines of dialogue provoke the protagonist to make the decision to reject his or her dystopian society.

Check Your Understanding

Quickwrite: Think back over the group discussion about dialogue and conflict that you participated in for question 6. Prepare a brief written summary of the points your group made.

Writing to Sources: Explanatory Text

In a paragraph, explain how the trials (conflicts) experienced by the main character in your novel and the evidence of unconditional love are representative of the Hero's Journey archetype. Be sure to:

   • Include a topic sentence.
   • Use evidence from the novel.
   • Show an understanding of the steps of the journey archetype.
   • Check your writing for correct subject-verb agreement.

My Notes

The End of the Journey

Learning Targets

- Analyze the transformational nature of conflicts and the hero's *boon* as it relates to the archetype of the Hero's Journey in the novel.
- Contrast the protagonist with another character.
- Determine and explain the novel's theme in written responses, citing evidence from the text as support.

Novel Study

In this activity, you will reflect on how your protagonist has changed over the course of the novel.

1. Think about the protagonist's Departure into the Hero's Journey (Stage 1) and his *Road of Trials*. How has the character changed as a result of these trials or conflicts? Use the sentence frame below to explain the change, and be sure to provide evidence to support your interpretation.

   In the beginning, the protagonist was _____, but after

   _____, he becomes _____.

2. What do you remember about the *boon* in Stage 2, the Initiation of the Hero's Journey?

   Step 6: The Ultimate Boon:

3. How do conflicts with society (including characters who believe in the society's way of life) transform the character into a hero? As you read, take notes in the chart below.

Conflict with Society	Heroic Traits Revealed Through Conflict	Connection to Theme Subjects

My Notes

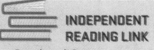

**INDEPENDENT
READING LINK**

Read and Connect

Find information on a person who is working to fight the challenge you are exploring. Does this person embody the concept of a "hero"? Why or why not? What has this person's journey been? Write your response in your Reader/Writer Notebook.

4. Use your Reader/Writer Notebook to continue adding to your personal vocabulary list. Identify, record, and define (in context) at least five new words.

5. Interpret the hero's *boon*: What did the hero achieve through this journey?

6. Which characteristics helped the hero to achieve the *boon*? Explain.

Writing Introductory Paragraphs

7. Read and analyze the samples of introductory paragraphs below. Which one would be used to write an essay structured as compare/contrast? Which would introduce an essay based on a different explanatory organizational structure?

Sample 1

People say that kids are a lot like their parents, but in Kurt Vonnegut's short story "Harrison Bergeron," this is definitely not the case. Harrison Bergeron, the protagonist, and Hazel Bergeron, Harrison's mother, have close to nothing in common. Hazel is completely average and therefore content, while her son is completely superior and therefore rebellious.

Sample 2

A hero must be willing to take risks and have the courage to go against the norm to help others. "Harrison Bergeron" by Kurt Vonnegut is a story of how society holds back its most talented members in search of the supposed ideal of equality. Harrison Bergeron, the protagonist, is a would-be hero who is struck down before he has the opportunity to begin, much less complete, his hero's journey.

My Notes

The End of the Journey

My Notes

Check Your Understanding

In small groups, discuss the trials experienced by the main character in your novel. With your classmates, determine whether these trials are examples of the Hero's Journey archetype.

Writing to Sources

Analyze the prompts below. Notice that each prompt requires a different organizational structure. Choose one of the prompts and write a response.

Explanatory Writing Prompt 1: Think about the protagonist's characteristics, what he achieved, and how he changed by the end of the story. Contrast the protagonist with another character from his society. Be sure to:

- Introduce the topic clearly, establishing a clear controlling idea.
- Provide examples from the text (including at least one direct quotation) and analysis to support your ideas.
- Sequence ideas logically using the appropriate compare/contrast structure.
- Choose the appropriate verbal mood for the ideas you want to express.
- Write in active voice unless the passive voice is specifically needed.

Explanatory Writing Prompt 2: Think about the final stage in the Hero's Journey: the Crossing, or Return Threshold. What does the hero learn about life as a result of the journey (theme)? Be sure to:

- Introduce the topic clearly, establishing a clear controlling idea.
- Provide examples from the text (including at least one direct quotation) and analysis to support your ideas.
- Sequence ideas logically to explain how the protagonist's transformation connects to what he learns.
- Choose the appropriate verbal mood for the ideas you want to express.
- Write in active voice unless the passive voice is specifically needed.

Independent Reading Checkpoint

Discuss the challenge you researched with a partner. Take notes on what your partner says, and hand in your notes at the end of the discussion.

Writing an Explanatory Essay

ASSIGNMENT

Think about how writers organize and develop ideas in explanatory writing. Use an explanatory organizational structure to communicate your understanding of the concept of dystopia or the concept of the Hero's Journey. Select one of the prompts below:

- Write an essay that compares and contrasts life in the dystopian society of the novel you read with our modern-day society.
- Write an essay that explains how the protagonist (hero) changes as a result of conflict with his dystopian society (Road of Trials) and how this change connects to the novel's theme (the Crossing, or Return Threshold).

Planning and Prewriting: Take time to plan your essay.	▥ Which prompt do you feel best prepared to respond to with examples from literature and real life? ▥ What prewriting strategies (such as freewriting or graphic organizers) could help you brainstorm ideas and organize your examples?
Drafting: Write a multi-paragraph essay that effectively organizes your ideas.	▥ How will you introduce the topic clearly and establish a controlling idea (thesis)? ▥ How will you develop the topic with well-chosen examples and thoughtful analysis (commentary)? ▥ How will you logically sequence the ideas using an appropriate structure and transitions? ▥ How will your conclusion support your ideas?
Evaluating and Revising the Draft: Create opportunities to review and revise your work.	▥ During the process of writing, when can you pause to share and respond with others in order to elicit suggestions and ideas for revision? ▥ How can the Scoring Guide help you evaluate how well your draft meets the requirements of the assignment?
Checking and Editing for Publication: Confirm your final draft is ready for publication.	▥ How will you proofread and edit your draft to demonstrate command of the conventions of standard English capitalization, punctuation, spelling, grammar and usage? ▥ How did you use TLQC (transition/lead-in/quote/citation) to properly embed quotations? ▥ How did you ensure use of the appropriate voice and mood in your writing?

Reflection

After completing this Embedded Assessment, think about how you went about accomplishing this task, and respond to the following:

- How has your understanding of utopia and dystopia developed through the reading in this unit?

Writing an Explanatory Essay

SCORING GUIDE

Scoring Criteria	Exemplary	Proficient	Emerging	Incomplete
Ideas	The essay • maintains a focused thesis in response to one of the prompts • develops ideas thoroughly with relevant supporting details, facts, and evidence • provides insightful commentary and deep analysis.	The essay • responds to one of the prompts with a clear thesis • develops ideas adequately with supporting details, facts, and evidence • provides sufficient commentary to demonstrate understanding.	The essay • has an unclear or unrelated thesis • develops ideas unevenly or with inadequate supporting details, facts, or evidence • provides insufficient commentary to demonstrate understanding.	The essay • has no obvious thesis • provides minimal supporting details, facts, or evidence • lacks commentary.
Structure	The essay • has an engaging introduction • uses an effective organizational structure for a multi-paragraph essay • uses a variety of transitional strategies to create cohesion and unity among ideas • provides an insightful conclusion.	The essay • has a complete introduction • uses an appropriate organizational structure for a multi-paragraph essay • uses transitional strategies to link, compare, and contrast ideas • provides a conclusion that supports the thesis.	The essay • has a weak or partial introduction • uses an inconsistent organizational structure for a multi-paragraph essay • uses transitional strategies ineffectively or inconsistently • provides a weak or unrelated conclusion.	The essay • lacks an introduction • has little or no obvious organizational structure • uses few or no transitional strategies • provides no conclusion.
Use of Language	The essay • conveys a consistent academic voice by using a variety of literary terms and precise language • embeds quotations effectively • demonstrates command of the conventions of standard English capitalization, punctuation, spelling, grammar, and usage (including a variety of syntax).	The essay • conveys an academic voice by using some literary terms and precise language • embeds quotations correctly • demonstrates adequate command of the conventions of standard English capitalization, punctuation, spelling, grammar, and usage (including a variety of syntax).	The essay • uses insufficient language and vocabulary to convey an academic voice • embeds quotations incorrectly or unevenly • demonstrates partial or inconsistent command of the conventions of standard English capitalization, punctuation, spelling, grammar, and usage.	The essay • uses limited or vague language • lacks quotations • lacks command of the conventions of standard English capitalization, punctuation, spelling, grammar, and usage; frequent errors obscure meaning.

Previewing Embedded Assessment 2 and Effective Argumentation

Learning Targets

- Reflect on learning and make connections to new learning specific to vocabulary and concept knowledge introduced thus far.
- Collaboratively analyze and identify the skills and knowledge necessary for success in the Embedded Assessment.

Making Connections

It can be said that writers of fiction, especially dystopian novels, are trying to make a point or criticize some aspect of society. In this part of the unit, you will think about how you can have an impact by creating a well-reasoned argument about a social issue important to you.

Essential Questions

1. Reflect on your understanding of the first Essential Question: *To what extent can a perfect society exist?*

2. How has your understanding of the concept of *utopia* changed over the course of this unit?

3. How would you change your original response to Essential Question 2, *What makes an argument effective?*

Developing Vocabulary

4. Re-sort the Academic and Literary Vocabulary using the **QHT** strategy.

5. Return to your original list sorted at the beginning of the unit. Compare this list with your original. How has your understanding changed?

6. Select a word from the above chart and write a concise statement about your learning. How has your understanding changed over the course of this unit?

LEARNING STRATEGIES:
QHT, Close Reading, Paraphrasing, Graphic Organizer

My Notes

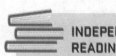

INDEPENDENT READING LINK

Read and Recommend

In this half of the unit, while working on creating an argumentative essay, you will have the opportunity to read on your own. Argumentative texts (speeches and essays) are recommended. The Resources section of your textbook, your Reading Lists and Logs, and your teacher can hep you with your selections. With your class, brainstorm and recommend argumentative text options.

Previewing Embedded Assessment 2 and Effective Argumentation

Unpacking Embedded Assessment 2

Closely read the Embedded Assessment 2 assignment.

> Write an argumentative essay in which you convince an audience to support your claim about a debatable idea. Use your research and experience or observations to support your argument.

Now consult the Scoring Guide and work with your class to paraphrase the expectations. Create a graphic organizer to use as a visual reminder of the required concepts and skills.

After each activity, use this graphic organizer to guide reflection about what you have learned and what you still need to learn in order to be successful in completing the Embedded Assessment.

Looking Ahead to Argumentative Writing

7. Based on your current understanding, how are explanatory and argumentative writing similar? How are they different?

Similarities:

Differences:

Understanding Elements of Argumentation

Learning Targets

- Evaluate a writer's ideas, point of view, or purpose in an argumentative essay.
- Determine how the writer manages counterclaims.
- Identify and apply the six elements of argumentation.

Preview

In this activity, you will read and analyze part of an eighth-grader's **argumentative** essay.

Setting a Purpose for Reading

- As you read the essay, use three different highlighters to identify the parts of the writer's argument. Mark text evidence with the first color, reasoning with the second color, and counterclaims used to support the claim with the third color.
- Circle unknown words and phrases. Try to determine the meaning of the words by using context clues, word parts, or a dictionary.

LEARNING STRATEGIES:
QHT, Marking the Text, Graphic Organizer

ACADEMIC VOCABULARY
An **argument** is a logical appeal, supported by reasons and evidence, to persuade an audience to take an action or agree with a point of view.

Essay

Private Eyes

by Brooke Chorlton (an eighth-grader from Washington State)

1 "Private eyes, they're watching you, they see your every move," sang the band Hall and Oates in their 80s hit "Private Eyes." A popular song three decades ago is quite relevant to life today. We do not live very private lives, mainly due to the Internet, whose sole purpose is to help people share everything. But there are still boundaries to what we have to share. Employers should not require access to the Facebook pages of potential or current employees because Facebook is intended to be private, is not intended to be work-related, and employers do not need this medium to make a good hiring decision.

2 It is true that the Internet is not private, and it is also true that Facebook was not created to keep secrets; it is meant for people to share their life with the selected people they choose as their "friends." However, Facebook still has boundaries or some limits, so that members can choose what to share. As a fourteen-year-old girl I know for a fact, because I have seen it, that when you are setting up your Facebook account, you are able to choose the level of security on your page. Some choose to have no security; if someone on Facebook were to search them, they would be able to see all of their friends, photos, and posts. And, according to *Seattle Times* journalists Manuel Valdes and Shannon McFarland, "It has become common for managers to review publically available Facebook Profiles." The key words are "publically available." The owners of these profiles have chosen to have no boundaries, so it is not as big a deal if an employer were to look at a page like this. But others choose to not let the rest of the world in; if you search them, all that would come up would be their name and profile picture. That is all: just a name and a picture. Only the few selected to be that person's friends are allowed into their online world, while the strangers and stalkers are left out in the cold. It is not likely that you would walk up to a stranger and share what you did that weekend. Orin Kerr, a George Washington University law professor and former federal **prosecutor**, states that requiring someone's password to their profile is, "akin to requiring [their] house keys." If we expect privacy in our real world life, shouldn't we be able to have privacy in our online life as well?

My Notes

prosecutor: a person, especially a public official, who institutes legal proceedings against someone

Understanding Elements of Argumentation

Second Read

- Reread the passage to answer these text-dependent comprehension questions.
- Write any additional questions you have about the text in your Reader/Writer Notebook.

1. **Craft and Structure:** What is the writer's purpose? Who is the writer's audience? How do you know? Use textual evidence to support your answer.

2. **Key Ideas and Details:** What is the writer's claim? Is it clear to the audience? Use textual evidence to support your answer.

3. **Craft and Structure:** Paragraph 2 mentions a counterclaim. Restate the counterclaim in your own words. What evidence and reasoning does the writer use to counter or refute the claim?

Working from the Text

4. Based on the thesis, what is the next point the writer will make about the right of employers to ask for access to Facebook?

5. Notice that the writer ends the paragraph with an interrogative sentence. Why is this an effective mood to use as a transition to the next major idea of the essay?

Beginning to Construct an Argument

6. Think of a technology-related topic that has two sides that can be argued. Decide which side of the issue you want to argue. Brainstorm possible topics and claims.

   Topics:

Claims:

My Notes

7. Choose one of the topics you brainstormed, and begin to structure your argument by using the graphic organizer below. First carefully consider all the elements in the left column as they relate to your topic. Then complete the response portion of the graphic organizer.

Element	Definition/Explanation	Response
Purpose	the specific reason(s) for writing or speaking; the goal the writer or speaker wishes to achieve	
Audience	the specific person or group of people the writer is trying to convince (the opposition); one must consider the audience's values and beliefs before writing the argument	
Claim	an assertion of something as true, real, or factual	
Evidence	knowledge or data on which to base belief; used to prove truth or falsehood; evidence may include: • testimony from experts and authorities • research-based facts and statistics • analogies (comparisons to similar situations) • references to history, religious texts, and classic literature	
Reasoning	logical conclusions, judgments, or inferences based on evidence	
Counterclaim (Concession/ Refutation)	a claim based on knowledge of the other side of a controversial issue; used to demonstrate understanding of the audience, expertise in the subject, and credibility (ethos) a writer or speaker briefly recognizes and then argues against opposing viewpoints	

Check Your Understanding

Sometimes when you debate you have to argue a position with which you do not necessarily agree. Choose another topic you feel strongly about and then argue the opposite position. List three pieces of evidence to support your argument.

Don't Hate—Debate!

LEARNING STRATEGIES:
Visualizing, KWHL, Debate, Brainstorming, Note-taking, Graphic Organizer

My Notes

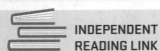

INDEPENDENT READING LINK

Read and Discuss

Choose one essay or speech from your Independent Reading List that contains a compelling claim or argument. What makes the claim or argument effective? Include the author's purpose and any elements of argument you see in the text. Document your response in your Reader/Writer Notebook. You will discuss your response in a small-group setting.

Learning Targets

- Identify and analyze persuasive appeals.
- Orally present valid reasoning, well-chosen details, and relevant evidence to support a debatable claim.
- Identify and evaluate arguments as *logos*, *pathos*, and/or *ethos*.
- Assess the soundness of arguments based on reasoning, relevance, and sufficient evidence.

Persuasive Appeals

1. Persuasive appeals are an important part of creating a convincing argument. Read the definitions below to understand how writers or speakers use each type of appeal.

Appeal	Meaning
Logos	an appeal to reason; providing logical reasoning and evidence in the form of *description*, *narration*, and/or *exposition*
Pathos	an appeal to emotions; using descriptive, connotative, and figurative language for effect; providing an emotional anecdote; developing tone
Ethos	an appeal based on trust or character; demonstrating that you understand the audience's point of view; making the audience believe that you are knowledgeable and trustworthy; showing that you have researched your topic by supporting reasons with appropriate, logical evidence and reasoning

2. Create a visual of each type of appeal to help you remember its definition.

Introducing the Strategy: Debate

The purpose of a **debate** is to provide an opportunity to collect and orally present evidence supporting the affirmative and negative arguments of a proposition or issue. During a debate, participants follow a specific order of events and often have a time limit for making their points.

Preparing to Debate

A debate provides an opportunity to practice creating a reasoned argument and to identify and use appeals when trying to convince others of your point of view. You will engage in an informal debate on a debatable topic arising from the article below.

3. Read and respond to the following news article, first by circling any words you don't know that you think are important, and next by deciding whether you are for or against the legislation.

Article

Representative Urges Action on the Media

In order to combat what he calls the dangerous increases in teens' harmful media habits, Representative Mark Jenkins has recently introduced legislation that would make it a crime for anyone under the age of 18 to engage with more than two hours of media a day on the weekdays and three hours a day on the weekends. The bill defines "media" as television, radio, commercial magazines, non-school related Internet and any blogs or podcasts with advertising. Penalties for violation can range from **forfeiture** of driver's licenses and media counseling to fines for parents or removal of media tools (TVs, computers, phones, etc.). Monitoring systems will be set up in each Congressional district through the offices of Homeland Security and the National Security Agency. Rep. Jenkins could not be reached for comment because he was appearing on television.

forfeiture: the giving up of something as a penalty for wrongdoing

4. Read the debate prompt (always posed as an interrogative sentence).

   Debate: Should the government restrict media usage for anyone under the age of 18 to two hours a day on weekdays and three hours a day on weekends?

5. Brainstorm valid reasons for both sides of the issue. Focus on *logos* (logical) appeals, though you may use other appeals to develop your argument. During the debate, you will use these notes to argue your side.

YES, the government should restrict media usage because:		NO, the government should not restrict media usage because:	
Reason 1:	Evidence:	Reason 1:	Evidence:
Reason 2:	Evidence:	Reason 2:	Evidence:

Don't Hate—Debate!

WORD CONNECTIONS

Cognates

A cognate is a word that has the same root meaning as a word in the same or another language. The English word *evaluate* comes from the French verb *evaluer*, which means "to find the value of." It has the same meaning as *evaluar*, a similar word in Spanish. Both *evaluate* and *evaluar* mean "to assess."

My Notes

6. When it is your turn to speak, engage in the debate. Be able to argue either claim. Keep in mind the elements of argument and the different types of appeals. Be sure to use appropriate eye contact, volume, and a clear voice when speaking in a debate.

Sentence Starters

- I agree with your point about . . . , but it is also important to consider . . .
- I disagree with your point about . . . , and would like to counter with the idea that . . .
- You made a good point about . . . , but have you considered . . .
- Your point about . . . is an appeal to emotions and so is not a logical reason/ explanation.

7. When it is your turn to listen, evaluate others' arguments for their use of logical appeals. Record notes in the chart below as you identify examples of effective and ineffective *logos*, and provide a brief explanation for each example.

Effective Use of *Logos*	Other Appeals

Check Your Understanding

Answer these questions in your Reader/Writer Notebook: What types of persuasive appeals were most effective in supporting the topic during the debate? Why? Was any *logos* appeal convincing enough to make you change your mind about the issue? Explain.

Argument Writing Prompt

Think of a topic that is important to you and write a paragraph that details your position. Decide whether you are going to make the argument using mostly *logos*, *ethos*, or *pathos* appeals. Be sure to:

- Provide a clear thesis statement outlining your position.
- Use primarily one form of appeal to shape your writing.
- Review your work for correct subject-verb agreement.

Highlighting Logos

Learning Targets
- Identify and evaluate logical reasoning and relevant evidence in an argument.
- Understand the relationship between logic and fallacy.
- Write arguments based on logical reasoning and evidence to support a claim.

Preview

In this activity, you will read two articles about distracted driving and evaluate the logic presented in each.

Setting a Purpose for Reading
- As you read, underline precise adjectives and verbs the writer uses for impact.
- Circle unknown words and phrases. Try to determine the meaning of the words by using context clues, word parts, or a dictionary.

LEARNING STRATEGIES:
Marking the Text, Close Reading, Rereading

My Notes

Online Article

Parents Share Son's Fatal Text Message to Warn Against Texting & Driving

1 DENVER (AP) – Alexander Heit's final text cut off in mid-sentence. Before he could send it, police say the 22-year-old University of Northern Colorado student drifted into oncoming traffic, jerked the steering wheel and went off the road, rolling his car.

2 Heit died shortly after the April 3 crash, but his parents and police are hoping the photo of the mundane text on his iPhone will serve as a stark reminder to drivers.

3 The photo, published Wednesday in *The Greeley Tribune*, shows Heit was responding to a friend by typing "Sounds good my man, seeya soon, ill tw" before he crashed.

4 Witnesses told police that Heit appeared to have his head down when he began drifting into the oncoming lane in the outskirts of Greeley, where the University of Northern Colorado is located. According to police, an oncoming driver slowed and moved over just before Heit looked up and jerked the steering wheel.

5 Police say Heit, a Colorado native who loved hiking and snowboarding, had a spotless driving record and wasn't speeding.

6 In a statement released through police, Heit's mother said she doesn't want anyone else to lose someone to texting while driving.

7 "In a split second you could ruin your future, injure or kill others, and tear a hole in the heart of everyone who loves you," Sharon Heit said.

Source: CBS News, © 2013 The Associated Press

Highlighting Logos

Second Read

- Reread the passage to answer this text-dependent comprehension question.
- Write any additional questions you have about the text in your Reader/Writer Notebook.

1. **Key Ideas and Details:** What kind of appeal does the writer use at the beginning of this article: *logos*, *pathos*, or *ethos*? Why is it effective?

Working from the Text

2. What evidence is used to convince others that texting and driving is dangerous? Is this evidence logical, relevant, and convincing?

3. Now that you have examined and identified the use of the three "appeals" used to convince an audience, explain why *logos* is the most important appeal to be able to use skillfully.

4. Notice how the different appeals overlap in an argument.

WORD CONNECTIONS

Multiple Meaning Word

When you hear the word "sound," you probably think of noise, but "sound" has many meanings. It can mean free from error, showing good judgment, or being logically valid, such as in "sound advice" or a "sound argument." A "sound heart" is one free from defects, and a "sound sleep" describes sleep that was deep and undisturbed.

What Is Sound Reasoning?

Sound reasoning stems from a valid argument whose conclusion follows from its premises. A **premise** is a statement upon which an argument is based or from which a conclusion is drawn. In other words, a premise is an assumption that something is true

For example, consider this argument:

Premise: A implies B;

Premise: B implies C;

Conclusion: Therefore, A implies C.

Although we do not know what statements A, B, and C represent, we are still able to judge the argument as valid. We call an argument "sound" if the argument is valid *and* all the statements, including the conclusion, are true.

This structure of **two premises** and **one conclusion** forms the basic argumentative structure. Aristotle held that any logical argument could be reduced to two premises and a conclusion.

| **Premises:** | If Socrates is a man, and all men are mortal, |
| **Conclusion:** | then Socrates is mortal. |

A **logical fallacy** is an error in reasoning that makes an argument invalid or unsound. Common fallacies include:

- claiming too much
- oversimplifying a complex issue
- supporting an argument with abstract generalizations
- false assumptions
- incorrect premises

Example: *We need to pass a law that stupid people cannot get a driver's license.* This statement incorrectly equates driving skills with intelligence.

Avoid logical fallacies by being sure you present relevant evidence and logical and sound reasoning—the cornerstones of effective argumentation.

5. Examine this statement of the premises and conclusion of the argument of the article you just read. Is it valid and sound? Explain why or why not.

> **Premises:** If texting is distracting, and distracted driving can result in an accident,
>
> **Conclusion:** then texting can result in an accident.

Setting a Purpose for Reading

- As you read this article, underline words and phrases that indicate the science behind the article.
- Circle unknown words and phrases. Try to determine the meaning of the words by using context clues, word parts, or a dictionary.

Online Article

The Science Behind
Distracted Driving

from KUTV, Austin

1 Texting while driving can be deadly, but what is it that makes it so dangerous?

2 No longer are people simply talking on their cellphones, they're multi-tasking—checking email, updating social media and texting.

3 "Particularly texting, that seems to be a really hazardous activity, much more dangerous than talking on a cellphone, rising to a level that exceeds what we see with someone who's driving drunk," David Strayer says. He has been studying distracted driving for 15 years.

4 Strayer says we're becoming a nation of distracted drivers. He says that when you take your eyes off the road, hands off the steering wheel, and your mind off driving, it's a deadly mix. "That combination of the three: the visual, the manual, and the cognitive distraction significantly increase the crash risk," says Strayer.

5 With two sophisticated driving **simulators**, an instrumented vehicle, an eye tracker, and a way to measure brain activity, Strayer and his team at the University of Utah have been able to pinpoint what's happening when a person texts while driving. He says, "They're not looking at the road. They're not staying in their lane. They're missing traffic lights," creating a crash risk that is eight times greater than someone giving the road their undivided attention. "That's a really significant crash risk. It's one of the reasons many states have enacted laws to outlaw texting."

6 Thirty-nine states have banned texting while driving.

GRAMMAR & USAGE
Conditional Statements

Statements of premises and conclusions, also known as syllogisms, are always formed as **conditional statements** that are finished with a conclusion. Syllogisms contain two premises, which lead to the conclusion. The first premise is the major premise and the second is the minor. This is also called deductive reasoning because you can deduce the conclusion based on the premises given.

A conditional statement based on this article, written as a syllogism, would be "texting is distracting; driving while distracted is dangerous; therefore, texting while driving is dangerous."

As you read, look for an idea or argument that presents two premises and a conclusion, and try writing it as a syllogism.

WORD CONNECTIONS

Roots and Affixes

Distracted comes from the prefix *dis-*, meaning "away" and the Latin root word *tract*, meaning "to drag or pull." "Distracted driving" happens when your attention is being pulled away to something other than driving.

simulators: machines that model certain environmental and other conditions for purposes of training or experimentation

---

Highlighting Logos

7 Strayer's work has been featured at National Distracted Driving summits, used by states to enact no-texting while driving laws, he's even testified in criminal court proceedings—often meeting the families of those killed in distracted driving crashes.

Second Read

- Reread the passage to answer this text-dependent comprehension question.
- Write any additional questions you have about the text in your Reader/Writer Notebook.

6. **Knowledge and Ideas:** What is David Strayer's argument? Is it sound? Cite textual evidence in your response.

Working from the Text

7. Effective arguments use quotes and accurately paraphrased evidence from sources to support claims. For example, David Strayer, who has been studying distracted driving for 15 years, calls texting "hazardous" and "more dangerous than . . . driving drunk." Write a quote and/or paraphrase evidence from the article above. Be sure not to misinterpret or misrepresent the author's statement.

My Notes

Check Your Understanding

The article on page 151 uses *pathos*—an appeal to the reader's emotions—to make its argument against driving while texting. What types of evidence could the author add to create a *logos* appeal?

Writing to Sources: Argument

Choose one quote from each of the articles you have just read to support the claim *Texting while driving is distracting and increases the risk of crashes.* Use the TLQC format, as you learned in Unit 1 (Activity 1.14), to state the importance of the evidence. Be sure to:

- Use the TLQC format for introducing quoted material.
- Write in the active voice.
- Use ellipses when necessary to show that words have been left out.

Forming and Supporting a Debatable Claim

Learning Targets
- Identify the difference between a debatable and a non-debatable claim.
- Develop an argument to support a debatable claim about a controversial topic, using valid reasons and relevant evidence.

Debatable and Non-Debatable Claims

You have already brainstormed topics and possible claims. It may seem obvious, but it is important to be sure your topic and claim are debatable.

- If a claim is **debatable**, it is **controversial**; that is, two logical people might disagree based on evidence and reasoning used to support the claim. Example: *Using a cellphone while driving puts you and other drivers in danger.*

- If a claim is **non-debatable**, it is a fact and therefore it cannot be argued. Example: *Cellphones are a popular form of modern communication.* This could be an explanatory topic, but is not suitable for argument.

1. Summarize the difference between a debatable and a non-debatable claim.

2. Write one debatable and one non-debatable claim relating to each topic below.
   Topic: the amount of time teens spend using technology
   - Debatable:

   - Non-debatable:

   Topic: the age at which someone should have a social media account
   - Debatable

   - Non-debatable:

My Notes

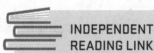

INDEPENDENT READING LINK

Read and Recommend
Select one essay or speech from your Independent Reading List that provides a clear use of *logos*, *pathos*, or *ethos*. Prepare to give an oral recommendation of this essay or speech by connecting an explanation of the persuasive appeal with specific examples from the text. Document your response in a paragraph in your Reader/Writer Notebook.

Forming and Supporting a Debatable Claim

Forming and Supporting a Debatable Claim

3. Use the following steps to form and support a debatable claim for the topic you chose in Activity 2.11.

Step 1: Write a debatable claim for each side of an issue relating to the topic.

Texting	
Side 1 Claim:	**Side 2** Claim:

Step 2: Highlight the claim you will support.

Step 3: Freewrite: How can you support the claim you chose? How much logical reasoning can you use? Will you depend on *pathos*? How can you support your claim with evidence and sound reasoning?

Step 4: Identify and analyze your **audience**. Who would support the other side? Be specific! Consider the kind of information, language, and overall approach that will appeal to your audience. Ask yourself the following questions:

- What does the audience know about this topic (through personal experience, research, etc.)?
- What does the audience value related to this topic?
- How might the audience disagree with me? What objections will the audience want me to address or answer?
- How can I best use *logos* to appeal to and convince this audience?
- How will I use language to show I am worth listening to on this subject?

Step 5: Now that you better understand your audience, plan to address at least two counterclaims by identifying potential weaknesses of your argument within opposing reasons, facts, or testimony. Use this format:

My audience might argue_____, so I will counter by arguing or pointing out that _____.

Check Your Understanding

Quickwrite: Why is it necessary to identify your audience as precisely and accurately as possible before you draft your argument? What might go wrong if you do not have a strong sense of who the audience is?

Conducting Effective Research

Learning Targets
- Form effective questions to focus research.
- Identify appropriate sources that can be used to support an argument.

Using the Research Process

Once you have chosen your topic, created a claim, and considered possible counterclaims, you are ready to conduct additional **research** on your topic to find evidence to support your claim and refute counterclaims.

1. What are the steps of the research process? Are the steps logical? Why?

Writing Research Questions

2. What makes an effective research question?

3. How will gathering evidence affect my research questions?

4. What is an example of an effective research question?

Locating and Evaluating Sources

Many people rely on the Internet for their research, since it is convenient and it can be efficient. To find relevant information on the Internet, you need to use effective **search terms** to begin your research. Try to choose terms that narrow your results. For example, searching on the term "driving accidents" will return broad information, whereas searching on the term "distracted driving" will return results more closely in line with that topic.

The Internet has a lot of useful information, but it also has a great deal of information that is not reliable or credible. You must carefully examine the websites that offer information, since the Internet is plagued with unreliable information from unknown sources. Faulty information and unreliable sources undermine the validity of one's argument.

LEARNING STRATEGIES:
Skimming/Scanning, Close Reading, Marking the Text, Note-taking

ACADEMIC VOCABULARY
Research (*v.*) is the process of locating information from a variety of sources.
Research (*n.*) is the information found from investigated sources.

 WORD CONNECTIONS

Etymology

Refute comes from the prefix *re-*, meaning "back/ backward" and the Latin root word *futare*, meaning "to beat." The Latin word *refutare* came to mean "to drive back or rebut." *To refute* now means "to disprove or invalidate." For example, if you refute an argument, you're proving the argument to be false.

ACADEMIC VOCABULARY
Search terms are the words or phrases entered into an online search engine to find information related to the words or phrases.

Conducting Effective Research

WORD CONNECTIONS

Multiple Meaning Words

Currency often refers to money or financial exchanges, but it can also mean "the state of being current," such as the *currency of information*, or "general use or acceptance," such as an idea gaining *widespread currency*.

My Notes

5. What do you know about the following criteria that define reliable Internet sites? Fill in the chart with your current knowledge.

Criteria for Evaluating Websites	
Accuracy	
Validity	
Authority	
Currency	
Coverage	

6. What types of websites are reliable and trustworthy? Why?

7. Now it is time to find additional evidence from a variety of outside sources to strengthen your argument. First, form two or three research questions that will help you to support your claim:

8. Which types of sources are best for the information you seek? List at least three and explain your choices.

9. What search terms will you use to narrow your search for sources with relevant information on the topic and claim?

Researching and Reading Informational Texts

Much research information is taken from informational texts, which can be challenging to read. An effective strategy for reading these texts is to pay attention to their **text features**.

There are five broad categories of text features found in informational texts:

- **Text organization** identifies text divisions (e.g., chapters, sections, introductions, summaries, and author information).
- **Headings** help readers understand the information (e.g., titles, labels, and subheadings).
- **Graphics** show information visually to add or clarify information (e.g., diagrams, charts and tables, graphs, maps, photographs, illustrations, paintings, timelines, and captions).
- **Format and font size** signal to the reader that certain words are important (e.g., boldface, italics, or a change in font).
- **Layout** includes aids such as insets, bullets, and numbers that point readers to important information.

Preview

In this activity, you will read an article and evaluate its validity.

Setting a Purpose for Reading

- As your read, put a star next to the writer's claim. Underline information you think would be logical evidence to support the claim.
- Circle unknown words and phrases. Try to determine the meaning of the words by using context clues, word parts, or a dictionary.
- Note whether the text features lend the article credibility or not.

ABOUT THE AUTHOR

Marcel Just is the D.O. Hebb Professor of Psychology and director of the Center for Cognitive Brain Imaging at Carnegie Mellon University.

Tim Keller is a senior research psychologist at the center.

They are co-authors of the study "A Decrease in Brain Activation Associated with Driving When Listening to Someone Speak."

My Notes

WORD CONNECTIONS

Content Connections

In general terms, *spatial* means "relating to, occupying, or having the character of space." Scientifically speaking, *spatial* refers to the location of objects and the metric relationships between them. Specific to how the brain reacts, *spatial processing* indicates the brain activity required to engage spatial memory and orientation so that driving can occur.

My Notes

concurrently: occurring at the same time

deterioration: the act or process of becoming worse

Article

How the **Brain** Reacts

http://roomfordebate.blogs.nytimes.com/2009/07/18/should-cellphone-use-by-drivers-be-illegal/

1 Behavioral studies have shown that talking on a cellphone diverts the driver's attention and disrupts driving performance. We investigated that question by looking at brain activity that occurs during driving. In our study, using functional magnetic resonance imaging (fMRI), we examined the effect of listening to someone speak on the brain activity associated with simulated driving.

Brain activity associated with spatial processing when driving without distraction (left) and when driving while listening to sentences (right).

Center for Cognitive Brain Imaging, Carnegie Mellon University

2 Participants steered a vehicle along a curving virtual road, either undisturbed or while listening to spoken sentences that they judged as true or false. The parietal lobe activation associated with spatial processing in driving decreased by 37 percent when participants **concurrently** listened to the sentences. We found that listening comprehension tasks drew mental resources away from driving and produced a **deterioration** in driving performance, even though the drivers weren't holding or dialing a phone.

3 These brain activation findings show the biological basis for the deterioration in driving performance (in terms of errors and staying in a lane) that occurs when one is also processing language. They suggest that under mentally demanding circumstances, it may be dangerous to combine processing of spoken language with a task like driving a car in demanding circumstances.

4 Our listening experiment did not require the participants to speak, so it was probably less disruptive to driving than an actual two-way conversation might be. It's likely that our study actually underestimates the reduction in driving performance.

5 If listening to sentences degrades driving performance, then probably a number of other common driver activities—including tuning or listening to a radio, eating and drinking, monitoring children or pets, or even conversing with a passenger—would also cause reduced driving performance.

6 It would be incorrect, however, to conclude that using a cellphone while driving is no worse than engaging in one of these other activities. First, it's not known how much these other distractions affect driving (though that would be an interesting study).

7 Second, talking on a cellphone is a particular social interaction, with demands different from a conversation with a passenger. Not responding in a cellphone conversation, for instance, can be interpreted as rude behavior.

8 By contrast, a passenger in a car is more likely to be aware of the competing demands for a driver's attention. Indeed there is recent experimental evidence suggesting that passengers and drivers suppress conversation in response to driving demands.

9 Third, with spoken language, a listener cannot willfully stop the processing of a spoken utterance. These considerations suggest that talking on cellphones while driving can be a risky choice, not just for common sense reasons, but because of the way our brains work.

Second Read

- Reread the passage to answer these text-dependent comprehension questions.
- Write any additional questions you have about the text in your Reader/Writer Notebook.

10. **Knowledge and Ideas:** What evidence do the writers provide to support their claim that spoken language can degrade driving performance?

11. **Craft and Structure:** What transition words do the writers use to navigate the reader through their argument?

Working from the Text

12. Choose two pieces of relevant and convincing information that support the authors' claim. Quote as much of the original material as is necessary. Write your responses in the My Notes section on this page.

Examples:
- "We found that listening comprehension tasks drew mental resources away from driving and produced a deterioration in driving performance."
- "The parietal lobe activation associated with spatial processing in driving decreased by 37 percent when participants concurrently listened to the sentences."

My Notes

Check Your Understanding

What are three reliable sources you could consult to find evidence to support the claim that texting while driving is dangerous? List these three sources and briefly explain why they would be reliable.

Writing to Sources: Argument

One of the arguments the author makes in "How the Brain Reacts" is that talking to a passenger is less distracting than talking on a phone. Write a paragraph analyzing the author's argument in support of this position. Be sure to:

- Provide a clear thesis statement.
- Paraphrase the author's argument.
- List specific details that support the author's premise.
- Include your own commentary on whether the author was successful.

Learning Targets
- Create annotated bibliography entries and show how to use this information to strengthen an argument.
- Refine research questions to guide the research process.

Conducting Research
You have begun to conduct research on a topic and claim of your choice, creating research questions, using effective search terms, and finding appropriate sources from which you can take information to use as evidence.

Citing Sources and Creating a Bibliography
When using information from research in your writing, you should cite the source of the information. In addition to giving credit in your essay, you may also be asked to provide a **Works Cited** page or an **Annotated Bibliography** to document your research and strengthen your ethos. A Works Cited page includes a properly formatted citation for each source you use. An **Annotated Bibliography** includes both the full citation of the source and a summary of information in the source or commentary on the source.

Citation Formats
Works Cited Entry:

Burke, Kenneth. *Language as Symbolic Action: Essays on Life, Literature, and Method. Berkeley*: U of California P, 1966. Print.

In-text Citation:

Human beings have been described as "symbol-using animals" (Burke 3).

1. To practice note-taking and generating a bibliography entry, complete the *research card* below using information from "How the Brain Reacts."

> **Source Citation:**
>
>
>
> **How can this source help you to support your argument?**
>
>
>
> **What makes this source credible?**

In this activity, you will read another article about cellphones and driving and connect it to previous texts you have read on the subject.

Setting a Purpose for Reading
- As you read, note conflicting information the writer brings up. Underline words that indicate these transitions.
- Circle unknown words and phrases. Try to determine the meaning of the words by using context clues, word parts, or a dictionary.

LEARNING STRATEGIES:
Predicting, Graphic Organizer, Summarizing, Paraphrasing, Note-taking, Marking the Text, Questioning the Text

My Notes

INDEPENDENT READING LINK
Read and Respond
Choose a text from your Independent Reading List that shows effective research and use of relevant text. List examples from the text to support your opinion in your Reader/Writer Notebook.

Gathering and Citing Evidence

GRAMMAR & USAGE
Passive Voice

You have learned that the **passive voice** places the emphasis on the person or thing being acted upon.

Notice that the first part of the second sentence in paragraph 4 is in the passive voice. The phone records are the thing being acted upon.

> *But phone records are not easily obtained in the United States, forcing researchers in this country to find less direct ways to analyze the danger of cellphone distraction.*

Why do you think the author chose to use the passive voice? What information would you need to revise the sentence so that it is in the active voice?

Find one more example of passive voice in the article. Remember that verbs in the passive voice start with a form of *be* (*is, was, were*) and end with a past form of the main verb.

ordinance: statute; law

conclusive: definitive; clear

consensus: general agreement

prohibition: the action of forbidding something, especially by law

WORD CONNECTIONS

Roots and Affixes

The word *correlation* is made from the Latin prefix *cor-*, meaning "together; with" and the root word *relation*, meaning "connection."

ABOUT THE AUTHOR
Matthew Walberg is an investigative reporter for the *Chicago Tribune*, specializing in criminal justice and a wide range of governmental topics.

Article

Cellphones and driving:
As dangerous as we think?

Despite calls for cellphone bans, there's no conclusive data on handheld devices and safe driving

March 26, 2012 | By Matthew Walberg, *Chicago Tribune* reporter

Source: http://articles.chicagotribune.com/2012-03-26/news/ct-met-cellphone-safety-studies-20120326_1_handheld-cellphones-cellphone-restrictionscellphone-subscribers

1 A bill pending in Springfield would ban all drivers in Illinois from using handheld cellphones in Illinois. An **ordinance** being considered in Evanston would go further and prohibit motorists in that town from talking on cellphones of any kind—including hands-free.

2 It's a matter of safety, proponents of both measures say.

3 But two decades of research done in the U.S. and abroad have not yielded **conclusive** data about the impact cellphones have on driving safety, it appears. Nor is there a **consensus** that hands-free devices make for safer driving than handheld cellphones.

4 In theory, the effect of cellphones on driver performance should be relatively easy to determine: Compare crash data against phone records of drivers involved in accidents. But phone records are not easily obtained in the United States, forcing researchers in this country to find less direct ways to analyze the danger of cellphone distraction. The issue is further clouded because auto accidents overall have been decreasing, even as cellphones become more common.

5 "The expectation would be that as cellphone use has skyrocketed we would see a correlation in the number of accidents, but that hasn't happened," said Jonathan Adkins, spokesman for the Governors Highway Safety Association.

6 Adkins said the association believes that states should simply enforce their current cellphone laws, if any, and wait for further research to better understand exactly how much of a role cellphone use plays in automobile accidents.

7 "We know it's distracting, we know it increases the likelihood of a crash," Adkins said. "It just hasn't shown up in data in a lot of cases—in other words, it's hard to prove that a crash was caused because someone was on their cellphone."

8 Proponents of cellphone restrictions—whether total bans or **prohibition** of handheld phones—can cite some studies to back up their positions.

9 A 2005 study published in the British Medical Journal looked at crash data for 456 cellphone subscribers in Perth, Australia, who had an auto accident that required medical attention. The study, which essentially confirmed a similar 1997 study

conducted in Toronto, concluded that drivers talking on their phones were about four times more likely to be involved in an accident than those who were not on the phone.

10 Another highly publicized 2006 study from the University of Utah concluded that drivers who talked on cellphones were as impaired as drivers who were intoxicated at the legal blood-alcohol limit of 0.08. The study, however, found that using hands-free devices did little to improve drivers' performances.

11 There is some evidence suggesting state and local bans have caused some drivers to talk less while on the road.

12 This month, California's Office of Traffic Safety released the results of a study showing a sharp decrease in the number of accidents caused by cellphone use that resulted in death or injury.

13 Researchers tracked the number of accident reports that listed cellphone use as a factor during the two-year periods before and after the 2008 passage of a statewide ban on handheld devices. The study concluded that while overall traffic **fatalities** of all kinds dropped by 22 percent, fatalities caused by drivers who were talking on a handheld phone at the time of the crash dropped nearly 50 percent. Similar declines were found for drivers using hands-free devices.

14 The study followed the agency's 2011 survey of more than 1,800 drivers that found that only about 10 percent of drivers reported that they regularly talked on the phone while driving—down from 14 percent from the previous year's survey. In addition, the survey saw increases in the number of people who said they rarely or never use their cellphone behind the wheel.

15 Those surveyed, however, overwhelmingly believed that hands-free devices made cellphone use safer, a perception that runs counter to research showing such tools do little to reduce the distraction.

16 "If there is an advantage, it's only because a person may have two hands on the wheel, but most people drive with one hand all the time anyway," said Chris Cochran, spokesman for the Office of Traffic Safety. "In reality, it's the conversation, not the phone itself."

Second Read
* Reread the passage to answer these text-dependent comprehension questions.
* Write any additional questions you have about the text in your Reader/Writer Notebook.
2. **Craft and Structure:** What clues in the text tell you the meaning of the word *intoxicated*?

3. **Knowledge and Ideas:** What is the writer's purpose for citing studies? How do you know?

My Notes

fatalities: deaths

Gathering and Citing Evidence

4. **Craft and Structure:** How does the writer transition between pieces of opposing information? Cite some examples.

5. **Knowledge and Ideas:** In what way does the writer of this article disagree with the other writers in these activities on matters of fact or interpretation? Cite textual evidence to support your answer.

Working from the Text

6. Choose two pieces of relevant and convincing information from the article. Then prepare the information to be included in an argumentative essay. Paraphrase the first piece of information. Combine quoting and paraphrasing in the second piece of information, and add your own commentary to it.

   Paraphrase:

   Quote and paraphrase:

Check Your Understanding

In your Reader/Writer Notebook, create a research card for the article you just read. Be sure to include all of the required information.

Writing to Sources: Argument

Based on the research you have gathered from reading the sources, write a paragraph that states a claim about cellphone use while driving. Be sure to:

- State your claim.
- Incorporate evidence by paraphrasing and/or quoting.
- Show your reasoning with commentary.
- Properly cite your source(s).

Independent Reading Checkpoint

You have read a variety of sources relating to your topic. Which information supports your claim? Which information counters your claim? How can you use this information to strengthen your argument? Prepare your answers in the form of a brief oral presentation.

Organizing and Revising Your Argument

Learning Targets
- Use research to support a claim(s) and frame an argument.
- Share and respond to preliminary drafts in a discussion group using questions and comments with relevant evidence, observation, and ideas.
- Use new information to revise an argument to reflect Scoring Guide Criteria.

LEARNING STRATEGIES:
Writer's Checklist, Discussion Groups, Oral Reading, Sharing and Responding, Self-Editing/ Peer-Editing

Monitor Progress by Creating and Following a Plan

You have gone through a model of the research process and conducted research on your own topic for the argumentative essay you will write for the Embedded Assessment.

Now you will focus on completing your research and finding evidence for your argument. You will also work on organizing and communicating your argument.

1. First, look at the chart below. Where are you in the process of researching for your essay? Check off the steps you have already completed, but remember that you can go back to revise your claim or find additional support for your argument, if necessary. In the third column, add planning notes for completing each step of the process.

My Notes

_____

_____

_____

_____

_____

Research Plan for My Argumentative Essay

Check Progress	Step of Research Process	Notes
	Identify the issue or problem; establish a claim.	
	Form a set of questions that can be answered through research.	
	Locate and evaluate sources. Gather evidence for claims and counterclaims.	
	Interpret evidence.	
	Communicate findings.	

2. Reflect on your research. Which questions have you answered? What do you still need to know? What new questions do you have? You should keep research notes on a computer, on note cards, or in a log such as the one that follows.

Argumentative Essay Research Log

Topic/Issue: _____

My claim: _____

_____

_____

_____

_____

_____

_____

_____

_____

_____

_____

Organizing and Revising Your Argument

My Notes

Research Questions:

Works Consulted Source + Citation	Notes/Examples/Quotes
Sample citation for a website: Just, Marcel, and Tim Heller. "How the Brain Reacts." *Room for Debate Blogs*. *The New York Times*, 18 July 2009. Web. 1 Feb. 2012.	

Outlining an Essay

3. A clear organizational structure is essential to a successful essay. Fill in the blank spaces in the following outline with your claim and the reasons and evidence you will use to support it.

   I. **Introduction**

   A. Attention-getting hook

   B. Background information/definition of terms

   C. Claim (Thesis):

   II. **Body paragraphs**

   A. Reason 1:

      Evidence:

   B. Reason 2:

      Evidence:

   C. Reason 3:

      Evidence:

III. **Conclusion follows from and supports the argument**

A. Restate claim

B. Connect back to hook

C. State specific call to action

Sharing and Responding in Writing Groups

4. Prepare for discussion by doing the following:

- Revisit your outline and think about its organization.
- Think about your research notes and decide where the information fits in your argument.
- At the top of your draft, make a list of vocabulary and transitions you might use while discussing your ideas.
- Determine whether you should revise your claim to reflect the new information.
- Listen, comprehend, and evaluate as others read their claims.
- Review the rules for collegial discussions and decision-making from Activity 2.6.

5. Gather the materials you will need in the discussion group: the draft outline of your argument, your research cards, and a pen or pencil.

6. Set speaking and listening goals for the discussion:

Speaking: I will _____

Listening: I will _____

7. When you write your essay for Embedded Assessment 2, use the Writer's Checklist below to get feedback from others in your writing group and to self-edit before finalizing your essay draft. Also, use the Language and Writer's Craft suggestions as you consider revising your essay for effective use of language.

My Notes

Organizing and Revising Your Argument

Writer's Checklist

Use this checklist to guide the sharing and responding in your writing group.

IDEAS

☐ The writer has a clear claim (thesis).

☐ The writer supports his or her claim with logical reasoning and relevant evidence from accurate, credible sources.

☐ The writer effectively uses appeals to *logos* and *pathos*.

☐ The writer addresses counterclaims effectively.

ORGANIZATION

☐ The writer clearly introduces the claim at the beginning of the argument.

☐ The writer organizes reasons and evidence logically.

☐ The writer effectively uses transitional words, phrases, and clauses to create cohesion and clarify the relationships among ideas.

☐ The writer provides a concluding statement or section that follows from and supports the argument presented.

USE OF LANGUAGE

☐ The writer effectively and correctly embeds quotations and paraphrases clearly to strengthen evidence and create convincing reasoning.

☐ The writer uses a formal style, including proper referencing to sources to express ideas and add interest.

☐ The writer uses precise and clear language in the argument rather than vague or imprecise vocabulary.

My Notes

Language and Writer's Craft: Shifts in Voice and Mood

In a previous activity you learned that a sentence can be in either the active or passive voice. When you write a sentence, it is important that the voice stays consistent. The following sentence has an unnecessary shift:

*When the player **scored** the point, a roar **was heard** from the crowd.*

The sentence should be rewritten so that both verbs are in the active voice.

*When the player **scored** the point, the crowd **roared**.*

A shift in mood occurs when a sentence shifts from the imperative—a command—to the indicative—a simple statement of fact.

***Read** the assignment, and then **you should** answer the questions.*

This sentence can be rewritten in either the imperative or the indicative.

***Read** the assignment and **answer** the questions.*

*You **should read** the assignment, and then **you should** answer the questions.*

PRACTICE Review the paragraph you wrote for the Activity 2.16 writing prompt. Look for shifts in voice or mood. If necessary, revise your writing.

Check Your Understanding

Create a flow chart that shows the order in which the five steps of a research project should be completed. Clearly label each step.

Writing an Argumentative Essay

ASSIGNMENT

Write an argumentative essay in which you convince an audience to support your claim about a debatable idea. Use your research and experience or observations to support your argument.

Planning and Prewriting: Take time to make a plan for generating ideas and research questions.	▨ What prewriting strategies (such as outlining or webbing) can you use to select and explore a controversial idea? ▨ How will you draft a claim that states your position? ▨ What questions will guide your research?
Researching: Gather information from a variety of credible sources.	▨ What types of sources are best for the information you seek? ▨ What criteria will you use to evaluate sources? ▨ How will you take notes to gather and interpret evidence? ▨ How will you create a bibliography or Works Cited page?
Drafting: Convince your audience to support your claim.	▨ How will you select the best reasons and evidence from your research to support your claim? ▨ How will you use persuasive appeals (*logos, ethos, pathos*) in your essay? ▨ How will you introduce and respond to counterclaims? ▨ How will you organize your essay logically with an introduction, transitions, and concluding statement?
Evaluating and Revising the Draft: Create opportunities to review and revise your work.	▨ During the process of writing, when can you pause to share and respond with others in order to elicit suggestions and ideas for revision? ▨ How can the Scoring Guide help you evaluate how well your draft meets the requirements of the assignment?
Checking and Editing for Publication: Confirm that your final draft is ready for publication.	▨ How will you proofread and edit your draft to demonstrate command of the conventions of standard English capitalization, punctuation, spelling, grammar, usage, and formal style? ▨ How did you use TLQC (transition/lead-in/quote/citation) to properly embed quotations?

Reflection

After completing this Embedded Assessment, think about how you went about accomplishing this task, and respond to the following:

• How can you use discussion and/or debate in the future to explore a topic?

 Technology Tip

Consider publishing your essay on a website, blog, or online student literary magazine.

Writing an Argumentative Essay

SCORING GUIDE

Scoring Criteria	Exemplary	Proficient	Emerging	Incomplete
Ideas	The essay • supports a claim with compelling, relevant reasoning and evidence • provides extensive evidence of the research process • addresses counterclaim(s) effectively • uses a variety of persuasive appeals.	The essay • supports a claim with sufficient reasoning and evidence • provides evidence of the research process • addresses counterclaim(s) • uses some persuasive appeals (*logos*, *ethos*, *pathos*).	The essay • has an unclear or unfocused claim and/or inadequate support • provides insufficient evidence of the research process • addresses counterclaims ineffectively • uses inadequate persuasive appeals.	The essay • has no claim or claim lacks support • provides little or no evidence of research • does not reference a counterclaim • fails to use persuasive appeals.
Structure	The essay • has an introduction that engages the reader and defines the claim's context • follows a logical organizational structure • uses a variety of effective transitional strategies • contains an insightful conclusion.	The essay • has an introduction that includes a hook and background • follows an adequate organizational structure • uses transitional strategies to link ideas • has a conclusion that supports and follows from the argument.	The essay • has a weak introduction • uses an ineffective or inconsistent organizational strategy • uses basic or insufficient transitional strategies • has an illogical or unrelated conclusion.	The essay • lacks an introduction • has little or no obvious organizational structure • uses few or no transitional strategies • lacks a conclusion.
Use of Language	The essay • uses precise diction and language effectively to convey tone and persuade an audience • demonstrates command of the conventions of standard English capitalization, punctuation, spelling, grammar, and usage • includes an accurate, detailed annotated bibliography.	The essay • uses diction and language to convey tone and persuade an audience • demonstrates adequate command of the conventions of standard English capitalization, punctuation, spelling, grammar, and usage • includes a generally correct and complete annotated bibliography.	The essay • uses basic or weak diction and language • demonstrates partial command of the conventions of standard English capitalization, punctuation, spelling, grammar, and usage; for the most part, errors do not impede meaning • includes an incorrect or insufficient annotated bibliography.	The essay • uses confusing or vague diction and language • lacks command of the conventions of standard English capitalization, punctuation, spelling, grammar, and usage • does not include an annotated bibliography.

The Challenge to Make a Difference

Visual Prompt: What do you notice about this art? How does the artist use visual techniques for effect? How do you think the arts (artwork, music, literature, etc.) can help change the world?

Unit Overview

The world has dark pages in its history, and at times the challenge of righting such immeasurable wrongs seems impossible. Reading narratives about the Holocaust will reveal the worst in human behavior, but it will also show how individuals can find light in the darkness. In this unit, you will present the voices of fictional or real people who fought the darkness of the Holocaust by helping, hoping, or persevering. You will also apply the lessons of the past to start making a difference today by raising awareness and encouraging people to take action about a significant national or global issue.

GOALS:

- To engage effectively in a range of collaborative discussions
- To analyze the development of a theme or central idea of a text
- To research an issue of national or global significance
- To create an informative and persuasive multimedia presentation
- To strengthen writing through the effective use of voice and mood

ACADEMIC VOCABULARY
communication
résumé
euphemism
slogan
media

Literary Terms
found poem

Contents

Activities

Texts not included in these materials.

Language and Writer's Craft
- Active Versus Passive Voice (3.8)
- Reviewing Participial Phrases (3.14)
- Reviewing Clauses (3.15)

MY INDEPENDENT READING LIST

Previewing the Unit

LEARNING STRATEGIES:
Think-Pair-Share, QHT, Close Reading, Marking the Text, Paraphrasing, Graphic Organizer

My Notes

Learning Targets

- Examine the big ideas and the vocabulary for the unit.
- Identify the skills and knowledge necessary to be successful in completing the Embedded Assessment.

Making Connections

In the first part of this unit, you will read texts about the Holocaust that show both the tragedy of historical events and the ways in which people reacted to those events. This study will help prepare you to research current issues from around the world and choose one for which to create a persuasive multimedia campaign.

Essential Questions

The following **Essential Questions** will be the focus of the unit study. Respond to both questions.

1. Why is it important to learn about the Holocaust?

2. How can one person make a difference?

Developing Vocabulary

3. Use a QHT chart to sort the Academic Vocabulary and Literary Terms in the Contents.

INDEPENDENT READING LINK

You will be reading a narrative related to events preceding and during World War II and the genocide of a people based on their religion. You may want to read an additional novel or nonfiction narrative from the additional titles mentioned in this unit. Book lists are available in the back of this textbook, and you can use book discussions and recommendations from classmates to help you choose. Use your Reader/ Writer Notebook and your Independent Reading Logs to keep notes on what you are reading and answer questions that will come up. As you read, look for the thematic focus of this unit: "finding light in the darkness."

Unpacking Embedded Assessment 1

Read the assignment for Embedded Assessment 1:

Present a panel discussion that includes an oral reading of a significant passage from the narrative read by your group. Your discussion should explain how the theme or central idea of "finding light in the darkness" is developed in the entire narrative.

After you closely read the Embedded Assessment 1 assignment and use the Scoring Guide to further analyze the requirements, work with your class to paraphrase the expectations. Create a graphic organizer to use as a visual reminder of the required concepts and skills.

Collaborating to Preview Holocaust Narratives

Learning Targets
- Demonstrate effective communication in collaborative discussions.
- Analyze and discuss text in a collaborative group.

Preparing for Listening and Speaking

1. As a student, you have probably spent years observing teachers and other students who demonstrate both effective and ineffective speaking and listening skills. To help you identify good speaking and listening skills, create two T charts in your Reader/Writer Notebook, one for Listening and one for Speaking. Brainstorm effective and ineffective listening and speaking habits and practices. Add to your chart during the class discussion.

2. Read the following information to learn more about effective **communication** in collaborative groups. All members of a group need to communicate effectively to help the group work smoothly to achieve its goals. Group members should allow opportunities for everyone to participate. To help ensure a successful group experience, follow these guidelines.

As a speaker:
- Come prepared to the discussion, having read or researched the material being studied.
- Organize your thoughts before speaking.
- Ask questions to clarify and to connect to others' ideas.
- Respond to others' questions and comments with relevant evidence, observations, and ideas.
- Use appropriate eye contact, adequate volume, and clear pronunciation.

As a listener:
- Listen to comprehend, analyze, and evaluate others' ideas.
- Avoid barriers to listening such as daydreaming, fidgeting, or having side conversations.
- Take notes to prepare a thoughtful response.

3. On the following page are quotations about the topic of light and darkness. Take turns reading aloud, interpreting, and discussing the meaning and figurative language used in each quotation. Follow the guidelines for effective communication.

LEARNING STRATEGIES:
Note-taking, Graphic Organizer, Previewing, Predicting, Summarizing, Discussion Groups

ACADEMIC VOCABULARY
Communication is a process of exchanging information between individuals. It can include both verbal (words) and nonverbal (expressions, gestures) language.

My Notes

Collaborating to Preview Holocaust Narratives

Quotation	Interpretation
A. "We've all got both light and darkness inside us. What matters is the part we choose to act on. That's who we really are." —J.K. Rowling	
B. "Darkness cannot drive out darkness; only light can do that. Hate cannot drive out hate; only love can do that." —Martin Luther King, Jr.	
C. "It is better to light a candle than curse the darkness." —Eleanor Roosevelt	
D. "Sometimes our light goes out, but is blown into flame by another human being. Each of us owes deepest thanks to those who have rekindled the light." —Albert Schweitzer	
E. "Maybe it's the very presence of one thing—light or darkness—that necessitates the existence of the other. Think about it, people couldn't become legendary heroes if they hadn't first done something to combat darkness. Doctors could do no good if there weren't diseases for them to treat." —Jessica Shirvington	

4. Reflect on your group's discussion of the quotes. Identify challenges and set specific goals for improving your speaking, listening, and reading skills.

	Challenges	Goals
Speaking		
Listening		
Reading		

5. For this activity, you will be reading and discussing Holocaust narratives. In your discussion group, choose a different Holocaust narrative for each group member to preview.

6. Form a new group with other students who are previewing the same Holocaust narrative. Use the graphic organizer below to prepare a book preview.

WORD CONNECTIONS

Etymology

The word *holocaust* comes from the Greek words *holos*, meaning "whole" or "entire," and *caustos*, meaning "burn."

During World War II, the mass killing of European Jews, Roma, Slavs, and people with physical or mental disabilities during Hitler's regime was referred to as a *holocaust*. It wasn't until 1957, however, before it became a proper name, *Holocaust*.

Title:	Author:
Genre:	Length:

Predictions based on significant imagery from the book cover design:

Summary of the information provided in the book description or review:

Information about the author:

Personal response after reading a passage:

This book sounds . . .

This book reminds me of . . .

Someone who would like this book . . .

My Notes

7. Go back to your original discussion group and take turns presenting your book previews. Use the chart on the next page to take notes on each book as you hear it described. If needed, continue on a new page in your Reader/Writer Notebook.

Collaborating to Preview Holocaust Narratives

Book Preview Note-Taking Graphic Organizer

Book Title	An Interesting Point Made About the Book	My Thoughts/Comments/Questions

8. Record your top three choices and explain the reasons for your selection.

9. Once you have formed your Literature Circle group, formulate a plan for reading your Holocaust narrative.

Reading Schedule

Title of Book: _____

Author: _____

Total Number of Pages: _____

Date Assigned	Date Due	Pages to Read	Role	Number of Journal Entries

Understanding Literature Circle Discussions

Learning Targets
- Analyze Literature Circle role descriptions and communicate an understanding of the qualifications for one role by creating a résumé.
- Apply learning about Literature Circle roles while participating in a text-based collaborative discussion.

Understanding Literature Circle Roles

Read the following information about Literature Circle roles. For each role, think about the skills required and consider your personal strengths.

My Notes

Discussion Leader

Your job is to develop a list of questions you think your group should discuss about the assigned section of the book. Use your knowledge of Levels of Questions to create thought-provoking interpretive (Level 2) and universal (Level 3) questions that connect to understanding the content and themes of the book. Try to create questions that encourage your group to consider many ideas. Help your group to explore these important ideas and share their reactions. You are in charge of facilitating the day's discussion.

Diction Detective

Your job is to carefully examine the diction (word choice) in the assigned section. Search for words, phrases, and passages that are especially descriptive, powerful, funny, thought-provoking, surprising, or even confusing. List the words or phrases and explain why you selected them. Then, analyze the intended effect, asking and answering questions such as the following: What is the author trying to say? How does the diction help the author achieve his or her purpose? What tone do the words indicate?

Bridge Builder

Your job is to build bridges between the events of the book and other people, places, or events in school, the community, or your own life. Look for connections between the text, yourself, other texts, and the world. Also, make connections between what has happened before and what might happen as the narrative continues. Look for the character's internal and external conflicts and the ways that these conflicts influence his or her actions.

Reporter

Your job is to identify and report on the key points of the reading assignment. Make a list or write a summary that describes how the setting, plot, and characters are developed in this section of the book. Consider character interactions, major events that occur, and shifts in the setting or mood that seem significant. Share your report at the beginning of the group meeting to help your group focus on the key ideas presented in the reading. Like that of a newspaper reporter, your report must be concise, yet thorough.

Understanding Literature Circle Discussions

ACADEMIC VOCABULARY
A **résumé** is a brief written account of personal, educational, and professional qualifications and experience, prepared by an applicant for a job.

Artist

Your job is to create an illustration to clarify information, communicate an important idea (e.g., about setting, character, conflict, or theme), and/or to add interest to the discussion. It can be a sketch, cartoon, diagram, flow chart, or a piece that uses visual techniques for effect. Show your illustration to the group without any explanation. Ask each group member to respond, either by making a comment or asking a question. After everyone has responded, explain your picture and answer any questions that have not been answered.

Assigning Literature Circle Roles

1. Create a **résumé** using the template below to apply for a role.

> **Name:**
>
> **Role (Job Description):** Choose one of the roles and summarize the requirements.
>
> **Skills:** Describe the skills you have that will help you perform this role (e.g., reading, artistic skills, etc.).
>
> **Experience:** Describe similar experiences you have had and how they will help you in this role.
>
> **Activities:** Describe any class work or extracurricular activities that have prepared you for the role.

2. Use your résumés to distribute role assignments in your group. Record these assignments on your reading schedule.

3. Create a table tent for your role by folding an index card or construction paper. On the side facing your group, write the role title and a symbolic image. On the side facing you, write a description of your role and bullet points listing the requirements. Be specific so that the next person who has this role will understand what to do.

Practicing Literature Circle Roles

4. Before you begin reading, think about these questions: How old do you think someone should be when they first learn about the Holocaust? Why would someone write a children's book about such a disturbing subject?

My Notes

5. Create a double-entry journal in your Reader/Writer Notebook, keeping your Literature Circle role in mind. For example, the discussion leader may want to record passages that inspire questions, while the artist might record interesting imagery.

6. After you read, use the notes from your double-entry journal to prepare for your role. When everyone in the group is ready, practice conducting a Literature Circle meeting. As you listen, take notes on interesting ideas presented by group members, and form questions in response.

My Notes

_____

_____

_____

_____

Discussion Note-Taking Graphic Organizer

An Interesting Point Made by a Member of My Group	My Thoughts/Comments/Questions

7. Reflect on your discussion. Review your responses in the graphic organizer.

• What contributed most to your understanding or appreciation of the text?

• What did you learn about the Holocaust through the narrative and discussion?

Understanding Literature
Circle Discussions

Check Your Understanding

Quickwrite: In your Reader/Writer Notebook, write three facts you learned in your discussion about the Holocaust. Describe how your discussion group helped you learn them.

Writing to Sources: Explanatory Text

Using the information from your Literature Circle discussion, write an analysis of the theme of the narrative you read. Be sure to:

- Include a clear statement of the theme.
- Expand on the statement of theme by providing your own analysis.
- Refer to the notes you took in your chart.
- Provide textual evidence to support your analysis.

Making Thematic Connections

Learning Target
- Analyze an excerpt from an autobiographical narrative and a poem.
- Compare the themes of two literary texts in a formal collaborative discussion.

Preview
In this activity, you will read a passage from a memoir and a poem and compare their themes.

Setting a Purpose for Reading
- As you read the passage, underline words and phrases that describe how Moishe changed after returning to Sighet.
- Circle unknown words and phrases. Try to determine the meaning of the words by using context clues, word parts, or a dictionary.

> **LEARNING STRATEGIES:**
> Choral Reading, Rereading, Close Reading, Questioning the Text, Visualizing, Marking the Text, Discussion Groups

My Notes

ABOUT THE AUTHOR
Elie Wiesel (1928–2016) was a teenager in 1944 when he and his whole family were taken from their home to the Auschwitz concentration camp and then to Buchenwald. Wiesel wrote his internationally acclaimed memoir *Night* about his experiences in the camps. In addition to writing many other books, Wiesel became an activist who spoke out about injustices in many countries around the world. He was awarded the Nobel Peace Prize in 1986.

Memoir

from

Night

by Elie Wiesel

1   AND THEN, one day all foreign Jews were expelled from Sighet.[1] And Moishe the Beadle[2] was a foreigner.

2   Crammed into cattle cars by the Hungarian police, they cried silently. Standing on the station platform, we too were crying. The train disappeared over the horizon; all that was left was thick, dirty smoke.

3   Behind me, someone said, sighing, "What do you expect? That's war …"

4   The **deportees** were quickly forgotten. A few days after they left, it was rumored that they were in Galicia,[3] working, and even that they were content with their fate.

deportees: people forced to leave a country by an authority

---

[1] **Sighet:** a town in Romania
[2] **Beadle:** a minor church official; a caretaker of a synagogue
[3] **Galicia:** a former province of Austria, now in parts of Poland and Ukraine

synagogue: a building that houses
Jewish religious services

My Notes

_____

_____

_____

_____

Kabbalah: a Jewish religious
tradition that strives to explain
how the universe works

insinuated: implied; hinted at

GRAMMAR &USAGE
Participle Verb Forms

The participle forms of verbs
can be used as adjectives.
There are two participial
forms: present (ending
in -ing) and past (usually
ending in -d). Note the use of
these participles as adjectives
in the text: "**reassuring**
wind"(paragraph 5)
and "**waiting** trucks"
(paragraph 7).

A participle may occur in a
participial phrase, which
includes the participle
plus any complements and
modifiers. The whole phrase
serves as an adjective.
For example: "**Crammed
into cattle cars by the
Hungarian police**, they . . ."
(paragraph 2).

As you read the memoir,
look for more examples of
participles and participial
phrases.

5 Days went by. Then weeks and months. Life was normal again. A calm, reassuring wind blew through our homes. The shopkeepers were doing good business, the students lived among their books, and the children played in the streets.

6 One day, as I was about to enter the **synagogue**, I saw Moishe the Beadle sitting on a bench near the entrance.

7 He told me what had happened to him and his companions. The train with the deportees had crossed the Hungarian border and, once in Polish territory, had been taken over by the Gestapo.[4] The train had stopped. The Jews were ordered to get off and onto waiting trucks. The trucks headed toward a forest. There everybody was ordered to get out. They were forced to dig huge trenches. When they had finished their work, the men from the Gestapo began theirs. Without passion or haste, they shot their prisoners, who were forced to approach the trench one by one and offer their necks. Infants were tossed in the air and used as targets for the machine guns. This took place in the Galician forest, near Kolomay. How had he, Moishe the Beadle, been able to escape? By a miracle. He was wounded in the leg and left for dead …

8 Day after day, night after night, he went from one Jewish house to the next, telling his story and that of Malka, the young girl who lay dying for three days, and that of Tobie, the tailor who begged to die before his sons were killed.

9 Moishe was not the same. The joy in his eyes was gone. He no longer sang. He no longer mentioned either God or **Kabbalah**. He spoke only of what he had seen. But people not only refused to believe his tales, they refused to listen. Some even **insinuated** that he only wanted their pity, that he was imagining things. Others flatly said that he had gone mad.

10 As for Moishe, he wept and pleaded:

11 "Jews, listen to me! That's all I ask of you. No money. No pity. Just listen to me!" he kept shouting in the synagogue, between the prayer at dusk and the evening prayer.

12 Even I did not believe him. I often sat with him, after services, and listening to his tales, trying to understand his grief. But all I felt was pity.

13 "They think I'm mad," he whispered, and tears, like drops of wax, flowed from his eyes.

14 Once, I asked him the question: "Why do you want people to believe you so much? In your place I would not care whether they believed me or not …"

15 He closed his eyes, as if to escape time.

16 "You don't understand," he said in despair. "You cannot understand. I was saved miraculously. I succeeded in coming back. Where did I get my strength? I wanted to return to Sighet to describe to you my death so you might ready yourselves while there is still time. Life? I no longer care to live. I am alone. But I wanted to come back to warn you. Only no one is listening to me …"

17 This was toward the end of 1942.

18 Thereafter life seemed normal once again. London radio, which we listened to every evening, announced encouraging news: the daily bombings of Germany and Stalingrad, the preparation of the Second Front. And so we, the Jews of Sighet, waited for better days that surely were soon to come.

---

[4] **Gestapo:** the secret police in Nazi Germany

Second Read

- Reread the passage to answer these text-dependent questions.
- Write any additional questions you have about the text in your Reader/Writer Notebook.

1. **Craft and Structure:** Who are the people represented by the pronouns "they" and "we" in paragraph 2? What is the intended effect?

2. **Craft and Structure:** What is the intended effect of the following line from paragraph 7: "Infants were tossed in the air and used as targets for the machine guns"?

3. **Key Ideas and Details:** Why did the Jews of Sighet refuse "to believe his tales, and refused to listen"?

4. **Key Ideas and Details:** What are the two main events of this narrative? What is Wiesel's purpose in focusing on these two events?

Setting a Purpose for Reading

- As you read the poem, underline words and phrases that identify what the author is not.
- Circle unknown words and phrases. Try to determine the meaning of the words by using context clues, word parts, or a dictionary.

ABOUT THE AUTHOR
Martin Niemöller (1892–1984) was a German Protestant pastor. During World War II, he opposed Hitler's religious policies and was sent to concentration camps. He survived and, after the war, joined the World Peace Movement. This poem is his response to the question "How could it happen?"

My Notes

WORD CONNECTIONS

Roots and Affixes

The Latin root *-commun-* in *communist* means "common." There are a few distinctions in the definition of *common*. In this case it refers to something that is shared or owned together by several people or groups. In communism, land and factories are owned by the community. This root occurs in *communal, communicate,* and *communion.*

The word *democrat* contains the Greek root *demo-*, which means "people," and the Greek suffix *-crat*, which means "rule." Democracy is a government run by the people.

My Notes

Poetry

FIRST THEY CAME FOR THE COMMUNISTS

by Martin Niemöller

> When the Nazis came for the communists,
> I remained silent;
> I was not a communist.
>
> When they locked up the social democrats,
> 5 I remained silent;
> I was not a social democrat.
>
> When they came for the trade unionists,
> I did not speak out;
> I was not a trade unionist.
>
> 10 When they came for the Jews,
> I did not speak out;
> I was not a Jew.
>
> When they came for me,
> there was no one left to speak out.

Second Read

- Reread the poem to answer these text-dependent questions.
- Write any additional questions you have about the text in your Reader/Writer Notebook.

5. **Key Ideas and Details:** How does each stanza contribute to a developing sense of doom?

Working from the Text

6. Work collaboratively to apply each of the different Literature Circle roles to the autobiographical narrative and the poem. Use the Text-Dependent Questions, as well as questions you develop during your discussion, to compare and analyze these texts. Consider each text's structure, language, and theme.

7. How is the autobiographical narrative's theme similar to and different from the poem's theme?

8. Use the graphic organizer that follows as a reminder of the roles and to guide your thinking for your Literature Circle discussion of both texts.

Artist: Choose one image. Visualize and sketch it.

Diction Detective: Analyze how the author uses descriptive and figurative imagery for effect.

Reporter: Write a brief summary of the text. What is it about? What is the theme or central idea?

Central text

Discussion Leader:
Use Levels of Questions to create three discussion questions:

Literal

Interpretive

Universal

Bridge Builder: Make a text-to-self, text-to-text, and text-to-world connection.
- Text to Self
- Text to Text
- Text to World

Check Your Understanding

Compare and contrast the structure of the poem and the autobiographical narrative excerpt. How does each text's structure contribute to its meaning and style?

Writing to Sources: Explanatory Text

Choose one of the Holocaust survivors you learned about in the texts. Write a short essay explaining what you think of this person. Be sure to:

- Include a clear opening statement identifying your selected person as well as your reasons for choosing that person.
- Provide textual evidence and support.
- Provide a conclusion that reinforces your opening statement.

My Notes

Analyzing an Allegory

My Notes

Learning Targets

- Present an oral dramatic interpretation of a passage from the text.
- Analyze how the themes in multiple genres are connected.

Preview

In this activity, you will be read a children's story and analyze it as an allegory of the Holocaust.

Setting a Purpose for Reading

- As you hear the story, listen for all the different types of animals.
- Write down unknown words and phrases. Try to determine the meaning of the words by using context clues, word parts, or a dictionary.

ABOUT THE AUTHOR

Eve Bunting was born in 1928 in Ireland and moved to California in 1958. After taking a writing class, Bunting started to get her children's stories and books published. Several of her books have received awards. Bunting has also taught many classes of her own on writing.

Second Read

- Write any questions you have about the text in your Reader/Writer Notebook.
- Take notes on the animals' reactions to the Terrible Things. Use the graphic organizer on the next pages for your notes.
- As you listen to and discuss this story, think about why a children's story of the Holocaust is best told as an allegory.

How do the other animals respond to the demand of the Terrible Things?	How do the other animals respond after the Terrible Things have taken the animals?
When the Terrible Things come for "every creature with feathers on its back"	
Frogs, squirrels, porcupines, rabbits, fish:	Porcupine, squirrels:
	Little Rabbit:
	Big Rabbit:
When the Terrible Things come for "every bushy-tailed creature"	
Frogs, porcupines, fish, rabbits:	Little Rabbit:
	Big Rabbit:

My Notes

_____

_____

_____

_____

_____

_____

_____

_____

Analyzing an Allegory

How do the other animals respond to the demand of the Terrible Things?	How do the other animals respond after the Terrible Things have taken the animals?
When the Terrible Things come for "every creature that swims"	
Rabbits, porcupines:	Little Rabbit:
	Big Rabbit:
When the Terrible Things come for "every creature that sprouts quills"	
Rabbits:	Little Rabbit:
	Big Rabbit:
When the Terrible Things come for "any creature that is white"	
	Little Rabbit:

Working from the Text

1. Why would authors choose to use an allegory to tell a story?

2. After listening and taking notes, meet with your Literature Circle groups and, using your notes and insights, discuss how this text connects to the previous two texts you have read. Discuss the three different genres presented and why they are effective and appropriate for the topic, audience, and purpose.

3. Work collaboratively to plan and perform a dramatic interpretation of your assigned passage. Mark the text for pauses, emphasis, volume, and tone to convey important ideas and to add interest.

4. Rehearse your interpretation, and then present to the other group that shares your passage.

5. Reflect on your group's dramatic interpretation. What did your group do well? What will you do differently next time?

Check Your Understanding

Quickwrite: What method of telling the story about the Terrible Things is most effective? Why?

Writing to Sources: Explanatory Text

Write a paragraph explaining how the theme of this story is similar to the theme of Wiesel's excerpt and the Niemöller poem. Be sure to:

• Begin with a topic sentence that responds to the prompt and states a theme.

• Provide textual evidence from the texts and commentary for support.

• Use precise diction to inform or explain.

My Notes

Dangerous Diction

Learning Target

• Understand the Holocaust-related diction of euphemism and explain new
learning about the Holocaust using new vocabulary words.

Understanding Euphemism

The Nazis deliberately used **euphemisms** to disguise the true nature of their crimes.
Euphemisms replace disturbing words using diction with more positive connotations.

1. Work with a small group to analyze how the Nazis manipulated language to
disguise the horror of their policies. Research the term *euphemism* and its use
in Nazi Germany. If doing an online search, use an effective search term to find
the true meanings of the terms below.

Euphemism	Denotation (Literal Definition)	Meaning in Context of the Holocaust	Analyze the Difference in Connotation
Relocation			
Disinfecting or Delousing Centers			
Camp			
The Final Solution			

WORD
CONNECTIONS

Etymology

Euphemism contains the Greek
prefix *eu-*, meaning "well"
or "pleasing," and the Greek
root -*pheme*-, which has the
meaning of "speak." A person
who uses a euphemism speaks
with pleasing words.
People in ancient Greece were
superstitious about using
certain words in religious
ceremonies. Euphemisms
were used instead to be more
pleasing.

2. To discuss the Holocaust, you will need to be familiar with Holocaust-related
diction. In your Literature Circle groups, use a dictionary or other resource to
find a definition or explanation for each of the terms in the list on the next page.

Holocaust Vocabulary	Definition/Explanation
Antisemitism	
Concentration Camp	
Death Camp	
Genocide	
Gestapo	
Holocaust	
Nazi	
Persecution	
Propaganda	
SS (Schutzstaffel)	
Star of David	

Check Your Understanding

Illustrate one of the Holocaust vocabulary words on an index card. Share the illustration with classmates and discuss why you illustrated the word as you did. Compare and contrast illustrations for similar vocabulary words.

WORD CONNECTIONS

Roots and Affixes

Genocide comes from the Greek word *genos*, which means "race" or "line of descent." The root *-gen-* occurs in such words as *gene, genesis,* and *genus.*

The suffix *-cide* forms nouns with the meaning of "kill" or "causing death," as in *homicide* and *pesticide.*

Exploring the Museum

LEARNING STRATEGIES:
Oral Reading, Note-taking, Discussion Groups, Graphic Organizer, Summarizing

My Notes

Learning Targets

- Summarize information from a Holocaust website and contribute events to a historical timeline.
- Create and organize talking points and deliver an effective collaborative presentation.

Researching the Holocaust

1. Setting (time and place) is important in any story, but why is it especially important in a Holocaust narrative?

2. The United States Holocaust Memorial Museum in Washington, D.C., has a large collection of artifacts and educational displays about the events and people of the Holocaust. Work collaboratively to research and take notes on your assigned topics by exploring the museum's website, starting with the page "The Holocaust: A Learning Site for Students."

3. Each of the topics on the Learning Site links to a different webpage. Visit the website to explore your topics. Take notes on a graphic organizer like the one below in order to prepare your talking points for a presentation on the Holocaust. Your talking points should contain interesting information that leads to an exploration of the theme, or central idea.

   On the next page is a list of topics about the Holocaust. Your teacher will assign each group a topic (column) and individual subjects within that topic to research. As you research, neatly copy your key dates and events onto individual index cards to add to the collaborative timeline after your presentation.

My Group's Topic:	
Topic 1:	Topic 2:
Notes for Talking Points:	Notes for Talking Points:
Summaries and Dates of Key Events:	Summaries and Dates of Key Events:

4. Mark the chart to indicate your assignment by circling the title of your group's topic (column) and highlighting or placing a check mark by the topics you are responsible for.

Nazi Rule	Jews in Prewar Germany	The "Final Solution"	Nazi Camp System	Rescue and Resistance
• Hitler Comes to Power • The Nazi Terror Begins • SS Police State • Nazi Propaganda and Censorship • Nazi Racism • World War II in Europe • The Murder of the Handicapped • German Rule in Occupied Europe	• Jewish Life in Europe Before the Holocaust • Antisemitism • The Boycott of Jewish Businesses • The Nuremberg Race Laws • The "Night of Broken Glass" • The Evian Conference • Voyage of the *St. Louis* • Locating the Victims	• Ghettos in Poland • Life in the Ghettos • Mobile Killing Squads • The Wannsee Conference and the "Final Solution" • At the Killing Centers • Deportations • Auschwitz	• Prisoners of the Camps • "Enemies of the State" • Forced Labor • Death Marches • Liberation • The Survivors • The Nuremberg Trials	• Rescue in Denmark • Jewish Partisans • The Warsaw Ghetto Uprising • Killing Center Revolts • The War Refugee Board • Resistance Inside Germany

Source: Copyright © United States Holocaust Memorial Museum, Washington, D.C.

5. Present your talking points to your peer group, and then prepare a collaborative presentation based on your group's most interesting or important talking points. Each person in your group should prepare and present at least one talking point. Use the outline that follows to organize your presentation. Draft an introduction and conclusion, arrange the order of talking points into broader categories, and assign a speaker to each part of the presentation.

My Notes

_____

_____

_____

_____

_____

_____

_____

_____

Exploring the Museum

Organization of Presentation	Assignment
Introduction: Begin with a dramatic interpretation of a startling fact, statistic, or anecdote from the site and preview what is to follow in the presentation.	Dramatic Interpretation: Preview:
Transition: **Talking Point 1:** Topic:	
Transition: **Talking Point 2:** Topic:	
Transition: **Talking Point 3:** Topic:	
Transition: **Talking Point 4:** Topic:	
Conclusion: Summarize the main points of your discussion and end with a thoughtful question or thematic connection.	Brief Summary: Question or Connection:

My Notes

6. As you rehearse your presentation, turn to the chart on page 201 and use it to evaluate yourself and the rest of your group.

7. Deliver your presentation and add the information from your index cards to the collaborative timeline.

8. As you view the other presentations, take notes in your Reader/Writer Notebook. Use a chart like the one below, drawing a line under each new presentation.

Presentation Topic and Speaker Names	Facts and Information About the Topic	My Opinion and Evaluation of the Talking Points

9. Reflect on your group's collaborative presentation:
   - What did your group do well?
   - What will you do differently next time?

Check Your Understanding

In your Reader/Writer Notebook, make three inferences about the Holocaust. Then make a list of any additional questions you have about the presentations or timeline.

Presenting Voices

Learning Targets

- Research a specific Holocaust victim and present a narrative that captures his or her story.
- Apply an understanding of active and passive voice, by using voice for effect.

Researching the Holocaust

1. During the Holocaust, many people fit into one of the following categories based on either their circumstances or decisions that they made. Try to think of individual examples of each from your reading, research, and/or prior knowledge. Which group do you think was the largest? Which was the smallest?

   Victims:

   Perpetrators:

   Rescuers:

   Bystanders:

2. Choose an ID card from the Holocaust Museum website. Take notes on each section of your card, using the chart to organize information.

   Name:

   Date of Birth:

   Place of Birth:

   Biographical Background:

   Experiences from 1933–1939:

   War Years:

   Future and Fate:

WORD CONNECTIONS

Roots and Affixes

Perpetrator contains the Latin root *-petrare-*, which means "to bring about." It derives from *pater*, which means "father," as seen in *paternity* and *patriarch*. Adding the suffix *-or*, which means "one that performs a specific action," makes *perpetrator* refer to the person who brings about, or commits, a certain action. It is commonly associated with doing something wrong or illegal.

My Notes

_____

_____

_____

_____

_____

_____

_____

INDEPENDENT READING LINK

Read and Respond

Find a few instances in the narrative you are reading independently where the author uses the active voice and the passive voice. Rewrite each sentence in the other voice.

Presenting Voices

Language and Writer's Craft: Active Versus Passive Voice

When writing or speaking, it is usually better to use active voice instead of passive voice. However, skilled writers and speakers use voice for effect, and sometimes the passive voice works best. Study the examples below. How is the effect different in each sentence?

Passive: Relocation camps were used to destroy whole villages.
Active: The Nazis used the camps to empty whole villages of their citizens.

Notice that the passive voice sentence does not mention the people who were doing the destroying. It has a softer effect. The active voice sentence is more engaging and powerful. Depending on what tone the writer wants to create, either sentence could be effective.

PRACTICE Find some examples of active and passive voice in your reading or writing. Write several examples in your Reader/Writer Notebook and try changing them to the opposite voice to see which has more impact.

Narrative Writing Prompt

Using the information you learned in your research about a Holocaust victim, draft a story about the victim's experiences. Be sure to:

- Use narrative techniques (dialogue, pacing, description, and reflection) to develop events and characters.
- Establish a context and use first-person point of view.
- Sequence events logically and naturally using your notes as a guide.
- Use active and passive voice effectively.

3. Revise your writing to show your understanding of voice and mood by adding or substituting for effect. Also, be sure you have included transitions to convey sequence, signal shifts, and connect the relationships among experiences and events. Reflect on your editing: How does using voice and mood for effect strengthen your writing?

Presenting the Narrative

4. Before you prepare an oral reading of your narrative, examine the criteria for evaluation below. These criteria also apply to speaking.

> **WORD CONNECTIONS**
>
> **Roots and Affixes**
>
> Both *pronounce* and *enunciate* contain the Latin root *-nuntius-* which means "messenger." There is a delicate distinction between the two words. To *pronounce* means to say words correctly. To *enunciate* means to say words clearly as you are pronouncing them.

Element of Expressive Oral Reading/Speaking	Proficient	Emerging
Enunciation: Pronunciation of words	Enunciation is clear, correct, and effective throughout the reading and enhances the listener's understanding.	Mumbling, incorrect, or indistinct pronunciation hinders the listener's understanding.
Pitch: Vocal highs and lows	Variety in vocal highs and lows enhances the listener's understanding of the passage.	Mostly monotone
Volume: Variety in volume	Variety in volume enhances the listener's understanding of the passage.	Too quiet
Tempo: Appropriate pacing (fast or slow)	Appropriate pacing enhances the listener's understanding of the passage.	Too fast or too slow
Phrasing: Pausing at appropriate points and for emphasis	Pauses and emphasis enhance the listener's understanding of the passage.	No pauses or emphasized words

5. Prepare and present an oral reading of your revised narrative to a small group of your peers. Use the chart above to provide feedback about each speaker's strengths and weaknesses.

>
>
> **WORD CONNECTIONS**
>
> **Roots and Affixes**
>
> The word *monotone* includes the prefix *mono-*, meaning "one," as in *monologue*, *monomania*, and *monocle*. Thus *monotone* means "one tone," or "without inflection."

Check Your Understanding

How did the process of researching a person from the Holocaust and assuming that person's identity add to your understanding of the Holocaust? Discuss with a partner.

Finding Light in Film

My Notes

Learning Targets

- Explain how screenwriters use literary elements such as setting, character, plot, and mood to develop a theme.
- Present an effective oral reading and transform a written draft into talking points for discussion.

Finding Light in the Darkness

1. Return to Activity 3.2 and reread the quotes. Notice that each speaker uses the imagery of light and darkness to express his or her ideas about good and evil, love and hatred, hope and depression—all of which are opposites. How do you think this conflict between opposites might be portrayed in film?

Life Is Beautiful is a fictional story about a family in Italy that is sent to a concentration camp. The father and son are Jewish, but the mother is not. The father tries to protect his son from the ugly realities of the Holocaust by making it seem as if they are playing a game whose prize is a real tank.

2. Based on the information above, predict conflicts that the father might encounter as he tries to convince his son that the concentration camp is just a game.

3. Work in groups of four to take notes on setting, character, plot, and mood in each film clip. Share notes and trade jobs after each clip to complete the graphic organizer on the next page.

Setting	Character(s)	Plot	Mood
Clip 1			
Clip 2			
Clip 3			
Clip 4			

Finding Light in Film

Check Your Understanding

Was the mood of the film appropriate for the topic of the film? Why or why not? Discuss your opinions in a small group using the following discussion prompts.

Discussion Prompts:

a. Is it disrespectful to make a film about the Holocaust that has so much comedy in it?

b. What aspects of the Holocaust, as portrayed in the film, are similar to or different from what you learned in your research?

c. How and when did the mood change during the film clips, and what settings, characters, or events caused those shifts?

Writing to Sources: Explanatory Text

One of the themes of *Life Is Beautiful* is the ability to find the good in a very difficult situation. Write a draft of an explanatory essay that describes some of the ways Holocaust victims found light in the dark reality of their lives. Make sure you use at least two examples from the movie and/or the texts in your writing. Be sure to:

- Begin with a meaningful topic sentence that responds to the prompt.
- Provide two or more examples from the movie and texts.
- Use transitions to clarify your points.
- Provide a conclusion that summarizes your response.

Prepare and present an oral reading of your written draft. Use the chart in the previous activity to guide your preparation. Present your response to another pair of students. Provide feedback about ideas and oral reading.

Dramatic Tone Shifts

Learning Target

- Analyze how dialogue is used in a play to develop character and plot, convey tone, and reveal theme.

Preview

In this activity, you will read part of a play. Pay attention to the tone at the beginning of the scene and at the end.

Setting a Purpose for Reading

- As you read the dialogue, underline words and phrases that indicate the tone of how the characters are feeling.
- Circle unknown words and phrases. Try to determine the meaning of the words by using context clues, word parts, or a dictionary.
- Actors often highlight their lines when they get a new script. The beginning of the passage lists the characters involved in the scene. Choose one and highlight each instance they speak.

> **ABOUT THE AUTHOR**
>
> Frances Goodrich (1891–1984) and Albert Hackett (1900–1995) were both writers and actors who married in 1931. Together they wrote numerous plays and film screenplays. In 1955 they adapted Anne Frank's *The Diary of a Young Girl* for the stage, where it received several Tony Award nominations, including a win for Best Play. The play also was awarded the Pulitzer Prize for Drama in 1956.

LEARNING STRATEGIES:
Skimming/Scanning, Marking the Text, Close Reading, Rereading, Oral Reading, Discussion Groups, Drafting, Adding

My Notes

Drama

from

The Diary of **Anne Frank**

by Frances Goodrich and Albert Hackett

Families living in the hidden attic:

Mr. Frank and Mrs. Frank: Anne and Margot Frank's parents

Margot and Anne: sisters, 18 and 13 years old

Mr. van Daan and Mrs. van Daan: Mr. van Daan worked with Otto Frank in Amsterdam

Peter van Daan: their son

Mr. Dussel: older; dentist who also lives in the attic

Others:

Miep Gies: close friend of the Frank family

Eisenhower: the voice of the American general

Scene: Anne, Mr. Dussel, Mr. van Daan, Mr. Frank, Mrs. van Daan, Mrs. Frank, Margot, Peter, Miep, Eisenhower

(Night. Everyone is asleep. Suddenly, Mrs. Frank sits up in bed.)

Mrs. Frank: *(In a whisper.)* Otto. Listen. The rat!

INDEPENDENT READING LINK

Read and Connect

Find an instance in the narrative you are reading independently where the tone shifts dramatically. How is it similar to or different than the tone shift in the play in Activity 3.10?

Dramatic Tone Shifts

gnawing: biting or chewing

Mr. Frank: Edith, please. Go back to sleep. (*He turns over. Mrs. Frank gets up, quietly creeps to the main room, standstill. There is a tiny crunching sound. In the darkness, a figure is faintly illuminated, crouching over, gnawing on something. Mrs. Frank moves closer, turns on the light. Trembling, Mr. van Daan jumps to his feet. He is clutching a piece of bread.*)

Mrs. Frank: My God, I don't believe it! The bread! He's stealing the bread! (*Pointing at Mr. van Daan.*) Otto, look!

Mr. van Daan: No, no. Quiet.

Mr. Frank: (*As everyone comes into the main room in their nightclothes.*) Hermann, for God's sake!

Mrs. van Daan: (*Opening her eyes sleepily.*) What is it? What's going on?

Mrs. Frank: It's your husband. Stealing our bread!

Mrs. van Daan: It can't be. Putti, what are you doing?

Mr. van Daan: Nothing.

Mr. Dussel: It wasn't a rat. It was him.

Mr. van Daan: Never before! Never before!

Mrs. Frank: I don't believe you. If he steals once, he'll steal again. Every day I watch the children get thinner. And he comes in the middle of the night and steals food that should go to them!

Mr. van Daan: (*His head in his hands.*) Oh my God. My God.

Mr. Frank: Edith. Please.

Margot: Mama, it was only one piece of bread.

Mr. van Daan: (*Putting the bread on the table. In a panic.*) Here. (*Mrs. Frank swats the bread away.*)

Mr. Frank: Edith, he couldn't help himself! It could happen to any one of us.

Mrs. Frank: (*Quiet.*) I want him to go.

Mrs. van Daan: Go? Go where?

Mrs. Frank: Anywhere.

Mrs. van Daan: You don't mean what you're saying.

Mr. Dussel: I understand you, Mrs. Frank. But it really would be impossible for them—

Mrs. Frank: They have to! I can't take it with them here.

Mr. Frank: Edith, you know how upset you've been these past—

Mrs. Frank: That has nothing to do with it.

Mr. Frank: We're all living under terrible strain. (*Looking at Mr. van Daan.*) It won't happen again.

Mr. van Daan: Never. I promise.

Mrs. Frank: I want them to leave.

Mrs. van Daan: You'd put us out on the street?

Mrs. Frank: There are other hiding places. Miep will find something. Don't worry about the money. I'll find you the money.

Mrs. van Daan: Mr. Frank, you told my husband you'd never forget what he did for you when you first came to Amsterdam.

Mrs. Frank: If my husband had any **obligation** to you, it's paid for.

Mr. Frank: Edith, I've never seen you like this, for God's sake.

Anne: You can't throw Peter out! He hasn't done anything.

Mrs. Frank: Peter can stay.

Peter: I wouldn't feel right without Father.

Anne: Mother, please. They'll be killed on the street.

Margot: Anne's right. You can't send them away.

Mrs. Frank: They can stay till Miep finds them a place. But we're switching rooms. I don't want him near the food.

Mr. Dussel: Let's divide it up right now.

Margot: *(As he gets a sack of potatoes.)* We're not going to divide up some rotten potatoes.

Mr. Dussel: *(Dividing the potatoes into piles.)* Mrs. Frank, Mr. Frank, Margot, Anne, Peter, Mrs. van Daan, Mr. van Daan, myself… Mrs. Frank, Mr. Frank…

Margot: *(Overlapping.)* Mr. Dussel, please. Don't! No more. No more, Mr. Dussel! I beg you. I can't bear it. *(Mr. Dussel continues counting nonstop. In tears.)* Stop! I can't take it …

Mrs. Frank: All this … all that's happening …

Mr. Frank: Enough! Margot. Mr. Dussel. Everyone—back to your rooms. Come, Edith. Mr. Dussel, I think the potatoes can wait. *(Mr. Dussel goes on counting. Tearing the sack from Mr. Dussel, the potatoes spilling.)* Just let them wait! *(He holds out his hand for Mrs. Frank. They all go back to their rooms. Peter and Mrs. van Daan pick up the scattered potatoes. Not looking at each other, Mr. and Mrs. van Daan move to their separate beds. The buzzer rings frantically, breaking the silence.)* Miep? At this hour? *(Miep runs up the stairs, as everyone comes back into the main room.)*

Miep: *(Out of breath.)* Everyone … everyone … the most wonderful, incredible news!

Mr. Frank: What is it?

Miep: *(Tears streaming down her cheeks.)* The invasion. The invasion has begun! *(They stare at her, unable to grasp what she is telling them.)* Did you hear me? Did you hear what I said? The invasion! It's happening—right now! *(As Mrs. Frank begins to cry.)* I rushed to tell you before the workmen got here. You can feel it in the streets—the excitement! This is it. They've landed on the coast of Normandy.

Peter: The British?

Miep: British, Americans … everyone! More than four thousand ships! Look—I brought a map. *(Quickly she unrolls a map of Normandy on the table.)*

Mr. Frank: *(Weeping, embracing his daughters.)* For over a year we've hoped for this moment.

obligation: legal or moral duty or commitment

GRAMMAR & USAGE
Pronoun Antecedents

A pronoun that takes the place of a noun or another pronoun is called its **antecedent**. Mrs. Frank says, "They have to! I can't take it with them here." To whom is she referring? The preceding part of the play indicates that Mrs. Frank is referring to the van Daans. This statement would be confusing if readers did not know the antecedent (in this example, the van Daans).

As you read, notice pronouns and make sure you know their antecedents. Being clear about antecedents can often improve your comprehension of a text.

My Notes

convulsive: marked by violent shaking

Miep: *(Pointing.)* Cherbourg. The first city. They're fighting for it right now.

Mr. Dussel: How many days will it take them from Normandy to the Netherlands?

Mr. Frank: *(Taking Mrs. Frank in his arms.)* Edith, what did I tell you?

Mr. Dussel: *(Placing the potatoes on the map to hold it down as he checks the cities.)* Cherbourg. Caen. Pont L'Eveque. Paris. And then ... Amsterdam! *(Mr. van Daan breaks into a* **convulsive** *sob.)*

Mrs. van Daan: Putti.

Mr. Frank: Hermann, didn't you hear what Miep said? We'll be free ... soon. *(Mr. Dussel turns on the radio. Amidst much static, Eisenhower's voice is heard from his broadcast of June 6, 1944.)*

Eisenhower: *(Voice-over.)* People of Western Europe, a landing was made this morning on the coast of France by troops of the Allied Expeditionary Force. This landing is part of the concerted United Nations plan for the liberation of Europe ...

Mr. Frank: *(Wiping tears from his eyes.)* Listen. That's General Eisenhower. *(Anne pulls Margot down to her room.)*

Eisenhower: *(Voice-over, fading away.)* ... made in conjunction with our great Russian allies. I have this message for all of you. Although the initial assault may not have been made in your own country, the hour of your liberation is approaching. All patriots ...

Anne: *(Hugging Margot.)* Margot, can you believe it? The invasion! Home. That means we could be going home.

Margot: I don't even know what home would be like anymore. I can't imagine it—we've been away for so long.

Anne: Oh, I can! I can imagine every little detail. And just to be outside again. The sky, Margot! Just to walk along the canal!

Margot: *(As they sit down on Anne's bed.)* I'm afraid to let myself think about it. To have a real meal—*(They laugh together.)* It doesn't seem possible! Will anything taste the same? Look the same? *(Growing more and more serious.)* I don't know if anything will ever feel normal again. How can we go back ... really?

Second Read

- Reread the scene to answer these text-dependent questions.
- Write any additional questions you have about the text in your Reader/Writer Notebook.

1. **Key Ideas and Details:** Quote a line of dialogue that expresses Mrs. Frank's anger and explain why she is so angry.

2. **Key Ideas and Details:** Examine Mr. Frank's dialogue in this scene. How does it show his role in the family and in this particular scene?

3. **Key Ideas and Details:** How does Miep's news of the invasion change the tone of the scene? Characterize the new tone and explain how it has changed.

Working from the Text

4. In your group, assign roles for an oral reading of the scene.

5. Prepare for an oral reading by skimming/scanning the scene independently, marking and annotating your character's lines:

   • Mark connotative diction and label the tone you intend to use in speaking lines of dialogue.

   • Mark words of the dialogue that you will emphasize with a shift in volume or pitch.

   • Place slash marks in places where you will pause for effect.

6. Conduct an oral reading in your group, using your marks and annotations as a guide.

7. Discuss how and when the tone shifted in the play. Did setting, character, or plot cause the shift in tone?

Check Your Understanding

What is the mood of the play? Find evidence in the text to support your answer. Discuss with a partner or in a small group.

Writing to Sources: Explanatory Text

Think about the characters in the scene from *The Diary of Anne Frank*. How does their dialogue reveal the characters and the conflicts of the story? How does it increase the reader's understanding of an aspect of the Holocaust experience? Draft a response that explains how specific dialogue is used to develop character(s) or plot and to reveal theme. Be sure to:

• Begin with a topic sentence that responds to the prompt.

• Provide textual evidence and commentary for support.

• Use transitional words and phrases to clarify how your ideas are related.

• Include a conclusion that summarizes your major points and supports your opening statement.

My Notes

Language Checkpoint:
Using Punctuation Within Sentences

Learning Targets
- Understand and recognize the uses of punctuation to indicate pauses and breaks within sentences.
- Use dashes correctly when writing and editing.

Recognizing Punctuation Marks Within Sentences

Punctuation marks make texts easier to read and understand. They can show a writer's tone as well as organize thoughts. You already use many different punctuation marks in your formal writing.

1. **Quickwrite:** Write a brief explanation of how each punctuation mark below is used.

   period (.):

   question mark (?):

   exclamation point (!):

   comma (,):

   ellipsis (. . .):

   dash (—):

2. Read the following lines of dialogue taken from *The Diary of Anne Frank* (Activity 3.10). After each line, describe what the purpose or function of each punctuation mark is.

   MR. FRANK: Edith, you know how upset you've been these past—

   MRS. FRANK: That has nothing to do with it.

   dash (—):

   MIEP: British, Americans . . . everyone! More than four thousand ships! Look—I brought a map.

   ellipsis (. . .):

   dash (—):

Punctuating Pauses

A long sentence without *internal punctuation*—that is, punctuation that appears inside the sentence—runs the risk of being confusing to readers. Internal punctuation marks can clarify ideas in a sentence. They can also be used to create pauses that make dialogue sound more realistic.

Quick Guide to Internal Punctuation		
Comma (,)	indicates a brief pause in a sentence	Well, I didn't think about it that way.
Ellipsis (. . .)	indicates thought or speech that trails off or pauses	I wonder if . . . I don't know if it'll work, but . . . sure, let's try it.
Dash (—)	indicates a sudden break or interruption in thought or speech	If you push the start button first—hey, are you paying attention to my instructions?

3. Work with a partner to revise each sentence below, using the punctuation mark indicated after the sentence.

   a. And then she opened up my book/ Hey!/ Did you just see that?

   Dash (—):

   b. The rocket wasn't tested/ so I wonder if it will even succeed.

   Comma (,):

c. There's a way this plan can work/ If we put our heads together/ Yeah, we'll have some ideas.
   Ellipsis (. . .):

4. Rewrite the following lines of dialogue to include appropriate internal punctuation, based on context.

   a. I'm just not sure. It's not coming to me. Maybe if I sleep on that idea for tonight.

   b. The way the performers are staging the action is incredible. Whoa! Did you see that?

   c. Joe may not appreciate that option so I will reconsider our plans for tonight.

Revising

Sometimes writers do not choose the most appropriate punctuation in their first drafts. Read the student paragraph below, and decide how to revise each numbered sentence.

The Diary of Anne Frank is a drama written by Frances Goodrich and Albert Hackett. [1] Together the two writers adapted Anne Frank's book for the stage. [2] One of the greatest accomplishments of their work is how natural the dialogue sounds it feels like you're right there in the room with the characters! For example, Mrs. Frank says, "If he steals once, he'll steal again . . . And he comes in the middle of the night and steals food that should go to them!" [3] The tone and punctuation really make the emotion of the scene very clear and much more believable. [4] In real life, people interrupt each other all the time, so characters in a play should do the same—it's necessary in order to make the scenes realistic.

Check Your Understanding

What question(s) can you ask yourself whenever you write, in order to ensure you are using internal punctuation correctly? Add the question(s) to your Editor's Checklist.

Practice

Reread the excerpt from *The Diary of Anne Frank* from Activity 3.10, and notice how the playwrights use special punctuation to make the characters' dialogue believable. Then craft a small scene from your own imagination. Be sure to:

• Include dialogue for at least three characters in your scene.

• Use ellipses, dashes, or commas to indicate pauses, sudden interruptions, or dialogue that trails off.

• Ask a partner to review your work for correct use of punctuation.

The Wrong Side of the Fence

My Notes

Learning Targets

- Analyze an excerpt of a Holocaust narrative and prepare talking points to present in a panel discussion.
- Deliver an oral reading and orally explain the thematic focus of a passage.

Preview

In this activity, you will read about two boys with different perspectives of the Holocaust.

Setting a Purpose for Reading

- As you read the passage, underline words and phrases that describe the setting.
- Draw squiggly lines under words and phrases that describe the boys' characters.
- Circle unknown words and phrases. Try to determine the meaning of the words by using context clues, word parts, or a dictionary.

ABOUT THE AUTHOR

John Boyne (1971–) is an Irish writer who began his writing career creating short stories. He published *The Boy in the Striped Pajamas* in 2006, and this novel proceeded to win multiple international awards. The novel also was made into a film.

Fiction

from
The Boy in the Striped Pajamas

by John Boyne

1 Two boys were sitting on opposite sides of a fence.

2 "All I know is this," began Shmuel. "Before we came here I lived with my mother and father and my brother Josef in a small flat above the store where Papa makes his watches. Every morning we ate our breakfast together at seven o'clock and while we went to school, Papa mended the watches that people brought to him and made new ones too. I had a beautiful watch that he gave me but I don't have it anymore. It had a golden face and I wound it up every night before I went to sleep and it always told the right time."

3 "What happened to it?" asked Bruno.

4 "They took it from me," said Shmuel.

5 "Who?"

6 "The soldiers of course," said Shmuel as if it was the most obvious thing in the world.

7 "And then one day things started to change," he continued. "I came home from school and my mother was making armbands for us from a special cloth and drawing a star on each one. Like this." Using his finger he drew a design in the dusty ground beneath him.

The star of David.

8 "And every time we left the house, she told us we had to wear one of these armbands."

9 "My father wears one too," said Bruno. "On his uniform. It's very nice. It's bright red with a black-and-white design on it." Using his finger he drew another design in the dusty ground on his side of the fence.

A swastika.

10 "Yes, but they're different, aren't they?" said Shmuel.

11 "No one's ever given me an armband," said Bruno.

12 "But I never asked to wear one," said Shmuel.

13 "All the same," said Bruno, "I think I'd quite like one. I don't know which one I'd prefer though, your one or father's."

14 Shmuel shook his head and continued with his story. He didn't often think about these things anymore because remembering his old life above the watch shop made him very sad.

15 "We wore the armbands for a few months," he said. "And then things changed again. I came home one day and Mama said we couldn't live in our home any more."

16 "That happened to me too!" said Bruno, delighted that he wasn't the only boy who'd been forced to move. "The Fury came for dinner, you see, and the next thing I knew we moved here. And I *hate* it here," he added. "Did he come to your house and do the same thing?"

17 "No, but when we were told we couldn't live in our house we had to move to a different part of Cracow, where the soldiers built a big wall and my mother and father and my brother and I all had to live in one room."

18 "All of you?" asked Bruno. "In one room?"

"And not just us," said Shmuel. "There was another family there and the mother and father were always fighting with each other and one of the sons was bigger than me and hit me even when I did nothing wrong."

19 "You can't have all lived in the one room," said Bruno. "That doesn't make any sense."

20 "All of us," said Shmuel. "Eleven in total."

Bruno opened his mouth to **contradict** him again—he didn't really believe that eleven people could live in the same room together—but changed his mind.

contradict: to express an opposite thought

The Wrong Side of the Fence

My Notes

21 "We lived there for some more months," continued Shmuel, "all of us in that one room. There was one small window in it but I didn't like to look out of it because then I would see the wall and I hated the wall because our real home was on the other side of it. And this part of town was a bad part because it was always noisy and it was impossible to sleep. And I hated Luka, who was the boy who kept hitting me even when I did nothing wrong."

22 "Gretel hits me sometimes," said Bruno. "She's my sister," he added. "And a Hopeless Case. But soon I'll be bigger and stronger than she is and she won't know what's hit her then."

23 "Then one day the soldiers all came with huge trucks," continued Shmuel, who didn't seem all that interested in Gretel. "And everyone was told to leave the houses. Lots of people didn't want to and they hid wherever they could find a place but in the end I think they caught everyone. And the trucks took us to a train and the train …" He hesitated for a moment and bit his lip. Bruno thought he was going to start crying and couldn't understand why.

24 "The train was horrible," said Shmuel. "There were too many of us in the carriages for one thing. And there was no air to breathe. And it smelled awful."

25 "That's because you all crowded onto one train," said Bruno, remembering the two trains he had seen at the station when he left Berlin. "When we came here, there was another one on the other side of the platform but no one seemed to see it. That was the one we got. You should have got on it too."

26 "I don't think we would have been allowed," said Shmuel, shaking his head. "We weren't able to get out of our carriage."

27 "The door's at the end," explained Bruno.

28 "There weren't any doors," said Shmuel.

29 "Of course there were doors," said Bruno with a sigh. "They're at the end," he repeated. "Just past the **buffet** section."

30 "There weren't any doors," insisted Shmuel. "If there had been, we would have gotten off."

31 Bruno mumbled something under his breath along the lines of "Of course there were," but he didn't say it very loud so Shmuel didn't hear.

32 "When the train finally stopped," continued Shmuel, "we were in a very cold place and we all had to walk here."

33 "We had a car," said Bruno, out loud now.

34 "And Mama was taken away from us, and Papa and Josef and I were put into the huts over there and that's where we've been since."

35 Shmuel looked very sad when he told this story and Bruno didn't know why; it didn't seem like such a terrible thing to him, and after all much the same thing happened to him.

36 "Are there many other boys over there?" asked Bruno.

37 "Hundreds," said Shmuel.

38 Bruno's eyes opened wide. "Hundreds?" he said, amazed. "That's not fair at all. There's no one to play with on this side of the fence. Not a single person."

buffet: a counter or table where food is served

WORD CONNECTIONS

Multiple Meaning Words

The word *carriage* can refer to many things, all stemming from its root meaning "carry." We know it as a wheeled vehicle drawn by a horse, a device to transport babies (a baby carriage), or any general support frame to carry a heavy object (like a car's undercarriage). The British use it specifically to refer to a railroad passenger car. It can also be used to describe a person's bearing, or the manner in which they move their head and body.

39 "We don't play," said Shmuel.

40 "Don't play? Why ever not?"

41 "What would we play?" he asked, his face looking confused at the idea of it.

42 "Well, I don't know," said Bruno. "All sorts of things. Football, for example. Or exploration. What's the exploration like over there anyway? Any good?"

43 Shmuel shook his head and didn't answer. He looked back towards the huts and turned back to Bruno then. He didn't want to ask the next question but the pains in his stomach made him.

44 "You don't have any food on you, do you?" he asked.

45 "Afraid not," said Bruno. "I meant to bring some chocolate but I forgot."

46 "Chocolate," said Shmuel very slowly, his tongue moving out from behind his teeth. "I've only ever had chocolate once."

47 "Only once? I love chocolate. I can't get enough of it although Mother says it'll rot my teeth."

48 "You don't have any bread, do you?"

49 Bruno shook his head. "Nothing at all," he said. "Dinner isn't served until half past six. What time do you have yours?"

50 Shmuel shrugged his shoulders and pulled himself to his feet. "I think I'd better get back," he said.

51 "Perhaps you can come to dinner with us one evening," said Bruno, although he wasn't sure it was a very good idea.

52 "Perhaps," said Shmuel, although he didn't sound convinced.

53 "Or I could come to you," said Bruno. "Perhaps I could come and meet your friends," he added hopefully. He had hoped that Shmuel would suggest this himself but there didn't seem to be any sign of that.

54 "You're on the wrong side of the fence though," said Shmuel.

55 "I could crawl under," said Bruno, reaching down and lifting the wire off the ground. In the centre, between two wooden telegraph poles, it lifted quite easily and a boy as small as Bruno could easily fit through.

My Notes

The Wrong Side of the Fence

56 Shmuel watched him do this and backed away nervously. "I have to get back," he said.

57 "Some other afternoon then," said Bruno.

58 "I'm not supposed to be here. If they catch me I'll be in trouble."

59 He turned and walked away and Bruno noticed again how small and skinny this new friend was. He didn't say anything about this because he knew only too well how unpleasant it was being criticized for something as silly as your height, and the last thing he wanted to do was be unkind to Shmuel.

60 "I'll come back tomorrow," shouted Bruno to the departing boy and Shmuel said nothing in reply; in fact he started to run off back to the camp, leaving Bruno all on his own.

Second Read

- Reread the passage to answer these text-dependent questions.
- Write any additional questions you have about the text in your Reader/Writer Notebook.

1. **Key Ideas and Details:** Analyze the description and dialogue. Why is the watch so important to Shmuel? What does it symbolize for him?

2. **Key Ideas and Details:** What does Bruno not seem to understand about their different situations, as shown in the conversation about the armbands?

3. **Key Ideas and Details:** What inferences can you make about the setting? Provide details that help form your inferences.

4. **Craft and Structure:** Examine paragraph 16 that talks about "The Fury." Who is this and why does Bruno call him "The Fury"?

5. **Key Ideas and Details:** Quote one or more lines of dialogue that show Bruno's perspective lacks an understanding of Shmuel's situation and explain why.

6. **Craft and Structure:** What specifically are the carriages mentioned in paragraph 24?

7. **Craft and Structure:** The conversation about train travel between Bruno and Shmuel uses the phrases "said Shmuel, shaking his head" and "said Bruno with a sigh." How do these phrases reveal what both boys are feeling?

8. **Key Ideas and Details:** How does the following dialogue reveal theme: "You're on the wrong side of the fence though"?

Working from the Text

9. How does the theme "finding light in the darkness" connect to the passage about Shmuel and Bruno?

10. Why would an author write a Holocaust narrative from a child's perspective? How would that change a reader's understanding of the story?

The Wrong Side of the Fence

Character 1:	Character 2:	Setting:

Plot		
Beginning:	Middle:	End:

Theme:

11. Fill in the graphic organizer above with information from the passage. Use your notes to prepare talking points that will guide a meaningful discussion of the text. Be sure to:

- Discuss how an individual (character), event (plot), or place (setting) contributes to the development of a theme.
- Include details from text, commentary (analysis), and questions to spark discussion.

12. Work collaboratively to prepare the content of your panel discussion. Use the outline to organize your presentation. Draft an introduction and conclusion, select and arrange talking points into broader categories, and assign a speaker to each part of the presentation. This time, have at least two people present the dramatic interpretation of the text.

Organization of Presentation	Assignment
Introduction: Begin with a dramatic interpretation of an important section of the narrative, and preview what is to follow in the presentation.	**Dramatic Interpretation:** **Preview:**
Transition: **Talking Point 1:** Topic:	
Transition: **Talking Point 2:** Topic:	
Conclusion: Summarize the main points of your discussion. Connect the story to the theme of "finding light in the darkness."	**Brief Summary:** **Connection to Theme:**

My Notes

13. Review the criteria from the Scoring Guide on page 224 to prepare the delivery of your panel discussion.

14. After rehearsing your panel discussion, present it to another group. Use the Scoring Guide to provide specific feedback and suggestions for improvement (focus on the quality of speakers' interpretation and evidence).

Check Your Understanding

Quickwrite: Do you think Bruno and Schmuel are likely to become friends? Why or why not? Compare and contrast their characters in your Reader/Writer Notebook.

Writing to Sources: Explanatory Text

Write a short, objective summary of the excerpt from *The Boy in the Striped Pajamas*, including its theme and how the characters, setting, and plot relate to the theme. Be sure to:

- Include a topic sentence that states the theme.
- Include details and quotes from the text in the summary.
- Explain how characters, setting, and plot relate to the theme.

Technology Tip

Remember that dashes can be used to show pauses in your writing. To make a dash quickly, type two hyphens followed by text.

Creating a Memorable Opening

LEARNING STRATEGIES:
Rereading, Close reading,
Oral Reading, Choral Reading,
Discussion Groups

My Notes

Learning Targets
- Transform a prose selection into a "found poem."
- Orally present a dramatic interpretation.

Preview
In this activity, you will read an excerpt from Anne Frank's diary and create a found poem.

Setting a Purpose for Reading
- As you read the diary entry, underline words and phrases that indicate why Anne is so upset.
- Circle unknown words and phrases. Try to determine the meaning of the words by using context clues, word parts, or a dictionary.

ABOUT THE AUTHOR
Anne Frank (1929–1945) is one of the Holocaust's most famous victims. The Frank family fled Germany for Amsterdam, but eventually the Nazis also occupied the Netherlands. The family spent two years in hiding, during which Anne wrote of her thoughts and feelings to her imaginary friend, Kitty. The German authorities found the family's hiding place and sent them to concentration camps, where Anne perished at age 15. Her diary was found years later, and it continues to be read today as a moving narrative from the Holocaust.

Diary

from The Diary of a Young Girl

Wednesday, 13 January, 1943

by Anne Frank

Dear Kitty,

1 Everything has upset me again this morning, so I wasn't able to finish a single thing properly.

2 It is terrible outside. Day and night more of those poor miserable people are being dragged off, with nothing but a rucksack and a little money. On the way they are deprived even of these possessions. Families are torn apart, the men, women, and children all being separated. Children coming home from school find that their parents have disappeared. Women return from shopping to find their homes shut up and their families gone.

3 The Dutch people are anxious too, their sons are being sent to Germany. Everyone is afraid.

4 And every night hundreds of planes fly over Holland and go to German towns, where the earth is plowed up by their bombs, and every hour hundreds and thousands of people are killed in Russia and Africa. No one is able to keep out of it, the whole globe is waging war and although it is going better for the allies, the end is not yet in sight.

5   And as for us, we are fortunate. Yes, we are luckier than millions of people. It is quiet and safe here, and we are, so to speak, living on **capital**. We are even so selfish as to talk about "after the war," brighten up at the thought of having new clothes and new shoes, whereas we really ought to save every penny, to help other people, and save what is left from the wreckage after the war.

capital: wealth kept after paying expenses

6   The children here run about in just a thin blouse and clogs; no coat, no hat, no stockings, and no one helps them. Their tummies are empty; they chew an old carrot to **stay** the pangs, go from their cold homes out into the cold street and, when they get to school, find themselves in an even colder classroom. Yes, it has even got so bad in Holland that countless children stop the passers-by and beg for a piece of bread. I could go on for hours about all the suffering the war has brought, but then I would only make myself more dejected. There is nothing we can do but wait as calmly as we can till the misery comes to an end. Jews and Christians wait, the whole earth waits, and there are many who wait for death.

stay: to delay or postpone

Yours,

Anne

My Notes

_____

_____

_____

_____

_____

_____

_____

_____

_____

_____

Second Read

- Reread the diary entry to answer these text-dependent questions.
- Write any additional questions you have about the text in your Reader/Writer Notebook.

1. **Key Ideas and Details:** Why does Anne feel that she is fortunate?

2. **Craft and Structure:** Based on the mood Anne portrays in this passage, what does she mean in paragraph 6 by "more dejected"?

Literary Terms
A **found poem** is verse that is created from a prose text by using the original words, phrases, images, and/or sentences, but manipulating them and reformatting them into poetic lines.

Working from the Text

3. In a previous activity, you read a play based on Anne Frank's diary. What could you learn from her diary that you could not learn from the play?

4. The opening two paragraphs of the diary entry have been transformed into a model of a **found poem**. With a partner, conduct an oral reading using choral reading for effect.

"Wednesday, 13 January, 1943"

Everyone is afraid:

It is terrible outside.
Day and night
more of those poor miserable people
are being dragged off.

INDEPENDENT READING LINK
Read and Respond

Choose a passage from the Holocaust narrative you are reading independently to transform into a found poem. Perform an oral reading of your poem at the final literature circle meeting.

Creating a Memorable Opening

Families are torn apart.
Children coming home from school
find that their parents
have disappeared.

Women
return from shopping to find
their homes shut up and
their families gone.

The Dutch people,
their sons are being sent
to Germany.
Everyone is afraid ...

5. The author of the found poem selected particular lines from the text and then transformed them into poetry. How does this transformation change the power of the language?

6. How does the structure of the lines in the found poem transform the text from prose to poetry? Which lines stand out? Why?

7. How would a dramatic interpretation of this found poem successfully open a panel discussion about the Holocaust?

8. Reread the diary entry again, highlighting words, phrases, and images you think are important. Then create your own found poem using the words and images you find compelling.

Check Your Understanding

Plan a dramatic interpretation (i.e., oral reading) of the found poem you created. Present your oral reading to a partner and listen and provide feedback to your partner's oral reading.

Independent Reading Checkpoint

Respond to the first Reflection question in Embedded Assessment 1 as it relates to your independent reading narrative: How was the theme or central idea of "finding light in the darkness" developed in the narrative you read independently?

Presenting Voices of the Holocaust

ASSIGNMENT

Present a panel discussion that includes an oral reading of a significant passage from the narrative read by your group. Your discussion should explain how the theme or central idea of "finding light in the darkness" is developed in the entire narrative.

Planning: Discuss your ideas with your group to prepare a focus for your panel discussion.	■ How was the theme or central idea of "finding light in the darkness" developed in your Holocaust narrative? ■ How did supporting details such as character, plot, and setting contribute to the theme? ■ How will you find a significant passage for your oral reading that will help communicate the idea of "finding light in the darkness"? ■ How will you assign talking points to each group member to include an introduction, at least two supporting details, and a conclusion?
Drafting: Write a draft of your talking point(s) that includes details from the text, commentary (analysis), and discussion questions.	■ How will the introductory talking point present a hook, summary of the text, and thematic statement? ■ How will the supporting talking points explain how an individual, event, or place contributed to theme? ■ How will the concluding talking point restate the theme, summarize the main points of the discussion, and elicit textual connections (text to self, text, or world) from the entire group?
Rehearsing: Rehearse and revise your panel discussion to improve the final presentation.	■ How will you prepare notes to constructive feedback and build on ideas and questions presented by other group members? ■ How will your group create smooth transitions between speakers? ■ How will you include your oral reading as you introduce and develop your explanation? ■ How will you use precise diction in order to establish and maintain a formal style? ■ How will you use eye contact, volume, and pronunciation to express your ideas clearly?

Reflection

After completing this Embedded Assessment, think about how you went about accomplishing this task, and respond to the following:

- How was the theme or central idea of "finding light in the darkness" developed in the different Holocaust narratives that you heard about in the panel discussions?

- What did you learn from studying and discussing narratives about the Holocaust that you can apply to your own life?

 Technology Tip

If possible, consider projecting an outline of your panel discussion to provide your audience with an "agenda" to follow.

Presenting Voices of the Holocaust

SCORING GUIDE

Scoring Criteria	Exemplary	Proficient	Emerging	Incomplete
Ideas	The discussion • includes an effective oral reading of a significant text passage • presents a variety of significant ideas to explain how literary elements contribute to the development of a theme • provides relevant elaboration to develop the topic, including textual evidence, details, commentary, and questions.	The discussion • includes an oral reading of a text passage • presents adequate ideas to explain how literary elements in a narrative contribute to the development of a theme • provides sufficient elaboration to develop the topic, including textual evidence, details, commentary, and questions.	The discussion • includes an ineffective passage or reading of a passage • presents unfocused or undeveloped ideas to explain how literary elements in a narrative contribute to the development of a theme • provides insufficient or weak elaboration to develop the topic.	The discussion • does not include an oral reading of a passage • does not explain how literary elements in a narrative contribute to the development of a theme • provides minimal or irrelevant elaboration.
Structure	The discussion • demonstrates strong evidence of effective collaboration and preparation • follows a logical and smooth organizational structure • uses transitional strategies effectively and purposefully.	The discussion • demonstrates sufficient evidence of collaboration and preparation • follows an adequate organizational structure • uses transitional strategies to create cohesion and clarify relationships.	The discussion • demonstrates insufficient evidence of collaboration and preparation • follows an uneven or ineffective organizational structure • uses transitional strategies inconsistently.	The discussion • demonstrates little or no collaboration and/or preparation • lacks any obvious organizational structure • does not use transitional strategies.
Use of Language	The speaker • communicates effectively with group members and the audience • uses consistently precise diction and academic language • demonstrates deep command of the conventions of standard English grammar, usage, and language (including active/passive voice).	The speaker • communicates appropriately with group members and the audience • uses sufficiently precise diction and academic language • demonstrates adequate command of the conventions of standard English grammar, usage, and language (including active/passive voice).	The speaker • communicates inappropriately or inconsistently with group members and/or the audience • uses insufficiently precise diction and academic language • demonstrates partial command of the conventions of standard English grammar, usage, and language.	The speaker • does not communicate well with the group or audience • uses flawed, confusing, or basic diction and language • has frequent errors in standard English grammar, usage, and language.

Previewing Embedded Assessment 2 and Looking at Multimedia

Learning Targets

- Reflect on and make connections between the lessons of the Holocaust and "taking action."
- Analyze the skills and knowledge needed to complete Embedded Assessment 2 successfully.

Making Connections

During your study of narratives of the Holocaust, you were asked to think about the concept of "finding the light in the darkness." This idea is developed further in the last half of the unit by building on the idea of people taking action to create positive change in their communities and the world.

Essential Questions

Reflect on your understanding of the relationship between the first Essential Question (*Why is it important to learn about the Holocaust?*) and the second Essential Question (*How can one person make a difference?*).

Developing Vocabulary

Return to the **Academic Vocabulary** and **Literary Terms** at the beginning of the unit. Using the QHT strategy, re-sort the words based on your new learning.

1. Compare this sort with your original sort. How has your understanding changed?

2. Select a word from the chart (or a Holocaust-related term) and write a concise statement about your learning. How has your understanding of this word changed over the course of this unit?

Unpacking Embedded Assessment 2

Closely read the Embedded Assessment 2 assignment and the Scoring Guide.

> Develop a multimedia presentation that informs your peers about an issue of national or global significance and convinces them to take action. Work collaboratively to conduct and synthesize research into an engaging campaign that challenges your audience to make a difference.

Work with your class to paraphrase the expectations and create a graphic organizer to use as a visual reminder of the required concepts (what you need to know) and skills (what you need to do).

After each activity, use this graphic organizer to guide reflection about what you have learned and what you still need to learn in order to be successful in the Embedded Assessment.

LEARNING STRATEGIES:
QHT, Close Reading, Paraphrasing, Graphic Organizer

My Notes

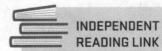

INDEPENDENT READING LINK

To support your learning in the second half of the unit, select a fiction or nonfiction narrative about someone who made a difference in the world or who tried to confront social injustice.

3. How would you define *multimedia*? Think of the meanings of each part of the word: *multi-* and *media*. What is the connection between the words *medium* and *media*?

4. Work with a partner to create a web showing the different types of media that you use.

Media

5. Explain how you use the different types of media and for what purposes.

Learning Targets

- Analyze imagery and slogans in public service announcements for purpose and effect.

- Evaluate how diverse media enhance presentations of information.

LEARNING STRATEGIES:
Discussion Groups

Communicating with Visuals

1. How effective are visuals in making a point about a significant issue? How do they compare with other media channels: speeches, articles, videos, radio announcements, and so on?

ACADEMIC VOCABULARY
A **slogan** is a memorable phrase or motto used to identify or promote a product or group.

2. Look at the two images below. Each is intended as a "call to action" as part of a public service campaign to make a difference. Examine each of the visuals and determine its purpose. Note also that each image has text, including a **slogan**. How does a slogan help promote a goal?

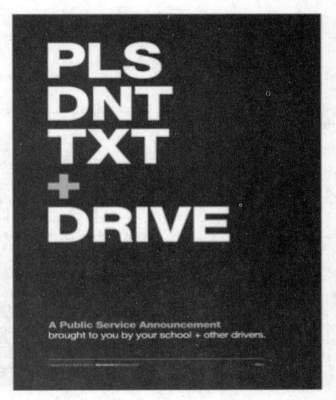

3. Evaluate the effectiveness of the imagery and the slogan. Each image is associated with a website. What can you tell about the sponsors of the visuals by their Web addresses? In groups, explore the websites and find other images, text, and perhaps video associated with the campaigns.

4. In addition to the websites above, explore the following government site, which has PSA (public service announcement) images and videos: https://www.dhs.gov/see-something-say-something. As you explore each website, analyze the purpose of the information presented. In your groups, discuss and evaluate the purpose or purposes of the information. Is it presented for social, commercial, public safety, or political purposes?

Making a Difference

5. Choose a recorder to capture the insights and conclusions of your group discussion.

Poster	Visit the website and take notes about the images, slogans, and additional media formats present. Describe how the purpose is helped by the format.	Why has this visual been created? Is it for social, commercial, public safety, or political purposes?
1	http://www.nature.org/photosmultimedia/psas/index.htm	
2	https://www.dhs.gov/see-something-say-something	
3	Search wfp.org	

6. **Quickwrite:** What kind of music would you combine with these campaigns to make them memorable?

My Notes

Language and Writer's Craft: Reviewing Participial Phrases

The **participle** forms of verbs can be used as adjectives. There are two participial forms: present (ending in -*ing*) and past (usually ending in -*d* or -*ed*).

> **rising** world concerns
>
> widely **used** mediums

A participle may be part of a participial phrase, which includes the participle plus any complements and modifiers. The whole phrase serves as an adjective.

> **Located 275 miles north of San Francisco,** Arcata is . . .

PRACTICE In your Reader/Writer Notebook, write one sentence using a participle and one sentence using a participial phrase.

Check Your Understanding

Find or create a paper advertisement for a cause you care about. Include a simple illustration and slogan. In small groups, evaluate the advertisements.

Explanatory Writing Prompt

Write a paragraph explaining a cause you believe in, why you support it, and the imagery and slogans you think would draw people to your cause. Be sure to:

• Include an opening statement that introduces your cause and why you support it.

• Provide clear descriptions of how you would advertise your cause.

• Explain why the images and slogans will help draw people to the cause.

Never Forget, Never Again

Learning Targets
- Analyze the purpose, audience, and tone of a speech.
- Analyze a speech for the elements of argumentation.

Preview
In this activity, you will read a speech by Elie Wiesel and think about its audience and tone.

Setting a Purpose for Reading
- As you read the speech, underline words and phrases that help set the tone of the speech.
- Circle unknown words and phrases. Try to determine the meaning of the words by using context clues, word parts, or a dictionary.

ABOUT THE AUTHOR
Elie Wiesel (1928–2016) was a Holocaust survivor. Taken to a concentration camp in Poland at age 15, Wiesel endured great hardships, including the death of his mother, his sister, and eventually his father, who died just after being released. Wiesel's experiences led him to spend his life writing books and working to end intolerance and injustice around the world. This life mission earned him a Nobel Peace Prize.

Speech

from The Nobel Acceptance Speech Delivered by Elie Wiesel
in Oslo on December 10, 1986

1 I am moved, deeply moved by your words, Chairman Aarvik. And it is with a profound sense of **humility** that I accept the honor—the highest there is—that you have chosen to bestow upon me. I know your choice transcends my person.

2 Do I have the right to represent the multitudes who have perished? Do I have the right to accept this great honor on their behalf? I do not. No one may speak for the dead, no one may interpret their **mutilated** dreams and visions. And yet, I sense their presence. I always do—and at this moment more than ever. The presence of my parents, that of my little sister. The presence of my teachers, my friends, my companions …

3 This honor belongs to all the survivors and their children and, through us, to the Jewish people with whose destiny I have always identified.

4 I remember: it happened yesterday, or eternities ago. A young Jewish boy discovered the Kingdom of Night. I remember his bewilderment, I remember his **anguish**. It all happened so fast. The ghetto. The **deportation**. The sealed cattle car. The fiery altar upon which the history of our people and the future of mankind were meant to be sacrificed.

5 I remember he asked his father: "Can this be true? This is the twentieth century, not the Middle Ages. Who would allow such crimes to be committed? How could the world remain silent?"

LEARNING STRATEGIES:
SOAPSTone, Close Reading, Discussion Groups, Drafting, Rehearsal, Oral Reading

My Notes

WORD CONNECTIONS
Etymology
The word *deportation* derives from an Old French word meaning "to carry off." When first used, it referred to the way a person behaved or acted. In the 1640s people began using it to mean "banishment."

humility: modesty
mutilated: damaged beyond repair
anguish: agonizing pain
deportation: removal to another country

Never Forget, Never Again

6 And now the boy is turning to me. "Tell me," he asks, "what have you done with my future, what have you done with your life?" And I tell him that I have tried. That I have tried to keep memory alive, that I have tried to fight those who would forget. Because if we forget, we are guilty, we are accomplices.

7 And then I explain to him how **naïve** we were, that the world did know and remained silent. And that is why I swore never to be silent whenever wherever human beings endure suffering and humiliation. We must take sides. Neutrality helps the oppressor, never the victim. Silence encourages the tormentor, never the tormented. Sometimes we must interfere. When human lives are endangered, when human dignity is in **jeopardy**, national borders and sensitivities become irrelevant. Wherever men and women are persecuted because of their race, religion, or political views, that place must—at that moment—become the center of the universe.

8 There is so much injustice and suffering crying out for our attention: victims of hunger, of racism and political persecution—in Chile, for instance, or in Ethiopia— writers and poets, prisoners in so many lands governed by the Left and by the Right.

9 Human rights are being violated on every continent. More people are oppressed than free. How can one not be sensitive to their plight? Human suffering anywhere concerns men and women everywhere.

10 There is so much to be done, there is so much that can be done. One person—a Raoul Wallenberg, an Albert Schweitzer, Martin Luther King, Jr.—one person of **integrity**, can make a difference, a difference of life and death. As long as one **dissident** is in prison, our freedom will not be true. As long as one child is hungry, our life will be filled with anguish and shame. What all these victims need above all is to know that they are not alone; that we are not forgetting them, that when their voices are stifled we shall lend them ours, that while their freedom depends on ours, the quality of our freedom depends on theirs.

11 This is what I say to the young Jewish boy wondering what I have done with his years. It is in his name that I speak to you and that I express to you my deepest gratitude as one who has emerged from the Kingdom of Night. We know that every moment is a moment of grace, every hour an offering; not to share them would mean to betray them.

12 Our lives no longer belong to us alone; they belong to all those who need us desperately.

naïve: simple; unsophisticated
jeopardy: peril; danger

integrity: adherence to an ethical code
dissident: one who disagrees

Second Read

- Reread the speech to answer these text-dependent questions.
- Write any additional questions you have about the text in your Reader/Writer Notebook.

1. **Craft and Structure:** What can you infer about the meaning of "bestow" in paragraph 1?

2. **Key Ideas and Details:** In paragraphs 2–5, Elie Wiesel makes reference to or alludes to what central event? Why does he use fragments to evoke the memory?

3. **Craft and Structure:** What does Wiesel mean when he says that human dignity is "in jeopardy" in paragraph 7?

4. **Key Ideas and Details:** Closely examine paragraphs 6 and 7. What is Wiesel saying about memory and silence?

Working from the Text

5. The purpose of "a call to action" is to provide a concluding statement or section that supports the argument by making clear to the audience what the writer or speaker wants them to think or do. How is Wiesel's last sentence a "call to action"?

6. You will be assigned a specific element from the SOAPSTone strategy below. Annotate the speech for this element.

Introducing the Strategy: SOAPSTone

SOAPSTone stands for Speaker, Occasion, Audience, Purpose, Subject, and Tone. It is a reading and writing tool for analyzing the relationship among a writer, his or her purpose, and the target audience of the text. SOAPSTone guides you in asking questions to analyze a text or to plan for writing a composition.

- **Speaker:** The speaker is the voice that tells the story.
- **Occasion:** The occasion is the time and place of the story; it is the context that prompted the writing.
- **Audience:** The audience is the person or persons to whom the piece is directed.
- **Purpose:** The purpose is the reason behind the text or what the writer wants the audience to think as a result of reading the text.
- **Subject:** The subject is the focus of the text.
- **Tone:** Tone is the speaker's attitude toward the subject.

My Notes

Never Forget, Never Again

7. Use your annotations of the speech and take notes on analyzing the argument in a SOAPSTone graphic organizer like the one below. Refer to the Resources section of your book for a SOAPSTone graphic organizer that you can copy and use for your analysis. The questions in the Analysis column below should help guide your analysis of the speech.

Element	Analysis	Textual Evidence
Speaker	Who is the speaker?	
Occasion	What event(s) or situation(s) prompted the creation of this text?	
Audience	Who is the intended audience?	
Purpose	What is the speaker's claim? What is the speaker's reason for creating this text? What is the speaker's call to action?	
Subject	How does the speaker appeal to *logos* (i.e., how does the speaker use facts, examples, statistics, research, and logical reasoning for effect)? How does the speaker use counterclaims or concession and rebuttal? How does the speaker appeal to *pathos* (emotion)?	
Tone	What is the speaker's attitude toward the subject? How does the speaker use connotative diction and/ or imagery to create tone?	

My Notes

_____

_____

_____

_____

_____

_____

_____

_____

_____

_____

Check Your Understanding

Elie Wiesel says that if we forget that injustices are taking place, we become accomplices. How does he support this argument? Do you agree? Discuss with a partner.

Language and Writer's Craft: Reviewing Clauses

A clause is a group of words with both a subject and a verb. Common clauses include adverbial and adjectival clauses.

Adverbial: An adverbial clause is a dependent clause that functions as an adverb. It modifies a verb, adjective, or adverb. The writer can place the adverbial clause in different parts of the sentence, depending on where it best adds to the desired effect. An adverbial clause begins with a subordinating conjunction (such as *if, when, although, because,* or *as*).

> **Example:** "Experience is what you get **when you didn't get what you wanted.**" (Randy Pausch, "The Last Lecture," 2008)

Adjectival: An adjectival clause is a dependent clause that is used as an adjective in a sentence. Since the adjectival clause modifies a noun or pronoun, it cannot be moved around. It should stay close to the word it modifies. An adjectival clause generally begins with a relative pronoun (*that, which, who, whom,* or *whose*).

> **Example:** "He **who can no longer pause to wonder and stand rapt in awe** is as good as dead." (Albert Einstein)

PRACTICE Look over your response to the Explanatory Writing Prompt on page 228. Did you use an adverbial or adjectival clause in your writing? If you did, write it in your Reader/Writer Notebook. If you didn't, add one to your writing.

Writing to Sources: Argument

Write a brief essay arguing for or against this statement by Miles Lehrman, who helped create the Holocaust Museum: "A perpetrator is not the most dangerous enemy. The most dangerous part is the bystander because neutrality always helps the killer." Be sure to:

- Assert a clear claim and address a counterclaim.
- Support your claim using *logos* and/or *ethos* appeals.
- Use adverbial and adjectival clauses effectively.
- Use dashes appropriately to punctuate any abrupt pauses in thought.

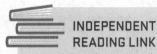

INDEPENDENT READING LINK

Read and Respond

Explain how the subject of your biography or autobiography has chosen an issue and hopes to make a difference in the lives of others who might be suffering.

Students Taking Action

LEARNING STRATEGIES:
Predicting, Marking the Text,
Summarizing, Brainstorming,
Graphic Organizer, Note-taking

ACADEMIC VOCABULARY
Media is the plural of
medium, which is a
means of expression or
communication.

My Notes

Learning Targets
- Evaluate a variety of multimedia campaigns.
- Generate ideas for research in preparation for creating an original campaign.

Preview
In this activity, you will read and evaluate an informational text about taking action.

Setting a Purpose for Reading
- As you read the excerpt, underline words and phrases that are targeted for a youthful audience.
- Circle unknown words and phrases. Try to determine the meaning of the words by using context clues, word parts, or a dictionary.

Informational Text

from
Do Something!
A Handbook for Young Activists

Listen up! You don't have to be a rock star or the president or even have a driver's license to change the world. You can do something important right now—like, before your head hits the pillow tonight—that can make a difference in someone's life, change something for the better, or fix an important problem.

Young people rocking change isn't just possible; it's happening every day. Like the 12-year-old who registered over 10,000 people to donate bone marrow for people with cancer. Or the 7-year-old who taught other kids to swim. Or the 10-year-old who raised $30 by selling lemonade—and it was enough to buy dog food at a shelter for one night. If they can do it, so can you.

▶ Facts About **DoSomething.org** in 2012

1. 2.4 million young people took action through our campaigns in 2012.
2. We have 1,666,208 members doing stuff to improve their communities and the world.
3. Our 977,781 mobile subscribers take action and text us all about it.
4. We gave young people $240,000 in scholarships in 2012.
5. Our members collected 1,020,041 pairs of jeans for homeless youth through our Teens for Jeans campaign.
6. Our members recycled over 1.2 million aluminum cans through our 50 Cans campaign.
7. Our members donated 316,688 books to school libraries through our Epic Book Drive.
8. 67,808 members stood up to bullying through our Bully Text campaign.

WORD CONNECTIONS

Etymology

Campaign comes from a French word meaning "open country," and it referred to military engagement in open fields. It later came to denote any large-scale military operation, and now it is used to refer to any involved pursuit of a goal. You may be familiar with its use in political campaigns and fundraising campaigns.

Second Read

- Reread the excerpt to answer these text-dependent questions.
- Write any additional questions you have about the text in your Reader/Writer Notebook.

1. **Craft and Structure:** How effective is the diction of the piece in appealing to the target audience? Cite examples in your explanation.

Working from the Text

2. Mark the text of the following campaign summaries to identify the what, why, and how of each issue.
   - What is the issue or problem the student wanted to do something about?
   - Why did the student care about this issue?
   - How did the student make a difference?

Student 1: Sarah Cronk **State:** IA **Issue:** Disability Rights

Sarah watched her older brother Charlie struggle to fit in during high school because of his disabilities. He was depressed and anxious, until the captain of the swim team invited him to join. Suddenly the cool kids welcomed him, and he found a new group of friends. Inspired by Charlie, Sarah co-founded the first high school–based inclusive cheerleading squad in the nation. Today, the Sparkle Effect has generated 26 squads in 15 states and South Africa, encouraging a culture of acceptance in every community.

Student 2: Danny Mendoza **State:** CA **Issue:** Foster Care

While in college, Danny learned that his 9-year-old cousin, Roger, was living in a car. After lots of maneuvering, Danny helped him move from the Honda to a house, but he was deeply disturbed by how little control Roger had over his own situation. Danny took action and created Together We Rise, a youth-led organization dedicated to running programs that not only bring a sense of normalcy and stability to children in foster care, but also allow foster children to make their own choices. Through programs like music lessons, mentoring, sports and athletics, résumé building, and job readiness, Together We Rise provides the resources for foster kids to prepare for success at age 18, when they are kicked out of the foster care system and left to fend for themselves. Together, Danny and Together We Rise have reached 3,000 foster care youth through these programs, providing a better opportunity for long-term success.

My Notes

Students Taking Action

GRAMMAR & USAGE

Commas

A comma after an introductory element in a sentence indicates a pause before the main part of the sentence.

Look at these examples:

Introductory participial phrase: **Inspired by Charlie,** . . .

Introductory prepositional phrase: **At age 14,** . . .

Look for introductory elements like these as you read, and note how you pause after them.

Student 3: Jordan Coleman **State:** NJ **Issue:** Education

Jordan was angry when he learned that fewer than half of African American boys graduate from high school. He's an actor, so he decided to make a movie called *Say It Loud* (at age 13) to raise awareness about the importance of education. He toured with the film to spread his message to young people in community centers and schools around the country. He even got to speak at an education rally during the Presidential Inauguration in 2009!

Student 4: Evan Ducker **State:** NY **Issue:** Discrimination

Evan was born with a large birthmark on his face. At age 14, he decided to educate the public about the medical and psychological issues facing kids born with these kinds of birthmarks through his book, *Buddy Booby's Birthmark*, and his annual International *Buddy Booby's Birthmark* Read-Along for Tolerance and Awareness.

3. In the My Notes section, summarize the kinds of kids that are featured and how they have made a difference.

4. Form a personal response to connect to the text by answering these questions:
   - To which student do you most relate? Why?
   - Which student do you most respect? Why?

5. Create a web to brainstorm issues of community, national, and global significance that you are aware of and/or care about.

6. Choose a cause from the website your teacher assigns you to explore as a group.
   Our Cause:

7. Have each person in your group focus on a different issue related to your cause. For example, if your cause is "Animals," you can have one person research animal testing, another animal cruelty, and a third animal homelessness. (You will find links to different issues under each cause.)

My Issue:
- Complete the first row of the graphic organizer on the next page by taking notes on the what, why, and how of your issue. Add your own ideas as well as the ones you find on the website.
- Present your issue to your group members. As group members present their issues, take notes in the graphic organizer.

My Notes

_____

_____

_____

_____

_____

_____

_____

_____

_____

WORD
CONNECTIONS

Word Relationships

Cause and *issue* are two related words. *Cause* is used to refer to an often broad area of concern that needs to be addressed. An *issue* refers to a specific item under that cause. For example, global warming, overpopulation, and pollution are all issues within the cause of helping the environment.

8. Reflect on your research: Is there an issue that stands out to your group as a potential subject for your multimedia campaign? If so, where can you find more information about it?

Graphic Organizer

WHAT is the issue or problem?	WHY should you care?	HOW can you make a difference?
List informative and compelling facts.	Record appeals to *logos*, *pathos*, and *ethos*.	Record a clear and reasonable call to action.
Issue: _____		
Issue: _____		
Issue: _____		

Our cause:

Check Your Understanding

Brainstorm a list of causes or organizations you support and would like to volunteer with. Work in small groups to gather more information about some of these volunteer opportunities.

My Notes

_____

_____

_____

_____

_____

From Vision to Action

WORD CONNECTIONS

Content Connections

Deforestation and *desertification* are terms learned in both social studies and science. *Deforestation* is the large scale removal of trees and forest. *Desertification* is the transformation of habitable land to desert. Desertification sometimes happens after an area has been deforested.

My Notes

_____
_____
_____
_____
_____

curtail: to cut short
devastating: highly destructive
erosion: the process of wearing away

_____
_____
_____
_____
_____

Learning Targets

- Analyze informational texts about efforts that have made a difference on a global scale.
- Create a Web page to represent a campaign to make a difference.

Preview

In this activity, you will read about two ways that people can make a difference in the world. Then you will think about how you can make a difference for an issue you care about.

Setting a Purpose for Reading

- As you read the informational texts, underline verbs that describe what the activists are doing, or trying to do, to solve a problem.
- Circle unknown words and phrases. Try to determine the meaning of the words by using context clues, word parts, or a dictionary.

Informational Text

Wangari Maathai

Wangari Maathai rose to prominence fighting for those most easily marginalized in Africa—poor women.

1 The first African woman to win the Nobel Peace Prize (2004) was praised by the awarding committee as "a source of inspiration for everyone in Africa fighting for sustainable development, democracy and peace."

2 A pioneering academic, her role as an environmental campaigner began after she planted some trees in her back garden.

3 This inspired her in 1977 to form an organization—primarily of women—known as the Green Belt Movement aiming to **curtail** the **devastating** effects of deforestation and desertification.

4 Her desire was to produce sustainable wood for fuel use as well as combating soil **erosion**.

5 Her campaign to mobilize poor women to plant some 30 million trees has been copied by other countries.

6 Speaking as recently as Wednesday on the BBC's Africa Live program, she said her tree planting campaign was not at all popular when it first began.

7 "It took me a lot of days and nights to convince people that women could improve their environment without much technology or without much financial resources."

8 The Green Belt Movement went on to campaign on education, nutrition, and other issues important to women.

Political role

9 Mrs. Maathai has been arrested several times for campaigning against deforestation in Africa.

10 In the late 1980s, she became a prominent opponent of a skyscraper planned for the middle of the Kenyan capital's main park—Uhuru Park.

11 She was **vilified** by Kenyan President Daniel arap Moi's government but succeeded in **thwarting** the plans.

12 More recently, she evolved into a leading campaigner on social matters.

13 Once she was beaten unconscious by heavy-handed police. On another occasion she led a demonstration of naked women.

14 In 1997, she ran for president against Mr. Moi but made little impact.

Esteem

15 But in elections in 2002, she was elected as MP with 98% of the votes as part of an opposition **coalition** which swept to power after Mr. Moi stepped down.

16 She was appointed as a deputy environment minister in 2003.

17 Mrs. Maathai says she usually uses a biblical analogy of creation to stress the importance of the environment.

18 "God created the planet from Monday to Friday. On Saturday he created human beings.

19 "The truth of the matter is … if man was created on Tuesday, I usually say, he would have been dead on Wednesday, because there would not have been the essential elements that he needs to survive," she told the BBC.

20 The Nobel Peace Prize committee praised her for taking "a **holistic** approach to **sustainable** development that embraces democracy, human rights and women's rights in particular."

21 She thinks globally and acts locally, they said.

22 She was born in 1940 and has three children.

23 Her former husband, whom she divorced in the 1980s, was said to have remarked that she was "too educated, too strong, too successful, too stubborn and too hard to control."

My Notes

vilified: subjected to vicious statements
thwarting: preventing

coalition: an alliance of people or groups

holistic: emphasizing the whole of something, as opposed to its parts
sustainable: able to be maintained

From Vision to Action

My Notes

Informational Text

About Freerice.com

1 Freerice is a nonprofit website that is owned by and supports the United Nations World Food Programme. Freerice has two goals:

- Provide education to everyone for free.

- Help end world hunger by providing rice to hungry people for free.

2 Whether you are CEO of a large corporation or a street child in a poor country, improving your education can improve your life. It is a great investment in yourself.

3 Perhaps even greater is the investment your donated rice makes in hungry human beings, enabling them to function and be productive. Somewhere in the world, a person is eating rice that you helped provide.

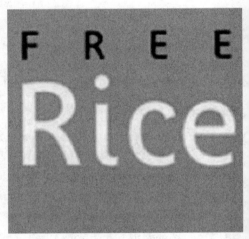

Informational Text

Free Rice Online Quiz Game

4 Freerice is an online internet game that donates 20 grains of rice to the World Food Programme (WFP) for every word that is correctly defined. WFP, the United Nations frontline organization fighting hunger, distributes the rice to the hungry. WFP uses the donations from the site to purchase rice locally, both feeding people in need and **stimulating** local economies.

5 Already, the site has raised enough rice to feed over 1.5 million people for a day. The game has been embraced by young and old alike, proving to be an excellent tool for prepping for the SATs or to brush up on vocabulary words. Teachers have been using the game to teach both vocabulary and the value of helping others in need.

stimulating: causing increased activity in

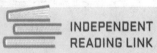

INDEPENDENT READING LINK

Read and Respond

Think about the cause or issue that the person is fighting for in your independent reading book. What personal, political, or social connections exist between that cause or issue and the person?

Second Read

- Reread the informational texts to answer these text-dependent questions.
- Write any additional questions you have about the text in your Reader/Writer Notebook.

1. **Key Ideas and Details:** What were some of the obstacles Wangari Maathai struggled against in creating and campaigning for the Green Belt Movement?

2. **Key Ideas and Details:** Why do you think the Nobel Peace Prize committee praised Wangari Maathai for thinking globally and acting locally?

3. **Key Ideas and Details:** How does the game on freerice.com achieve its two goals?

Working from the Text

4. What is the meaning of the slogan "Think Globally, Act Locally"?

5. Wangari Maathai and Freerice.com each made a difference on a global scale by organizing their goals around a specific mission and taking action. Use the chart on the next page to evaluate different elements from the homepages of their websites.

My Notes

From Vision to Action

My comments:	Wangari Maathai	World Food Programme
Organization Name	The Green Belt Movement	World Food Programme Freerice
Logo		
Slogan		
Mission Statement		
Call to Action		

Check Your Understanding

Create a small newspaper advertisement for FreeRice.com. Include facts about the program as well as a slogan in the advertisement. Share your advertisement with a partner.

Learning Targets

- Identify and explain how specific media types appeal to different target audiences.
- Evaluate the effectiveness of specific elements of multimedia campaigns.
- Create a visual that shows how to use persuasive appeals in different types of media to convince a target audience to take action.

Preview

In this activity, you will read about multimedia campaigns and think about how to create your own.

Setting a Purpose for Reading

- As you read the informational text, underline words and phrases that describe what public service announcements (PSAs) are like.
- Circle unknown words and phrases. Try to determine the meaning of the words by using context clues, word parts, or a dictionary.

LEARNING STRATEGIES:
Graphic Organizer, Note-taking, Discussion Groups, Sketching

WORD CONNECTIONS

Word Relationships

You can see that *commercial* derives from the word *commerce*, which is the buying and selling of goods. As a noun a *commercial* refers to an advertisement on television or radio. As an adjective, it describes a business or enterprise where the main goal is to make money and earn profits.

Informational Text

Public Service Announcements

1 Broadcast media—radio and television—are required by the Federal Communications Commission (FCC) to serve "in the public interest." Most stations use PSAs as one of the ways they meet this requirement. While they aren't required to donate a fixed percentage of air time per day to PSAs, stations do have to state in their licensing and renewal applications how much air time they plan to devote to PSAs. Most stations donate about a third of their commercial spots to non-commercial causes; in other words, if a station has 18 minutes of commercials in a given hour, six minutes of that will probably be devoted to PSAs.

2 Public service announcements, or PSAs, are short messages produced on film, videotape, DVD, CD, audiotape, or as a computer file and given to radio and television stations. Generally, PSAs are sent as ready-to-air audio or video tapes, although radio stations sometimes prefer a script that their announcers can read live on the air.

3 Since World War II, public service announcements (PSAs) have informed and attempted to persuade the public about a variety of issues.

4 If people find an ad or PSA entertaining enough, they might talk about it with a friend or share it online. When this happens, many more people will receive the intended message.

Second Read

- Reread the informational text to answer these text-dependent questions.
- Write any additional questions you have about the text in your Reader/Writer Notebook.

My Notes

_____

_____

_____

_____

_____

_____

INDEPENDENT READING LINK

Read and Discuss

Suppose you were to help the subject of your independent reading narrative make a PSA to promote his or her cause. Discuss with a classmate who the target audience of the PSA would be. What words or phrases would you use to appeal to that audience?

Examining Media Campaigns

_____
_____
_____
_____
_____
_____
_____
_____
_____
_____
_____
_____
_____
_____

1. **Key Ideas and Details:** What evidence in this text suggests that public service announcements are not intended for commercial purposes?

Working from the Text

2. Brainstorm types of media you could use to raise awareness and encourage action about an issue of national or global significance.

3. What is meant by a target audience? How does audience affect how an argument is developed and presented?

4. Research examples of public service announcements and campaigns. You might use the Internet, listen to radio, watch television, or look at newspaper or magazine ads to find examples. Find at least three examples that appeal to you, and **evaluate** them for the clarity of their messages, use of visuals and multimedia elements, and effectiveness.

Description of PSA	Clarity of Message	Use of Visuals/ Multimedia Elements	Effectiveness
Name: Purpose: Audience: Content:			
Name: Purpose: Audience: Content:			
Name: Purpose: Audience: Content:			

5. Analyze the campaigns' use of persuasive appeals for effect. How did each campaign use *pathos*, *ethos*, and *logos* to convince the target audience to take action? Give examples from your research. For a quick review of persuasive appeals, see Activity 2.12.

Pathos:

Ethos:

Logos:

6. Of the different media and appeals used, which would you use in your own multimedia campaign? Who is your target audience? Which type of media would appeal to them? What type of ads would you create (magazine, newspaper, poster, billboard, Web banner), and where would you put them in order to reach your target audience?

7. Choose one of the public service campaigns you researched and identify the types of media it uses to get the word out. For each type of media used, analyze the persuasive appeals for effect. Do the various ads appeal to *pathos, ethos,* or *logos*? Are these appeals effective?

Public Service Announcement Campaign:

Sponsor Organization:

Volunteer Agency:

Type of Media	Target Audience	Types of Appeals Used/ Effectiveness

8. Revisit the target audiences and types of media you are considering for your campaign. How can you use persuasive appeals in different types of media to convince your target audience to take action? Sketch a visual to show your thinking. Think about these guidelines for creating a PSA:

- Aim for a sticky slogan.
- Use one powerful image.
- Use one shocking statistic.
- Search for images by idea or create your own images.
- Include a "Credits" slide for images as well as content. Document with this text: "This image is used under a CC license from [insert URL for image]."

Check Your Understanding

Quickwrite: Briefly write about two commercials—one that you think positively influences people and one that you think negatively influences people. Why do you think commercials have these effects on viewers?

Raising Awareness

pic

LEARNING STRATEGIES:
Diffusing, Graphic Organizer, Note-taking, Collaborative Discussion

My Notes

WORD CONNECTIONS

Content Connections

Neuroblastoma is a tumor that affects young children. It commonly begins in the abdomen and develops from tissues in the part of the nervous system that controls body functions.

GRAMMAR & USAGE
Verb Tenses

The present progressive verb tense describes an ongoing action that is happening at the same time the statement is written. This tense is formed by using *am*, *is*, or *are* with the verb form ending in *-ing*. For example, look at the first sentence in paragraph 10: "In McFarland . . . **are being reported** . . ." The words "are being reported" show that the action is happening as the writer is writing. Look for another example of present progressive verb tense in the text.

Learning Target
• Evaluate the effectiveness of arguments in print texts.

Preview
In this activity, you will read part of a speech and think about how to make an argument effectively.

Setting a Purpose for Reading
• As you read the speech, mark with *L* words and phrases that use *logos* (facts) to support the argument, and mark with *P* words and phrases that use *pathos* (emotion).
• Circle unknown words and phrases. Try to determine the meaning of the words by using context clues, word parts, or a dictionary.

ABOUT THE AUTHOR
Cesar Chavez (1927–1993) was born in Yuma, Arizona, to a family that worked as migrant farm workers. As a migrant worker himself in 1962, he founded the National Farm Workers Association (NFWA). This group led strikes throughout California against agricultural businesses, including grape growers and lettuce growers. The NFWA changed its name to the United Farm Workers of America, and Chavez continued to campaign for fair labor practices and worker safety with nonviolent protests. A year after his death, Chavez was awarded the Presidential Medal of Freedom.

Speech

ADDRESS BY
CAESAR CHAVEZ,
PRESIDENT, UNITED FARM WORKERS OF AMERICA, AFL-CIO

Pacific Lutheran University
March 1989, Tacoma, Washington

1 What is the worth of a man or a woman? What is the worth of a farm worker? How do you measure the value of a life?

2 Ask the parents of Johnnie Rodriguez.

3 Johnnie Rodriguez was not even a man; Johnnie was a five year old boy when he died after a painful two year battle against cancer.

4 His parents, Juan and Elia, are farm workers. Like all grape workers, they are exposed to pesticides and other agricultural chemicals. Elia worked in the table grapes around Delano, California until she was eight months pregnant with Johnnie.

5 Juan and Elia cannot say for certain if pesticides caused their son's cancer. But neuroblastoma is one of the cancers found in McFarland, a small farm town only a few miles from Delano, where the Rodriguezes live.

6 "Pesticides are always in the fields and around the towns," Johnnie's father told us. "The children get the chemicals when they play outside, drink the water or when they hug you after you come home from working in fields that are sprayed.

7 "Once your son has cancer, it's pretty hard to take," Juan Rodriguez says. "You hope it's a mistake, you pray. He was a real nice boy. He took it strong and lived as long as he could."

8 I keep a picture of Johnnie Rodriguez. He is sitting on his bed, hugging his Teddy bears. His sad eyes and cherubic face stare out at you. The photo was taken four days before he died.

9 Johnnie Rodriguez was one of 13 McFarland children diagnosed with cancer in recent years; and one of six who have died from the disease. With only 6,000 residents, the rate of cancer in McFarland is 400 percent above normal.

10 In McFarland and in Fowler childhood cancer cases are being reported in excess of expected rates. In Delano and other farming towns, questions are also being raised.

11 The chief source of **carcinogens** in these communities are **pesticides** from the vineyards and fields that encircle them. Health experts believe the high rate of cancer in McFarland is from pesticides and nitrate-containing fertilizers **leaching** into the water system from surrounding fields.

****

12 Farm workers and their families are exposed to pesticides from the crops they work. The soil the crops are grown in. Drift from sprays applied to adjoining fields— and often to the very field where they are working.

13 The fields that surround their homes are heavily and repeatedly sprayed. Pesticides pollute irrigation water and groundwater.

14 Children are still a big part of the labor force. Or they are taken to the fields by their parents because there is no child care.

15 Pregnant women labor in the fields to help support their families. **Toxic** exposure begins at a very young age—often in the womb.

16 What does acute pesticide poisoning produce?

17 Eye and respiratory irritations. Skin rashes. Systemic poisoning.

18 Death.

19 What are the chronic effects of pesticide poisoning on people, including farm workers and their children, according to scientific studies?

20 Birth defects. Sterility. Still births. Miscarriages. Neurological and neuropsychological effects. Effects on child growth and development.

21 Cancer.

22 Do we feel deeply enough the pain of those who must work in the fields every day with these poisons? Or the anguish of the families that have lost loved ones to cancer? Or the heartache of the parents who fear for the lives of their children? Who are raising children with deformities? Who agonize the outcome of their pregnancies?

My Notes

carcinogen: a substance that causes cancer
pesticides: chemicals used to kill insects
leaching: draining
toxic: poisonous

GRAMMAR & USAGE
Sentence Fragments

In almost all cases, incomplete sentences are not proper grammar in the English language. There are instances, however, where they can be used for effect. For example, look at paragraphs 17 and 18. The elements in these paragraphs are sentence fragments because they have no verbs. The writer used these sentence fragments for effect. By following the question about the effects of pesticide with sentence fragments, the author emphasizes each danger more than it would be in a regular sentence separated by commas. Find more sentence fragments in the speech. Notice what effect they create.

Raising Awareness

plague: a highly fatal epidemic affliction

wanton: immoral and excessive

23 Who ask in fear, 'where will this deadly **plague** strike next?'

24 Do we feel their pain deeply enough?

25 I didn't. And I was ashamed.

26 I studied this **wanton** abuse of nature. I read the literature, heard from the experts about what pesticides do to our land and our food.

27 I talked with farm workers, listened to their families, and shared their anguish and their fears. I spoke out against the cycle of death.

28 But sometimes words come too cheaply. And their meaning is lost in the clutter that so often fills our lives.

29 That is why, in July and August of last year, I embarked on a 36-day unconditional, water-only fast.

30 The fast was first and foremost directed at myself. It was something I felt compelled to do to purify my own body, mind and soul.

31 The fast was an act of penance for our own members who, out of ignorance or need, cooperate with those who grow and sell food treated with toxins.

32 The fast was also for those who know what is right and just. It pains me that we continue to shop without protest at stores that offer grapes; that we eat in restaurants that display them; that we are too patient and understanding with those who serve them to us.

33 The fast, then, was for those who know that they could or should do more—for those who, by not acting, become bystanders in the poisoning of our food and the people who produce it.

34 The fast was, finally, a declaration of noncooperation with supermarkets that promote, sell, and profit from California table grapes. They are as culpable as those who manufacture the poisons and those who use them.

35 It is my hope that our friends everywhere will resist in many nonviolent ways the presence of grapes in the stores where they shop.

Second Read

- Reread the speech to answer these text-dependent questions.
- Write any additional questions you have about the text in your Reader/Writer Notebook.

1. **Craft and Structure:** What can you predict about this article given the opening question of the speech? Is the question intended to appeal to *logos*, *pathos*, or *ethos*? Explain.

2. **Key Ideas and Details:** The speaker opens his speech with an anecdote. What kind of persuasive appeal is he using and what effect does it have?

3. **Key Ideas and Details:** What is the claim Cesar Chavez is making?

4. **Key Ideas and Details:** Summarize the logic of Chavez's argument about the relationship between human health and pesticides. How has the author depended on logical reasoning and relevant evidence (*logos*)?

5. **Key Ideas and Details:** How does Cesar Chavez satisfy the call to action part of the argument he is making?

Working from the Text

6. Who is the article's target audience? How do you know?

7. Based on the target audience, use your analysis to evaluate each element of the authors' argument.

8. Overall, is the argument effective? Why or why not?

My Notes

INDEPENDENT READING LINK

Read and Research

Go online to research another person who supported the same cause as the person in your independent reading narrative. How were their actions similar or different than your subject's?

Raising Awareness

9. Find an online site (probably a site that ends in ".org") that advocates for the use of safe pesticides and the protection of the environment, for instance: http://www.beyondpesticides.org/. Use the organizer below to take notes on the website you find and the elements of a multimedia campaign to create change.

Logos Facts used to help me understand the issue.	**Pathos** Images used to create emotion and to convince me to act.

Check Your Understanding

Quickwrite: How does the text use *ethos* to raise awareness of the use of pesticides in farming? How can you use *ethos* in your own multimedia campaign?

 Independent Reading Checkpoint

You are going to participate in book talks in small groups to share insights into the narratives you have each read. You should consider the challenge to society presented in your independent reading book and how that challenge was confronted. What did it take for one person to address that challenge, and how was that person successful? How has he or she left a positive impact on our society or on the world?

Language Checkpoint: Understanding Verb Tense

Learning Targets

- Understand how to use appropriate verb tenses in writing.
- Revise writing to correct inappropriate shifts in verb tense.

Understanding Verb Tense

Verbs do more than express action or a state of being: they also tell *when* something happened—in the past, present, or future. The expression of a verb's time is called **verb tense.**

1. Read the following excerpt from Cesar Chavez's speech. Identify each verb.

   What is the worth of a man or a woman? What is the worth of a farm worker? How do you measure the value of a life?

2. With a partner, decide whether the verbs are in the past, present, or future tense. Why do you think Chavez uses this tense?

3. Look at the next passage from Chavez's address. Identify each verb.

   Johnnie Rodriguez was not even a man; Johnnie was a five year old boy when he died after a painful two year battle against cancer.

   His parents, Juan and Elia, are farm workers. Like all grape workers, they are exposed to pesticides and other agricultural chemicals. Elia worked in the table grapes around Delano, California until she was eight months pregnant with Johnnie.

4. With a partner, look at the verbs and identify the verb tense or tenses. What does Chavez's use of verb tense tell you about the actions in this passage?

5. Look at this passage from Chavez's address. Identify the verbs.

   It is my hope that our friends everywhere will resist in many nonviolent ways the presence of grapes in the stores where they shop.

6. With a partner, look at the verbs and identify the tenses. Why do you think Chavez uses these tenses?

7. Look at this passage and underline the verbs.

   In McFarland and in Fowler childhood cancer cases are being reported in excess of expected rates. In Delano and other farming towns, questions are also being raised.

8. What do the verbs tell you about the timing of the action?

Language Checkpoint: Understanding Verb Tense

Inappropriate Verb Tense Shifts

Chavez changes his verb tense throughout his address, sometimes even within the same sentence. He uses a variety of tenses to narrate details about events that have happened in the past, to describe realities of the moment, and to express his wishes for the future. Using a variety of tenses as Chavez does can be a powerful rhetorical tool. But switching tenses unintentionally can make writing unclear. In your writing, use tenses consistently unless you have a good reason to switch them.

9. Read the following sentences about Chavez's speech. Underline the verbs that incorrectly shift in tense. Write each sentence correctly in the space provided, and underline the correction you made.

   a. During his talk at Pacific Lutheran University, Chavez was speaking about the difficult lives of farmworkers, and he asks the audience, "Do we feel their pain deeply enough?"

   b. Chavez fought for the rights of farmworkers because he believes in the value of every human life.

   c. Just because people who pick crops do not have as much money as other people, and some of them can't afford the same healthcare, it doesn't mean their lives had less value.

Revising

Read the following paragraph from a student's essay about Cesar Chavez's address. Work with a partner to check whether the verbs maintain an appropriate and consistent tense. Circle any mistakes you notice, and then mark the text to correct the mistakes.

[1] Cesar Chavez is the President of the United Farm Workers of America. [2] He was speaking to a group of people at a university when he tells the story of Johnnie Rodriguez, a young boy who is dying of cancer. [3] There were so many people dying of cancer in McFarland that Chavez says the disease must be linked to the pesticides the farmers use. [4] For instance, Johnnie's mother picked grapes while she was pregnant with Johnnie, so Chavez believes the pesticides must be the cause of his illness. [5] Chavez decides that he must fight the unjust treatment of farm workers.

Check Your Understanding

Imagine you are editing a classmate's writing, and you notice incorrect shifts in verb tense. In your own words, write an explanation to help your classmate understand the mistakes and how to correct them. Then add an item to your Editor's Checklist to help you remember how to revise your writing to correct inappropriate shifts in verb tense.

Practice

Using what you have learned about verb tense, write an introductory paragraph to an essay about Cesar Chavez. The claim should address whether Cesar Chavez's argument for workers' rights is effective. Trade your work with a partner to:

- Underline verbs.
- Make sure your verbs are in appropriate tenses.
- Ensure that you do not shift verb tenses unnecessarily.

Presenting a Multimedia Campaign

ASSIGNMENT

Develop a multimedia presentation that informs your peers about an issue of national or global significance and convinces them to take action. Work collaboratively to conduct and synthesize research into an engaging campaign that challenges your audience to make a difference.

Planning and Researching: Collaborate with a group of peers to select and gather information on an issue for your campaign.	▥ Which of the issues from the list your class has developed are of interest to you? ▥ Where could you look online to find out about more issues of national or global significance? ▥ How will you evaluate the credibility and timeliness of sources? ▥ How will you investigate what others are doing about your issue in order to evaluate possible solutions to incorporate into your call to action? ▥ How will you give credit for information found in your sources and prepare a Works Cited page or an Annotated Bibliography?
Drafting: Collaborate with your group to design a multimedia campaign.	▥ How will you use rhetorical appeals (*pathos*, *logos*, and *ethos*) to persuade your audience to care? ▥ How can you raise awareness by informing your peers about compelling facts related to your issue? ▥ What will be your group's name, mission statement, logo, and/or slogan? ▥ What media channels will you use in your presentation, such as presentation tools, audio/visual components, social media, or others? ▥ How will you organize talking points to inform your audience about the issue, convince them to care, and provide a call to action (what, why, and how)?
Rehearsing and Presenting: Use effective speaking and listening to prepare, present, and observe.	▥ How can you use feedback from a dress rehearsal to improve your presentation? ▥ How will you use the scoring guide to provide feedback on your own and others' presentations? ▥ How will you listen and take notes on the what, why, and how of each multimedia presentation?

Reflection

After completing this Embedded Assessment, think about how you went about accomplishing this task, and respond to the following:

- Which presentations were effective in convincing you to care about the issue, and why?

- What were the most effective media channels you observed, and what were the strengths of each?

📶 Technology Tip

Using a presentation tool such as Prezi or PowerPoint can help organize your presentation, but be careful to focus on your audience instead of the screen. Using note cards can help you maintain eye contact instead of reading directly from your slides.

Presenting a Multimedia Campaign

SCORING GUIDE

Scoring Criteria	Exemplary	Proficient	Emerging	Incomplete
Ideas	The presentation • supports a clear claim and addresses counterclaim(s) with relevant reasons and evidence from a variety of accurate sources • uses persuasive appeals effectively • integrates engaging multimedia and campaign features to clarify ideas.	The presentation • supports a claim and addresses counterclaim(s) with sufficient reasons and evidence from reliable sources • uses persuasive appeals (*logos*, *pathos*, and *ethos*) • includes adequate multimedia and campaign features to clarify ideas.	The presentation • has an unclear or unsupported claim, addresses counterclaim(s) ineffectively, and/or uses research from insufficient or unreliable sources • uses persuasive appeals unevenly • includes inadequate multimedia and campaign features.	The presentation • has no claim or counterclaim, and/or shows little or no evidence of research • does not use persuasive appeals • lacks multimedia or campaign features.
Structure	The presentation • demonstrates extensive evidence of collaboration and preparation • has an introduction that engages and informs the audience • sequences ideas and quotations smoothly with transitions • concludes with a clear call to action.	The presentation • demonstrates adequate evidence of collaboration and preparation • has an introduction that informs and orients the audience • sequences ideas and embeds quotations with transitions • includes a conclusion with a call to action.	The presentation • demonstrates insufficient or uneven collaboration and/or preparation • has a weak introduction • uses flawed or illogical sequencing; quotations seem disconnected • includes a weak or partial conclusion.	The presentation • demonstrates a failure to collaborate or prepare • lacks an introduction • has little or no evidence of sequencing or transitions • lacks a conclusion.
Use of Language	The speaker • communicates to a target audience with a persuasive tone and precise diction • demonstrates command of the conventions of standard English grammar, usage, and language (including correct mood/voice) • cites and evaluates sources thoroughly in an annotated bibliography.	The speaker • communicates to a target audience with appropriate tone and some precise diction • demonstrates adequate command of the conventions of standard English grammar, usage, and language (including correct mood/voice) • cites and evaluates sources in an annotated bibliography.	The speaker • communicates to a target audience inappropriately; may use basic diction • demonstrates partial command of the conventions of standard English grammar, usage, and language • begins to cite and/or evaluate sources in an annotated bibliography; may use improper format.	The speaker • does not communicate clearly; uses vague or confusing diction • has frequent errors in standard English grammar, usage, and language • lacks an annotated bibliography.

The Challenge of Comedy

Visual Prompt: What makes people laugh?

Unit Overview

If laughter is truly the best medicine, then a study of challenges would not be complete without a close examination of the unique elements of comedy. Overcoming challenges is often easier when we are able to look at the humorous side of life. However, finding humor is not always easy; it can be a challenge in itself. In this unit, you will learn how authors create humor and how they use humor to reveal a universal truth (theme).

The Challenge of Comedy

GOALS:

- To analyze how a variety of authors create humor in print and nonprint texts
- To analyze how humor is used to reveal a universal truth (theme)
- To write a well-developed analysis of a humorous text
- To analyze and perform a scene from a Shakespearean comedy
- To understand verbals and how they are used in writing

ACADEMIC VOCABULARY
juxtaposition
derision
denounce
caricature

Literary Terms
persona
satire
irony
dialect
hyperbole
yarn
alliteration

Contents

Activities:

Texts not included in these materials.

Language and Writer's Craft
- Verbals (4.2)
- Using Verbals (4.4)

MY INDEPENDENT READING LIST

Previewing the Unit

My Notes

Learning Targets

- Preview the big ideas in the unit and make predictions about the topics of study.
- Demonstrate an understanding of the skills and knowledge needed to complete Embedded Assessment 1 successfully.

Making Connections

In the final unit you will encounter the challenging task of appreciating humorous texts and Shakespearean texts. You will use all your collaborative, speaking and listening, reading, and writing skills as you examine the ways in which authors create humor.

Essential Questions

Based on your current knowledge, respond to the following Essential Questions:

1. How do writers and speakers use humor to convey truth?

2. What makes an effective performance of a Shakespearean comedy?

Developing Vocabulary

Use a QHT chart to sort the terms on the Contents page. Remember, one academic goal is to move all words to the "T" column by the end of the unit.

Unpacking Embedded Assessment 1

Closely read the assignment for Embedded Assessment 1.

Write an essay that explains how an author creates humor for effect and uses it to communicate a universal truth.

Then, find the Scoring Guide and work with your class to paraphrase the expectations. Create a graphic organizer to use as a visual reminder of the required concepts (what you need to know) and skills (what you need to do).

After each activity, use this graphic to guide reflection about what you have learned and what you still need to learn in order to be successful in the Embedded Assessment.

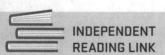

INDEPENDENT READING LINK

Read and Respond

For your outside reading for this unit, choose texts by writers whom you find humorous. You might look for humorous short stories as well as narrative essays and poetry. Create a list of titles in your Independent Reading List of at least five texts based on recommendations from your teacher as well as your own research.

Understanding the Complexity of Humor

Learning Targets
- Write an objective summary of an informational text.
- Demonstrate understanding of the denotations and connotations of words related to humor.

Preview
In this activity, you will read an essay on the topic of humor. As you read, think about your own sense of humor and what makes you laugh.

Setting a Purpose for Reading
- As you read, underline key words and phrases that explain the main idea of each section.
- Circle unknown words and phrases. Try to determine the meaning of the words by using context clues, word parts, or a dictionary.

LEARNING STRATEGIES:
Skimming/Scanning, Predicting, Close Reading, Marking the Text, Summarizing, Revisiting Prior Work, Discussion Groups

My Notes

ABOUT THE AUTHOR
Marc Tyler Nobleman (b. 1972) has written more than 70 books. His current writing interest is picture books for readers of all ages. He is also a cartoonist whose work has been published in numerous well-known publications, including *The Wall Street Journal, Forbes, The Saturday Evening Post*, and *New York Daily News*.

Essay

Made You Laugh

by Marc Tyler Nobleman

1 Would you like to know a language everyone in the world understands? You already do—because you laugh. Any two people from vastly different cultures who don't speak a word of the other's language still know exactly what is meant when the other person laughs.

2 Think of laughter as the unofficial language of Earth. Yet how much do any of us really understand about humor?

On the Laugh Track

3 What makes things funny? READ asked John Ficarra, the editor of MAD magazine. After all, he should know. Here's what he said: "Monkeys. They're unbeatable. For example, show a photo of

Understanding the Complexity of Humor

GRAMMAR &USAGE
Subject-Verb Agreement

Subjects and verbs should always agree with each other. A singular subject always takes a singular verb, and a plural subject takes a plural verb. For example:

"My **friend is** dead!"
The word *friend* is singular, so the verb *be* also has to be in the singular form (*is*).

"Ok, so **monkeys are** funny."
The word *monkeys* is plural, so the verb *be* is also in the plural form (*are*).

The words *each, either, neither, anybody, anyone, nobody, somebody, someone,* and *no one* are singular subjects and thus require a singular verb form. Do not be confused by words that appear between the subject and the verb. For example:

"**Everyone** who writes comedy **needs** to know the audience."

Everyone is a singular subject and takes a singular form of the verb *need*.

Read "Made You Laugh" one more time and select three sentences. Identify the subject and verb of each sentence and note whether they are singular or plural.

My Notes

_____

_____

_____

_____

_____

_____

_____

a dentist—not funny. Show a photo of a dentist with a monkey in his chair, and it's comedy gold. Try this theory out on a few of your family photos, and you'll see." OK, so monkeys are funny. What else? How about this?

4 Two hunters were in the woods, when one collapsed. He didn't seem to be breathing. The other called the emergency number and said, "My friend is dead! What can I do?" The operator said, "Calm down, I can help. First, let's make sure he's dead." After a second of silence on the hunter's end, the operator heard a gunshot. The hunter came back on the phone and said, "OK, now what?"

5 If you laughed, you're not alone. In the year 2001, that joke was voted the funniest in the world as part of a project called LaughLab. Psychologist Richard Wiseman's goal was to determine what makes people laugh and what is found to be funny among men and women, older and younger people, and people from different countries. His research team tested people in person and asked others to submit opinions online using a "Giggleometer," which ranked jokes on a scale of 1–5. More than 40,000 jokes were tested.

6 You may be saying to yourself, "Studying jokes? Is that science?" But plenty of smart people say yes. Laughter is a biological function. It has a certain rhythm; laughter syllables build, then trail off, and they come out in a repetitive, not random, sequence. For example, "ha-ha-ho-ho-he" is typical, but "ha-ho-ha-ho-ha" or "he-ho-he" just doesn't happen.

7 Babies begin to laugh instinctively when they're about four months old, perhaps to form a connection with parents. Those born blind and deaf also laugh, so laughter is not dependent on sight and hearing. Other animals, notably chimps, exhibit laugh-like behavior when playing with one another. Even rats, when tickled, make high-pitched squeals that can be interpreted as laughter. (As you might guess, only a dedicated few know this firsthand.)

Comedy Is Serious Stuff

8 Comics know that the same jokes are not funny to everyone everywhere. Ed Hiestand, a writer for comedy great Johnny Carson, told READ, "Everyone who writes comedy needs to know the audience. On the Carson show, everybody would laugh on a Friday night. Nobody would laugh on a Monday." Even within one state or town or family, senses of humor are as varied as the people are. Professional comics do not assume a 10 p.m. audience will like a joke because a 7 p.m. audience did.

9 Comedians who test jokes for a living say it's hit or miss. "It's a tough gig, and you have to have a large threshold for pain," said stand-up Jay Nog. Performers whose jokes get a two-second laugh consider that a significant accomplishment.

10 Timing is critical. Starting stand-up Zubair Simonson said he's learning the hard way that "good timing can cause a weak joke to soar, while poor timing can cause a strong joke to falter." Authors and film actors do not often get immediate public feedback. But comics do.

11 What keeps the funny guys going? The laughs and after-effects. "The best humor has some sort of layer to it; it makes a statement of some kind or comment," said Margy Yuspa, a director at Comedy Central. "An example is [Dave] Chappelle. His comedy is funny on the surface and also often comments on race or social issues."

Funny You Said That

12 Comedians have their own theories about humor. "What makes us laugh is a surprise change in perspective that connects an unknown with a known idea in a

unique manner," said Ronald P. Culberson, a humorist at FUNsulting.com. "For instance, a three-legged dog walks into an Old West saloon and says, "I'm looking for the man who shot my paw.""

13 Ask an average person why humans laugh, and he or she would probably say, "Because something was funny." But comics need to know what gives the giggles; their livelihood depends on it.

14 Comedian Anthony DeVito told READ that "people tend to laugh at things that reinforce what they already believe. Comedy tells them they're right."

15 Gary Gulman, a finalist in Last Comic Standing, a reality TV show and comedy competition, gave specifics. "Sometimes it's a keen observation about something you thought you lived through. Sometimes it's a **juxtaposition** of words. Sometimes it's a gesture or a sound. An encyclopedia couldn't do this question justice."

What Are You Laughing At?

16 Yet laughter is not always a planned response to a joke. One study found that 80 percent of the time, we laugh at something that just happens. People often laugh just because someone else does. Like a yawn, a laugh is contagious. That's why some sit-coms use laugh tracks.

17 Laughter is also social, a way to bond with others. After all, how often do you laugh alone? When two or more people laugh at the same thing, it is as if nature reminds them of what they have in common.

18 Behavioral neuroscientist Robert R. Provine conducted a 10-year experiment in which he eavesdropped on 2,000 conversations in malls, at parties, and on city sidewalks. He found that the greatest guffaws did not follow intentionally funny statements; people laughed hardest at everyday comments that seemed funny only in a certain social context.

19 "Do you have a rubber band?" is not in and of itself humorous, but it is if it's said in response to "I like Amelia so much. I wish I could get her attention."

Theories of Funniness

20 There are three main theories about humor.

21 **Release theory**—Humor gives a break from tension. In a horror movie, as a character creeps through a dark house (often idiotically) to follow an eerie noise, he might open a door to find a cat playing with a squeeze toy. The audience laughs in relief. Humor also lets us deal with unpleasant or forbidden issues, such as death and violence. People are often more comfortable laughing at something shocking said by someone else, though they would never say it themselves. Comedian Keenen Ivory Wayans once said, "Comedy is the flip side of pain. The worst things that happen to you are hysterical—in retrospect. But a comedian doesn't need retrospect; he realizes it's funny while he's in the eye of the storm."

22 **Superiority theory**—Audience members laugh at those who appear to be more stupid than they judge themselves to be. Slapstick humor, such as seeing a guy slip on a banana peel, often falls into this category. This theory dates back to Plato in ancient Greece and was prominent in the Middle Ages, when people with deformities were often employed as court jesters.

23 Some comedians exploited this theory by building a routine—or even a **persona**—around the idea that they were losers who couldn't catch a break. Larry David, David Letterman, and Woody Allen are comedians who have done this, each in his own way.

My Notes

ACADEMIC VOCABULARY
Juxtaposition, a technique used by artists and writers, places normally unassociated ideas, words, and phrases next to one another for effect (e.g., surprise or wit).

Literary Terms
A **persona** is the voice or character speaking or narrating a story.

Understanding the Complexity of Humor

WORD CONNECTIONS

Roots and Affixes

Superiority has the Latin root *super*, which means "placed above." This root is found in many English words, including *superb, superlative, supreme, supervise, superintendent,* and *supernatural.*

An *incongruity* happens when things do not match as they are expected to. The word *incongruity* has the root *-congru-*, which means "to come together," "to agree," or "to coincide." The prefix *in-* means "not" or "without."

Literary Terms

Satire is a form of comedy that uses humor, irony, or exaggeration to expose and criticize issues in society or people's weaknesses.

My Notes

24 **Incongruity theory**—People laugh when things that are not normally associated with each other are put together. Many comedy duos, from Laurel and Hardy to David Spade and Chris Farley, feature a thin man and a fat man, a visual contrast.

25 People also laugh when there is a difference between what they expect to happen and what actually occurs. They are being led in a certain direction, and then that direction abruptly changes, and the unpredictability makes them laugh. Children see birds all the time without reaction, but if one flies into their classroom through an open window, they will probably explode in giggles.

Got Laughs?

26 What we laugh at changes as we age. Here are some examples.

Audience	Often Likes
Young children	Slapstick, or silly **physical humor**
Elementary-school children	**Puns,** simple jokes that play off the sound rather than the meaning of a word, such as "Lettuce all go to the salad bar"
Teens	**Jokes** about topics that authority figures would consider rebellious, a way to use humor to deal with nerve-racking subjects
Adults, particularly well-educated ones	**Satire,** which makes fun of the weaknesses of people and society

27 Generally, children laugh more than adults. One study found that adults laugh 20 times a day, while children laugh 200 times!

The Secrets of Humor

28 Certain comedic devices turn up again and again in jokes, comic strips, and filmed entertainment—because they succeed.

29 "There were tricks," said Hiestand of his days writing for *The Tonight Show* hosted by Johnny Carson, "things you would see, certain things always got laughs." One of the most popular is often called the rule of threes. That is a pattern in which two nonfunny elements are followed by a third that is funny (yet still makes sense within the context). Many jokes start off with a list of three, such as "A rabbi, a lawyer, and a duck walk into a bar." As the joke unfolds, the rabbi says something straightforward, then the lawyer does as well, but the duck finishes with something witty or absurd.

30 Three guys were stranded on an island. An antique lamp washed ashore. When the guys touched it, a genie came out. "I'll grant each of you one wish," the genie said. The first guy said, "I want to go home," then disappeared. The second guy said, "I also want to go home," and he too disappeared. The third man suddenly looked sad. He said, "I want my two friends back to keep me company."

31 Certain concepts seem to be more amusing than others. If you tell any joke involving an animal, and it doesn't matter which one you use, think Donald and Daffy. In the LaughLab experiment, scientists determined that the funniest animal is the duck. (It's not arbitrary that a duck was used in the rule-of-threes joke.)

Do Tell—But Do It Right

32 There are also known techniques for telling jokes well.

- **Keep it short**—Don't include any details that are not necessary to bring you to the punch line. In the genie joke, there was no need to specify it was a tropical island or to name the castaways. The quicker you tell a joke, the funnier it will be.

- **Be specific**—Some comedians swear that a joke is funnier if you say "Aquafresh" instead of "toothpaste." The attention to detail makes the story seem more real.

- **Keep a straight face**—Deliver the joke deadpan, or without emotion. That way, any strangeness in the joke will seem even stranger because the person telling it doesn't seem to notice.

- **Don't laugh at your own joke**—Let your audience decide whether it is funny or foolish—or both.

33 Theories and techniques aside, much about humor remains a mystery. According to Hiestand, Carson many times said, "I don't understand what makes comedy a sure thing. There's no 100-percent surefire formula." Meanwhile, for most of us, laughter is never a problem. It does not need to be solved, just enjoyed.

Second Read

- Reread the essay to answer these text-dependent questions.
- Write any additional questions you have about the text in your Reader/Writer Notebook.

1. **Key Ideas and Details:** Why does laughter seem to qualify as a biological function? What might be the biological function of laughter?

My Notes

Understanding the Complexity of Humor

My Notes

2. **Craft and Structure:** In paragraph 7, what purpose does the sentence in parentheses serve?

3. **Key Ideas and Details:** As discussed in paragraphs 16–19, why is unplanned humor often funnier than planned humor?

4. **Craft and Structure:** What context clues in paragraph 21 help you understand the meaning of the word "retrospect"?

5. **Key Ideas and Details:** Based on paragraphs 26–27, what distinction can you make between what makes children laugh and what makes adults laugh? Why might children laugh more often than adults?

6. **Key Ideas and Details:** There are four known techniques for telling jokes well as explained in paragraph 32. How do the first two techniques relate to narrative writing?

7. **Knowledge and Ideas:** What is the author's argument in this essay? Cite specific evidence from the text in your response.

Working from the Text

8. Referring back to the words and phrases you've underlined, write an objective summary of a section of the text by putting the main points into your own words. Remember that a summary is a broad overview of the text; stick to the main points by writing about big ideas and excluding smaller details.

Using Precise Diction to Analyze Humor

9. To analyze a text carefully, one must use specific words to describe the humor and explain the intended effect. Work collaboratively to define terms and to understand the nuances of words with similar denotations (definitions). You have already encountered some of these words.

Words to Describe Humor	Denotation	Connotations
amusing		
cute		
facetious		
hysterical		
ironic		
irreverent		
laughable		
light-hearted		
ludicrous		
mocking		
sarcastic		
satirical		
witty		

My Notes

Understanding the Complexity of Humor

My Notes

Words to Describe a Response to Humor	Denotation	Connotations
chuckle		
giggle		
groan		
guffaw		
snort		
scoff		
smile		
smirk		
snicker		
titter		

Language and Writer's Craft: Verbals

A **verbal** is a form of a verb that functions as something other than a verb. For example, a verbal might be used as a noun, an adjective, or an adverb.

An **infinitive** is the *to* form of a verb, such as *to chuckle* or *to snort*. Infinitives can be used as nouns, adjectives, or adverbs.

A **participle** is a verbal that is used as an adjective. There are present and past participles.
Present: giggling, snickering
Past: gnarled, destroyed

A **gerund** is a verbal that acts as a noun and ends in *–ing*. It can sometimes be difficult to tell the difference between a gerund and a present participle because both end in *–ing*. The key is to determine whether the word acts as an adjective or a noun.

Participle: The **giggling** child made lots of noise.
Giggling is an adjective describing the noun *child*.

Gerund: His **giggling** was distracting.
Giggling is the subject of the sentence, so it is a noun.

PRACTICE Review your response to question 7. Look for two sentences you could revise by using verbals.

Check Your Understanding

Reread "Made You Laugh" and write a paragraph summarizing the author's arguments about what makes things funny.

Explanatory Writing Prompt

Create a detailed paragraph that uses precise diction to explain your sense of humor. Use at least two words each from the "Words to Describe Humor" and "Words to Describe a Response to Humor" charts. Explain what does and does not make you laugh and how you typically respond to humorous texts. Be sure to:

• Begin with a clear thesis statement explaining your sense of humor.
• Include some specific examples of things that make you laugh.
• Use at least one infinitive, one participle, and one gerund.
• Use verb tenses correctly and consistently.

My Notes

Classifying Comedy

WORD CONNECTIONS

Cognates

The English word *comedy* comes from the Latin word *comoedia*, meaning "an amusing play or performance." It has the same meaning as the Spanish word, *comedia*.

My Notes

Learning Targets
- Categorize humorous texts into levels of comedy.
- Write an analysis of how an artist creates humor.

Understanding Levels of Comedy

Comedy occurs in different ways.

1. Read and mark the text to indicate information that is new to you.

Low comedy refers to the type of humor that is focused primarily on the situation or series of events. It includes such things as physical mishaps, humor concerning the human body and its functions, coincidences, and humorous situations. With low comedy, the humor is straightforward and generally easy to follow and understand.

Since the primary purpose of most low comedy is to entertain, the action is frequently seen as hilarious or hysterical and the effect is often side-splitting laughter and guffaws. Many times, the characters are exaggerated caricatures rather than fully developed characters. These caricatures are often caught in unlikely situations or they become victims of circumstances seemingly beyond their control. Thus, the plot takes priority over the characters. Examples of low comedy might include *Madea's Family Reunion*, *Meet the Parents*, and *America's Funniest Home Videos*. Shakespeare's comedies, such as *A Midsummer Night's Dream* and *Twelfth Night*, are full of low comedy.

High comedy refers to the type of humor that is focused primarily on characters, dialogue, or ideas. It includes such things as clever wordplay, wit, and pointed remarks regarding larger issues. Many times, high comedy takes an irreverent or unconventional look at serious issues.

Sometimes the humor of high comedy is not immediately obvious; it can take a bit of reflection in order to realize the humorous intent. Frequently, the purpose of high comedy is to express an opinion, to persuade, or to promote deeper consideration of an idea. Often described as amusing, clever, or witty, high comedy typically results in chuckles, grins, and smiles rather than loud laughter. Clever use of language and interesting characters receive more attention than the circumstances that surround them. Examples of high comedy include *Modern Family*, *The Middle*, and, at times, *The Simpsons*. Shakespeare's tragedies, such as *Hamlet* and *Romeo and Juliet*, also include instances of high comedy.

2. Why do we distinguish between different kinds of comedy?

3. With a partner, take notes to complete each chart on the next page. Brainstorm a strong example at each level of comedy.

Low Comedy

Purpose	Common Subjects	Emphasis	Descriptions	Intended Responses

High Comedy

Purpose	Common Subjects	Emphasis	Descriptions	Intended Responses

Classifying Comedy

My Notes

_____
_____
_____
_____
_____
_____
_____
_____
_____
_____
_____
_____
_____
_____
_____
_____
_____
_____
_____
_____
_____
_____
_____
_____
_____
_____
_____
_____

Analyzing Humorous Texts

4. Brainstorm what you already know about comic strips and political cartoons. Think about format, audience, topics, descriptions of humor, intended effects, etc.

Comic Strips:

Political Cartoons:

5. Read and mark the text of the following definitions for information that is new to you:

Comic strips are meant primarily to entertain. They have a beginning and middle that lead to a humorous ending. They tend to be a low-level comedy that is easily understood by a wide audience.

Political cartoons deal with larger issues and are often meant to communicate a particular political or social message. They often have a single panel with a powerful statement to reinforce humor displayed through a picture (characters or symbols). They tend to be high-level comedy, appealing to a smaller population that is well-informed about a specific topic.

Check Your Understanding

In order to compare and contrast comics and political cartoons, create a Venn diagram that lists the characteristics of each. Are there any areas where they overlap?

Introducing the Strategy: RAFT

RAFT is an acronym that stands for role, audience, format, and topic. RAFT is a strategy that can be used for responding to and analyzing a text by identifying and examining its role, audience, format, and topic.

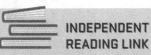

INDEPENDENT READING LINK

Read and Respond

Analyze one of the humorous texts you are reading. Does the text reflect high comedy or low comedy? Cite specific examples from the text to support your answer, and record your responses in your Reader/ Writer Notebook.

6. Use the graphic organizer and the RAFT strategy on the next page to analyze the humor in comics and political cartoons based on the previous definitions.

Title _____

Role	Comics:	Political Cartoon:
Who is the author? Where is this comic or political cartoon found? What is the attitude (tone) of the author toward the topic? How can you tell?		
Audience Who does this comic or political cartoon target? How do you know?		
Format Describe the use of print and non-print techniques (dialogue, narration frames, and angles) used for effect.		
Topic What is this comic/cartoon about? Who are the characters? What is happening? How would you describe the humor? What is the intended effect?		

Writing to Sources: Explanatory Text

Think about your selected cartoon or comic. How does the author create humor? Write a paragraph explaining your answer. Be sure to:

- Establish a controlling idea that describes the humor and its effect.
- Include specific details from the cartoon or comic to support your ideas.
- Explain whether the cartoon or comic is high or low humor and why.
- Use precise diction to describe humor.

My Notes

_____
_____
_____
_____
_____
_____
_____
_____
_____
_____

Humorous Anecdotes

LEARNING STRATEGIES:
Graphic Organizer, Discussion
Groups, Rereading, Close
Reading, Marking the Text,
Brainstorming, TWIST,
Oral Reading

WORD CONNECTIONS

Etymology

The word *anecdote* comes from the Greek word *anekdota*, meaning "things unpublished." Think about the connotation this brings to the modern word.

My Notes

Learning Targets

- Analyze how authors convey humor in speech and writing.
- Write and present an oral reading of an original anecdote.
- Analyze the effect of verbals in a humorous text.

Humorous Anecdotes

1. Read the following information to see how the use of anecdotes applies to a study of humor.

   An **anecdote** is a brief, entertaining account of an incident or event. Often, anecdotes are shared because of their humorous nature, but anecdotes can also help illustrate larger ideas and concepts. Families sometimes share anecdotes about the humorous things family members have done. Frequently, the stories become more and more absurd as the details are exaggerated with each retelling.

2. Do you or your family have a humorous anecdote that is shared over and over? What is it? Why is it retold? Who tells it? How does it change over time?

Viewing a Humorous Monologue

The following monologue provides humorous accounts of somewhat ordinary events. Finding and describing the humor in the people, places, and events you encounter can enrich your conversations as well as your writing.

3. As you watch the clip for the first time, listen for different topics in the monologue and take notes.

Comedian's Persona	People	Places	Events

4. The second time you view the clip, pay attention to *how* the comedian delivers the anecdote. Take notes on your assigned section.

1. Describe the comedian's delivery. What is the effect on the audience?

Tone:

Facial Expressions:

Gestures:

Volume:

Pacing:

Inflection (emphasis):

Effect:

2. Record the comedian's transitions between topics within his anecdote. What words or phrasing does he use?

3. Describe the imagery the comedian uses. List details that describe a person, place, or event. Why does the comedian include these specific details?

Topic:

Descriptive Details:

Figurative Language:

4. Does the speaker's tone shift? Record his attitude about the topic at the beginning of the monologue and if his attitude changes. How does he communicate this shift?

Humorous Anecdotes

Check Your Understanding

List three ways the comedian in the clip makes the audience laugh with a simple anecdote. Does he use his persona? people in the story? humorous events?

5. Discuss how you would describe the humor the comedian uses. What do you think is the intended response? During your discussion, be sure to:
   • Use precise diction to describe the humor.
   • Provide examples from the text to support your analysis.

Preview

In this activity, you will read a humorous essay and think about any funny memories you've had related to a road trip or riding in a car.

Setting a Purpose for Reading

• As you read the essay, underline words and phrases that make you think of your own experiences and memories.
• Circle unknown words and phrases. Try to determine the meaning of the words by using context clues, word parts, or a dictionary.

ABOUT THE AUTHOR

Jon Scieszka (b. 1954) is the oldest of six brothers in his family. He became an elementary school teacher and found that his students liked the funny stories that he enjoyed telling. He has since published a number of children's books, which are illustrated by his friend Lane Smith. In 2008, the Librarian of Congress named him National Ambassador for Young People's Literature.

Essay

from Brothers

by Jon Scieszka

1   Brothers are the guys you stick with and stick up for.

2   The Scieszka brothers are scattered all over the country now, but we still get together once a year to play a family golf tournament. We named it after our dad, Lou, and his favorite car—his old Cadillac Coupe de Ville. It is the Coupe de Lou Classic. We all grew up playing golf, because Dad Lou, an elementary

school principal, taught Junior Golf and gave us lessons during summers off. And I'm sure my brothers would want me to point out the amazing fact that I am the winner of both the very first Coupe de Lou 1983 and the latest Coupe de Lou 2004.

3   But of all the Scieszka brother memories, I believe it was a family car trip that gave us our finest moment of brotherhood. We were driving cross-country from Michigan to Florida, all of us, including the family cat (a guy cat, naturally), in the family station wagon. Somewhere mid-trip we stopped at one of those Stuckey's rest-stop restaurants to eat and load up on Stuckey's candy.

4   We ate lunch, ran around like maniacs in the warm sun, then packed back into the station wagon—Mom and Dad up front, Jim, Jon, Tom, Gregg, Brian, Jeff, and the cat in back. Somebody dropped his Stuckey's Pecan Log Roll® on the floor. The cat found it and must have scarfed every bit of it, because two minutes later we heard that awful ack ack ack sound of a cat getting ready to barf.

5   The cat puked up the pecan nut log. Jeff, the youngest and smallest (and closest to the floor) was the first to go. He got one look and whiff of the pecan nut cat yack and blew his own sticky lunch all over the cat. The puke-covered cat jumped on Brian, Brian barfed on Gregg. Gregg upchucked on Tom. Tom burped a bit of Stuckey lunch back on Gregg. Jim and I rolled down the windows and hung out as far as we could, yelling in group puke horror.

6   Dad Lou didn't know what had hit the back of the car. No time to ask questions. He just pulled off to the side of the road. All of the brothers—Jim, Jon, Tom, Gregg, Brian, and Jeff—spilled out of the puke wagon and fell in the grass, gagging and yelling and laughing until we couldn't laugh anymore.

7   What does it all mean? What essential guy wisdom did I learn from this?

8   Stick with your brothers. Stick up for your brothers. And if you ever drop a pecan nut log in a car with your five brothers and your cat ... you will probably stick to your brothers.

Second Read

- Reread the essay to answer these text-dependent questions.
- Write any additional questions you have about the text in your Reader/Writer Notebook.

6. **Craft and Structure:** How does the author use dashes and parentheses for comic effect?

7. **Key Ideas and Details:** How are the golf tournament and the road trip incident connected?

My Notes

Humorous Anecdotes

Working from the Text

8. Review the essay and make connections between the essay and your own experiences. Also think about other humorous texts you have read and how the essay connects to those texts. Finally, make connections between the essay and the world around you. Use the following symbols to mark the text.

    E/S = Essay to Self

    E/T = Essay to other Texts

    E/W =Essay to World

Introducing the Strategy: TWIST

TWIST is an acronym for tone, word choice, imagery, style, and theme. This writing strategy helps a writer analyze each of these elements in a text in order to write a response to an analytical writing prompt about the text.

9. Reread the excerpt from "Brothers," and use the TWIST strategy to guide your analysis of the text.

Acronym	Text: "Brothers" by Jon Scieszka
Tone *What is the author's attitude about the topic?*	
Word choice *What specific diction does the author use for effect?*	
Imagery *What specific descriptive details and figurative language does the author use for effect?*	

Style

How does the author use language to create humor?

What is the intended response the author hopes to achieve?

Theme

What is the central idea of this text? What idea about life is the author trying to convey through humor?

10. Once you have found textual evidence from the text "Brothers," and made an inference about the theme, you are ready to write an analytical topic sentence. State the title, author, and genre (TAG) in your thesis or topic sentence. For example:

    <u>Jon Scieszka's</u> <u>anecdote</u> <u>"Brothers"</u> is a low-level comedy that uses a comic situation, exaggeration, and comic diction to reveal a universal truth about how brothers who laugh together stick together.

    Practice writing a topic sentence about the stand-up comedy using the TAG format.

Humorous Anecdotes

Writing and Presenting Your Own Anecdote

11. Use the TWIST graphic organizer below to plan your own anecdote.

Subject of Humorous Memory:	People/Places/Events:

Tone:

What is your attitude about the topic? How will you convey that attitude?

Word Choice:

What specific diction can you use for effect?

Imagery:

What specific descriptive and figurative language can you use for effect?

Style:

How can you use language (diction and syntax) to create humor?
What is the intended response you hope to achieve?

Theme:

What idea about life are you trying to convey through humor?

12. Draft your anecdote. Be sure to include a beginning, middle, and end. As you write your draft, think about using verbals. Study the material below to learn about using verbals.

13. Present an oral reading of your draft to a partner. After your partner presents, provide feedback relating to his or her ideas, organization, language, and the humorous effect.

Language and Writer's Craft: Using Verbals

You have learned that a verbal is a verb form that does not function as a verb. Types of verbals are gerunds, participles, and infinitives. Writers use verbals for variety and effect. Look at these examples:

Golfing was an activity that the Scieszka family enjoyed. (*Golfing* is a gerund because it acts as a noun. It is the subject of the sentence.)

"Jim and I rolled down the windows and hung out as far as we could, **yelling** in group puke horror." (*Yelling* is a present participle. It modifies *Jim and I*.)

"We still get together once a year **to play** a family golf tournament." (*To play* is an infinitive. It functions as an adverb, modifying the verb *get* by answering the question "why.")

PRACTICE In your Reader/Writer Notebook, write a brief summary of Joe Scieszka's anecdote using one infinitive, one gerund, and one participle.

Writing to Sources: Explanatory Text

Select an anecdote in audio or visual format, or print a copy of the anecdote you read in this activity. Write a paragraph explaining the humor the author creates and its intended response. Be sure to:

- Clearly state how the anecdote uses the elements of humor.
- Include examples from the text to support your analysis.
- Use precise diction.
- Use participles, gerunds, and infinitives in your writing.

My Notes

Finding Truth in Comedy

My Notes

Learning Targets
- Collaborate to analyze a humorous essay in a Socratic Seminar.
- Write to explain how an author conveys universal truths through humor.

Preview
In this activity, you will read a humorous essay and think about how people use comedy to discuss serious or important topics.

Setting a Purpose for Reading
- As you read the essay, underline words and phrases that are intended to be humorous.
- Circle unknown words and phrases. Try to determine the meaning of the words by using context clues, word parts, or a dictionary.
- Place an exclamation point by text that deals with a universal truth.

ABOUT THE AUTHOR
Dave Barry (b. 1947) was a humor columnist for the *Miami Herald* until 2005. His work there won him the Pulitzer Prize for Commentary in 1988. He has also written novels and children's books and continues to write articles for a variety of magazines. Much of Barry's work provides humorous commentary on current social issues.

Essay

i've got a few pet peeves about sea creatures

by Dave Barry

Chunk 1

1 Pets are good, because they teach children important lessons about life, the main one being that, sooner or later, life kicks the bucket.

2 With me, it was sooner. When I was a boy, my dad, who worked in New York City, would periodically bring home a turtle in a little plastic tank that had a little plastic island with a little plastic palm tree, as is so often found in natural turtle habitats. I was excited about having a pet, and I'd give the turtle a fun pet name like Scooter. But my excitement was not shared by Scooter, who, despite residing in a tropical paradise, never did anything except mope around.

3 Actually, he didn't even mope "around": He moped in one place without moving, or even blinking, for days on end, displaying basically the same vital signs as an ashtray. Eventually I would realize—it wasn't easy to tell—that Scooter had passed on to that

Big Pond in the Sky, and I'd bury him in the garden, where he'd decompose and become food for the zucchini, which in turn would be eaten by my dad, who would in turn go to New York City, where, compelled by powerful instincts that even he did not understand, he would buy me another moping death turtle. And so the cycle of life would repeat.

Chunk 2

4 I say all this to explain why I recently bought fish for my 4-year-old daughter, Sophie. My wife and I realized how badly she wanted an animal when she found a beetle on the patio and declared that it was a pet, named Marvin. She put Marvin into a Tupperware container, where, under Sophie's loving care and feeding, he thrived for maybe nine seconds before expiring like a little six-legged parking meter. Fortunately, we have a beetle-intensive patio, so, unbeknownst to Sophie, we were able to replace Marvin with a parade of stand-ins of various sizes ("Look! Marvin has grown bigger!" "Wow! Today Marvin has grown smaller!"). But it gets to be tedious, going out early every morning to wrangle patio beetles. So we decided to go with fish.

5 I had fish of my own, years ago, and it did not go well. They got some disease like Mongolian Fin Rot, which left them basically just little pooping torsos. But I figured that today, with all the technological advances we have such as cellular phones and "digital" things and carbohydrate-free toothpaste, modern fish would be more reliable.

6 So we got an aquarium and prepared it with special water and special gravel and special fake plants and a special scenic rock so the fish would be intellectually stimulated and get into a decent college. When everything was ready I went to the aquarium store to buy fish, my only criteria being that they should be 1) hardy digital fish; and 2) fish that looked a LOT like other fish, in case God forbid we had to Marvinize them. This is when I discovered how complex fish society is. I'd point to some colorful fish and say, "What about these?" And the aquarium guy would say, "Those are great fish but they do get aggressive when they mate." And I'd say, "Like, how aggressive?" And he'd say, "They'll kill all the other fish."

7 This was a recurring theme. I'd point to some fish, and the aquarium guy would inform me that these fish could become aggressive if there were fewer than four of them, or an odd number of them, or it was a month containing the letter "R," or they heard the song "Who Let the Dogs Out." It turns out that an aquarium is a powder keg that can explode in deadly violence at any moment, just like the Middle East, or junior high school.

Chunk 3

8 TRUE STORY: A friend of mine named David Shor told me that his kids had an aquarium containing a kind of fish called African cichlids, and one of them died. So David went to the aquarium store and picked out a replacement African cichlid, but the aquarium guy said he couldn't buy that one, and David asked why, and the guy said: "Because that one is from a different lake."

9 But getting back to my daughter's fish: After much thought, the aquarium guy was able to find me three totally pacifist fish-Barney Fife fish, fish so nonviolent that, in the wild, worms routinely beat them up and steal their lunch money. I brought these home, and so far they have not killed each other or died in any way. Plus, Sophie LOVES them. So everything is working out beautifully. I hope it stays that way, because I hate zucchini.

Second Read

* Reread the essay to answer these text-dependent questions.
* Write any additional questions you have about the text in your Reader/Writer Notebook.

My Notes

Finding Truth in Comedy

1. **Craft and Structure:** What is the effect of the repetition of "a little plastic" in paragraph 2?

2. **Key Ideas and Details:** What is the effect of the juxtaposed ideas "grown bigger" and "grown smaller" in paragraph 4?

3. **Craft and Structure:** What is the impact of the phrase "little pooping torsos" in paragraph 5?

4. **Key Ideas and Details:** What specific details does the author include in paragraph 7 in order to have a comic effect?

Working from the Text

5. Read and respond to the following quote.

Quote by George Bernard Shaw	Interpretation	Personal Commentary
"The power of comedy is to make people laugh, and when they have their mouths open and they least expect it— you slip in the truth."		

6. How would you classify this essay (high or low comedy)? Explain.

7. How would you describe the humor? What is the author's intended response? Use precise diction in your response.

8. How does the author use language (diction, syntax, imagery) to create a humorous tone?

9. How does the author appeal to the audience's emotions, interests, values, and/or beliefs?

10. What is the universal truth (theme) of the text? How does the author develop the idea through humorous characters and plot?

11. Develop Levels of Questions based on your analysis to prepare for a Socratic Seminar discussion. Remember to maintain a formal style in your speaking during the Socratic Seminar. Be sure to:

- Use precise verbs such as *communicates, creates, emphasizes,* or *illustrates* when discussing the author's purpose.
- Use the author's last name: "Barry creates humor by ..."
- Cite textual evidence to support your opinion.

Levels of Questioning	"I've got a few pet peeves about sea creatures"
Level 1: Literal	
Level 2: Interpretive	
Level 3: Universal (thematic)	

My Notes

Finding Truth in Comedy

12. Brainstorm other precise verbs that will help in your discussion. Do you have any other tips for using formal language?

13. Use your analysis and questions to engage in a Socratic Seminar discussion.

Check Your Understanding

In preparation for your Writing to Sources activity, discuss in a small group how you think Barry uses humor to express the universal truth in the story.

Writing to Sources: Explanatory Text

Write a paragraph that explains how Barry uses humor to convey a truth about life. Be sure to:

- Establish a clear controlling idea about conveying a truth.
- Cite specific evidence from the text.
- Use precise diction to describe humorous effects.
- Use verb tenses correctly and consistently.

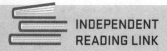

INDEPENDENT READING LINK

Read and Discuss

For independent practice, choose one of the humorous texts from your list and explain the theme using specific evidence for support. Write several Levels of Questions for a specific section of reading in your Reader/Writer Notebook. Use the Level 3 questions to have a discussion about themes with your peers.

Satirical Humor

Learning Targets

- Analyze satire in print and nonprint texts.
- Write an analytical paragraph that includes appropriate and varied transitions.

1. You will next view a film clip your teacher shows and take notes on the satire you observe.

This clip is from:	
TOPIC (vice or folly exposed)	SATIRE (examples of irony, sarcasm, or ridicule used)

ACADEMIC VOCABULARY
Satiric comedy is not always funny. Sometimes it mocks or derides the subject. This kind of **derision** allows a satirist to **denounce** or express strong disapproval of an attitude or topic.

Preview

In this activity, you will read a satirical article and think about how the author uses satire to express disapproval on a particular topic.

Setting a Purpose for Reading

- As you read the article, underline words and phrases that make you laugh or that you recognize as humor.
- Circle unknown words and phrases. Try to determine the meaning of the words by using context clues, word parts, or a dictionary.
- Place a * by any words or phrases that indicate irony, sarcasm, or ridicule.

My Notes

Article

Underfunded Schools Forced to Cut Past Tense from Language Programs

from *The Onion*

1 WASHINGTON—Faced with ongoing budget crises, underfunded schools nationwide are increasingly left with no option but to cut the past tense—a grammatical construction traditionally used to relate all actions and states that have transpired at an earlier point in time—from their standard English and language arts programs.

2 A part of American school curricula for more than 200 years, the past tense was deemed by school administrators to be too expensive to keep in primary and secondary education.

Satirical Humor

GRAMMAR & USAGE
Active and Passive Voice

Writers use active and passive voice to emphasize different ideas in their writing.

The **active voice** emphasizes who or what is doing the action.

For example:
"The past tense provides students with a unique and consistent outlet for self-expression."

In this example, *past tense* is the thing doing the providing.

The **passive voice** emphasizes the person or thing being acted upon. Passive voice can be used effectively when the actor in the situation is unknown or not important.

For example:
"School districts in California have been forced to cut addition and subtraction from their math departments."

The emphasis is on the school districts, the things being acted upon.

As you read, look for other examples of active and passive voice and notice the different effects they create.

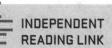

INDEPENDENT READING LINK
Read and Connect

Choose a humorous text from your list that demonstrates satire. Create a graphic organizer to explore the satire and compare your results to the graphic organizer you completed in Activity 4.6, question 8. List the similarities and differences in your Reader/Writer Notebook.

3 "This was by no means an easy decision, but teaching our students how to conjugate verbs in a way that would allow them to describe events that have already occurred is a luxury that we can no longer afford," Phoenix-area high school principal Sam Pennock said.

4 "With our current budget, the past tense must unfortunately become a thing of the past."

5 In the most dramatic display of the new trend yet, the Tennessee Department of Education decided Monday to remove "-ed" endings from all of the state's English classrooms, saving struggling schools an estimated $3 million each year. Officials say they plan to slowly phase out the tense by first eliminating the past perfect; once students have adjusted to the change, the past progressive, the past continuous, the past perfect progressive, and the simple past will be cut. Hundreds of school districts across the country are expected to follow suit.

6 "This is the end of an era," said Alicia Reynolds, a school district director in Tuscaloosa, AL. "For some, reading and writing about things not immediately taking place was almost as much a part of school as history class and social studies."

7 "That is, until we were forced to drop history class and social studies a couple of months ago," Reynolds added.

8 Nevertheless, a number of educators are coming out against the cuts, claiming that the embattled verb tense, while outmoded, still plays an important role in the development of today's youth.

9 "Much like art and music, the past tense provides students with a unique and consistent outlet for self-expression," South Boston English teacher David Floen said. "Without it I fear many of our students will lack a number of important creative skills. Like being able to describe anything that happened earlier in the day."

10 Despite concerns that cutting the past tense will prevent graduates from communicating effectively in the workplace, the home, the grocery store, church, and various other public spaces, a number of lawmakers, such as Utah Sen. Orrin Hatch, have welcomed the cuts as proof that the American school system is taking a more forward-thinking approach to education. "Our tax dollars should be spent preparing our children for the future, not for what has already happened," Hatch said at a recent press conference. "It's about time we stopped wasting everyone's time with who 'did' what or 'went' where. The past tense is, by definition, outdated." Said Hatch, "I can't even remember the last time I had to use it."

11 Past-tense instruction is only the latest school program to face the chopping block. School districts in California have been forced to cut addition and subtraction from their math departments, while nearly all high schools have reduced foreign language courses to only the most basic phrases, including "May I please use the bathroom?" and "No, I do not want to go to the beach with Maria and Juan." Some legislators are even calling for an end to teaching grammar itself, saying that in many inner-city school districts, where funding is most lacking, students rarely use grammar at all.

12 Regardless of the recent upheaval, students throughout the country are learning to accept, and even embrace, the change to their curriculum.

13 "At first I think the decision to drop the past tense from class is ridiculous, and I feel very upset by it," said David Keller, a seventh-grade student at Hampstead School in Fort Meyers, FL. "But now, it's almost like it never happens."

Second Read

- Reread the article to answer these text-dependent questions.
- Write any additional questions you have about the text in your Reader/Writer Notebook.

2. **Craft and Structure:** What role does the first paragraph play in the structure of this article?

3. **Key Ideas and Details:** How do quotes from specific people throughout the article add to the development of ideas?

4. **Key Ideas and Details:** How does the use of present tense in the last quote in paragraph 13 emphasize the satire?

Working from the Text

5. Work collaboratively to diffuse and paraphrase the definition of satire.

Satire, a form of high comedy, is the use of <u>irony</u>, <u>sarcasm</u>, and/or <u>ridicule</u> in exposing, <u>denouncing</u>, and/or <u>deriding</u> human <u>vice</u> and <u>folly</u>.

Paraphrase:

My Notes

Satirical Humor

6. Reread the text and place an exclamation point by the highly connotative diction that stands out to you. Note the effect of those words in the My Notes space.

7. Circle and explain your response to this text. I think this text is:

   hilarious   funny   clever   ridiculous   because ...

   Discuss the parts of the text that made you laugh, and describe how the connotative words help create the humor.

8. Collaboratively, use the graphic organizer to explore the satire.

The vice or folly exposed in the text:	Textual Evidence: Irony:
	Sarcasm:
	Ridicule:

Writing an Analytical Paragraph

When writing about texts, use the "literary present" (e.g., "The article *states* ...," not "The article *stated* ...").

Also, remember to maintain coherence in your writing. Using a well-chosen transition word or phrase can help show the relationship (connection) between the ideas in your writing. The following is a list of commonly used transitional words and phrases.

Purpose	Example
Add	*and, again, and then, besides, equally important, finally, further, furthermore, nor, too, next, lastly, what's more, moreover, in addition, first (second, etc.)*
Compare	*whereas, but, yet, on the other hand, however, nevertheless, on the contrary, by comparison, where, compared to, up against, balanced against, but, although, conversely, meanwhile, after all, in contrast, although this may be true*
Prove	*because, for, since, for the same reason, obviously, evidently, furthermore, moreover, besides, indeed, in fact, in addition, in any case, that is*
Show Exception	*yet, still, however, nevertheless, in spite of, despite, of course, once in a while, sometimes*
Show Time	*immediately, thereafter, soon, after a few hours, finally, then, later, previously, formerly, first (second, etc.), next, and then*
Repeat	*in brief, as I have said, as I have noted, as has been noted, to reiterate*
Emphasize	*definitely, extremely, obviously, in fact, indeed, in any case, absolutely, positively, naturally, surprisingly, always, forever, perennially, eternally, never, emphatically, unquestionably, without a doubt, certainly, undeniably, without reservation*
Show Sequence	*first, second, third, next, then, following this, at this time, now, at this point, after, afterward, subsequently, finally, consequently, previously, before this, simultaneously, concurrently, thus, therefore, hence, next, and then, soon*
Give an Example	*for example, for instance, in this case, in another case, on this occasion, in this situation, take the case of, to demonstrate, to illustrate, as an illustration, to illustrate*
Summarize or Conclude	*in brief, on the whole, summing up, to conclude, in conclusion, as I have shown, as I have said, hence, therefore, accordingly, thus, as a result, consequently*

Check Your Understanding

Which instances of satire in the article do you think went the furthest to make the author's point? Why? Discuss with a partner.

Writing to Sources: Explanatory Text

Analyze how the text about underfunded schools uses satirical humor to expose human vice or folly. Be sure to:

- Establish and support a controlling idea.
- Use transitions to create cohesion and clarify the relationships among ideas and concepts.
- Use precise diction and maintain a formal style.
- Support your analysis with evidence from the text.

My Notes

Elements of Humor: Comic Characters and Caricatures

LEARNING STRATEGIES:
Graphic Organizer, Note-taking, Diffusing, Marking the Text, Visualizing, Discussion Groups, Rehearsal

Learning Targets
- Define and recognize comic characters and caricatures.
- Collaborate to analyze characters and caricatures in a literary text.

Comic Caricatures and Characters

Characterization is the way a writer reveals a character's personality through what the character says, thinks, and feels or through how the character looks, acts, or interacts with others.

A **caricature** is a pictorial, written, and/or acted representation of a person who exaggerates characteristics or traits for comic effect. Caricatures are often used in cartoon versions of people's faces and usually exaggerate features for comic effect.

ACADEMIC VOCABULARY
To use a **caricature** or to **caricaturize** someone is to exaggerate or imitate certain characteristics to create a comic or distorted idea of a person.

1. You will next view some comic scenes. As you view the opening sequence, take notes in the graphic organizer.

Characters Sketch the caricature.	Details Describe the characterization.	Interpretation What idea is conveyed through the characterization?
Bart	Bart is repetitively writing sentences on the board that say ...	He is the stereotype of the bad kid in the classroom.
Homer		
Marge		
Lisa		
Family		

My Notes

2. With your discussion group, discuss what truth about life the author is conveying through humor. Cite specific examples from the graphic organizer.

Preview

In this activity, you will read a short story and think about the author's use of characterization.

Setting a Purpose for Reading

- As you read the short story, underline words and phrases that reveal something about Nuttel and the niece.
- Circle unknown words and phrases. Try to determine the meaning by using context clues, word parts, or a dictionary.

ABOUT THE AUTHOR

Hector Hugh Munro (1870–1916), better known by the pen name Saki, was a British writer and satirist known for his masterful short stories poking fun at Edwardian society. His witty and intelligent stories are considered among the best the genre has to offer.

Short Story

The Open Window

by Saki (H. H. Munro)

1 "My aunt will be down presently, Mr. Nuttel," said a very self-possessed young lady of fifteen; "in the meantime you must try and put up with me."

2 Framton Nuttel endeavoured to say the correct something which should **duly** flatter the niece of the moment without unduly discounting the aunt that was to come. Privately he doubted more than ever whether these formal visits on a succession of total strangers would do much towards helping the nerve cure which he was supposed to be undergoing.

duly: properly or fittingly

3 "I know how it will be," his sister had said when he was preparing to migrate to this rural retreat; "you will bury yourself down there and not speak to a living soul, and your nerves will be worse than ever from moping. I shall just give you letters of introduction to all the people I know there. Some of them, as far as I can remember, were quite nice."

4 Framton wondered whether Mrs. Sappleton, the lady to whom he was presenting one of the letters of introduction, came into the nice division.

5 "Do you know many of the people round here?" asked the niece, when she judged that they had had sufficient silent communion.

My Notes

Elements of Humor: Comic Characters and Caricatures

rectory: the house in which a parish priest or minister lives

My Notes

6 "Hardly a soul," said Framton. "My sister was staying here, at the **rectory**, you know, some four years ago, and she gave me letters of introduction to some of the people here."

7 He made the last statement in a tone of distinct regret.

8 "Then you know practically nothing about my aunt?" pursued the self-possessed young lady.

9 "Only her name and address," admitted the caller. He was wondering whether Mrs. Sappleton was in the married or widowed state. An undefinable something about the room seemed to suggest masculine habitation.

10 "Her great tragedy happened just three years ago," said the child; "that would be since your sister's time."

11 "Her tragedy?" asked Framton; somehow in this restful country spot tragedies seemed out of place.

12 "You may wonder why we keep that window wide open on an October afternoon," said the niece, indicating a large French window that opened on to a lawn.

13 "It is quite warm for the time of the year," said Framton; "but has that window got anything to do with the tragedy?"

moor: boggy grassland

14 "Out through that window, three years ago to a day, her husband and her two young brothers went off for their day's shooting. They never came back. In crossing the **moor** to their favourite snipe-shooting ground they were all three engulfed in a treacherous piece of bog. It had been that dreadful wet summer, you know, and places that were safe in other years gave way suddenly without warning. Their bodies were never recovered. That was the dreadful part of it." Here the child's voice lost its self-possessed note and became falteringly human. "Poor aunt always thinks that they will come back some day, they and the little brown spaniel that was lost with them, and walk in at that window just as they used to do. That is why the window is kept open every evening till it is quite dusk. Poor dear aunt, she has often told me how they went out, her husband with his white waterproof coat over his arm, and Ronnie, her youngest brother, singing 'Bertie, why do you bound?' as he always did to tease her, because she said it got on her nerves. Do you know, sometimes on still, quiet evenings like this, I almost get a creepy feeling that they will all walk in through that window—"

15 She broke off with a little shudder. It was a relief to Framton when the aunt bustled into the room with a whirl of apologies for being late in making her appearance.

16 "I hope Vera has been amusing you?" she said.

17 "She has been very interesting," said Framton.

18 "I hope you don't mind the open window," said Mrs. Sappleton briskly; "my husband and brothers will be home directly from shooting, and they always come in this way. They've been out for snipe in the marshes to-day, so they'll make a fine mess over my poor carpets. So like you men-folk, isn't it?"

19 She rattled on cheerfully about the shooting and the scarcity of birds, and the prospects for duck in the winter. To Framton it was all purely horrible. He made a desperate but only partially successful effort to turn the talk on to a less ghastly topic; he was conscious that his hostess was giving him only a fragment of her attention, and her eyes were constantly straying past him to the open window and the lawn beyond. It was certainly an unfortunate coincidence that he should have paid his visit on this tragic anniversary.

20 "The doctors agree in ordering me complete rest, an absence of mental excitement, and avoidance of anything in the nature of violent physical exercise," announced Framton,

who **laboured under** the tolerably wide-spread **delusion** that total strangers and chance acquaintances are hungry for the least detail of one's ailments and infirmities, their cause and cure. "On the matter of diet they are not so much in agreement," he continued.

21 "No?" said Mrs. Sappleton, in a voice which only replaced a yawn at the last moment. Then she suddenly brightened into alert attention—but not to what Framton was saying.

22 "Here they are at last!" she cried. "Just in time for tea, and don't they look as if they were muddy up to the eyes!"

23 Framton shivered slightly and turned towards the niece with a look intended to convey sympathetic comprehension. The child was staring out through the open window with dazed horror in her eyes. In a chill shock of nameless fear Framton swung round in his seat and looked in the same direction.

24 In the deepening twilight three figures were walking across the lawn towards the window; they all carried guns under their arms, and one of them was additionally burdened with a white coat hung over his shoulders. A tired brown spaniel kept close at their heels. Noiselessly they neared the house, and then a hoarse young voice chanted out of the dusk: "I said, Bertie, why do you bound?"

25 Framton grabbed wildly at his stick and hat; the hall-door, the gravel-drive, and the front gate were dimly-noted stages in his headlong retreat. A cyclist coming along the road had to run into the hedge to avoid an imminent collision.

26 "Here we are, my dear," said the bearer of the white **mackintosh**, coming in through the window; "fairly muddy, but most of it's dry. Who was that who bolted out as we came up?"

27 "A most extraordinary man, a Mr. Nuttel," said Mrs. Sappleton; "could only talk about his illnesses, and dashed off without a word of good-bye or apology when you arrived. One would think he had seen a ghost."

28 "I expect it was the spaniel," said the niece calmly; "he told me he had a horror of dogs. He was once hunted into a cemetery somewhere on the banks of the Ganges by a pack of pariah dogs, and had to spend the night in a newly dug grave with the creatures snarling and grinning and foaming just above him. Enough to make anyone lose their nerve."

29 Romance at short notice was her speciality.

Second Read

- Reread the short story to answer these text-dependent questions.
- Write any additional questions you have about the text in your Reader/Writer Notebook.

3. **Key Ideas and Details:** Why is it significant that Framton Nuttel is described as undergoing a "nerve cure" in paragraph 2? Predict how this detail could be used for humorous effect.

4. **Craft and Structure:** What phrase in paragraph 3 helps you understand what "moping" means?

laboured under: be misled by a mistaken belief
delusion: a persistent false belief

My Notes

mackintosh: raincoat

Elements of Humor: Comic Characters and Caricatures

My Notes

5. **Craft and Structure:** What is the meaning of the word "habitation" in paragraph 9? What clues in the text leading up to and including paragraph 9 support your response?

6. **Key Ideas and Details:** What tone does the niece convey with her description of the "tragedy" in paragraph 14? What effect might this precise detail have on her guest?

7. **Craft and Structure:** What context clues tell you the meaning of the word "bog" in paragraph 14?

8. **Key Ideas and Details:** Why is it "horrible" for Framton to listen to Mrs. Sappleton as noted in paragraph 19?

9. **Craft and Structure:** What is the meaning of the word "ailments" in paragraph 20? What clues in the text support your response?

10. **Key Ideas and Details:** What does the author tell the reader in his narration that makes Framton Nuttel appear silly and pathetic in paragraph 20? Why?

11. **Key Ideas and Details:** Why is Nuttel's reaction to the return of the men in paragraph 25 comic rather than appropriate?

12. **Key Ideas and Details:** What aspects of the niece's character are revealed in her last line of dialogue in paragraph 28?

Working from the Text

13. For each unfamiliar word you circled, write a synonym in My Notes.

14. **Quickwrite** using a 3–2–1 reflection.

   3 – Describe three things you notice about the author's use of humor in the story.

   2 – Describe two characters you can picture most vividly.

   1 – Share one question you have.

15. Use the graphic organizer to express ideas you have about the characters and humor in this text.

Details	Characters	Interpretation
How does the author develop the character? (actions, words, thoughts)	Describe the character using precise adjectives. Would any of them be considered a caricature?	What truth about life is revealed through the comic character?
Framton Nuttel		
Mrs. Sappleton		
The niece		

Elements of Humor

Explaining why something is funny can be a challenge, but there are some common things authors do that usually make people laugh. Writers create humor by focusing on descriptions and actions that make characters funny, comic situations, and comic language. Humor often depends on some combination of these three elements.

16. Preview the Elements of Humor graphic organizer in Activity 4.11 and add notes about the comic characters and caricatures you explored in this activity. After you explore each new element of humor in the upcoming activities, return to this graphic organizer to add notes about new learning.

Check Your Understanding

Mr. Nuttel might be considered a caricature of a nervous person. Find examples in the story that support this idea and note them in your Reader/Writer Notebook.

My Notes

Elements of Humor: Comic Situations

Literary Terms
Irony is a literary device that plays on readers' expectations by portraying events in a way that is actually different from reality.

Learning Targets

- Investigate how humor is created by comic situations.
- Analyze comic situations in a literary text collaboratively.
- Determine the impact of word choice on meaning and tone in a comic situation.

Comic situations can be created in many different ways:

- by placing a character in an unlikely situation in which he or she obviously does not belong
- by portraying characters as victims of circumstances who are surprised by unusual events and react in a comical way
- by creating **situational irony** where there is contrast between what characters or readers might reasonably expect to happen and what actually happens

1. While you watch a film clip, think about how the situation contributes to the humor.
2. As you view the clip a second time, take notes using the graphic organizer below.

Clip: Director:

Comic Character _____	Comic Situation	Film Techniques That Help Create Humor
Appearance/Facial Expressions:	Setting:	Framing:
Actions:	Humorous Events:	Angles:
Words:		Sound:

Preview

In this activity, you will read an excerpt from a novel and think about the author's use of irony to create comic situations.

Setting a Purpose for Reading

- As you read the excerpt, underline words and phrases that explain what is happening in the plot.
- Circle unknown words and phrases. Try to determine the meaning of the words by using context clues, word parts, or a dictionary.
- Place a "D" by examples of dialect.

ABOUT THE AUTHOR
Born Samuel Langhorne Clemens, Mark Twain (1835–1910) was an American author and humorist. He is noted for his novels *The Adventures of Huckleberry Finn* (1885), called "the Great American Novel," and *The Adventures of Tom Sawyer* (1876). He has been lauded as the "greatest American humorist of his age," and William Faulkner called Twain "the father of American literature."

> **Literary Terms**
>
> **Dialect** is a regional or social variety of a language distinguished by pronunciation, grammar, or vocabulary. This section of the story includes a depiction of Tom's and Jim's dialects.

Novel

FROM
The Adventures of TOM SAWYER

by Mark Twain

"A DAY'S WORK"

Chunk 1

1 SATURDAY morning was come, and all the summer world was bright and fresh, and brimming with life. There was a song in every heart; and if the heart was young the music issued at the lips. There was cheer in every face and a spring in every step. The locust-trees were in bloom and the fragrance of the blossoms filled the air. Cardiff Hill, beyond the village and above it, was green with vegetation and it lay just far enough away to seem a Delectable Land, dreamy, reposeful, and inviting.

Chunk 2

2 Tom appeared on the sidewalk with a bucket of whitewash and a long-handled brush. He surveyed the fence, and all gladness left him and a deep melancholy settled down upon his spirit. Thirty yards of board fence nine feet high. Life to him seemed hollow, and existence but a burden. Sighing, he dipped his brush and passed it along the topmost plank; repeated the operation; did it again; compared the insignificant whitewashed streak with the far-reaching continent of unwhitewashed fence, and sat down on a tree-box discouraged. Jim came skipping out at the gate with a tin pail, and singing Buffalo Gals. Bringing water from the town pump had always been hateful

My Notes

_____

_____

_____

_____

_____

_____

_____

Elements of Humor: Comic Situations

work in Tom's eyes, before, but now it did not strike him so. He remembered that there was company at the pump. White, mulatto, and negro boys and girls were always there waiting their turns, resting, trading playthings, quarrelling, fighting, skylarking. And he remembered that although the pump was only a hundred and fifty yards off, Jim never got back with a bucket of water under an hour—and even then somebody generally had to go after him. Tom said:

Chunk 3

3 "Say, Jim, I'll fetch the water if you'll whitewash some."

4 Jim shook his head and said:

5 "Can't, Mars Tom. Ole missis, she tole me I got to go an' git dis water an' not stop foolin' roun' wid anybody. She say she spec' Mars Tom gwine to ax me to whitewash, an' so she tole me go 'long an' 'tend to my own business—she 'lowed SHE'D 'tend to de whitewashin'."

6 "Oh, never you mind what she said, Jim. That's the way she always talks. Gimme the bucket—I won't be gone only a minute. SHE won't ever know."

7 "Oh, I dasn't, Mars Tom. Ole missis she'd take an' tar de head off'n me. 'Deed she would."

8 "SHE! She never licks anybody—whacks 'em over the head with her thimble—and who cares for that, I'd like to know. She talks awful, but talk don't hurt—anyways it don't if she don't cry. Jim, I'll give you a marvel. I'll give you a **white alley**!"

9 Jim began to waver.

10 "White alley, Jim! And it's a bully taw."

11 "My! Dat's a mighty gay marvel, I tell you! But Mars Tom I's powerful 'fraid ole missis—"

12 "And besides, if you will I'll show you my sore toe."

13 Jim was only human—this attraction was too much for him. He put down his pail, took the white alley, and bent over the toe with absorbing interest while the bandage was being unwound. In another moment he was flying down the street with his pail and a tingling rear, Tom was whitewashing with vigor, and Aunt Polly was retiring from the field with a slipper in her hand and triumph in her eye.

14 But Tom's energy did not last. He began to think of the fun he had planned for this day, and his sorrows multiplied. Soon the free boys would come tripping along on all sorts of delicious expeditions, and they would make a world of fun of him for having to work—the very thought of it burnt him like fire. He got out his worldly wealth and examined it—bits of toys, marbles, and trash; enough to buy an exchange of WORK, maybe, but not half enough to buy so much as half an hour of pure freedom. So he returned his **straitened** means to his pocket, and gave up the idea of trying to buy the boys. At this dark and hopeless moment an inspiration burst upon him! Nothing less than a great, magnificent inspiration.

Chunk 4

15 He took up his brush and went tranquilly to work. Ben Rogers hove in sight presently—the very boy, of all boys, whose ridicule he had been dreading. Ben's gait was the hop-skip-and-jump—proof enough that his heart was light and his anticipations high. He was eating an apple, and giving a long, melodious whoop, at intervals, followed by a deep-toned ding-dong-dong, ding-dong-dong, for he was personating a steamboat. As he drew near, he slackened speed, took the middle of the street, leaned far over to starboard and rounded to ponderously and with laborious pomp and circumstance—

WORD CONNECTIONS

Multiple Meaning Words

The word *whitewash* has come to have a second meaning. In this story, *whitewash* means "a whitening mixture used on fences and walls." The word has also come to mean "to conceal or cover up crimes, scandals, flaws, or failures." You can see how this usage comes from the idea of using whitewash to cover up something bad.

white alley: a kind of marble

WORD CONNECTIONS

Word Relationships

The words "great" and "magnificent" may seem similar; however, Twain uses **magnificent** to mean "splendid; impressive," while **great**, in this context, means important. Twain uses both words to inform the reader that a pivotal change is about to occur in the story because of Tom's idea.

straitened: characterized by poverty

for he was personating the *Big Missouri*, and considered himself to be drawing nine feet of water. He was boat and captain and engine-bells combined, so he had to imagine himself standing on his own hurricane-deck giving the orders and executing them:

16 "Stop her, sir! Ting-a-ling-ling!" The headway ran almost out, and he drew up slowly toward the sidewalk.

17 "Ship up to back! Ting-a-ling-ling!" His arms straightened and stiffened down his sides.

18 "Set her back on the stabboard! Ting-a-ling-ling! Chow! ch-chow-wow! Chow!" His right hand, mean-time, describing stately circles—for it was representing a forty-foot wheel.

19 "Let her go back on the labboard! Ting-a-ling-ling! Chow-ch-chow-chow!" The left hand began to describe circles.

20 "Stop the stabboard! Ting-a-ling-ling! Stop the labboard! Come ahead on the stabboard! Stop her! Let your outside turn over slow! Ting-a-ling-ling! Chow-ow-ow! Get out that head-line! LIVELY now! Come—out with your spring-line—what're you about there! Take a turn round that stump with the bight of it! Stand by that stage, now—let her go! Done with the engines, sir! Ting-a-ling-ling! SH'T! S'H'T! SH'T!" (trying the gauge-cocks).

21 Tom went on whitewashing—paid no attention to the steamboat. Ben stared a moment and then said: "Hi-YI! YOU'RE up a stump, ain't you!"

Chunk 5

22 No answer. Tom surveyed his last touch with the eye of an artist, then he gave his brush another gentle sweep and surveyed the result, as before. Ben ranged up alongside of him. Tom's mouth watered for the apple, but he stuck to his work. Ben said:

23 "Hello, old chap, you got to work, hey?"

24 Tom wheeled suddenly and said:

25 "Why, it's you, Ben! I warn't noticing."

26 "Say—I'm going in a-swimming, I am. Don't you wish you could? But of course you'd druther WORK—wouldn't you? Course you would!"

27 Tom contemplated the boy a bit, and said:

28 "What do you call work?"

29 "Why, ain't THAT work?"

30 Tom resumed his whitewashing, and answered carelessly:

31 "Well, maybe it is, and maybe it ain't. All I know, is, it suits Tom Sawyer."

32 "Oh come, now, you don't mean to let on that you LIKE it?"

33 The brush continued to move.

34 "Like it? Well, I don't see why I oughtn't to like it. Does a boy get a chance to whitewash a fence every day?"

35 That put the thing in a new light. Ben stopped nibbling his apple. Tom swept his brush daintily back and forth—stepped back to note the effect—added a touch here and there—criticized the effect again—Ben watching every move and getting more and more interested, more and more absorbed. Presently he said:

36 "Say, Tom, let ME whitewash a little."

37 Tom considered, was about to consent; but he altered his mind:

My Notes

Elements of Humor: Comic Situations

GRAMMAR & USAGE
Denotation and Connotation

A word's **denotation** is its actual meaning. Its **connotation** is the feeling or impression it gives the reader. When Ben enters the fence scene, he's described as "eating an apple." The connation of this description is very literal: He is actually eating an apple. But further along, he is described as "nibbling" the apple. The denotation of *nibbling* is "taking small bites." The use of *nibbling* implies that Ben has become too distracted to eat the apple, so he is taking tiny bites while he thinks. After Ben starts to paint and gives his apple to Tom, Tom "munched" his apple. The word *munched* carries a connotation of joy, so it helps show how happy Tom is with himself.

As you read, look for two more instances where the author has chosen words especially for their connotations.

My Notes

_____

_____

_____

_____

_____

_____

_____

_____

_____

_____

_____

_____

38 "No—no—I reckon it wouldn't hardly do, Ben. You see, Aunt Polly's awful particular about this fence—right here on the street, you know—but if it was the back fence I wouldn't mind and SHE wouldn't. Yes, she's awful particular about this fence; it's got to be done very careful; I reckon there ain't one boy in a thousand, maybe two thousand, that can do it the way it's got to be done."

39 "No—is that so? Oh come, now—lemme just try. Only just a little—I'd let YOU, if you was me, Tom."

40 "Ben, I'd like to, honest injun; but Aunt Polly—well, Jim wanted to do it, but she wouldn't let him; Sid wanted to do it, and she wouldn't let Sid. Now don't you see how I'm fixed? If you was to tackle this fence and anything was to happen to it—"

41 "Oh, shucks, I'll be just as careful. Now lemme try. Say—I'll give you the core of my apple."

42 "Well, here—No, Ben, now don't. I'm afeard—"

43 "I'll give you ALL of it!"

Chunk 6

44 Tom gave up the brush with reluctance in his face, but alacrity in his heart. And while the late steamer *Big Missouri* worked and sweated in the sun, the retired artist sat on a barrel in the shade close by, dangled his legs, munched his apple, and planned the slaughter of more innocents. There was no lack of material; boys happened along every little while; they came to jeer, but remained to whitewash. By the time Ben was fagged out, Tom had traded the next chance to Billy Fisher for a kite, in good repair; and when he played out, Johnny Miller bought in for a dead rat and a string to swing it with—and so on, and so on, hour after hour. And when the middle of the afternoon came, from being a poor poverty-stricken boy in the morning, Tom was literally rolling in wealth. He had besides the things before mentioned, twelve marbles, part of a jews-harp, a piece of blue bottle-glass to look through, a spool cannon, a key that wouldn't unlock anything, a fragment of chalk, a glass stopper of a decanter, a tin soldier, a couple of tadpoles, six fire-crackers, a kitten with only one eye, a brass door-knob, a dog-collar—but no dog—the handle of a knife, four pieces of orange-peel, and a dilapidated old window sash.

Second Read

- Reread the excerpt to answer these text-dependent questions.
- Write any additional questions you have about the text in your Reader/Writer Notebook.

3. **Craft and Structure:** What does the word "reposeful" mean in paragraph 1? What clues in the text help you understand the meaning of the word?

4. **Craft and Structure:** What does the word "melancholy" mean in paragraph 2? What clues in the text helped you understand the meaning of the word?

5. **Craft and Structure:** One of the notable characteristics of Twain's style is his use of verbals. Examine paragraph 2 and highlight all the verbals.

6. **Key Ideas and Details:** How does Tom try to get Jim to help him in Chunk 3? Why does he fail?

7. **Craft and Structure:** How does Twain use steamboat jargon for effect in Chunk 4?

8. **Key Ideas and Details:** Tom tries to manipulate his friends into doing whitewashing for him. How does he change his plan in Chunk 5 after Jim's refusal to help?

9. **Craft and Structure:** What does the word "alacrity" mean in paragraph 44? Cite the text to support your response.

10. **Craft and Structure:** What is the intended effect of listing Tom's "treasures" in such great detail in paragraph 44? What does the audience understand about the value of these things that is different from Tom's point of view?

My Notes

Elements of Humor: Comic Situations

Working from the Text

11. Review the definition of **dialect** on page 297. Referencing the words and phrases you have already marked with a "D," try to paraphrase a few lines of dialogue in My Notes.

12. Prepare for a collaborative discussion by annotating and reviewing the text as follows:
    - Review what you have already underlined as the plot and make changes as needed. Be prepared to **paraphrase** (retell in your own words) the plot.
    - Place a question mark next to any word or idea you would like to **clarify** (discuss to remove confusion).
    - Place a star next to any part of the text you would like to **analyze** (share an inference, assumption, prediction based on the text).

13. On a separate piece of paper or in your Reader/Writer Notebook, create a graphic organizer like the one below to answer comprehension questions about the story.

Tom is like a ... (create a simile)	It is ironic that ...
The part of the story that stands out in my head is ... (draw a picture) This is a comedic situation because ...	I wonder ...

14. What is the level of comedy of this text? What is a universal truth, or theme, of this text? Write a thematic statement. Be sure to support your ideas with textual evidence.

Twain – "All in a Day's Work"
Level of Comedy:
Theme subject(s):
Theme statement:

Check Your Understanding

In your Reader/Writer Notebook, record three specific comic situations from the text. Share them with a partner.

Writing to Sources: Explanatory Text

Explain how Mark Twain uses comic characters and situations to convey a universal truth through humor. Be sure to:

- Establish a controlling idea and support it with textual evidence and commentary.
- Use transitions to create cohesion and clarify the relationships among ideas and concepts.
- Use precise diction and maintain a formal style.
- Use verbals.

Elements of Humor

Add your notes about comic situations to the Elements of Humor graphic organizer in Activity 4.11.

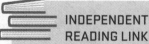

INDEPENDENT READING LINK

Read and Research

Research other humorous works by Mark Twain. Choose one of these works and create a one-paragraph summary of a comic situation in your Reader/Writer Notebook. Note the level of comedy and identify the theme statement.

Learning Targets

- Understand the difference between the frequently confused words *its/it' s*, *your/you' re*, and *their/ they' re/there*.
- Use frequently confused words correctly when writing and editing.

Recognizing Frequently Confused Words

In English, some of the most frequently confused words are *its*, *your*, and *their* and *it' s*, *you' re*, and *they' re*. The adverb *there* is also frequently misused.

1. **Quickwrite:** Why do you think a writer might confuse these words?

2. Read the following sentences from *The Adventures of Tom Sawyer*:

   He [Tom] remembered that there was company at the pump…[B]oys and girls were always <u>there</u> waiting <u>their</u> turns, resting, trading playthings, quarrelling, fighting, skylarking.

   What does each underlined word refer to?

   there: _____

   their: _____

Understanding Possessive Determiners

Quick Guide to Possessive Determiners	
your	Thank you for letting me borrow <u>your</u> book about Mark Twain.
its	I didn't know the word "straitened," so I read <u>its</u> meaning in the margin.
their	The characters give Tom <u>their</u> prized possessions for a chance to paint.

Possessive determiners are words that show to whom something belongs. Writers use possessive determiners—which include the words *my*, *your*, *his*, *her*, *its*, *our*, and *their*—to make sentences more cohesive and less repetitive. For this reason, the sentence "Tom worked very hard, so Tom's energy did not last" is not typical. The more typical version of the sentence would be "Tom worked very hard, so his energy did not last."

3. Work with a partner to revise the following sentences to include possessive determiners.

   a. Tom, give me Tom's paintbrush!
      Revised:

   b. The children shared the children's wealth.
      Revised:

   c. The fence got the fence's paint, and all was well.
      Revised:

4. Take turns with your partner to read each pair of sentences aloud. How do the two versions sound different? Which sounds clearer? Why?

Understanding Contractions

A contraction is a shortened word, or two words spliced together, with an apostrophe. Writers use contractions to add variety to their sentences, or to create more realistic dialogue.

Quick Guide to Contractions		
Phrase	**Contraction**	**Sample Sentence**
you are	you're	You're a clever boy, Tom Sawyer!
it is	it's	It's a nice summer day.
they are	they're	They're doing Tom's work for him.

5. Mark Twain uses several contractions in *The Adventures of Tom Sawyer* to show the dialect of the characters. With your partner, scan the passage in Activity 4.8 and find examples of the following contractions. The chunks have been provided to narrow your search. Write the quotes in the chart. Then rewrite each sentence to include both words in the contraction.

Contraction	Quote	Expanded Sentence
it's [Chunk 3]		
you're [Chunk 4]		

6. Take turns with your partner to read the sentences aloud. How do the two versions sound different? How does the character change when you change his or her speech?

Revising

Read the following paragraph from a student's essay. Choose the word that belongs in each sentence.

The Adventures of Tom Sawyer is a hilarious story that [your/you're] bound to like. Even though [its/it's] old, I found it entertaining. [Its/It's] central character is, of course, Tom Sawyer. Tom is a young boy who has to whitewash his aunt's fence one beautiful summer morning. He hates doing that chore, and he worries about what his friends will say when they pass by on [their/they're/there] way to play and have fun. Tom thinks [its/it's] unfair that he has to do work while [their/they're/there] free to roam about, so he comes up with a plan. As they walk by, he pretends he is having a good time painting the fence, and [their/they're/there] missing out. This tactic gets them to give Tom [their/they're/there] possessions in exchange for a chance to paint. He doesn't have to do the work, and he gets a lot of stuff he likes. Tom might not be [your/you're] favorite person, but no one can deny that he is clever.

Compare your choices with a partner's. Did you make the same choices? Work together to resolve any differences.

Check Your Understanding

What question(s) can you ask yourself whenever you write to be sure that you have used the word or contraction you meant to use? Add the question(s) to your Editor's Checklist.

Practice

Reread the explanatory essay you wrote in Activity 4.8. Highlight each instance where you wrote the following words and determine whether or not you selected the correct word in each case.

your, you' re, its, it' s, their, they' re, there

Elements of Humor: Hyperbole

Literary Terms

Hyperbole describes the literary technique of extreme exaggeration for emphasis, often used for comic effect.

My Notes

Literary Terms

A **yarn** is a long, often involved story, usually telling of incredible or fantastic events; an entertaining tale; a tall tale.

Learning Targets

- Analyze the effect of hyperbole in poetry.
- Identify hyperbole in previously studied print and nonprint texts.

Understanding Hyperbole

1. Finish the lines using hyperbolic language. The first line is shown as an example.
   - My dog is so big, he beeps when he backs up.
   - I'm so hungry, I could eat a _____.
   - My cat is so smart that _____.
   - She was so funny that _____.

Preview

In this activity, you will read poems and think about the authors' use of hyperbole.

Setting a Purpose for Reading

- As you read the poem, underline words and phrases that demonstrate hyperbole.
- Circle unknown words and phrases. Try to determine the meaning of the words by using context clues, word parts, or a dictionary.
- Mark lines you find humorous or strange with an exclamation point.

ABOUT THE AUTHOR

Carl Sandburg (1878–1967) was a journalist who also wrote poetry, novels, and historical books. He is perhaps best known as a poet, although his biography *Abraham Lincoln: The War Years* won a Pulitzer Prize.

Poetry

"They Have Yarns"

by Carl Sandburg

They have yarns
Of a skyscraper so tall they had to put hinges
On the two top stories so to let the moon go by,
Of one corn crop in Missouri when the roots

Went so deep and drew off so much water
The Mississippi riverbed that year was dry,
Of pancakes so thin they had only one side,
Of "a fog so thick we shingled the barn and six feet out on the fog,"
Of Pecos Pete straddling a cyclone in Texas and riding it to the west coast where
   "it rained out under him,"

Of the man who drove a swarm of bees across the Rocky Mountains and the Desert
  "and didn't lose a bee,"

Of a mountain railroad curve where the engineer in his cab can touch the caboose
  and spit in the conductor's eye,

Of the boy who climbed a cornstalk growing so fast he would have starved to death
  if they hadn't shot biscuits up to him,

Of the old man's whiskers: "When the wind was with him his whiskers
  arrived a day before he did,"

Of the hen laying a square egg and cackling, "Ouch!" and of hens laying eggs with
  the dates printed on them,

Of the ship captain's shadow: it froze to the deck one cold winter night,

Of mutineers on that same ship put to chipping rust with rubber hammers,

Of the sheep counter who was fast and accurate: "I just count their feet and divide
  by four,"

Of the man so tall he must climb a ladder to shave himself,

Of the runt so teeny-weeny it takes two men and a boy to see him,

Of mosquitoes: one can kill a dog, two of them a man,

Of a cyclone that sucked cookstoves out of the kitchen, up the chimney flue, and on
  to the next town,

Of the same cyclone picking up wagon-tracks in Nebraska and dropping them over
  in the Dakotas,

Of the hook-and-eye snake unlocking itself into forty pieces, each piece two inches
  long, then in nine seconds flat snapping itself together again,

Of the watch swallowed by the cow—when they butchered her a year later the
  watch was running and had the correct time,

Of horned snakes, hoop snakes that roll themselves where they want to go, and
  rattlesnakes carrying bells instead of rattles on their tails,

Of the herd of cattle in California getting lost in a giant redwood tree that had
  hollowed out,

Of the man who killed a snake by putting its tail in its mouth so it swallowed itself,

Of railroad trains whizzing along so fast they reach the station before the whistle,

Of pigs so thin the farmer had to tie knots in their tails to keep them from crawling
  through the cracks in their pen,

Of Paul Bunyan's big blue ox, Babe, measuring between the eyes forty-two
  ax-handles and a plug of Star tobacco exactly,

Of John Henry's hammer and the curve of its swing and his singing of it as
  "a rainbow round my shoulder."

WORD CONNECTIONS

Content Connections

One of the fantastic events in this poem deals with an event common to meteorology: a cyclone. A cyclone is a large, powerful, and destructive storm with high winds turning in an area of low pressure.

GRAMMAR & USAGE
Participial Phrases

In previous activities you learned that a participle is an –ing or –ed form of a verb that acts as an adjective. A **participial phrase** is made up of a participle plus any modifiers or complements the participle has. A participial phrase modifies a noun or pronoun.

Consider these examples from the poem:

"a cornstalk **growing so fast**"

"the dates **printed on them**"

"rattlesnakes **carrying bells instead of rattles on their tails**"

As you read, look for other examples of participial phrases. Note which noun or pronoun each participial phrase modifies.

My Notes

_____

_____

_____

_____

_____

Elements of Humor: Hyperbole

Second Read

- Reread the poem to answer these text-dependent questions.
- Write any additional questions you have about the text in your Reader/Writer Notebook.

2. **Knowledge and Ideas:** Reference the text and choose three of the yarns. Identify the real things they exaggerate. Provide examples of hyperbole related to these real things by citing the text.

3. **Key Ideas and Details:** What allusions does the author use? How might this add to the humor?

Working from the Text

4. Review the definitions of hyperbole and yarn on page 306. Based on Sandburg's poem, how might a yarn relate to a hyperbole?

5. In a collaborative discussion, share the lines you underlined as demonstrating hyperbole, the unknown words and phrases you circled, and the lines you marked as funny or strange.

6. Using the My Notes section on page 307, add a line or two to Sandburg's poem, using hyperbolic language and a participial adjective phrase. Consider using an allusion for humorous effect. Note how each line of hyperbole begins the same way.

7. Place a "V" next to lines in the text that contain verbals.

Setting a Purpose for Reading

- As you read the poem, underline words and phrases that demonstrate hyperbole.
- Circle unknown words and phrases. Try to determine the meaning of the words by using context clues, word parts, or a dictionary.
- Mark lines you find humorous or strange with an exclamation point.

ABOUT THE AUTHOR

Ted Hughes (1930–1998) is considered to be one of the twentieth century's greatest poets. He wrote almost 90 books during his long career and won numerous prizes and fellowships. In 1984, he was appointed England's poet laureate.

Poetry

"Mooses"

by Ted Hughes

The goofy Moose, the walking house frame,
Is lost
In the forest. He bumps, he blunders, he stands.

With massy bony thoughts sticking out near his ears—
Reaching out palm upwards, to catch whatever might be
falling from heaven—
He tries to think,
Leaning their huge weight
On the lectern of his front legs.
He can't find the world!
Where did it go? What
does a world look like?

The Moose
Crashes on, and crashes into a
lake, and stares at the
mountain and cries:
'Where do I belong? This is no place!'

He turns dragging half the lake out after him
And charges the crackling underbrush

He meets another Moose
He stares, he thinks: 'It's only a mirror!'
Where is the world?' he groans. 'O my lost world!

And why am I so ugly?
'And why am I so far away from my feet?'

My Notes

He weeps.

Hopeless drops drip from his droopy lips.

The other Moose just stands there doing the same.

Two dopes of the deep woods.

Second Read

- Reread the poem to answer these text-dependent questions.
- Write any additional questions you have about the text in your Reader/Writer Notebook.

8. **Craft and Structure:** Look for examples of parallel structure and repetition in the poem. How do these stylistic choices make the moose appear "goofy"?

9. **Key Ideas and Details:** Is this poem high or low comedy? How do you know?

Working from the Text

10. Cite the text to illustrate how the author uses hyperbole for effect.

11. What words and phrases show how the speaker's tone shifts throughout the poem?

12. How does Hughes's use of verbals, especially participial phrases, contribute to the hyperbole in the poem? Quote specific lines and analyze the use of verbals and hyperbole.

Setting a Purpose for Reading

- As you read the poem, underline words and phrases that demonstrate hyperbole.
- Circle unknown words and phrases. Try to determine the meaning of the words by using context clues, word parts, or a dictionary.
- Mark lines you find humorous or strange with an exclamation point.

WORD CONNECTIONS

Cognates

Chicle is a gummy substance obtained from trees and used to manufacture chewing gum. In Spanish, *el chicle*, means "gum."

> **ABOUT THE AUTHOR**
> Ana Castillo is a celebrated Chicana poet, activist, novelist, and translator. Her commitment to human rights, free expression, and cultural exchange has shaped her career as a writer and scholar. Castillo's work in poetry and prose is highly innovative and is based on oral and literary traditions.

Poetry

El Chicle

by Ana Castillo

Mi'jo and I were
laughing
ha, ha, ha—
when the gum he
chewed
fell out of his mouth
and into my hair
which, after I clipped
it,
flew in the air,
on the back
of a dragonfly
that dipped in the
creek
and was snapped
fast by a turtle
that reached high
and swam deep.
Mi'jo wondered
what happened to

My Notes

Elements of Humor: Hyperbole

My Notes

that gum,
worried that it stuck
to the back of my
seat
and Mami will be
mad
when she can't get it
out.
Meanwhile, the turtle
in the pond
that ate the dragonfly
that carried the hair
with the gum
swam south on
Saturday
and hasn't been seen
once since.

Second Read

- Reread the poem to answer these text-dependent questions.
- Write any additional questions you have about the text in your Reader/Writer Notebook.

13. **Craft and Structure:** Who do you think "Mi'jo" refers to? What clues in the poem support your answer?

14. **Key Ideas and Details:** What is the central event of the poem? How do you know?

Working from the Text

15. What is the consistent tone of the poem, and who is the intended audience? Cite words or phrases from the poem to support your response.

Check Your Understanding

Return to the humorous texts you have read in this unit and identify a couple examples of hyperbole. Share your examples in a small group and discuss how hyperbole creates a humorous effect. Record examples shared by your peers in the graphic organizer.

Title:

Example:

Title:

Example:

Hyperbole

Title:

Example:

Title:

Example:

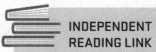

INDEPENDENT READING LINK

Read and Connect

Research humorous texts in which the author uses hyperbole for effect. Choose a text that exemplifies the use of hyperbole, tone, and verbals. Cite examples to support your choice in your Reader/Writer Notebook. Include a brief summary explaining why this humorous text appeals to you. You will use your notes to recommend the text to your peers in a small group setting.

Elements of Humor: Comic Wordplay

My Notes

Learning Targets
- Interpret the use of wordplay in poetry and drama.
- Collaborate to explore wordplay in previously studied texts.
- Create a visual representation of a pun.

Preview
In this activity, you will read a poem and think about the author's use of wordplay, specifically puns.

Setting a Purpose for Reading
- As you read the poem, underline words and phrases that demonstrate the author's use of puns.
- Circle unknown words and phrases. Try to determine the meaning of the words by using context clues, word parts, or a dictionary.
- Draw a question mark next to any puns that you do not understand.

ABOUT THE AUTHOR
Jack Prelutsky (b. 1940) says that he has always enjoyed playing with language, although he did not always like poetry. He rediscovered poetry in his twenties, when he began writing humorous verse for children. Since then, he has written more than fifty poetry collections. His poems are sometimes silly, sometimes playful, sometimes frightening, but always entertaining. In 2006, the Poetry Foundation named him the first-ever Children's Poet Laureate. Prelutsky also studied music, and he has set several of his poems to music for the audio versions of his poetry anthologies.

WORD CONNECTIONS

Roots and Affixes
The word *clamor* comes from a Latin word meaning "to call out." The root *-clam-*, also spelled *-claim-*, appears in *exclaim* and *exclamation*, *proclaim* and *proclamation*, and *acclaim* and *acclamation*.

Poetry

Is Traffic Jam Delectable?

by Jack Prelutsky

Is traffic jam delectable,
does jelly fish in lakes,
does tree bark make a racket,
does the clamor rattle snakes?

Can salmon scale a mountain,
does a belly laugh a lot,
do carpets nap in flower beds
or on an apricot?
Around my handsome bottleneck,

I wear a railroad tie,
my treasure chest puffs up a bit,
I blink my private eye.
I like to use piano keys
to open locks of hair,

then put a pair of brake shoes on
and dance on debonair.
I hold up my electric shorts
with my banana belt,
then sit upon a toadstool

and watch a tuna melt.
I dive into a car pool,
where I take an onion dip,
then stand aboard the tape deck
and sail my penmanship.

I put my dimes in riverbanks
and take a quarterback,
and when I fix a nothing flat
I use a lumberjack.
I often wave my second hand

to tell the overtime,
before I take my bull pen up
to write a silly rhyme.

Second Read

- Reread the poem to answer these text-dependent questions.
- Write any additional questions you have about the text in your Reader/Writer Notebook.

1. **Craft and Structure:** How does Prelutsky's understanding of children influence his choice of words? What is the result for the reader? Cite examples from the text to support your answer.

My Notes

Elements of Humor: Comic Wordplay

2. **Key Ideas and Details:** Puns depend on an audience's understanding of both possible meanings of a word or phrase. Why might someone older be more likely to understand what a "tape deck" or "brake shoes" are? What does this indicate about the level of comedy involved in puns?

Working from the Text

3. Referencing the text as an example, define *pun* and create some examples of your own.

4. Mark the text by highlighting at least three humorous puns that you can visualize.

5. Sketch at least one of the puns in the margin of the poem or on a separate piece of paper.

6. In your discussion groups, share your sketches and read aloud the corresponding pun. Explain the two meanings of the word or phrase that creates the pun. Be sure to use precise diction and discuss how the author uses puns for humorous effect.

7. As a group, review the poem and discuss the puns that you notated with question marks. Try to collaborate to make meaning of these.

Analyzing a Humorous Skit

You will next read and/or listen to the skit "Who's on First?" by Abbott and Costello.

8. Based on the title of the skit, what do you think is the subject?

9. Sketch a baseball diamond on a separate piece of paper. As you read the skit, try to fill in the names of each of the players mentioned.

10. Write answers to the following questions about "Who's on First?" and compare them with a peer.

- Why are Abbott and Costello having difficulty understanding each other?

- How does the wordplay create humor at a high level of comedy?

11. Add your notes about comic language (hyperbole and wordplay) to the Elements of Humor graphic organizer in Activity 4.11.

Check Your Understanding

Reread "Is Traffic Jam Delectable?" Choose two of the puns in the poem and draw pictures to illustrate them.

Writing to Sources: Explanatory Text

Choose one of the texts from this or the previous activity. Explain how the writer uses comic language (hyperbole and/or wordplay) to express a universal truth. Be sure to:

- Establish a controlling idea and support it with quotes from the text and commentary explaining the humor.
- Use the correct terms to refer to the elements of humor.
- Use verbals and precise diction.
- Check that frequently confused words are used correctly.

My Notes

Planning and Revising an Analysis of a Humorous Text

LEARNING STRATEGIES:
Graphic Organizer, Marking the Text, Note-taking, Drafting, Discussion Groups

Learning Targets

- Draft and revise an essay analyzing a humorous short story.
- Evaluate a sample student essay.

Identifying and Analyzing the Elements of Humor

1. Review the Elements of Humor graphic organizer below and rank how comfortable you are at understanding the elements (#1 being most comfortable, #2 being second most, etc.).

Elements of Humor			
Humorous Element	**Definition**	**Level of Comedy**	**Examples from Texts**
Comic Characters and Caricatures	A caricature is a pictorial, written, or acted representation of a person that exaggerates characteristics or traits for comic effect.		
Comic Situations and Situational Irony	Comic situations are when characters are in an unlikely situation or are victims of circumstances and react in a comical way. Situational irony involves a contrast between what characters or readers might reasonably expect to happen and what actually happens.		
Comic Language: Hyperbole	Hyperbole is extreme exaggeration used for emphasis, often used for comic effect.		
Comic Language: Wordplay • **One-liners** • **Puns**	A one-liner is a short joke or witticism expressed in a single sentence. A pun is the humorous use of a word or words to suggest another word with the same sound or different meaning.		

2. Your teacher will assign a text for you to analyze.
   - Closely read (or reread) the text.
   - Mark the text by highlighting evidence of humorous elements.
   - Annotate the text using precise diction to describe the intended humor and humorous effect.

My Notes

_____

_____

_____

_____

_____

_____

3. Collaborate with your group to complete the graphic organizer below and on the next page.

Title: _____   **Author:** _____

Humorous Element	Examples from Text	Comedic Effect
Comic Characters and Caricatures		
Comic Situations and Situational Irony		
Comic Language: Hyperbole		
Comic Language: Wordplay • **One-liners** • **Puns**		

Planning and Revising an Analysis of a Humorous Text

Level of Comedy	Explanation	Evidence

Description of Humor and Intended Effect	Examples from Text	Explanation (Commentary)

Universal Truth (Theme)	Evidence from Text

Reading and Analyzing a Sample Essay

An effective essay includes a clear introduction to the topic, body paragraphs that expand on the thesis and provide evidence and commentary to support it, and a conclusion that provides closure for the topic.

Introduction

- Begin with a **hook**.
- Set the **context** for the essay.
- Establish a **controlling idea** (**thesis** statement) that directly responds to the prompt.

Body Paragraphs

- Begin with a **topic sentence** related to the thesis.
- Include **evidence** from the text (paraphrased and directly quoted).
- Provide **commentary** that uses precise diction to describe humor and the intended effect.
- Use a variety of **transitions** to connect ideas and create coherence.

Concluding Paragraph

- Discuss the universal truth revealed through the text.
- Evaluate the effectiveness of the author's use of humor to communicate this truth.

Setting a Purpose for Reading

- As you read the explanatory essay, underline precise diction and academic vocabulary, especially humorous vocabulary.
- Circle unknown words and phrases. Try to determine the meaning of the words by using context clues, word parts, or a dictionary.
- Place a question mark by any sentences or sections that you think need to be revised.

My Notes

Planning and Revising an Analysis of a Humorous Text

Student Explanatory Essay

"The Power of Pets"

by Isha Sharma (an eighth-grade student)

1   Every child has gone through a phase in life when they have a sudden fixation with getting a pet, and parents often have to go through a lot of trouble in order to appease the child, at least until the obsession is replaced with another. In the light-hearted essay, "I've got a few pet peeves about sea creatures," Dave Barry uses hyperbole and verbal irony to show how a parent will often go through great lengths to satisfy his child, often hoping that the child will learn something in the process.

2   To point out the often ridiculous experiences parents go through for their children, Barry uses hyperbole to emphasize how complicated getting a pet fish can be. For example, he explains first how a "pet" beetle under his daughter's "loving care and feeding ... thrived for maybe nine seconds before expiring like a little six legged parking meter" (1). The additional use of simile and the exaggerated amount of time adds to the humor, as in any case, one's "loving care and feeding" should not cause the death of anything so quickly, no matter how terrible the "care" could actually be. The explanation of the parents replacing each beetle with another shows how willing parents are to support their children no matter how ridiculous the circumstances. Furthermore, Barry calls the fish he bought "so nonviolent that in the wild, worms routinely beat them up and steal their lunch money" (2). As known to all people, it is fish that eat worms and not the other way around. This is hyperbolic because worms are not known for "beating fish up" and animals do not have money, lunch money included. This also ties back to a metaphor/analogy Barry made that "an aquarium is a powder keg that can explode in deadly violence at any moment just like ... junior high" (2). Both of these situations are highly exaggerated. Through the use of hyperbole, Barry is able to convey how parents often feel about their struggle even in simple situations, to which a child might react to them as being overdramatic.

3   Also, Barry uses verbal irony/sarcasm to vent and display his frustration, which proves furthermore the lengths he is going to help his daughter. For instance, when complaining about the aggressive nature of fish, he says they could become aggressive if "it was a month containing the letter 'R', of if they hear the song "Who Let the Dogs Out"" (2). Months and songs are all aspects of human life, it is unlikely that fish will ever have fish months or fish songs. This adds to the sarcastic tone of the writer, which shows that even through his frustrations, he is struggling to find the right choice for his daughter, no matter how much of a nuisance it is to make it. Also, Barry uses sarcasm when explaining the variety of needs for a fish tank so that "the fish would be intellectually stimulated and get into a decent college" (1). The author, as with most intellectual people, knows that fish do not have colleges, and seeing

that their intelligence capacity is smaller than a human's, they cannot be "intellectually stimulated." The author uses this verbal irony to point out that even though the needs of a fish are not as significant as the needs of a human, caring for them still requires a lot of effort. Clearly, the author chooses to go through this effort for his daughter. The usage of verbal irony in this piece further points out the "struggles" of a father to appease his child.

4   Even in the most trivial instances, the parent will go though many obstacles to help his child, often in the hope that the child will learn something along the way. Whether or not the child actually learns this is questionable, yet the parent's effort should not go unnoticed.

Second Read

- Reread the explanatory essay to answer these text-dependent questions.
- Write any additional questions you have about the text in your Reader/Writer Notebook.

4. **Craft and Structure:** Identify and write the hook, context, and controlling idea or thesis in the introduction.

5. **Craft and Structure:** In each paragraph, identify the topic sentence, supporting detail, commentary, and transitions and write your responses below.

Planning and Revising an Analysis of a Humorous Text

6. **Key Ideas and Details:** In the concluding paragraph, identify and write the universal truth.

Working from the Text

7. Referring back to the question marks you notated in the text, create revision suggestions for each. Write your responses in the My Notes space next to the text.

8. Work with your writing group to revise the student essay. You may want to review the roles and responsibilities of writing group members in Activity 1.8. Select one or more of the following:

   - Write a new introduction.
   - Write a third support paragraph.
   - Write a new conclusion.

Check Your Understanding

Working with a partner, evaluate the revised student essay and briefly discuss any further revisions you think would improve it. Consult the steps in this activity to guide your discussion.

 Independent Reading Checkpoint

Consider the connections you made while reading humorous texts. In one paragraph, summarize one message (theme) a particular author tried to convey to the reader through humor. Briefly describe the level of comedy and the elements of humor used by the author.

Writing an Analysis of a Humorous Text

ASSIGNMENT

Write an essay that explains how an author creates humor for effect and uses it to communicate a universal truth.

Planning and Prewriting: Take time to make a plan for your essay.	▦ What reading strategies (such as marking or diffusing the text) will help you take notes on the author's use of humor as you read the text?
	▦ How can you correctly identify the level of comedy, elements of humor, and intended comedic effect on the reader?
	▦ What prewriting strategies (such as outlining or graphic organizers) could help you explore, focus, and organize your ideas?
Drafting: Write a multiparagraph essay that effectively organizes your ideas.	▦ What elements of an effective introductory paragraph will you use in your writing?
	▦ How will you develop support paragraphs with well-chosen examples (evidence) and thoughtful analysis (commentary) about at least two elements of humor?
	▦ How will you use transitions to create cohesion?
	▦ How will your conclusion support your ideas, identify and analyze the level(s) of comedy, and evaluate the author's effectiveness at communicating a universal truth?
Evaluating and Revising the Draft: Create opportunities to review and revise your work.	▦ During the process of writing, when can you pause to share and respond with others in order to elicit suggestions and ideas for revision?
	▦ How can the Scoring Guide help you evaluate how well your draft meets the requirements of the assignment?
	▦ How can you use a precise vocabulary of humor to enhance your critical analysis?
Checking and Editing for Publication: Confirm your final draft is ready for publication.	▦ How will you proofread and edit your draft to demonstrate command of the conventions of standard English capitalization, punctuation, spelling, grammar, and usage?
	▦ Did you effectively use verbals?
	▦ Did you establish and maintain a formal style?

Reflection

After completing this Embedded Assessment, think about how you went about accomplishing this task, and respond to the following:

- How has your understanding of how humor is created developed during this unit?

- Do you think your sense of humor will change as you mature? Explain.

 Technology Tip

Consider using an approved social media channel such as Edmodo or Wikispaces to collaboratively discuss your text online before drafting your essay.

Writing an Analysis of a Humorous Text

SCORING GUIDE

Scoring Criteria	Exemplary	Proficient	Emerging	Incomplete
Ideas	The essay • establishes and fully maintains a clearly focused controlling idea about the use of humor to convey a universal truth • develops the topic with relevant details, examples, and textual evidence • uses insightful commentary to analyze the effect of humorous elements.	The essay • establishes and maintains a controlling idea about the use of humor to convey a universal truth • develops the topic with adequate details, examples, and textual evidence • uses sufficient commentary to analyze the effect of humorous elements.	The essay • establishes and unevenly maintains a controlling idea that may be unclear or unrelated to the use of humor to convey a universal truth • develops the topic with inadequate details, examples, and textual evidence • uses insufficient commentary to analyze the humor.	The essay • lacks a controlling idea • fails to develop the topic with details, examples, and textual evidence • does not provide commentary or analysis.
Structure	The essay • introduces the topic and context in an engaging manner • uses a well-chosen organizational structure that progresses smoothly to connect ideas • uses a variety of effective transitional strategies • provides a satisfying conclusion.	The essay • introduces the topic and context clearly • uses an organizational structure that progresses logically to connect ideas • uses appropriate transitions to create cohesion and link ideas • provides a logical conclusion.	The essay • provides a weak or partial introduction • uses a flawed or inconsistent organizational structure • uses inappropriate, repetitive, or basic transitions • provides a weak or disconnected conclusion.	The essay • lacks an introduction • has little or no obvious organizational structure • uses few or no transitions • lacks a conclusion.
Use of Language	The essay • uses precise diction and language to maintain an academic voice and formal style • demonstrates command of the conventions of standard English capitalization, punctuation, spelling, grammar, and usage.	The essay • uses some precise diction to maintain a generally appropriate voice and style • demonstrates adequate command of the conventions of standard English capitalization, punctuation, spelling, grammar, and usage.	The essay • uses diction that creates an inappropriate voice and style • demonstrates partial or inconsistent command of the conventions of standard English capitalization, punctuation, spelling, grammar, and usage.	The essay • uses vague or confusing language • lacks command of the conventions of standard English capitalization, punctuation, spelling, grammar, and usage.

Previewing Embedded Assessment 2

Learning Targets

- Reflect on learning and make connections.
- Demonstrate an understanding of the skills and knowledge needed to complete Embedded Assessment 2 successfully.

Making Connections

You have written an analysis of a humorous text, which required you to know and understand how a writer uses words, characters, and situations to create a humorous effect. Now you will have an opportunity to understand humor from a different perspective—that of a performer.

Essential Questions

1. Reflect on your understanding of the first Essential Question from Activity 4:1: How do writers and speakers use humor to convey truth? How has your understanding of humor changed over the course of this unit?

2. Think about the second Essential Question from Activity 4:1 and respond to it: What makes an effective performance of a Shakespearean comedy?

Developing Vocabulary

3. Reflect on and list all the new humor-related vocabulary you have learned. Use the My Notes section for additional space if needed.

4. Re-sort the unit Academic Vocabulary and Literary Terms using the QHT strategy.

LEARNING STRATEGIES:
QHT, Close Reading, Paraphrasing, Graphic Organizer

My Notes

Q (unfamiliar)	H (familiar)	T (very familiar)

5. Compare your resorted terms with your original list. How has your understanding changed?

6. Select a word from the chart and write a **concise** statement about your learning. How has your understanding changed over the course of this unit?

Unpacking Embedded Assessment 2

Closely read the Embedded Assessment 2 assignment:

> Present your assigned scene in front of your peers to demonstrate your understanding of Shakespeare's text, elements of comedy, and performance.

Then, using the Scoring Guide on page 352, work with your class to paraphrase the expectations and create a graphic organizer to use as a visual reminder of the required concepts and skills. Copy the graphic organizer for future reference.

After each activity, use this graphic to guide reflection about what you have learned and what you still need to learn in order to be successful in completing the Embedded Assessment.

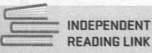

INDEPENDENT READING LINK

Read and Discuss

In this half of the unit, you will prepare to perform a scene from one of Shakespeare's plays. You will have the chance to read other humorous texts independently. Gather in a small group and discuss other humor writers you know about, and other comedies by Shakespeare. Prepare a reading list.

Creating Context for Shakespearean Comedy

Learning Targets

- Research to build knowledge about Shakespeare.
- Collaborate to build and share knowledge about Shakespeare.
- Make connections to establish context for the play *A Midsummer Night's Dream*.

> **LEARNING STRATEGIES:**
> Note-taking, Marking the Text, Skimming/Scanning, Discussion Groups

Drama Study

1. Complete the sentence starters about William Shakespeare in the first column below. Support your responses to the statements, and note any questions you have about him.

Who Is Shakespeare?	How Do I Know This?	Questions I Have
Shakespeare was an author of plays and poetry.	I have seen a movie based on one of his plays, called *Romeo and Juliet*.	How many of his other works have been made into movies?
Shakespeare lived …		
Shakespeare accomplished …		
Shakespeare …		

Creating Context for Shakespearean Comedy

Understanding Plot

2. Read these scenarios to determine how you would respond. Make notes about your reactions in the My Notes space.

Scenario One

The person you are in love with has invited you to your high school dance. Your parents, who disapprove of this person, lay down the law, saying, "You are absolutely not allowed to attend the dance with this person. If you wish to attend, you may go with *X*. Your choices are to go to the dance with *X* or not go at all." You are now faced with a dilemma. You are forbidden to go to the dance with the person you love, but you are permitted to attend with *X*, who has been in love with you forever and whom your parents adore.

Consider this: Would you still go to the dance under these conditions? Why or why not?

Scenario Two

Since you were forbidden by your parents to attend the dance with the person you love, the two of you devise a plan to sneak out and attend the dance anyway. All of a sudden you notice that your love is nowhere in sight. You begin to search the room for her/him. Eventually, you find her/him in the corner of the room talking with your best friend. You happily interrupt the conversation only to be horrified to discover that your love is confessing her/his love to your best friend.

Consider this: What would you do if you saw your girlfriend/boyfriend confessing her/his love to your best friend? How would you feel?

Scenario Three

You confront your love after seeing her/him kiss your best friend. Your girlfriend/boyfriend loudly announces that she/he is no longer interested in you and no longer wants anything to do with you. Your best friend seems confused about the situation as she/he has always been in love with your boyfriend or girlfriend, but the feeling was never shared.

Consider this: What would you do if your girlfriend/boyfriend treated you this way? Would you be mad at your best friend?

Check Your Understanding

Pick a question that you identified in the third column of the chart about Shakespeare. Do research to answer that question. Record the question and the answer in your Reader/Writer Notebook.

Connection to the Play

In Shakespeare's comedy *A Midsummer Night's Dream*, four characters—Lysander, Hermia, Helena, and Demetrius—are entangled in a very complicated love relationship that leaves them open to all sorts of comical mishaps.

3. Using the following information about the key characters from the play, create a visual that shows the relationship among the characters listed below. Practice pronouncing the characters' names. Study the pronunciation of the names, noting the long and short vowel sounds and silent letters as a guide to facilitate your oral pronunciation.

Character's Name	Pronunciation	I am ...	I love ...
Hermia	Hér-me-uh	The daughter of a wealthy nobleman	Lysander
Lysander	Lie-sánd-er	A prominent businessman	Hermia
Demetrius	De-mé-tree-us	Hermia's father's choice for her husband	Hermia too!
Helena	Héll-en-uh	Hermia's best friend	Demetrius

Visual Representation of Characters' Relationships

Narrative Writing Prompt

Using the information from the three scenarios, write your own scenarios for the four key characters described above. Be sure to:

- Incorporate an element of comedy examined earlier in this unit.
- Provide detail about the situation described in your scenario.
- Use precise diction.
- Check the spellings of any words that are frequently confused with similar words.

Insulting Language

Learning Targets

- Read closely to understand the meaning of Shakespeare's language.
- Prepare a dramatic text with proper inflection, tone, gestures, and movement.

Decoding Shakespeare's Language

Note that punctuation marks signal tone of voice, a crucial element of performance.

> "Hang off, thou cat, thou burr! Vile thing, let loose,
> Or I will shake thee from me like a serpent."

1. Use close reading to understand the meaning of each line below. Then, write a paraphrase of your interpretation.

Character	Quote/Insult	Paraphrase (Modern English)
Helena says to Hermia ...	"I will not trust you, Nor longer stay in your *curst* company."	
Lysander says to Hermia ...	"Out, *tawny Tartar*, out! Out, *loathed medicine*! O, *hated*, *potion*, hence!"	
Hermia says to Helena ...	"You *juggler*, you *canker-blossom*! You *thief of love*! What, have you come by night And stol'n my love's heart from him?	
Helena says to Hermia ...	"Fie, fie! You *counterfeit, you puppet, you!*"	

2. Once you have determined the meaning of the lines, select one and complete the chart below. Rehearse your line in preparation for a performance. Then, role play by becoming that character and feeling that emotion. Move throughout the room and deliver your insult with flair. Be sure to allow time for peers to react to your delivery.

Write the insult you have chosen below.	What inflection will you use? What words will you stress when you speak your lines?	How will you alter your tone when you deliver your line?	What gestures/ movements will you use to enhance your line?

3. What tone of voice do people usually use when delivering an insult? What emotions might someone be feeling when they insult another person, and why?

My Notes

Check Your Understanding

Reflect on your understanding of Shakespeare's language. What resources did you use to help you interpret his words? Were they useful? What would you do differently the next time you have to read his words? Discuss with a partner.

Close Reading of a Scene

LEARNING STRATEGIES:
Skimming/Scanning, Diffusing, Paraphrasing, Close Reading, Summarizing, Rereading, Visualizing

My Notes

_____

_____

_____

_____

_____

_____

_____

_____

_____

_____

_____

_____

_____

GRAMMAR & USAGE
Apostrophes

The **apostrophe** is used to indicate the absence of a letter or letters. *Do not* becomes *don' t*. Shakespeare used apostrophes in his writing, too, but in words you might not recognize.

In the line "Fine, i'faith" the apostrophe replaces the *n* in the word *in*.

When you read the line out loud, you should read it as it is written—in other words, leave out the *n*.

As you read more of Shakespeare's works, look for other examples of apostrophes replacing missing letters.

Learning Targets
- Collaborate to make meaning of a scene.
- Summarize and visualize the text to demonstrate understanding.

Preview
In this activity, you will read a scene from a Shakespearean play and think about its meaning.

Setting a Purpose for Reading
- As you read the scene, underline words and phrases that are meant to be insults.
- Circle unknown words and phrases. Try to determine the meaning of the words by using context clues, word parts, or a dictionary.

ABOUT THE AUTHOR
Little is known about the early life of William Shakespeare (1564–1616) except that he was born and grew up in Stratford-on-Avon in England. What is known is that he went to London as a young man and became an actor and playwright. He wrote 37 plays (comedies, tragedies, and histories) and is considered one of the greatest playwrights who ever lived. Performances of his plays occur regularly in theaters around the world.

Drama

from a midsummer night's dream

Act 3, Scene 2, Lines 282–305

by William Shakespeare

HERMIA	Oh me! you juggler! you canker-blossom!
	You thief of love! What, have you come by night
	And stolen my love's heart from him?
HELENA	Fine, i'faith!
285	Have you no modesty, no maiden shame,
	No touch of bashfulness? What, will you tear
	Impatient answers from my gentle tongue?
	Fie, fie! you counterfeit, you puppet, you!
HERMIA	Puppet? Why so? Ay, that way goes the game.
290	Now, I perceive that she hath made compare
	Between our statures; she hath urged her height;

And with her personage, her tall personage,

Her height, **forsooth**, she hath prevail'd with him.

And are you grown so high in his esteem;

295   Because I am so dwarfish and so low?

How low am I, thou painted maypole? speak;

How low am I? I am not yet so low

But that my nails can reach unto thine eyes.

HELENA   I pray you, though you mock me, gentlemen,

300   Let her not hurt me: I was never curst;

I have no gift at all in shrewishness;

I am a right maid for my cowardice:

Let her not strike me. You perhaps may think,

Because she is something lower than myself,

305   That I can match her.

HERMIA   Lower! hark, again.

forsooth: indeed; used to express surprise or indignation

Second Read

- Reread the scene to answer these text-dependent question.
- Write any additional questions you have about the text in your Reader/Writer Notebook.

1. **Key Ideas and Details:** What details in the text should a director consider when casting Helena and Hermia?

Working from the Text

2. Refer to the unknown words or phrases you circled and use reference books or online reference sources to define the words in context. Next to each word you circled, write a synonym or create a paraphrase in modern English.

3. Write a summary of this scene.

4. Reread the text orally with your group.

5. As you listen to the text being read a third time, visualize how the characters would be moving, gesturing, and speaking. Write comments, draw pictures, or stand to act what you are visualizing.

Check Your Understanding

Explain how this scene is intended to be comical on stage. What elements of comedy are represented?

GRAMMAR & USAGE
Punctuation

Punctuation gives clear cues as to how lines should be performed, particularly in poetry and plays.

An **exclamation mark** shows surprise, extreme happiness, or anger: *oh me! you juggler! you canker-blossom!*

A **question mark** indicates a question or confusion on the part of the speaker: *Puppet? Why so?*

A **comma** indicates a pause, usually for dramatic effect: *Fie, fie! you counterfeit, you puppet, you!*

A **semicolon** marks a pause that is longer than that for a comma but not as long as that for a period: *And are you grown so high in his esteem;/ Because I am so dwarfish and so low?*

As you prepare to read a piece out loud, highlight the different forms of punctuation and think about how they will affect your reading.

INDEPENDENT READING LINK
Read and Connect

Read an excerpt from another Shakespearean play classified as a comedy. Compare and contrast the use of punctuation in your reading to the excerpt from *A Midsummer Night's Dream*. Note the similarities and differences in your Reader/Writer Notebook.

Acting Companies and Collaborative Close Reading

Learning Targets
- Establish and follow collaborative norms.
- Analyze and rehearse a dramatic scene collaboratively.

Analyzing a Dramatic Scene

1. **Quickwrite:** Describe the attitudes and behaviors (norms) of a positive and productive member of an acting group.

My Notes

2. In the spaces below, write the names of the members of your acting company for the roles they will play. Write the scene you will perform, the names of the characters, and who will play each character.

   Acting Company Members

   Director:

   Actors:

   Scene:

   Characters:

Rehearsing a Dramatic Scene

3. You will next be assigned a scene from *A Midsummer Night's Dream* that your acting group will perform. Work collaboratively in your acting group to make meaning of the text. Follow these steps to guide your close reading and annotation of the text. You will be responsible for taking notes on your script and for using this script and notes as you plan and rehearse your scene.

- Skim/scan the text and circle unfamiliar words. Use a dictionary or thesaurus to replace each unfamiliar word with a synonym.

- Reread the scene and paraphrase the lines in modern English.

- Summarize the action. What is happening in the scene?

- Reread the scene and mark the text to indicate elements of humor (caricature, situation, irony, wordplay, hyperbole).

- Mark the punctuation, and determine how the punctuation affects the spoken lines. Discuss tone of voice and inflection.

- Analyze the movement in your scene:

  What is each character doing?

  When should characters enter and exit?

  How should characters enter and exit?

  What could you do to exaggerate the humor or create a humorous spin?

- Analyze the blocking in your scene, that is, the movement and placement of characters as they speak:

  Where is each character standing?

  To whom is each spoken line addressed?

4. Divide lines equally between group members. You may have to be more than one character. One person in your group will be both a player (actor) and the director.

Player (student's name)	Acting As (character's name)
Director:	

My Notes

Acting Companies and Collaborative Close Reading

My Notes

5. Rehearse your scene. To accurately portray your character and achieve your intended comic effect, be sure to focus on the following:

- tone and inflection
- correct pronunciation of words
- facial expression and gesture

Check Your Understanding

Reflect on the process of reading your scene and determining the meaning of the text, as well as your preparation for and rehearsal of the scene.

- What went well? What will you want to replicate in future rehearsals and in your performance?
- What is a revision or something new you plan to do as you continue to rehearse?

Facing the Challenge of Performance

Learning Targets
- Read and respond to an informational text about performance challenges.
- Memorize and rehearse lines for performance.

Preview
In this activity, you will read an informational text about performing and think about how these tips can help you prepare for your performance.

Setting a Purpose for Reading
- As you read the informational text, underline words and phrases that identify the main idea of each section.
- Circle unknown words and phrases. Try to determine the meaning of the words by using context clues, word parts, or a dictionary.
- Place an exclamation point by the tips you think most apply to you.

ABOUT THE AUTHOR
Gary Guwe is an award-winning speaker, entrepreneur, and public speaking trainer, specializing in effective communication. He has trained and helped more than 12,500 people.

LEARNING STRATEGIES:
Marking the Text, Discussion Groups, Note-taking, Rehearsal

My Notes

Informational Text

Adapted from
Fear Busters
10 Tips to Overcome Stage Fright!

by Gary Guwe

F – Focus on your most powerful Experience

Think about your most memorable and powerful experience when you accomplished a goal—maybe a time you worked extremely hard on a project or did well on a test. Reflect on your most powerful experience and remember the feeling of confidence; think about everything you did to create that feeling and how proud you felt after doing something challenging.

E – Energize Yourself

You have adrenaline pumping through your veins. Your heart is racing and your muscles are all tensed up. Your eyes are shifty and you are unsettled. You are ready to bolt for the door ... or are you?

An adrenaline rush is a built-in defense mechanism for human beings. It is a natural response mechanism that allows us to fight or take flight in the event of danger. That explains the heightened sensitivity we have when we are nervous and excited.

Facing the Challenge of Performance

Harness this nervous energy and make it work for you! One way we harness this nervous energy is to move around. Your character will at some point move and gesture. Use the times when your character can move and react as opportunities to dissipate your nervous energy.

A – Acknowledge Your Fears

It is said that fear is here to protect us, not paralyze us. Don't run away from being afraid. Acknowledge it as being part of you … use it to identify the possible pitfalls, then work to think about how you can avoid the pitfalls or how you can adjust or adapt if something goes wrong during your performance.

R – Relax … breathe!

Take deep breaths and regulate your breathing. Let the breathing regulate and calm your heart rate. Practice breathing when you rehearse.

B – Believe in Yourself

Know that your performance has the potential for being a powerful and memorable moment in your life. You will feel a huge sense of accomplishment and pride when you successfully perform your scene. Be knowledgeable about your part and prepared with your lines, and you will be ready to execute with confidence.

U – Understand the Audience

Understand that the audience is here to see you succeed. They know how it feels to perform, and they're not here to sabotage you, or poke fun at you … they're here to learn from you, to laugh, and to be entertained.

S – Smile!

Changing one's physiology can impact one's mental state.

Before your performance, when your character allows, and immediately afterwards—smile. Soon enough, your body will tell your brain that you're happy … and before you know it, any fear you have will melt away.

T – Talk to Yourself

Many people will begin telling themselves various reasons why they will not be able to perform well. Counter that.

Tell yourself that you will be able to do a good job and remind yourself of the reasons why you can ("I am prepared." "I will have fun." "I know my peers will laugh when … ").

E – Enjoy yourself

Get out on the stage and seek to have fun!

R – Rejoice!

Many people begin visualizing their worst case scenario as they ready themselves to perform.

Visualize yourself victorious at the end of the performance. Think of the amount of effort you will have put into preparing and think about the smiles and laughter which you will create and the skills and concepts you will have practiced and mastered.

Second Read

- Reread the informational text to answer these text-dependent questions.
- Write any additional questions you have about the text in your Reader/Writer Notebook.

1. **Key Ideas and Details:** Refer to the words and phrases you underlined and summarize the main idea of each section.

2. **Craft and Structure:** How is the text structured? Why do you think the author structured the text in this way?

Working from the Text

3. **Quickwrite:** What is the biggest challenge you face when it comes to performing your comic scene?

4. Refer to the text and write your personal response to each tip in the My Notes space. Use them as a guide for a collaborative discussion.

5. Discuss the ten tips with your acting group. Which tips did you notate as applying most to you? How will you use this advice?

My Notes

Facing the Challenge of Performance

Memorization Tips

Memorizing lines is a key part of delivering a good performance. Think about school plays you may have seen. Characters who deliver their lines clearly and without hesitation perform well.

Tip 1: Repeat, Repeat, Repeat, Repeat

Say the line over and over, but do it one word at a time, returning to the beginning of the line each time.

Example: Line 108 from Scene 5: "If we offend, it is with our good will."
"If." "If we." "If we offend." "If we offend, it." "If we offend, it is." "If we offend, it is with." "If we offend, it is with our." "If we offend, it is with our good." "If we offend, it is with our good will."

Tip 2: Recite and Erase

Write your line(s) on a whiteboard, and then practice the words.

- Recite the line.
- Erase a word or phrase, and recite the missing piece from memory.
- Repeat the process until all the words have disappeared and you are saying the line(s) from memory.

6. Discuss other tips your peers may have for memorizing lines. Then, select your hardest line to memorize and use the memorization tips to work on it.

Check Your Understanding

Describe at least three strategies you can use to overcome stage fright. How will you remind yourself of those strategies on the day of the performance?

INDEPENDENT READING LINK

Read and Discuss

Think about the play you are reading independently. Which of your friends or family members would you cast in the lead roles? Why? Come up with your cast and justify your choices based on personality, appearance, or other characteristics.

Working with Acting Companies and Focus Groups

Learning Targets
- Analyze a dramatic character to inform a performance.
- Collaborate to draft and implement a performance plan.

Character Focus Groups

1. **Players:** Reread your lines, using the graphic organizer to guide a close reading and analysis of your character.

   Meet in a focus group, whose members are all acting as the same character, and work collaboratively to interpret what the lines reveal about your character. Take turns sharing your individual analysis and add new insights to the graphic organizer.

I am playing:

_____

Aspects of Characterization	Detail from Text	Interpretation *What does this reveal about the character?*
Appearance		
Actions		
Words		
Thoughts/Feelings		

Working with Acting Companies and Focus Groups

Others' Reactions		
Comedic Actions/Words		

2. Take turns reading your character's lines. Practice making the analysis of your character come to life through your tone, inflection, facial expression, and gestures.

3. **Directors:** Select key action sequences and consider possible stage directions to determine how these scenes might be performed on stage.

Key Action Sequences	Stage Directions and Movement on Stage	What This Reveals About the Overall Scene (Comedic Effect)

Acting Groups

4. Return to your acting group and share your analysis in the order that your character speaks during your scene. Discuss the implications of each character's words and actions.

5. Develop a detailed performance plan by consulting the Scoring Guide.

   After reviewing the Scoring Guide criteria, I need to ...

6. Work with your acting company to complete the chart below and outline your performance plan.

Performance Plan				
Character	Played By	Contribution to Set Design	Prop(s)	Costume

Working with Acting Companies and Focus Groups

7. Individually, synthesize all the details of your performance plan.

Element of Performance	Ideas for Character	Explanation
Blocking		
Movements Enter/Exit		
Gestures		
Facial Expression(s)		
Emotion		
Comedic Emphasis		

8. Complete this section if you are the director. Share your plan with the members of your acting company.

We want to create a _____ mood. To accomplish this goal, we will ...

I will introduce the acting company and scene by ...

The scene will end when _____ so the audience will be left with a feeling of ...

We will focus on the comic effects listed below to ensure that ...

9. Use your performance plan to rehearse your scene to accurately portray your character and achieve your intended comic effect. Be sure to focus on the following:

- tone and inflection
- correct pronunciation of words
- gestures and movement

Check Your Understanding

Reflect on the process of planning for and rehearsing your scene. Think about what went well and what you will want to improve in future performances. In your Reader/Writer Notebook, write one improvement you would like to make on your own part, and one suggestion for improvement you can offer the group as a whole.

Same Text, Different Text

Learning Targets

- Analyze film and text in order to compare/contrast and evaluate the director's choices.
- Generate and evaluate performance choices.

Viewing Shakespeare on Film

1. Unlike comparing novels to film versions, turning a play script into a movie allows the viewer to make a close comparison. Think about the extent to which the film scripts adhere to or stray from the original Shakespeare scene and how the actors make the lines come alive through their voices, expressions, and movements.

2. As you view the film or a scene from *A Midsummer Night's Dream*, take notes on what you observe. Use the graphic organizer for either "Actors" or "Directors."

Actors:

Version of *A Midsummer Night's Dream* (Director/Year)	Physical Gestures and Movements	Costume and Makeup	Interpretive Choices in the Delivery of Lines
Film 1:			
Film 2:			

Same Text, Different Text

Actors' Questions

3. To what extent do these films stay faithful to or depart from the original script? Why might these particular choices have been made, and what effect do these choices have on the viewers' understanding of the scene?

4. How do your character's gestures, movements, and language achieve a comical effect? What elements of humor did you see?

Directors:

Version of *A Midsummer Night's Dream* (Director/Year)	Placement of Actors in Relationship to Props, Scenery, Each Other	Music or Other Sound Effects	Set Design, Lighting, Props
Film 1:			
Film 2:			

Directors' Questions

5. How has the director stayed faithful to or departed from the scene as written by Shakespeare? What effects do certain staging and technical choices have on the viewers' understanding of the scene?

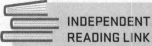

INDEPENDENT READING LINK

Read and Research

See if there is a modern-day retelling of the play you are reading independently. Watch it and fill out a similar graphic organizer for it.

6. How do the staging, set design, lighting, sound, and props achieve a comical effect? What elements of humor did you see?

My Notes

Check Your Understanding

Why would a film director choose to portray a scene differently than the way the author wrote it? What effects might the director be trying to achieve?

Dress Rehearsal

My Notes

Learning Targets

- Participate in a dress rehearsal of a dramatic scene.
- Reflect on strengths and challenges as a performer.

Dress Rehearsal

1. Participate in a dress rehearsal in which you perform your scene in front of another group. This rehearsal will help you determine what works well in your performance and what does not.

2. When you are in the role of a small group audience, use the Scoring Guide criteria to provide constructive feedback to enable the acting company to adjust its performance.

3. Consider using these questions to start your feedback conversation:

   - What elements of humor do you think you were most successful at using? Least successful?
   - Can you explain why you made the choice to ...
   - When did you feel the audience was most with you?
   - When did you feel the audience was least connected to your performance?
   - Did you ever have to adapt or adjust differently than you had planned? Explain. How did it work out?

Dress Rehearsal Reflection

4. What went well? What will you want to replicate in your performance?

5. What is the most significant thing you are going to do differently? How will you prepare?

 Independent Reading Checkpoint

Choose a short part of the play you have been reading independently and rewrite it in modern English. Read it out loud to your teacher or a partner.

Performing Shakespearean Comedy

ASSIGNMENT

Present your assigned scene in front of your peers to demonstrate your understanding of Shakespeare's text, elements of comedy, and performance.

Planning: As an acting company, prepare to perform your scene.	▪ How will you collaborate as a group on a performance plan that demonstrates an understanding of Shakespeare's humor?
	▪ Does each member of the acting company understand the scene's meaning as well as his or her role?
	▪ What elements of humor will your company focus on in performance?
	▪ How will you emphasize these elements through the delivery of lines, characterization, gestures, movements, props, and/or setting?
	▪ How will you mark your script to help you pronounce words correctly, emphasize words appropriately, and remember your lines and deliver them smoothly?
	▪ How will you use blocking and movement to interact onstage and emphasize elements of humor?
Rehearsing: Rehearse and revise your performance with your acting company.	▪ How will you show how characters, conflicts, and events contribute to a universal idea?
	▪ How will you introduce and conclude the scene?
	▪ How can the Scoring Guide help you evaluate how well your performance meets the requirements of the assignment?
	▪ How can you give and receive feedback about your use of eye contact, volume, and inflection in order to improve your own and others' performances?
Performing and Listening: Perform your scene and participate as an audience member.	▪ How will you convey ideas and emotions through your performance?
	▪ How will you take notes on the elements of humor emphasized in other performances?

Reflection

After completing this Embedded Assessment, think about how you went about accomplishing this task, and respond to the following:

- How did different performers emphasize the elements of humor in their scenes?

- Which performances were successful in eliciting a humorous response from the audience, and what made them effective?

 Technology Tip

As part of the rehearsal process, consider video recording your performance. Also, consider using a musical recording to introduce and/or conclude your performance.

Performing Shakespearean Comedy

SCORING GUIDE

Scoring Criteria	Exemplary	Proficient	Emerging	Incomplete
Ideas	The performance • demonstrates a deep understanding of Shakespeare's intended humor • uses a variety of effective performance elements (staging, set design, lighting, sound, props) for comic effect • shows evidence of extensive planning, rehearsal, and reflection.	The performance • demonstrates an adequate understanding of Shakespeare's intended humor • uses some performance elements (staging, set design, lighting, sound, props) for comic effect • shows evidence of sufficient planning, rehearsal, and reflection.	The performance • demonstrates a partial or uneven understanding of Shakespeare's intended humor • uses disconnected or basic performance elements (staging, set design, lighting, sound, props) • shows evidence of ineffective or insufficient planning, rehearsal, and reflection.	The performance • demonstrates little or no understanding of Shakespeare's intended humor • lacks performance elements • does not show evidence of planning, rehearsal, and reflection.
Structure	The performance • demonstrates extensive evidence of collaboration • provides context in an engaging introduction • communicates a satisfying ending to the audience.	The performance • demonstrates adequate evidence of collaboration • provides context in an appropriate introduction • communicates an ending to the audience.	The performance • demonstrates uneven or ineffective collaboration • provides a partial or weak introduction • communicates an abrupt or illogical ending to the audience.	The performance • demonstrates a failure to collaborate • provides no introduction • does not communicate an ending to the audience.
Use of Language	The performer • makes effective interpretive choices to deliver lines for comic effect and to convey meaning (including tone, pronunciation, inflection, facial expressions, gestures, movement, and blocking) • uses punctuation cues consistently and naturally to inform vocal delivery • memorizes lines fully and accurately.	The performer • makes appropriate interpretive choices to deliver lines for comic effect and to convey meaning (including tone, pronunciation, inflection, facial expressions, gestures, movement, and blocking) • uses some punctuation cues to inform vocal delivery • demonstrates an adequate ability to memorize lines.	The performer • makes undeveloped or inappropriate interpretive choices to deliver lines (including tone, pronunciation, inflection, facial expressions, gestures, movement, and blocking) • uses punctuation cues unevenly or inconsistently • demonstrates insufficient ability to memorize lines.	The performer • makes undeveloped or inappropriate interpretive choices to deliver lines • does not recognize punctuation cues or use them incorrectly • does not have any lines memorized.

Resources

Unit 1 Independent Reading List

Suggestions for Independent Reading

This list, divided into the categories of **Literature** and **Nonfiction/Informational Text**, comprises titles related to the themes and content of the unit. For your independent reading, you can select from this wide array of titles, which have been chosen based on complexity and interest. You can also do your own research and select titles that intrigue you.

Unit 1: The Challenge of Heroism		
Literature		
Author	**Title**	**Lexile**
Alexie, Sherman	*Reservation Blues*	670L
Alvarez, Julia	*Before We Were Free*	890L
Anderson, Laurie Halse	*Fever 1793*	580L
Avi	*Crispin: The Cross of Lead*	780L
Butler, Octavia	*The Parable of the Sower*	710L
Coelho, Paul	*The Alchemist*	910L
Crew, Linda	*Children of the River*	700L
Crutcher, Chris	*Whale Talk*	1000L
Dashner, James	*The Maze Runner*	770L
Ellis, Deborah	*The Breadwinner*	630L
Hinton, S.E.	*The Outsiders*	750L
Jeffrey, Gary	*African Myths*	N/A
Johnston, E.K.	*The Story of Owen: Dragon Slayer of Trondheim*	1020L
Jones, Diana Wynne	*Howl's Moving Castle*	800L
L'Engle, Madeline	*A Wrinkle in Time*	740L
Lewis, C.S.	*The Chronicles of Narnia* series	N/A
Lewis, Richard	*The Killing Sea*	760L
Lupica, Mike	*Hero*	730L
O'Connor, George	*Athena: Grey-Eyed Goddess*	720L
Paolini, Christopher	*Eragon*	710L
Park, Linda Sue	*When My Name Was Keoko*	610L
Paulsen, Gary	*Soldier's Heart*	1000L
Pierce, Tamora	*Alanna of Trebond*	690L
Riordan, Rick	*Heroes of Olympus* series	N/A
Robbins, Trina	*Freedom Songs: A Tale of the Underground Railroad*	580L
Robbins, Trina	*Lily Renee, Escape Artist: From Holocaust Survivor to Comic Book Pioneer*	510L
Selznick, Brian	*The Invention of Hugo Cabret* (Graphic Novel)	820L
Sepetys, Ruta	*Between Shades of Gray*	490L
Storrie, Paul	*Hercules: The 12 Labors*	N/A
White, T.E.	*The Once and Future King*	1080L

Nonfiction/Informational Text

Author	Title	Lexile
Bardhan-Quallen, Sudipta	*Up-Close: Jane Goodall*	N/A
Beales, Melba Pattilo	*Warriors Don't Cry*	N/A
Bradley, James	*Flags of Our Fathers*	950L
Chin-Lee, Cynthia	*Akira to Zoltan: 26 Men Who Changed the World*	N/A
Chin-Lee, Cynthia	*Amelia to Zora: 26 Women Who Changed the World*	N/A
Freedman, Russell	*Eleanor Roosevelt: A Life of Discovery*	1100L
Freedman, Russell	*Kids at Work: Lewis Hine and the Crusade Against Child Labor*	1140L
Hillenbrand, Laura	*Unbroken: An Olympian's Journey from Airman to Castaway to Captive* (Young Adult Adaptation)	850L
Hurley, Michael	*World's Greatest Olympians*	960L
Krull, Kathleen	*Lives of Extraordinary Women: Rulers, Rebels (and What the Neighbors Thought)*	1150L
Myers, Walter Dean	*The Greatest: Muhammad Ali*	N/A
Peet, Mal	*The Keeper*	780L
Wells, Susan	*Amelia Earhart: The Thrill of it All*	N/A
Yousafzai, Malala	*I Am Malala*	830L

Unit 2 Independent Reading List

Suggestions for Independent Reading

This list, divided into the categories of **Literature** and **Nonfiction/Informational Text**, comprises titles related to the themes and content of the unit. For your independent reading, you can select from this wide array of titles, which have been chosen based on complexity and interest. You can also do your own research and select titles that intrigue you.

Unit 2: The Challenge of Utopia		
Literature		
Author	**Title**	**Lexile**
Ada, Alma	*Love, Amalia*	940L
Asimov, Isaac	*I, Robot*	820L
Bradbury, Ray	*The Martian Chronicles: Something Wicked This Way Comes*	820L
Budhos, Marina	*Ask Me No Questions*	790L
Burg, Ann	*All the Broken Pieces*	680L
Carlson, Lori Marie	*Red Hot Salsa*	N/A
Cisneros, Sandra	*The House on Mango Street*	870L
Collins, Suzanne	*The Hunger Games*	810L
Dayton, Arwen Elys	*Seeker*	800L
Farmer, Nancy	*The House of the Scorpions*	660L
Frank, Pat	*Alas, Babylon*	870L
Heinlein, Robert	*Stranger in a Strange Land*	940L
Huxley, Aldous	*Brave New World*	870L
LeGuin, Ursula	*The Left Hand of Darkness*	970L
Lu, Marie	*Legend*	710L
Meyer, Marissa	*Cinder*	790L
More, Thomas	*Utopia*	1370L
O'Brien, Tim	*The Things They Carried*	880L
Orwell, George	*1984*	1090L
Orwell, George	*Animal Farm*	1170L
Reinhardt, Dana	*A Brief Chapter in My Impossible Life*	N/A
Roth, Veronica	*Divergent*	700L
Salisbury, Graham	*House of the Red Fish*	610L
Verne, Jules	*Twenty Thousand Leagues Under the Sea*	1030L
Wells, H.G.	*The Time Machine*	1070L
Wells, H.G.	*The War of the Worlds*	1040L
Westerfield, Scott	*Uglies*	770L
Yancey, Rick	*The Fifth Wave*	N/A
Yang, Dori Jones	*Daughter of Xanadu*	780L

Nonfiction/Informational Text

Author	Title	Lexile
Bausum, Ann	*Denied, Detained, Deported: Stories from the Dark Side of American Immigration*	1170L
Carson, Rachel,	*Silent Spring The Sea Around Us*	1340L
D'Aluisio, Faith and Peter Menzel	*What the World Eats*	1150L
Engle, Margarita	*The Lightening Dreamer: Cuba's Greatest Abolitionists*	N/A
Gore, Al	*Global Warming Is an Immediate Crisis*	N/A
Hatkoff, Juliana and Isabella Hatkoff	*Winter's Tail: How One Little Dolphin Learned to Swim Again*	930L
Hesse, Karen	*Aleutian Sparrow*	N/A
Hoose, Philip	*The Race to Save the Lord God Bird*	1150L
Kalan, Robert	*We Are Not Beasts of Burden*	1150L
Lasky, Kathryn	*John Muir: America's First Environmentalist*	1050L
Markle, Sandra	*How Many Baby Pandas?*	N/A
Pollan, Michael	*In Defense of Food: An Eater's Manifesto*	1390L
Schlosser, Eric	*Fast Food Nation*	1240L
Scholsser, Eric and Wilson, Charles,	*Chew on This: Everything You Don't Want to Know About Fast Food*	1110L
Sivertsen, Linda and Josh Sivertsen	*Generation Green: The Ultimate Teen Guide to Living an Eco-Friendly Life*	N/A
Somervill, Barbara	*Animal Survivors of the Wetlands*	1060L
Stearman, Kaye	*Taking Action Against Homelessness*	N/A
Waters, Alice	*Edible Schoolyard: A Universal Idea*	N/A
Welsbacher, Anne	*Earth-Friendly Design*	N/A

Unit 3 Independent Reading List

Suggestions for Independent Reading

This list, divided into the categories of **Literature** and **Nonfiction/Informational Text**, comprises titles related to the themes and content of the unit. For your independent reading, you can select from this wide array of titles, which have been chosen based on complexity and interest. You can also do your own research and select titles that intrigue you.

Unit 3: The Challenge to Make a Difference		
Literature		
Author	**Title**	**Lexile**
Adlington, L. J.	*The Diary of Pelly D.*	770L
Arato, Rona	*The Last Train: A Holocaust Story*	580L
Bergman, Tamar	*Along the Tracks*	650L
Boyne, John	*The Boy in the Striped Pajamas*	1080L
Chotjewitz, David	*Daniel, Half Human: And the Good Nazi,*	740L
Gratz, Alan and Gruener, Ruth	*Prisoner B-3087*	760L
Hesse, Karen	*The Cats in Krasinski Square*	990L
Hoestlandt, Jo	*Star of Fear, Star of Hope*	490L
Boom, Corrie Ten	*The Hiding Place*	900L
Isaacs, Anne	*Torn Thread*	880L
Lowry, Lois	*Number the Stars*	670L
Matas, Carol	Daniel's Story	720L
Drucker, Malka and Halperin, Michael	*Jacob's Rescue*	680L
Matas, Carol	*The Garden*	810L
Mazer, Norma Fox	*Good Night, Maman*	510L
Meminger, Neesha	*Shine, Coconut Moon*	740L
Morpurgo, Michael	*Waiting for Anya*	770L
Na, An	*The Fold*	700L
Napoli, Donna Jo	*Stones in Water*	630L
Nye, Naomi Shihab	*19 Varieties of Gazelle: Poems of the Middle East*	970L
Orgel, Doris	*The Devil in Vienna*	700L
Orlev, Uri	*Run, Boy, Run*	570L
Orlev, Uri	*The Island on Bird Street*	690L
Peacock, Carol Antionette	*Red Thread Sisters*	700L
Polacco, Patricia	*The Butterfly*	430L
Radin, Ruth Yaffe	*Escape to the Forest: Based on a True Story of the Holocaust*	660L
Spinelli, Jerry	*Milkweed*	510L
Venkatraman, Padma	*Climbing the Stairs*	750L
Yep, Laurence	*Golden Mountain Chronicles: Child of the Owl*	920L
Yolen, Jane	*The Devil's Arithmetic*	730L
Zullo, Allan	*We Fought Back: Teen Resisters of the Holocaust*	1070L
Zusak, Markus	*The Book Thief*	730L

Nonfiction/Informational Text		
Author	**Title**	**Lexile**
Bachrach, Susan D.	*Tell Them We Remember: The Story of the Holocaust*	1190L
Bitton-Jackson, Livia	*I Have Lived a Thousand Years: Growing Up in the Holocaust*	720L
Boas, Jacob	*We Are Witnesses: Five Diaries of Teenagers Who Died in the Holocaust*	970L
Deedy, Carmen Agra	*The Yellow Star: The Legend of King Christian X of Denmark*	550L
Frank, Anne	*The Diary of a Young Girl*	1080L
Freedman, Russell	*Kids at Work: Lewis Hine and the Crusade Against Child Labor*	1140L
Gregory, Josh	*Cesar Chavez*	930L
Herman, Gail	*Who Was Jackie Robinson?*	670L
Hoose, Philip	*The Race to Save the Lord God Bird*	1150L
Lobel, Anita	*No Pretty Pictures: A Child of War*	750L
Meltzer, Milton	*Rescue: The Story of How Gentiles Saved Jews in the Holocaust*	1020L
Millman, Isaac	*Hidden Child*	860L
Nir, Yehuda	*The Lost Childhood: A World War II Memoir*	920L
Opdyke, Irene Gut	*In My Hands: Memories of a Holocaust Rescuer*	890L
Perl, Lila and Lazan, Marion Blumenthal	*Four Perfect Pebbles: A Holocaust Story*	1080L
Sender, Ruth Minsky	*The Cage*	500L
Siegal, Aranka	*Upon the Head of the Goat: A Childhood in Hungary 1939–1944*	830L
van de Rol, Rudd and Verhoeven, Rian	*Anne Frank: Beyond the Diary: A Photographic Remembrance*	1030L
Warren, Andrea	*Charles Dickens and the Street Children of London*	1160L
Wiesel, Elie	*Night*	570L

Unit 4 Independent Reading List

Suggestions for Independent Reading

This list, divided into the categories of **Literature** and **Nonfiction/Informational Text**, comprises titles related to the themes and content of the unit. For your independent reading, you can select from this wide array of titles, which have been chosen based on complexity and interest. You can also do your own research and select titles that intrigue you.

Unit 4: The Challenge of Comedy

Literature

Author	Title	Lexile
Adams, Douglas	*The Hitchhiker's Guide to the Galaxy*	1000L
Alexie, Sherman	*The Absolutely True Diary of a Part-Time Indian*	600L
Allison, Jennifer	*Gilda Joyce, Psychic Investigator: A Mystery*	1000L
Dahl, Roald	*The Wonderful Story of Henry Sugar: And Six More*	850L
Eliott, Rob	*Laugh Out Loud Jokes for Kids*	N/A
Healey, Christopher	*Hero's Guide to Saving Your Kingdom Series*	750L
Kindl, Patrice	*Keeping the Castle*	1050L
Kinney, Jeff	*Diary of a Wimpy Kid*	900L
Kipling, Rudyard	*Just So Stories*	1190L
Korman, Gordon	*Don't Care High*	920L
Leavitt, Lindsey	*Princess for Hire*	670L
McAlpine, Gordon	*The Tell-Tale Start: The Misadventures of Edgar & Allan Poe (series)*	850L
McCloskey, Robert	*Homer Price*	1000L
Paulsen, Gary	*Molly McGinty Has a Really Good Day*	960L
Pilkey, Dav	*Captain Underpants Collection*	800L
Scieszka, Jon	*Frank Einstein and the Antimatter Motor*	730L
Snicket, Lemony	*The Bad Beginning*	1010L
Snicket, Lemony	*The Grim Grotto*	1120L
Sparknotes	*No Fear Shakespeare Graphic Novels*	N/A
Swift, Jonathan	*A Modest Proposal*	1520L
Twain, Mark	*The Celebrated Jumping Frog and Other Stories*	1000L
Vonnegut, Kurt	*Cat's Cradle*	790L

Nonfiction/Informational Text

Author	Title	Lexile
Crutcher, Chris	*King of the Mild Frontier: An Ill-Advised Autobiography*	1180L
Dahl, Roald	*Boy*	1090L
Fey, Tina	*Bossypants*	950L
Kimmel, Haven	*A Girl Named Zippy*	1010L
Martin, Steve	*Born Standing Up: A Comic's Life*	N/A
Mayfield, Katherine	*Acting A to Z: The Young Person's Guide to a Stage or Screen Career*	1030L

Independent Reading Log

NAME _____ DATE _____

Directions: This log is a place to record your progress and thinking about your independent reading during each unit. Add your log pages to your Reader/Writer Notebook or keep them as a separate place to record your reading insights.

Unit _____

Independent Reading Title _____

Author(s) _____ Text Type _____

Pages read: from _____ to _____

_____
_____
_____
_____
_____
_____

Independent Reading Title _____

Author(s) _____ Text Type _____

Pages read: from _____ to _____

_____
_____
_____
_____
_____
_____
_____

Independent Reading Title _____

Author(s) _____ Text Type _____

Pages read: from _____ to _____

_____
_____
_____
_____
_____
_____
_____

Unit _____

Independent Reading Title _____

Author(s) _____ Text Type _____

Pages read: from _____ to _____

_____

_____

_____

_____

Independent Reading Title _____

Author(s) _____ Text Type _____

Pages read: from _____ to _____

_____

_____

_____

_____

Independent Reading Title _____

Author(s) _____ Text Type _____

Pages read: from _____ to _____

_____

_____

_____

_____

_____

Independent Reading Title _____

Author(s) _____ Text Type _____

Pages read: from _____ to _____

_____

_____

_____

_____

_____

SpringBoard Learning Strategies
READING STRATEGIES

STRATEGY	DEFINITION	PURPOSE
Chunking the Text	Breaking the text into smaller, manageable units of sense (e.g., words, sentences, paragraphs, whole text) by numbering, separating phrases, drawing boxes	To reduce the intimidation factor when encountering long words, sentences, or whole texts; to increase comprehension of difficult or challenging text
Close Reading	Accessing small chunks of text to read, reread, mark, and annotate key passages, word-for-word, sentence-by-sentence, and line-by-line	To develop comprehensive understanding by engaging in one or more focused readings of a text
Diffusing	Reading a passage, noting unfamiliar words, discovering meaning of unfamiliar words using context clues, dictionaries, and/or thesauruses, and replacing unfamiliar words with familiar ones	To facilitate a close reading of text, the use of resources, an understanding of synonyms, and increased comprehension of text
Double-Entry Journal	Creating a two-column journal (also called Dialectical Journal) with a student-selected passage in one column and the student's response in the second column (e.g., asking questions of the text, forming personal responses, interpreting the text, reflecting on the process of making meaning of the text)	To assist in note-taking and organizing key textual elements and responses noted during reading in order to generate textual support that can be incorporated into a piece of writing at a later time
Graphic Organizer	Using a visual representation for the organization of information from the text	To facilitate increased comprehension and discussion
KWHL Chart	Setting up discussion that allows students to activate prior knowledge by answering "What do I know?"; sets a purpose by answering "What do I want to know?"; helps preview a task by answering "How will I learn it?"; and reflects on new knowledge by answering "What have I learned?"	To organize thinking, access prior knowledge, and reflect on learning to increase comprehension and engagement
Marking the Text	Selecting text by highlighting, underlining, and/or annotating for specific components, such as main idea, imagery, literary devices, and so on	To focus reading for specific purposes, such as author's craft, and to organize information from selections; to facilitate reexamination of a text
Metacognitive Markers	Responding to text with a system of cueing marks where students use a ? for questions about the text; a ! for reactions related to the text; and an * for comments ,about the text and underline to signal key ideas	To track responses to texts and use those responses as a point of departure for talking or writing about texts
OPTIC	**O** (Overview): Write notes on what the visual appears to be about. **P** (Parts): Zoom in on the parts of the visual and describe any elements or details that seem important. **T** (Title): Highlight the words of the title of the visual (if one is available). **I** (Interrelationships): Use the title as the theory and the parts of the visual as clues to detect and specify how the elements of the graphic are related.	To analyze graphic and visual images as forms of text

STRATEGY	DEFINITION	PURPOSE
OPTIC (continued)	**C** (Conclusion); Draw a conclusion about the visual as a whole. What does the visual mean? Summarize the message of the visual in one or two sentences.	
Predicting	Making guesses about the text by using the title and pictures and/or thinking ahead about events which may occur based on evidence in the text	To help students become actively involved, interested, and mentally prepared to understand ideas
Previewing	Making guesses about the text by using the title and pictures and/or thinking ahead about events which may occur based on evidence in the text	To gain familiarity with the text, make connections to the text, and extend prior knowledge to set a purpose for reading
QHT	Expanding prior knowledge of vocabulary words by marking words with a Q, H, or T (Q signals words students do not know; H signals words students have heard and might be able to identify; T signals words students know well enough to teach to their peers)	To allow students to build on their prior knowledge of words, to provide a forum for peer teaching and learning of new words, and to serve as a prereading exercise to aid in comprehension
Questioning the Text* The AP Vertical Teams Guide for English (109–112)	Developing levels of questions about text; that is, literal, interpretive, and universal questions that prompt deeper thinking about a text	To engage more actively with texts, read with greater purpose and focus, and ultimately answer questions to gain greater insight into the text; helps students to comprehend and interpret
Paraphrasing	Restating in one's own words the essential information expressed in a text, whether it be narration, dialogue, or informational text	To encourage and facilitate comprehension of challenging text.
RAFT	Primarily used to generate new text, this strategy can also be used to analyze a text by examining the role of the speaker (R), the intended audience (A), the format of the text (F), and the topic of the text (T).	To initiate reader response; to facilitate an analysis of a text to gain focus prior to creating a new text
Rereading	Encountering the same text with more than one reading.	To identify additional details; to clarify meaning and/or reinforce comprehension of texts
SIFT* The AP Vertical Teams Guide for English (17–20)	Analyzing a fictional text by examining stylistic elements, especially symbol, imagery, and figures of speech in order to show how all work together to reveal tone and theme	To focus and facilitate an analysis of a fictional text by examining the title and text for symbolism, identifying images and sensory details, analyzing figurative language and identifying how all these elements reveal tone and theme
Skimming/Scanning	Skimming by rapid or superficial reading of a text to form an overall impression or to obtain a general understanding of the material; scanning focuses on key words, phrases, or specific details and provides speedy recognition of information	To quickly form an overall impression prior to an in-depth study of a text; to answer specific questions or quickly locate targeted information or detail in a text
SMELL* The AP Vertical Teams Guide for English	• Sender-receiver relationship—What is the sender-receiver relationship? Who are the images and language meant to attract? Describe the speaker of the text. • Message—What is the message? Summarize the statement made in the text.	To analyze a persuasive speech or essay by focusing on five essential questions

STRATEGY	DEFINITION	PURPOSE
SMELL* (continued)	• Emotional Strategies—What is the desired effect? • Logical Strategies—What logic is operating? How does it (or its absence) affect the message? Consider the logic of the images as well as the words. • Language—What does the language of the text describe? How does it affect the meaning and effectiveness of the writing? Consider the language of the images as well as the words.	
SOAPSTone*	Analyzing text by discussing and identifying Speaker, Occasion, Audience, Purpose, Subject, and Tone	To facilitate the analysis of specific elements of non-fiction literary and informational texts and show the relationship among the elements to an understanding of the whole
Summarizing	Giving a brief statement of the main points or essential information expressed in a text, whether it be narration, dialogue, or informational text	To facilitate comprehension and recall of a text
Think Aloud	Talking through a difficult passage or task by using a form of metacognition whereby the reader expresses how he/she has made sense of the text	To reflect on how readers make meaning of challenging texts and facilitate comprehension
TP-CASTT* The AP Vertical Teams Guide for English (94–99)	Analyzing a poetic text by identifying and discussing Title, Paraphrase, Connotation, Attitude, Shift, Theme, and Title again	To facilitate the analysis of specific elements of a literary text, especially poetry. To show how the elements work together to create meaning
Visualizing	Forming a picture (mentally and/or literally) while reading a text	To increase reading comprehension and promote active engagement with text
Word Maps	Using a clearly defined graphic organizer such as concept circles or word webs to identify and reinforce word meanings	To provide a visual tool for identifying and remembering multiple aspects of words and word meanings

*Delineates AP strategy

WRITING STRATEGIES

STRATEGY	DEFINITION	PURPOSE
Adding	Making conscious choices to enhance a text by adding additional words, phrases, sentences, or ideas	To refine and clarify the writer's thoughts during revision and/or drafting
Brainstorming	Using a flexible but deliberate process of listing multiple ideas in a short period of time without excluding any idea from the preliminary list	To generate ideas, concepts, or key words that provide a focus and/or establish organization as part of the prewriting or revision process
Deleting	Providing clarity and cohesiveness for a text by eliminating words, phrases, sentences, or ideas	To refine and clarify the writer's thoughts during revision and/or drafting
Drafting	Composing a text in its initial form	To incorporate brainstormed or initial ideas into a written format

STRATEGY	DEFINITION	PURPOSE
Free writing	Write freely without constraints in order to capture thinking and convey the writer's purpose	To refine and clarify the writer's thoughts, spark new ideas, and/or generate content during revision and/or drafting
Generating Questions	Clarifying and developing ideas by asking questions of the draft. May be part of self-editing or peer editing	To clarify and develop ideas in a draft; used during drafting and as part of writer response
Graphic Organizer	Organizing ideas and information visually (e.g., Venn diagrams, flowcharts, cluster maps)	To provide a visual system for organizing multiple ideas, details, and/or textual support to be included in a piece of writing
Looping	After free writing, one section of a text is circled to promote elaboration or the generation of new ideas for that section. This process is repeated to further develop ideas from the newly generated segments	To refine and clarify the writer's thoughts, spark new ideas, and/or generate new content during revision and/or drafting
Mapping	Creating a graphic organizer that serves as a visual representation of the organizational plan for a written text	To generate ideas, concepts, or key words that provide a focus and/or establish organization during the prewriting, drafting, or revision process
Marking the Draft	Interacting with the draft version of a piece of writing by highlighting, underlining, color-coding, and annotating to indicate revision ideas	To encourage focused, reflective thinking about revising drafts
Note-taking	Making notes about ideas in response to text or discussions; one form is the double-entry journal in which textual evidence is recorded on the left side and personal commentary about the meaning of the evidence on the other side.	To assist in organizing key textual elements and responses noted during reading in order to generate textual support that can be incorporated into a piece of writing at a later time. Note-taking is also a reading and listening strategy.
Outlining	Using a system of numerals and letters in order to identify topics and supporting details and ensure an appropriate balance of ideas.	To generate ideas, concepts, or key words that provide a focus and/or establish organization prior to writing an initial draft and/or during the revision process
Quickwrite	Writing for a short, specific amount of time in response to a prompt provided	To generate multiple ideas in a quick fashion that could be turned into longer pieces of writing at a later time (May be considered as part of the drafting process)
RAFT	Generating a new text and/or transforming a text by identifying and manipulating its component parts of Role, Audience, Format, and Topic	To generate a new text by identifying the main elements of a text during the prewriting and drafting stages of the writing process
Rearranging	Selecting components of a text and moving them to another place within the text and/or modifying the order in which the author's ideas are presented	To refine and clarify the writer's thoughts during revision and/or drafting
Self-Editing/Peer Editing	Working individually or with a partner to examine a text closely in order to identify areas that might need to be corrected for grammar, punctuation, spelling	To facilitate a collaborative approach to generating ideas for and revising writing.

STRATEGY	DEFINITION	PURPOSE
Sharing and Responding	Communicating with another person or a small group of peers who respond to a piece of writing as focused readers (not necessarily as evaluators)	To make suggestions for improvement to the work of others and/or to receive appropriate and relevant feedback on the writer's own work, used during the drafting and revision process
Sketching	Drawing or sketching ideas or ordering of ideas. Includes storyboarding, visualizing	To generate and/or clarify ideas by visualizing them. May be part of prewriting
Substituting / Replacing	Replacing original words or phrases in a text with new words or phrases that achieve the desired effect	To refine and clarify the writer's thoughts during revision and/or drafting
TWIST* The AP Vertical Teams Guide for English 167–174	Arriving at a thesis statement that incorporates the following literary elements: tone, word choice (diction), imagery, style and theme	To craft an interpretive thesis in response to a prompt about a text
Webbing	Developing a graphic organizer that consists of a series of circles connected with lines to indicate relationships among ideas	To generate ideas, concepts, or key words that provide a focus and/or establish organization prior to writing an initial draft and/or during the revision process
Writer's Checklist	Using a co-constructed checklist (that could be written on a bookmark and/or displayed on the wall) in order to look for specific features of a writing text and check for accuracy	To focus on key areas of the writing process so that the writer can effectively revise a draft and correct mistake
Writing Groups	A type of discussion group devoted to sharing and responding of student work	To facilitate a collaborative approach to generating ideas for and revising writing.

SPEAKING AND LISTENING STRATEGIES

STRATEGY	DEFINITION	PURPOSE
Choral Reading	Reading text lines aloud in student groups and/or individually to present an interpretation	To develop fluency; differentiate between the reading of statements and questions; practice phrasing, pacing, and reading dialogue; show how a character's emotions are captured through vocal stress and intonation
Note-taking	Creating a record of information while listening to a speaker or reading a text	To facilitate active listening or close reading ; to record and organize ideas that assist in processing information
Oral Reading	Reading aloud one's own text or the texts of others (e.g., echo reading, choral reading, paired readings)	To share one's own work or the work of others; build fluency and increase confidence in presenting to a group
Rehearsal	Encouraging multiple practices of a piece of text prior to a performance	To provide students with an opportunity to clarify the meaning of a text prior to a performance as they refine the use of dramatic conventions (e.g., gestures, vocal interpretations, facial expressions)
Role Playing	Assuming the role or persona of a character	To develop the voice, emotions, and mannerisms of a character to facilitate improved comprehension of a text

COLLABORATIVE STRATEGIES

STRATEGY	DEFINITION	PURPOSE
Discussion Groups	Engaging in an interactive, small group discussion, often with an assigned role; to consider a topic, text or question	To gain new understanding of or insight into a text from multiple perspectives
Think-Pair-Share	Pairing with a peer to share ideas; before sharing ideas and discussion with a larger group	To construct meaning about a topic or question; to test thinking in relation to the ideas of others; to prepare for a discussion with a larger group

Graphic Organizer Directory

English Language Arts Graphic Organizers

Audience Notes and Feedback

Definition and Reflection

Editor's/Writer's Checklists

Evaluating Online Sources

Presenting Scoring Guide

RAFT

SMELL

SOAPSTone

TP-CASTT Analysis

TP-CASTT

Verbal & Visual Word Association

Web Organizer

Word Map

English Language Development Graphic Organizers

Active Listening Feedback

Active Listening Notes

Cause and Effect

Character Map

Collaborative Dialogue

Conclusion Builder

Conflict Map

Conversation for Quickwrite

Discourse Starters

Idea and Argument Evaluator

Idea Connector

Key Idea and Details Chart

Narrative Analysis and Writing

Notes for Reading Independently

Opinion Builder

Paragraph Frame for Conclusions

Paragraph Frame for Sequencing

Paraphrasing and Summarizing Map

Peer Editing

Persuasive/Argument Writing Map

Roots and Affixes Brainstorm

Round Table Discussion

Sequence of Events Time Line

Text Structure Stairs

Unknown Word Solver

Venn Diagram for Writing a Comparison

Word Choice Analyzer

Audience Notes and Feedback

Scoring Criteria	Notes/Feedback
Introduction/ Conclusion	
Timing	
Voice	
Eyes/Gestures	
Use of Media, Visuals, Props	
Audience Engagement	

Definition and Reflection

Academic Vocabulary Word

Definition in own words

Graphic Representation (literal or symbolic)

My experiences with this concept:

- I haven't really thought about this concept.

  _____

- I have only thought about this concept in Language Arts class.

  _____

- I have applied this concept in other classes.

  _____

- I have applied this concept outside of school.

  _____

My level of understanding:

- I am still trying to understand this concept.

  _____

- I am familiar with this concept, but I am not comfortable applying it.

  _____

- I am very comfortable with this concept and I know how to apply it.

  _____

- I could teach this concept to another classmate.

  _____

Editor's Checklist

Over the course of the year with SpringBoard, customize this Editor's Checklist as your knowledge of language conventions grows. The three examples below show you how to write a good checklist item.

	Are all the sentences complete?
	Are any sentence fragments intentional?
	Do all the sentences have correct punctuation?

Writer's Checklist

Ideas	
	Does your first paragraph hook the reader?
	Is the purpose of your writing clear (to inform, to make an argument, etc.)?
	Is the style of your writing correct for the type of text (narrative, argument, etc.)?
	Is your main idea clear and easy to summarize?
	Does your text contain details and information that support your main idea?
	Are the ideas in the text well organized?
	Do you connect your ideas by using transitions?
	Do you use parallel structure to keep your ideas clear?
	Does each paragraph have a conclusion that transitions to the next paragraph?
	Does your writing end with a strong conclusion that restates the original purpose of the text?
Language	
	Do you keep a consistent point of view throughout?
	Do you use the present tense when writing about a text?
	Are any shifts in verb tense easy to follow and necessary?
	Have you removed unnecessary or confusing words?
	Do you use vivid verbs and descriptive adjectives when appropriate?
	Do you use different styles of language (like figurative or sensory) when appropriate?
	Do you vary the length of your sentences?
	Do you vary the way you begin your sentences?
	Did you split up run-on sentences?
	Are your pronoun references clear?

Evaluating Online Sources

The URL
- What is its domain?
  - .com = a for-profit organization
  - .gov, .mil, .us (or other country code) = a government site
  - .edu = affiliated with an educational institution
  - .org = a nonprofit organization

- Is this URL someone's personal page?
- Why might using information from a personal page be a problem?
- Do you recognize who is publishing this page?
- If not, you may need to investigate further to determine whether the publisher is an expert on the topic.

Sponsor:
- Does the website easily give information about the organization or group that sponsors it?
- Does it have a link (often called "About Us") that leads you to that information?
- What do you learn?

Timeliness:
- When was the page last updated (usually this is posted at the top or bottom of the page)?
- How current a page is may indicate how accurate or useful the information in it will be.

Purpose:
- What is the purpose of the page?
- What is its target audience?
- Does it present information or opinion?
- Is it primarily objective or subjective?
- How do you know?

Author:
- What credentials does the author have?
- Is this person or group considered an authority on the topic?

Links
- Does the page provide links?
- Do they work?
- Are they helpful?
- Are they objective or subjective?

Presenting Scoring Guide

Scoring Criteria	Exemplary	Proficient	Emerging	Incomplete
Introduction / Conclusion	The presentation • provides a clear, engaging, and appropriate introduction to the topic or performance • provides a clear, engaging, and appropriate conclusion that closes, summarizes, draws connections to broader themes, or supports the ideas presented.	The presentation • provides a clear and appropriate introduction to the topic or performance • provides a clear and appropriate conclusion that closes, summarizes, draws connections to broader themes, or supports the ideas presented.	The presentation • provides an adequate introduction to the topic or performance • provides an adequate conclusion that closes, summarizes, draws connections to broader themes, or supports the ideas presented.	The presentation • does not provide an introduction to the topic or performance • does not provide a conclusion that closes, summarizes, draws connections to broader themes, or supports the ideas presented.
Timing	The presentation • thoroughly delivers its intended message within the allotted time • is thoughtfully and appropriately paced throughout.	The presentation • mostly delivers its intended message within the allotted time • is appropriately paced most of the time.	The presentation • delivers some of its intended message within the allotted time • is sometimes not paced appropriately.	The presentation • does not deliver its intended message within the allotted time • is not paced appropriately.
Voice (Volume, Pronunciation)	The presentation • is delivered with adequate volume enabling audience members to fully comprehend what is said • is delivered with clear pronunciation.	The presentation • is delivered with adequate volume enabling audience members to mostly comprehend what is said • is delivered with mostly clear pronunciation.	The presentation • is delivered with somewhat adequate volume enabling audience members to comprehend some of what is said • is delivered with somewhat clear pronunciation.	The presentation • is not delivered with adequate volume, so that audience members are unable to comprehend what is said • is delivered with unclear pronunciation.
Eyes/Gestures	The presentation • is delivered with appropriate eye contact that helps engage audience members • makes use of thoughtfully selected gestures and/or body language to convey meaning.	The presentation • is delivered with some appropriate eye contact that helps engage audience members • makes use of gestures and/or body language to convey meaning.	The presentation • is delivered with occasional eye contact that sometimes engages audience members • makes some use of gestures and/or body language to convey meaning.	The presentation • is not delivered with eye contact to engage audience members • makes little or no use of gestures and/or body language to convey meaning.
Use of Media, Visuals, Props	The presentation • makes use of highly engaging visuals, multimedia, and/or props that enhance delivery.	The presentation • makes use of visuals, multimedia, and/or props that enhance delivery.	The presentation • makes use of some visuals, multimedia, and/or props that somewhat enhance delivery.	The presentation • makes use of few or no visuals, multimedia, and/or props that enhance delivery.
Audience Engagement	The presentation • includes thoughtful and appropriate interactions with and responses to audience members.	The presentation • includes appropriate interactions with and responses to audience members.	The presentation • includes a few interactions with and responses to audience members.	The presentation • does not include interactions with and responses to audience members.

RAFT

Role	Who or what are you as a writer?
Audience	As a writer, to whom are you writing?
Format	As a writer, what format would be appropriate for your audience (essay, letter, speech, poem, etc.)?
Topic	As a writer, what is the subject of your writing? What points do you want to make?

SMELL

Sender-Receiver Relationship—Who are the senders and receivers of the message, and what is their relationship (consider what different audiences the text may be addressing)?

Message—What is a literal summary of the content? What is the meaning/significance of this information?

Emotional Strategies—What emotional appeals (*pathos*) are included? What seems to be their desired effect?

Logical Strategies—What logical arguments/appeals (*logos*) are included? What is their effect?

Language—What specific language is used to support the message? How does it affect the text's effectiveness? Consider both images and actual words.

SOAPSTone

SOAPSTone	Analysis	Textual Support
S What does the reader know about the writer?		
O What are the circumstances surrounding this text?		
A Who is the target audience?		
P Why did the author write this text?		
S What is the topic?		
Tone What is the author's tone, or attitude?		

TP-CASTT Analysis

Poem Title:

Author:

Title: Make a Prediction. What do you think the title means before you read the poem?

Paraphrase: Translate the poem in your own words. What is the poem about? Rephrase difficult sections word for word.

Connotation: Look beyond the literal meaning of key words and images to their associations.

Attitude: What is the speaker's attitude? What is the author's attitude? How does the author feel about the speaker, about other characters, about the subject?

Shifts: Where do the shifts in tone, setting, voice, etc., occur? Look for time and place, keywords, punctuation, stanza divisions, changes in length or rhyme, and sentence structure. What is the purpose of each shift? How do they contribute to effect and meaning?

Title: Reexamine the title. What do you think it means now in the context of the poem?

Theme: Think of the literal and metaphorical layers of the poem. Then determine the overall theme. The theme must be written in a complete sentence.

TP-CASTT

Poem Title:

Author:

T		
P		
C		
A		
S		
T		
T		

Verbal & Visual Word Association

Definition in Your Own Words	Important Elements

Academic Vocabulary Word

Visual Representation	Personal Association

Web Organizer

Word Map

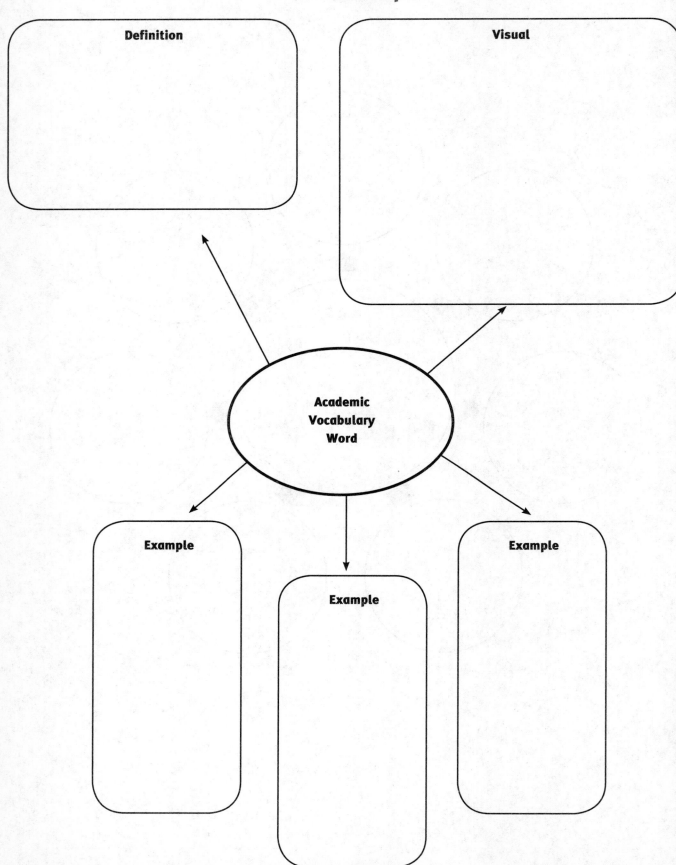

Definition

Visual

Academic
Vocabulary
Word

Example

Example

Example

Active Listening Feedback

Presenter's name: _____

Content

What is the presenter's purpose? _____

What is the presenter's main point? _____

Do you agree with the presenter? Why or why not? _____

_____

_____

Form

Did the presenter use a clear, loud voice? ☐ yes ☐ no

Did the presenter make eye contact? ☐ yes ☐ no

One thing I really liked about the presentation:

_____

_____

_____

One question I still have:

_____

_____

_____

Other comments or notes:

Active Listening Notes

Title: _____

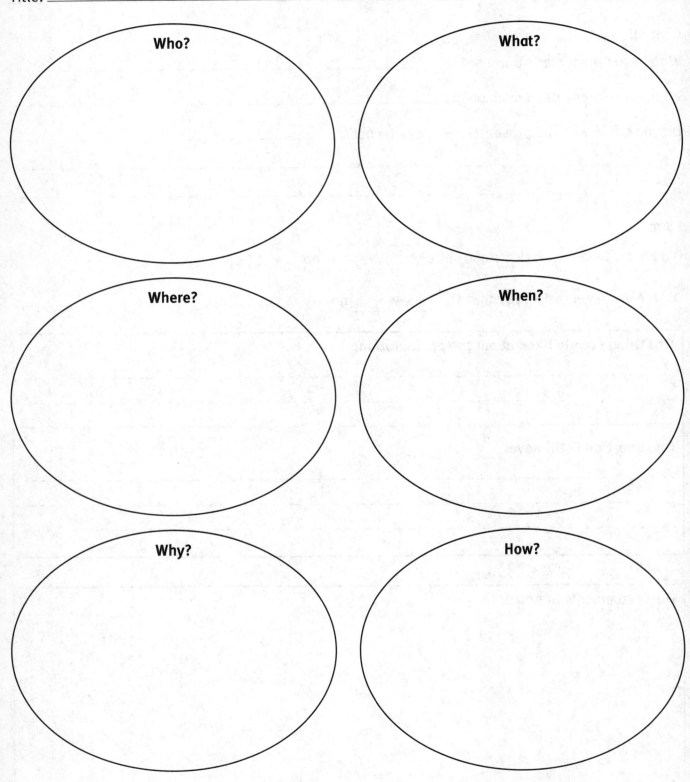

Who?

What?

Where?

When?

Why?

How?

Cause and Effect

Title: _____

Cause: What happened?	→	Effect: An effect of this is

Cause: What happened?	→	Effect: An effect of this is

Cause: What happened?	→	Effect: An effect of this is

Cause: What happened?	→	Effect: An effect of this is

Character Map

Character name: _____

What does the character look like?

How does the character act?

What do other characters say or think about the character?

Collaborative Dialogue

Topic: _____

"Wh-" Prompts

Who?   What?   Where?

When?   Why?

Speaker 1

Speaker 2

Conclusion Builder

Evidence

Evidence

Evidence

Based on this evidence, I can conclude

Conflict Map

Title: _____

What is the main conflict in this story?

What causes this conflict?

How is the conflict resolved?

What are some other ways the conflict could have been resolved?

Conversation for Quickwrite

1. Turn to a partner and restate the quickwrite in your own words.

2. Brainstorm key words to use in your quickwrite response.

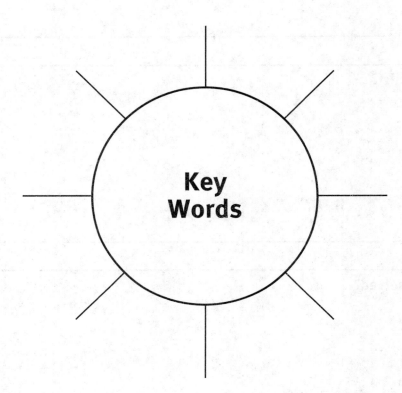

Key Words

3. Take turns explaining your quickwrite response to your partner. Try using some of the key words.

4. On your own, write a response to the quickwrite.

Discourse Starters

Questioning and Discussing a Text

One question I have is _____.

Could this mean _____?

What do you think the author means by _____?

Where in the text can we find _____?

Why do you think the author _____?

I understand _____, but I wonder _____.

I notice that _____.

I think this (word/sentence/paragraph) means _____.

I think _____ because the text says _____.

In paragraph _____, the author says _____.

According to the text, _____.

One way to interpret _____ is _____.

Based on the text, I can infer that _____.

Summarizing

The main events that take place are _____.

The major points of the text are _____.

The main idea of _____ is _____.

One central idea of this text is _____.

Another central idea is _____.

All in all, the message is _____.

The author's main purpose is to _____.

Basically, the author is saying that _____.

It can be concluded that _____ because _____.

How would you summarize the central idea(s)?

Comparing and Contrasting

_____ and _____ are similar because _____.

_____ and _____ are similar in that they both _____.

_____ is _____. Similarly, _____ is _____.

One thing _____ and _____ have in common is _____.

_____ and _____ are different because _____.

_____ and _____ are different in that _____.

_____ is _____. On the other hand, _____ is _____.

One difference between _____ and _____ is _____.

Clarifying

I'm not sure I understand the instructions.

Could you repeat that please?

I have a question about _____.

I am having trouble with _____.

Will you explain that again?

Could you clarify _____?

Could you please show me how to _____?

Would you mind helping me with _____?

Which (page/paragraph/section) are we reading?

How do you spell/pronounce _____?

Discourse Starters

Agreeing and Disagreeing

I agree with the idea that _____ because _____.

I share your point of view because _____.

You made a good point when you said _____.

I agree with (a person) that _____.

Although I agree that _____, I also think _____.

I see what you're saying, but _____.

I understand where you're coming from, but _____.

I disagree with the idea that _____ because _____.

I see it a different way because _____.

You have a point, but the evidence suggests _____.

Have you also considered _____?

Arguing and Persuading with Evidence

I believe that _____ because _____.

It is clear that _____ because _____.

One reason I think _____ is _____.

I have several reasons for thinking _____.

Let me explain why I think that _____.

Based on evidence in the text, I think _____.

Evidence such as _____ suggests that _____.

An example to support my position is _____.

This is evident because _____.

The text clearly indicates that _____.

What evidence supports the idea that _____?

Can you explain why you think _____?

Evaluating

This is effective because _____.

The evidence _____ is strong because _____.

This is convincing because _____.

The author's choice makes sense because _____.

I see why the author _____, but I think _____.

This is not very effective because _____.

The evidence _____ is weak because _____.

_____ would have been a better choice.

This would have been better if _____.

What do you think about the writer's choice to _____?

Why do you think _____ (is/isn't) effective?

Giving Feedback and Suggesting

The part where you _____ is strong because _____.

What impressed me the most is how you _____.

This is a good start. Maybe you should add _____.

I like how you _____, but I would try _____.

You might consider changing _____.

I would suggest revising _____ so that _____.

One suggestion would be to _____.

Why did you choose _____?

A better choice might be _____.

This would be clearer if _____.

Idea and Argument Evaluator

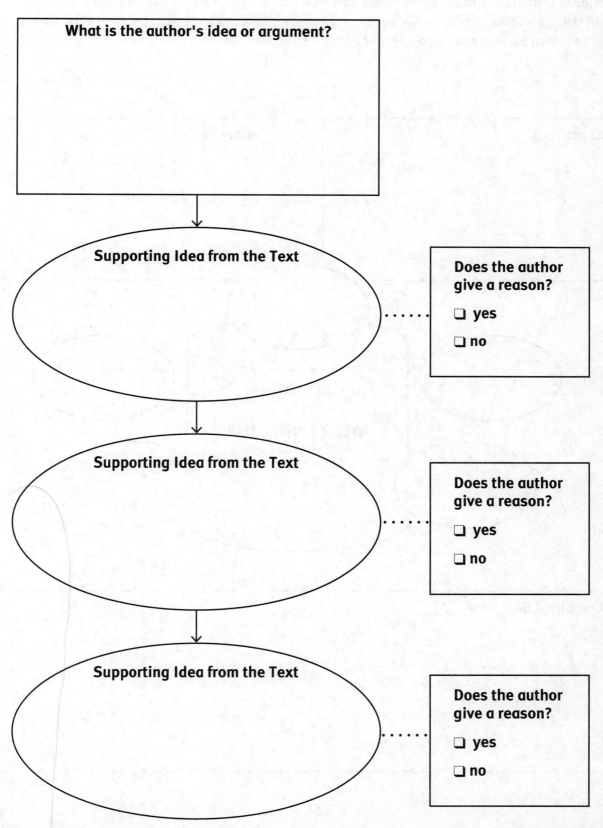

What is the author's idea or argument?

Supporting Idea from the Text

Does the author give a reason?

❏ yes

❏ no

Supporting Idea from the Text

Does the author give a reason?

❏ yes

❏ no

Supporting Idea from the Text

Does the author give a reason?

❏ yes

❏ no

Idea Connector

Directions: Write two simple sentences about the same topic. Next, write transition words around the Idea Connector. Then, choose an appropriate word to connect ideas in the two sentences. Write your combined sentence in the space below.

Sentence One

Sentence Two

IDEA CONNECTOR

Combined Sentence

Key Idea and Details Chart

Title/Topic _____

Key Idea _____

_____

_____

Supporting Detail 1 _____

_____

_____

Supporting Detail 2 _____

_____

_____

Supporting Detail 3 _____

_____

_____

Supporting Detail 4 _____

_____

_____

Restate topic sentence: _____

_____

Concluding sentence: _____

_____

_____

Narrative Analysis and Writing

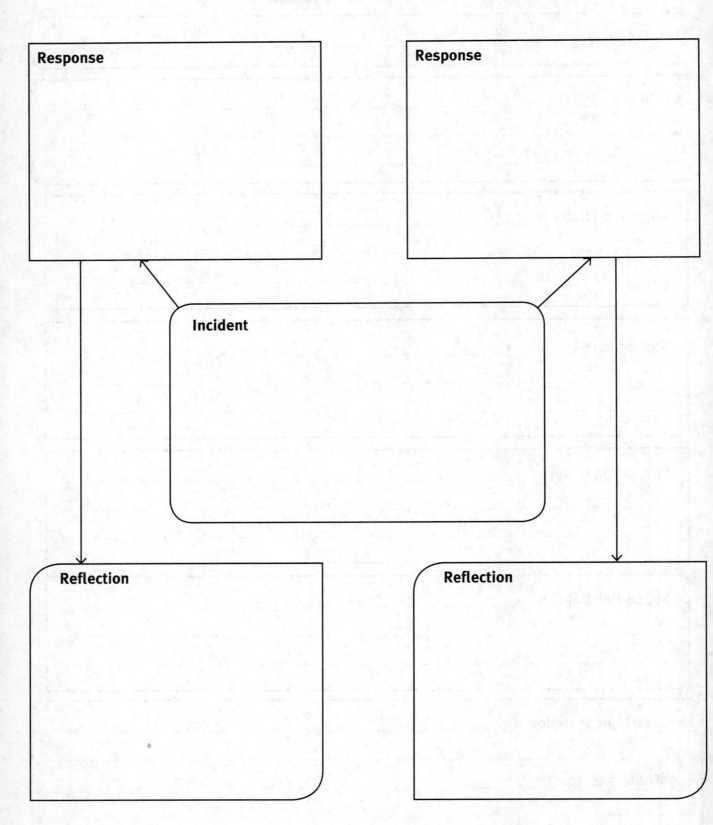

Response

Response

Incident

Reflection

Reflection

Notes for Reading Independently

Title: _____

The main characters are	The setting is	The main conflict is

The climax happens when	The conflict is resolved when

My brief summary of _____

Opinion Builder

Reason

Reason

Based on these reasons, my opinion is

Reason

Reason

Paragraph Frame for Conclusions

Conclusion Words and Phrases

shows that

based on

suggests that

leads to

indicates that

influences

The _____ (story, poem, play, passage, etc.)
shows that (helps us to conclude that) _____
_____
_____

There are several reasons why. First, _____
_____
_____
_____
_____

A second reason is _____
_____
_____
_____
_____
_____

Finally, _____
_____
_____
_____
_____

In conclusion, _____
_____
_____
_____

Paragraph Frame for Sequencing

Sequence Words and Phrases

at the beginning

in the first place

as a result

later

eventually

in the end

lastly

In the _____ (story, poem, play, passage, etc.)

there are three important _____

(events, steps, directions, etc.)

First, _____

_____

_____

_____

_____

Second, _____

_____

_____

_____

_____

Third, _____

_____

_____

_____

_____

Finally, _____

_____

_____

_____

Paraphrasing and Summarizing Map

What does the text say?	How can I say it in my own words?

How can I use my own words to summarize the text?

NAME _____ DATE _____

Peer Editing

Writer's name: _____

Did the writer answer the prompt? ☐ yes ☐ no

Did the writer provide evidence to support his or her reasons? ☐ yes ☐ no

Is the writing organized in a way that makes sense? ☐ yes ☐ no

Did the writer vary sentence structures to make the writing more interesting? ☐ yes ☐ no

Are there any spelling or punctuation mistakes? ☐ yes ☐ no

Are there any grammar errors? ☐ yes ☐ no

Two things I really liked about the writer's story:

1. _____
   _____
   _____

2. _____
   _____
   _____

One thing I think the writer could do to improve the writing:

1. _____
   _____
   _____

Other comments or notes:

Persuasive/Argument Writing Map

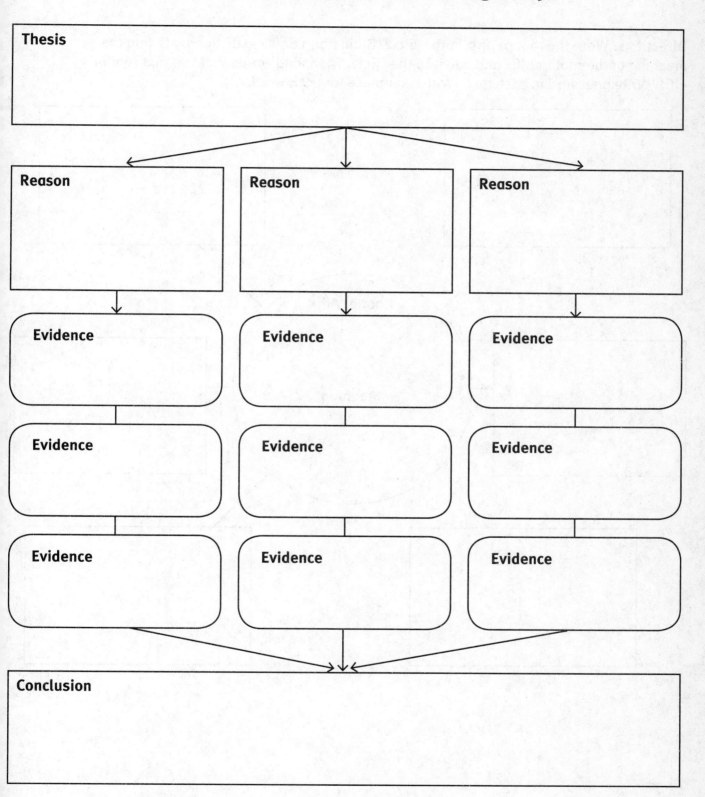

Thesis

Reason

Reason

Reason

Evidence

Evidence

Evidence

Evidence

Evidence

Evidence

Evidence

Evidence

Evidence

Conclusion

Roots and Affixes Brainstorm

Directions: Write the root or affix in the circle. Brainstorm or use a dictionary to find the meaning of the root or affix and add it to the circle. Then, find words that use that root or affix. Write one word in each box. Write a sentence for each word.

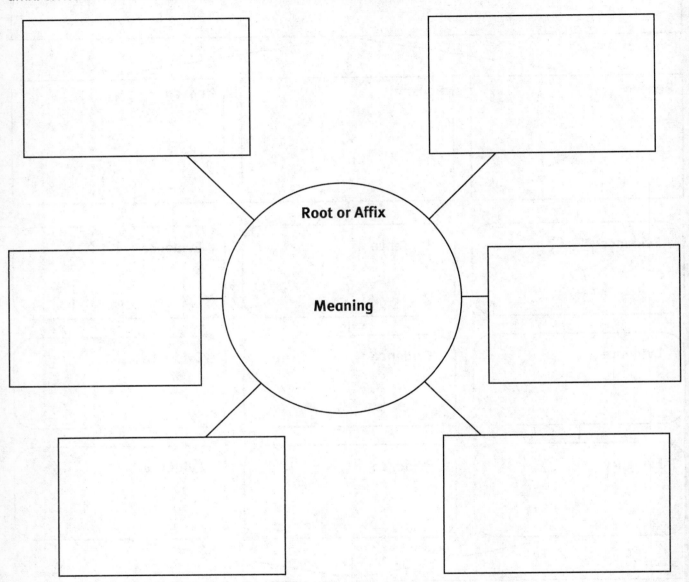

Round Table Discussion

Directions: Write the topic in the center box. One student begins by stating his or her ideas while the student to the left takes notes. Then the next student speaks while the student to his or her left takes notes, and so on.

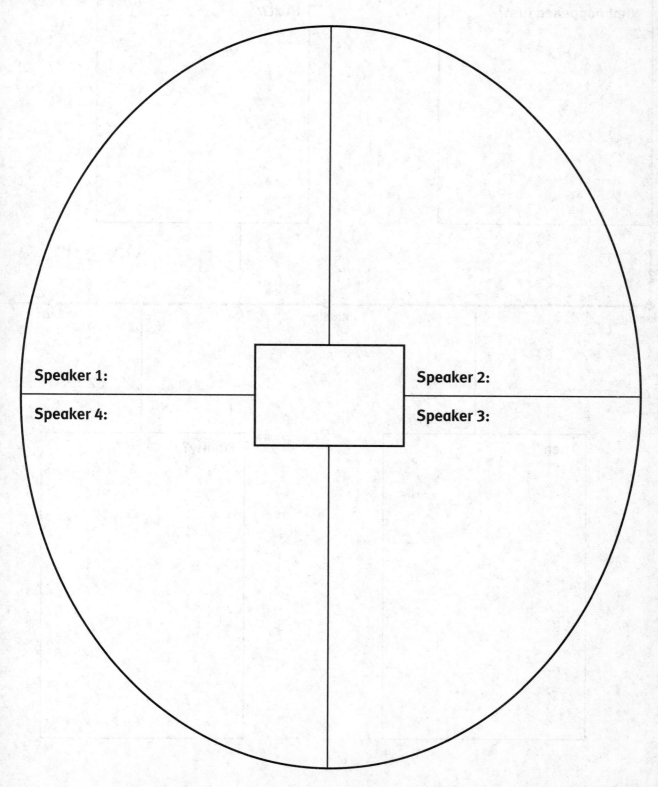

Speaker 1:

Speaker 2:

Speaker 4:

Speaker 3:

Sequence of Events Time Line

Title: _____

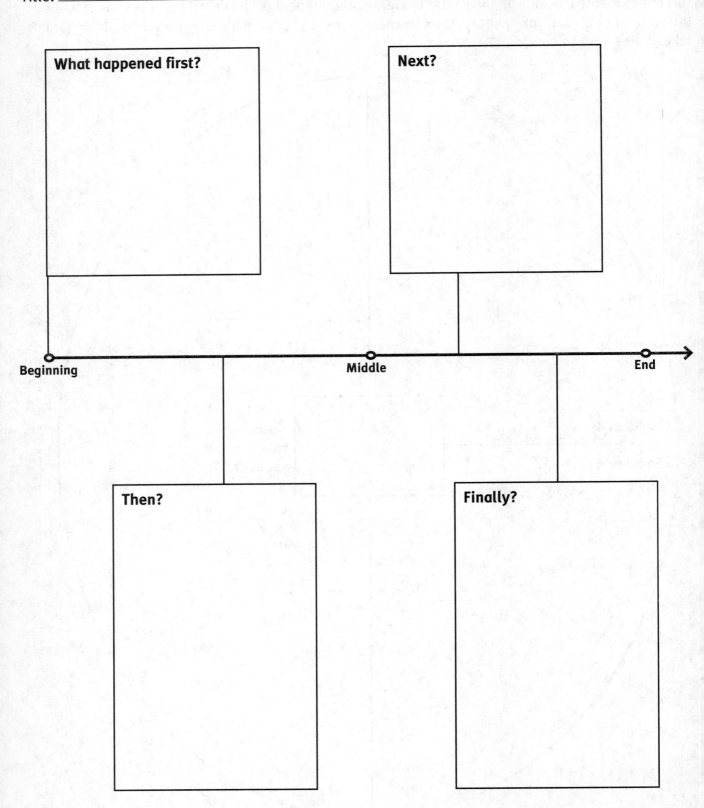

What happened first?		Next?

Beginning　　　　　　　　**Middle**　　　　　　　　**End**

Then?		Finally?

Text Structure Stairs

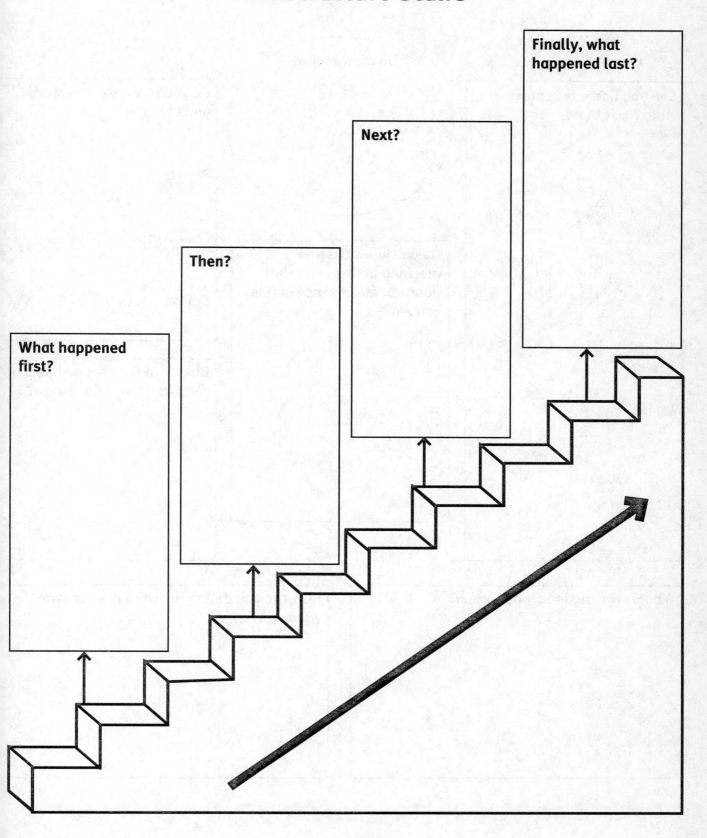

Finally, what happened last?

Next?

Then?

What happened first?

Unknown Word Solver

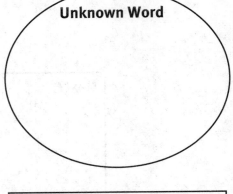

Unknown Word

Can you find any context clues? List them.

Do you recognize any word parts?

Prefix:

Root Word:

Suffix:

Do you know another meaning of this word that does not make sense in this context?

Does it look or sound like a word in another language?

What is the dictionary definition?

How can you define the word in your own words?

Venn Diagram for Writing a Comparison

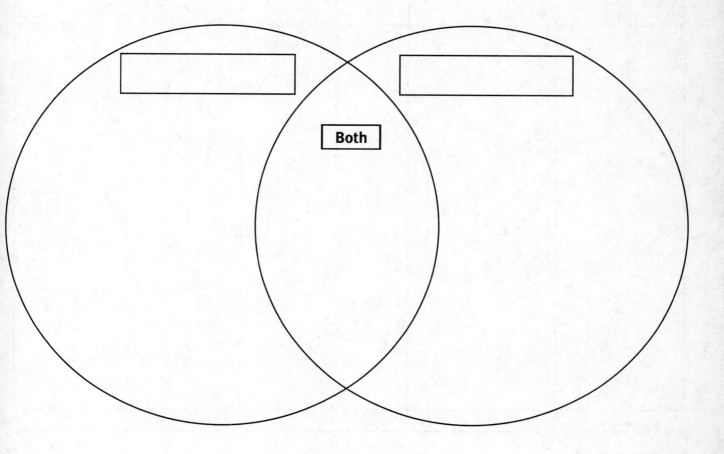

Both

They are similar in that _____

_____

_____

_____

_____

_____

They are different in that _____

_____

_____

_____

_____

_____

Word Choice Analyzer

Word or phrase from the text	What does the word or phrase mean?	What is another way to say the same thing?	What effect did the author produce by choosing these words?

Explain Your Analysis

The author uses the word or phrase _____ , which means

_____

Another way to say this is _____

_____

I think the author chose these words to _____

_____

_____

One way I can modify this sentence to add detail is to _____

_____

Glossary / Glosario

A

advertising: the use of print, graphics, or videos to persuade people to buy a product or use a service
publicidad: uso de impresos, gráfica o videos para persuadir a las personas a comprar un producto o usar un servicio

allegory: a story in which the characters, objects, or actions have a meaning beyond the surface of the story
alegoría: cuento en el que los personajes, objetos o acciones tienen un significado que va más allá de la superficie de la historia

alliteration: the repetition of consonant sounds at the beginnings of words that are close together
aliteración: repetición de sonidos consonánticos al comienzo de palabras que están cercanas

allusion: a reference to a well-known person, place, event, literary work, or work of art
alusión: referencia a una persona, lugar, obra literaria u obra de arte muy conocidos

analogy: a comparison of the similarity of two things; for example, comparing a *part to a whole* or the *whole to a part*
analogía: comparación de la semejanza de dos cosas; por ejemplo, comparar una *parte con un todo* o el *todo con una parte*

analysis (literary): to study details of a work to identify essential features or meaning
análisis (literario): estudio de los detalles de una obra para identificar características o significados esenciales

anecdote: a brief, entertaining account of an incident or event
anécdota: breve relato entretenido de un incidente o suceso

antagonist: the character who opposes or struggles against the main character
antagonista: personaje que se opone o enfrenta al personaje principal

antonyms: words with opposite meanings
antónimos: palabras con significados opuestos

archetype: a character, symbol, story pattern, or other element that is common to human experience across cultures and that occurs frequently in literature, myth, and folklore
arquetipo: personaje, símbolo, patrón de un cuento u otro elemento que es común a la experiencia humana a través de diversas culturas y que aparece con frecuencia en literatura, mitos y folclor

argument: facts or reasoning offered to support a position as being true
argumento: hechos o razonamiento entregados para apoyar una posición como verdadera

artifact: an object made by a human being, typically an item that has cultural or historical significance
artefacto: objeto hecho por un ser humano, habitualmente un objeto que tiene significación cultural o histórica

atmosphere: the feeling created by a literary work or passage
atmósfera: sentimiento creado por una obra o pasaje literario

audience: the intended readers of specific types of texts or the viewers of a program or performance
público: lectores objetivo de tipos específicos de textos o espectadores de un programa o actuación

B

balanced sentence: a sentence that presents ideas of equal weight in similar grammatical form to emphasize the similarity or difference between the ideas
oración balanceada: oración que presenta ideas de igual peso en forma gramatical similar para enfatizar la semejanza o diferencia entre las ideas

body paragraph: a paragraph that contains a topic sentence, supporting details and commentary, and a concluding sentence and that is usually part of a longer text
párrafo representativo: párrafo que contiene una oración principal, detalles de apoyo y comentarios, y una oración concluyente que normalmente forma parte de un texto más extenso

C

call to action: occurs at the end of an argumentative text to make clear what the writer or speaker wants the audience to think or do
llamado a la acción: ocurre en la conclusión de un texto argumentativo para establecer lo que el escritor o el orador quieren que el público piense o haga

caricature: a visual or verbal representation in which characteristics or traits are distorted for emphasis
caricatura: representación visual o verbal en la que las características o rasgos son distorsionados para dar énfasis

cause: an initial action; an event that makes something else happen
causa: acción inicial; suceso que hace que otra cosa ocurra

character: a person or animal that takes part in the action of a literary work
personaje: persona o animal que participa en la acción de una obra literaria

characterization: the methods a writer uses to develop characters; for example, through description, actions, and dialogue
caracterización: métodos que usa un escritor para desarrollar personajes; por ejemplo, a través de descripción, acciones y diálogo

citation: giving credit to the authors of source information
cita: dar crédito a los autores de información usada como fuente

cliché: an overused expression or idea
cliché: expresión o idea usada en exceso

climax: the turning point or the high point of a story
clímax: punto de inflexión o momento culminante de un cuento

coherence: the clear and orderly presentation of ideas in a paragraph or essay
coherencia: presentación clara y ordenada de las ideas en un párrafo o ensayo

comedy: an entertainment that is amusing or humorous
comedia: espectáculo que es divertido o cómico

commentary: explanation of the way the facts, details and/or examples in a paragraph or essay support the topic sentence
comentario: explicación de la manera en que los hechos, detalles y ejemplos de un párrafo o ensayo apoyan la oración principal

commercialism: an emphasis on gaining profits through advertising or sponsorship
mercantilismo: énfasis en obtener utilidades por medio de la publicidad o el auspicio

communication: the process of giving or exchanging information
comunicación: proceso de dar o intercambiar información

compare: to identify similarities in two or more items; *see also*, contrast
comparar: identificar semejanzas en dos o más elementos; *ver también*, contrastar

concise: brief and to the point
conciso: breve y al punto

concluding sentence: a final sentence that pulls together the ideas in a paragraph by restating the main idea or by summarizing or commenting on the ideas in the paragraph
oración concluyente: oración final que reúne las ideas de un párrafo, reformulando la idea principal o resumiendo o comentando las ideas del párrafo

conclusion: the ending of a paragraph or essay, which brings it to a close and leaves an impression with the reader
conclusión: fin de un párrafo o ensayo, que lo lleva a su término y deja una impresión en el lector

conflict: a struggle between opposing forces. In an **external conflict**, a character struggles with an outside force, such as another character or something in nature. In an **internal conflict**, the character struggles with his or her own needs, desires, or emotions.
conflicto: lucha entre fuerzas opuestas. En un **conflicto externo**, un personaje lucha contra una fuerza externa, como por ejemplo otro personaje o algo de la naturaleza. En un **conflicto interno**, el personaje lucha contra sus propias necesidades, deseos o emociones.

connotation: the suggested or implied meaning or emotion associated with a word—beyond its literal definition
connotación: significado o emoción sugerida o implícita que se asocia con una palabra—más allá de su definición literal

consumer: a buyer; a person who acquires goods and services
consumidor: comprador, persona que adquiere bienes y servicios

consumerism: the buying and consuming of goods and products; the belief that it is good to buy and consume goods and services
consumismo: compra y consumo de bienes y productos; creencia de que es bueno comprar y consumir bienes y servicios

context: the circumstances or facts that surround a particular event or situation
contexto: las circunstancias o los hechos que envuelven un suceso o situación particular

context clue: information in words and phrases surrounding an unfamiliar word that hint at the meaning of the unfamiliar word.
clave de contexto: información en las palabras y frases que rodean una palabra no conocida y que dan una pista acerca del significado de esa palabra.

contrast: to identify differences in two or more items; *see also*, compare
contrastar: identificar las diferencias entre dos o más elementos; *ver también*, comparar

controversy: a public debate or dispute concerning a matter of opinion
controversia: un debate público o disputa sobre una cuestión sujeta a opinión

copy: the actual text in an advertisement
texto publicitario: información actual en un anuncio publicitario

counter-argument: reasoning or facts given in opposition to an argument
contraargumento: razonamiento o hechos dados en oposición a un argumento

criteria: the facts, rules, or standards on which judgments are based.
criterios: hechos, reglas o estándares sobre las cuales están basadas las opiniones.

D

debate: *n.* a discussion involving opposing points of view; *v.* to present the sides of an argument by discussing opposing points
debate: *s.* discusión que involucra puntos de vista opuestos; *v.* presentar los lados de un argumento discutiendo puntos opuestos

definition: the process of making clear the meaning or nature of something

definición: proceso de aclarar el significado o naturaleza de algo

definition essay: a type of expository writing that explains, or defines, what a topic means

ensayo de definición: un tipo de escritura informativa que explica o define el significado de un tema

denotation: the exact, literal meaning of a word

denotación: significado exacto y literal de una palabra

denounce: declare something to be wrong in a public way

denunciar: declarar de manera pública que algo está mal

derision: strong disapproval of an attitude or topic

escarnio: fuerte desaprobación hacia una actitud o tema

detail: in writing, evidence (facts, statistics, examples) that supports the topic sentence

detalle: en la escritura, evidencia (hechos, estadística, ejemplos) que apoya la oracón principal

dialect: the distinctive language, including the sounds, spelling, grammar, and diction, of a specific group or class of people

dialecto: el lenguaje distintivo, incluyendo sonidos, ortografía, gramática y dicción, de un grupo específico o clase de personas

dialogue: conversation between characters

diálogo: conversación entre personajes

diction: a writer's or speaker's choice of words

dicción: selección de palabras por parte del escritor u orador

dissolve: the slow fading away of one image in a film as another fades in to take its place

desvanecimiento: desaparición lenta de una imagen en una película a medida que otra aparece progresivamente para tomar su lugar

drama: a genre of literature that is intended to be performed before an audience; a play

drama: género literario destinado a ser representado ante un público; obra teatral

dystopia: an imagined place or state in which the condition of life is imperfect or bad

distopía: lugar o estado imaginario en el que las condiciones de vida son imperfectas o malas

E

editorial: A short essay in which a publication, or someone speaking for a publication, expresses an opinion or takes a stand on an issue

editorial: ensayo corto en el que una publicación, o alguien que representa una publicación, expresa una opinión o toma partido acerca de un tema

effect: the result of an event or action

efecto: resultado de un suceso o acción

enunciation: how words are spoken so they can be clearly understood by an audience

enunciación: la manera en que se pronuncian las palabras para que sean entendidas claramente por un público

epic: a long narrative poem about the deeds of heroes or gods

épica: poema narrativo largo acerca de las proezas de héroes o dioses

epilogue: a section at the end of a book or play that extends or comments on the ending

epílogo: sección al final de un libro u obra teatral, que extiende o comenta el final

essay: a short literary composition on a single subject

ensayo: composición literaria corta acerca de un único tema

ethos: a rhetorical appeal that focuses on the character or qualifications of the speaker

ethos: recurso retórico centrado en el carácter o las capacidades del orador

euphemism: an inoffensive expression that is used in place of one that is considered harsh or blunt

eufemismo: expresión inofensiva usada en lugar de una considerada cruel o ruda

evaluate: make judgments based on criteria and standards to determine the value of something

evaluar: juzgar algo basándose en criterios y estándares para determinar el valor de algo

explanatory essay: an essay that makes an assertion and explains it with details, reasons, textual evidence, and commentary

ensayo explicativo: ensayo que hace una afirmación y la explica con detalles, razones, evidencia textual y comentarios

explanatory paragraph: a paragraph that makes an assertion and supports it with details and commentary

párrafo explicativo: párrafo que hace una afirmación y la apoya con detalles y comentarios

exposition: events that give a reader background information needed to understand a story

exposición: sucesos que entregan al lector los antecedentes necesarios para comprender un cuento

F

fable: a brief story that teaches a lesson or moral, usually through animal characters that take on human qualities

fábula: cuento breve que enseña una lección o moraleja, normalmente por medio de personajes animales que asumen cualidades humanas

fact: a statement that can be proven

hecho: enunciado que puede demostrarse

fairy tale: a story that involves fantasy elements such as witches, goblins, and elves. These stories often involve princes and princesses and today are generally told to entertain children.

cuento de hadas: cuento que involucra elementos fantásticos como brujas, duendes y elfos. A menudo, estos cuentos involucran a príncipes y princesas y hoy se cuentan generalmente para entretener a los niños.

falling action: events after the climax of a story but before the resolution

acción descendente: sucesos posteriores al clímax de un cuento, pero antes de la resolución

fantasy: a story based on things that could not happen in real life

fantasía: cuento basado en cosas que no podrían ocurrir en la vida real

figurative language: imaginative language that is not meant to be interpreted literally

lenguaje figurativo: lenguaje imaginativo que no pretende ser interpretado literalmente

flashback: a sudden and vivid memory of an event in the past; also, an interruption in the sequence of events in the plot of a story to relate events that occurred in the past

narración retrospectiva: recuerdo repentino y vívido de un suceso del pasado; además, interrupción en la secuencia de los sucesos del argumento de un cuento para relatar sucesos ocurridos en el pasado

fluency: the ability to use language clearly and easily

fluidez: capacidad de usar el lenguaje fácilmente y de manera clara

folk literature: the traditional literature of a culture, consisting of a variety of myths and folk tales

literatura folclórica: literatura tradicional de una cultura, consistente en una variedad de mitos y cuentos folclóricos

folklore: the stories, traditions, sayings, and customs of a culture or a society

folclor: historias, tradiciones, dichos y costumbres de una cultura o sociedad

folk tale: an anonymous traditional story passed on orally from one generation to another

cuento folclórico: cuento tradicional anónimo pasada oralmente de generación en generación

foreshadowing: clues or hints signaling events that will occur later in the plot

presagio: claves o pistas que señalan sucesos que ocurrirán mas adelante en el argumento

formal style: academic writing that shows care and appropriate language

estilo formal: estilo académico de escritura que demuestra atención y lenguaje adecuado

found poem: verse that is created from a prose text by using the original words, phrases, images, and/or sentences, but manipulating them and reformatting them into poetic lines

poema derivado: poema creado o derivado de un texto en prosa usando palabras, frases, imágenes u oraciones originales, pero manipulándolas y reorganizándolas para formar versos poéticos

free verse: a kind of poetry that does not follow any regular pattern, rhythm, or rhyme

verso libre: tipo de poesía que no sigue ningún patrón, ritmo o rima regular

function: how something is used
función: forma en que usa algo

G

genre: a category or type of literature, such as short story, folk tale, poem, novel, play

género: categoría o tipo de literatura, como el cuento corto, cuento folclórico, poema, novela, obra teatral

global revision: the process of deeply revising a text to improve organization, development of ideas, focus, and voice

revisión global: proceso de revisar en profundidad un texto para mejorar su organización, desarrollo de ideas, enfoque y voz

graphic novel: a narrative told through visuals and captions

novela gráfica: narrativa que se cuenta por medio de efectos visuales y leyendas

H

headline: a short piece of text at the top of an article, usually in larger type, designed to be the first words the audience reads

titular: trozo corto de texto en la parte superior de un artículo, habitualmente en letra más grande, diseñado para ser las primeras palabras que el público lea

humor: the quality of being comical or amusing
humor: cualidad de ser cómico o divertido

hook: *n.* a compelling idea or statement designed to get readers' attention in an introduction

gancho: *n.* idea o afirmación atractiva diseñada para captar la atención del lector en una introducción

hyperbole: extreme exaggeration used for emphasis, often used for comic effect

hypérbole: exageración extrema usada para dar énfasis, habitualmente usada para dar efecto cómico

I

idiom: a figure of speech that cannot be defined literally

expresión idiomatica: figura del discurso que no puede definirse literalmente

image: a picture, drawing, photograph, illustration, chart, or other graphic that is designed to affect the audience in some purposeful way

imagen: pintura, dibujo, fotografía, ilustración, cuadro u otra gráfica diseñada para producir algún efecto intencional sobre el público

imagery: descriptive or figurative language used to create word pictures; imagery is created by details that appeal to one or more of the five senses

imaginería: lenguaje descriptivo o figurativo utilizado para crear imágenes verbales; la imaginería es creada por detalles que apelan a uno o más de los cinco sentidos

improvise: to respond or perform on the spur of the moment
improvisar: reaccionar o representar impulsivamente

incident: a distinct piece of action as in an episode in a story or a play. More than one incident may make up an event.
incidente: trozo de acción distintivo como un episodio de un cuento o de una obra teatral. Más de un incidente puede conformar un suceso.

inference: a logical guess or conclusion based on observation, prior experience, or textual evidence
inferencia: conjetura o conclusión lógica basada en la observación, experiencias anteriores o evidencia textual

inflection: the emphasis a speaker places on words through change in pitch or volume
inflexión: énfasis que pone un orador en las palabras por medio del cambio de tono o volumen

interpretation: a writer's or artist's representation of the meaning of a story or idea
interpretación: representación que hace un escritor o artista del significado de un cuento o idea

interview: a meeting between two people in which one, usually a reporter, asks the other questions to get that person's views on a subject
entrevista: reunión entre dos personas, en la que una, normalmente un reportero, hace preguntas a la otra para conocer sus opiniones acerca de un tema

introduction: the opening paragraph of an essay, which must get the reader's attention and indicate the topic
introducción: párrafo inicial de un ensayo, que debe captar la atención del lector e indicar el tema

irony: a literary device that exploits readers' expectations; irony occurs when what is expected turns out to be quite different from what actually happens. *Dramatic irony* is a form of irony in which the reader or audience knows more about the circumstances or future events in a story than the characters within it; *verbal irony* occurs when a speaker or narrator says one thing while meaning the opposite; *situational irony* occurs when an event contradicts the expectations of the characters or the reader.
ironía: un recurso literario que explota las expectativas de los lectores; la ironía ocurre cuando lo que se espera resulta ser muy diferente de lo que realmente ocurre. La *ironía dramática* es una forma de ironía en la que el lector o la audiencia conocen más acerca de las circunstancias o sucesos futuros de una historia que los personajes mismo; la *ironía verbal* ocurre cuando un orador o narrador dice una cosa para expresar lo contrario; la *ironía situacional* ocurre cuando un suceso contradice las expectativas de los personajes o del lector

L

legend: a traditional story believed to be based on actual people and events. Legends, which typically celebrate heroic individuals or significant achievements, tend to express the values of a culture.
leyenda: cuento tradicional que se considera basado en personas y sucesos reales. Las leyendas, que típicamente celebran a individuos heroicos o logros importantes, tienden a expresar los valores de una cultura.

limerick: a light, humorous, nonsensical verse of few lines, usually with a rhyme scheme of a-a-b-b-a
quintilla: verso liviano, humorístico, disparatado y de pocas líneas, normalmente con un esquema a-a-b-b-a

listening: the process of receiving a message and making meaning of it from verbal and nonverbal cues
escuchar: proceso de recibir el mensaje y comprender su significado a partir de claves verbales y no verbales

literary analysis: the process of examining closely and commenting on the elements of a literary work
análisis literario: proceso de examinar atentamente y comentar los elementos de una obra literaria

revisión local: revisar un texto a nivel de palabras o de oraciones
local revision: revising a text on a word or sentence level

logo: a unique design symbol used to identify a company visually
logotipo: símbolo único de diseño, utilizado para identificar visualmente una empresa

logos: a rhetorical appeal to reason or logic through statistics, facts, and reasonable examples
logos: apelación retórica a la razón o la lógica por medio de estadísticas, hechos y ejemplos razonables

J

juxtaposition: the arrangement of two or more things for the purpose of comparison
yuxtaposición: la disposición de dos o más cosas con el propósito de comparar

M

media: the various means of mass communication, such as radio, television, newspapers, and magazines
medios de comunicación: los diversos medios de comunicación masiva, como radio, televisión, periódicos y revistas

media channel: a type of media, such as television or newspaper
canal mediático: tipo de medios de comunicación, como televisión o periódicos

metaphor: a comparison between two unlike things in which one thing becomes another
metáfora: comparación entre dos cosas diferentes en la que una cosa se convierte en otra

monologue: a speech or written expression of thoughts by a character
monólogo: discurso o expresión escrita de pensamientos por parte de un personaje

mood: the overall emotional quality of a work, which is created by the author's language and tone and the subject matter
carácter: la calidad emocional general de una obra, que es creada por el lenguaje y tono del autor y por el tema

motif: a recurring element, image, or idea in a work of literature
motivo: elemento, imagen o idea recurrente en una obra literaria

multiple intelligences: the variety of learning styles that everyone has in varying degrees. In each individual, different intelligences predominate.
inteligencias múltiples: diversidad de estilos de aprendizaje que todos tienen en diversos grados. En cada individuo predominan diferentes inteligencias.

myth: a traditional story that explains the actions of gods or heroes or the origins of the elements of nature
mito: cuento tradicional que explica las acciones de dioses o héroes o los orígenes de los elementos de la naturaleza

N

narrative: a type of writing that tells a story or describes a sequence of events in an incident
narrativa: tipo de escritura que cuenta un cuento o describe una secuencia de sucesos de un incidente

narrative poem: a story told in verse
poema narrativo: historia contada en verso

negate: to deny or make ineffective
denegar: negar o anular

negation: showing what something is not in order to prove what it is
negar: demostrar lo que algo no es para comprobar lo que es

news article: an article in a news publication that objectively presents both sides of an issue
artículo noticioso: artículo de una publicación noticiosa que presenta objetivamente ambos lados de un asunto

nonprint text: a text, such as film or graphics, that communicates ideas without print
texto no impreso: texto, como una película o gráfica, que comunica ideas sin imprimir

nonverbal communication: gestures, facial expressions, and inflection that form unspoken communication
comunicación no verbal: gestos, expresiones faciales e inflexión que forman la comunicación no hablada

novel: a type of literary genre that tells a fictional story
novela: tipo de género literario que cuenta una historia ficticia

nuance: a subtle difference or distinction in meaning
matiz: una diferencia sutil o distinción en significado

O

objective: supported by facts and not influenced by personal opinion
objetivo: apoyado por hechos y no influenciado por la opinión personal

objective camera view: in film, when the camera takes a neutral point of view
visión objetiva de la cámara: en el cine, cuando la cámara toma un punto de vista neutro

omniscient: a third-person point of view in which the narrator is all-knowing
omnisciente: punto de vista de una tercera persona, en la que el narador lo sabe todo

onomatopoeia: the use of words that imitate the sounds of what they describe
onomatopeya: el uso de palabras que imitan los sonidos de lo que describen

one-liner: a short joke or witticism expressed in a single sentence.
agudeza: chiste u comentario ingenioso que se expresa en una sola oración.

opinion: a perspective that can be debated
opinión: perspectiva que es debatible

oral interpretation: reading aloud a literary text with expression
interpretación oral: leer en voz alta un texto literario con expresión

oxymoron: a figure of speech in which the words seem to contradict each other; for example, "jumbo shrimp"
oxímoron: figura del discurso en la que las palabras parecen contradecirse mutuamente; por ejemplo, "audaz cobardía"

P

pacing: the amount of time a writer gives to describing each event and developing each stage in the plot
compás: el tiempo que un escritor da para describir un suceso y desarrollar cada etapa de la trama

pantomime: a form of acting without words, in which motions, gestures, and expressions convey emotions or situations
pantomima: forma de actuación sin palabras, en la que los movimientos, gestos y expresiones transmiten emociones o situationes

paraphrase: to restate in one's own words
parafrasear: reformular en nuestras propias palabras

parody: a humorous imitation of a literary work
parodia: imitación humorística de una obra literaria

pathos: a rhetorical appeal to the reader's or listener's senses or emotions through connotative language and imagery
pathos: apelación retórica a los sentidos o emociones del lector u oyente por medio de un lenguaje connotativo y figurado

performance: presenting or staging a play
actuación: presentar o poner en escena una obra teatral

persona: the voice or character speaking or narrating a story
persona: voz o personaje que habla o narra una historia

personal letter: a written communication between friends, relatives, or acquaintances that shares news, thoughts, or feelings
carta personal: comunicación escrita entre amigos, parientes o conocidos, que comparte noticias, pensamientos o sentimientos

personal narrative: a piece of writing that describes an incident and includes a personal response to and reflection on the incident
narrativa personal: texto escrito que describe un incidente e incluye una reacción personal ante el incidente y una reflexión acerca de él

personification: a kind of metaphor that gives objects or abstract ideas human characteristics
personificación: tipo de metáfora que da características humanas a los objetos o ideas abstractas

perspective: the way a specific character views a situation or other characters
perspectiva: manera en que un personaje específico visualiza una situación o a otros personajes

persuasion: the act or skill of causing someone to do or believe something
persuasión: acto o destreza de hacer que alguien haga o crea algo

persuasive essay: an essay that attempts to convince the reader of to take an action or believe an idea
ensayo persuasivo: ensayo que intenta convencer al lector de que realice una acción o crea una idea

phrasing: dividing a speech into smaller parts, adding pauses for emphasis
frasear: dividir un discurso en partes más pequeñas, añadiendo pausas para dar énfasis

pitch: the highness or lowness of a sound, particularly the voice in speaking
tono: altura de un sonido, especialmente de la voz al hablar

plagiarism: taking and using as your own the words and ideas of another
plagio: tomar y usar como propias las palabras e ideas de otro

plot: the sequence of related events that make up a story or novel
trama: secuencia de sucesos relacionados, que conforman un cuento o novela

point of view: the perspective from which a story is told. In **first-person** point of view, the teller is a character in the story telling what he or she sees or knows. In **third-person** point of view, the narrator is someone outside of the story.
punto de vista: perspectiva desde la cual se cuenta una historia. En el punto de vista de la **primera persona**, el relator es un personaje del cuento que narra lo que ve o sabe.

En el punto de vista de la **tercera persona**, el narrador es alguien que está fuera del cuento.

prediction: a logical guess or assumption about something that has not yet happened
predicción: conjetura lógica o suposición acerca de algo que aún no ha ocurrido

presentation: delivery of a formal reading, talk, or performance
presentación: entrega de una lectura, charla o representación formal

prose: the ordinary form of written language, using sentences and paragraphs; writing that is not poetry, drama, or song
prosa: forma común del lenguaje escrito, usando oraciones y párrafos; escritura que no es poesía, drama ni canción

protagonist: the central character in a work of literature, the one who is involved in the main conflict in the plot
protagonista: personaje principal de una obra literaria, el que participa en el conflicto principal de la trama

pun: the humorous use of a word or words to suggest another word with the same sound or a different meaning
retruécano: uso humorístico de una o varias palabras para sugerir otra palabra que tiene el mismo sonido o un significado diferente

purpose: the reason for writing; what the writer hopes to accomplish
propósito: razón para escribir; lo que el escritor espera lograr

Q

quatrain: a four-line stanza in poetry
cuarteta: en poesía, estrofa de cuatro versos

R

rate: the speed at which a speaker delivers words
rapidez: velocidad a la que el orador pronuncia las palabras

reflection: a kind of thinking and writing which seriously explores the significance of an experience, idea, or observation
reflexión: tipo de pensamiento y escritura que explora seriamente la importancia de una experiencia, idea u observación

reflective essay: an essay in which the writer explores the significance of an experience or observation
ensayo reflexivo: ensayo en que el autor explora la importancia de una experiencia u observación

refrain: a regularly repeated word, phrase, line, or group of lines in a poem or song
estribillo: palabra, frase, verso o grupo de versos de un poema o canción que se repite con regularidad

repetition: the use of the same words or structure over again
repetición: uso de las mismas palabras o estructura una y otra vez

research: (*v.*) the process of locating information from a variety of sources; (*n.*) the information found from investigating a variety of sources
investigar: (*v.*) proceso de buscar información en una variedad de fuentes; *también*, **investigación** (*n.*) información que se halla al investigar una variedad de fuentes

resolution: the outcome of the conflict of a story, when loose ends are wrapped up
resolución: resultado del conflicto de un cuento, cuando se atan los cabos sueltos

résumé: a document that outlines a person's skills, education, and work history
currículum vitae: un documento que resume las destrezas, educación y experiencia laboral de una persona

revision: a process of evaluating a written piece to improve coherence and use of language; *see also*, local revision, global revision
revisión: proceso de evaluar un texto escrito para mejorar la coherencia y el uso del lenguaje; *ver también*, revisión local, revisión global

rhetorical question: a question asked to emphasize a point or create an effect; no answer is expected
pregunta retórica: pregunta que se hace para enfatizar un punto o crear un efecto; no se espera una respuesta

rhyme: the repetition of sounds at the ends of words
rima: repetición de sonidos al final de las palabras

rhyme scheme: a consistent pattern of end rhyme throughout a poem
esquema de la rima: patrón consistente de una rima final a lo largo de un poema

rhythm: the pattern of stressed and unstressed syllables in spoken or written language, especially in poetry
ritmo: patrón de sílabas acentuadas y no acentuadas en lenguaje hablado o escrito, especialmente en poesía

rising action: major events that develop the plot of a story and lead to the climax
acción ascendente: sucesos importantes que desarrollan la trama de un cuento y conducen al clímax

S

satire: a manner of writing that mixes a critical attitude with wit and humor in an effort to improve mankind and human institutions
sátira: una forma de escritura que combina una actitud crítica con ingenio y humor en un esfuerzo por mejorar la humanidad y las instituciones humanas

science fiction: a genre in which the imaginary elements of the story could be scientifically possible
ciencia ficción: género en que los elementos imaginarios del cuento podrían ser científicamente posibles

search term: a single word or short phrase used in a database search
clave de búsqueda: una palabra o frase corta que se usa para investigar en una base de datos

seminar: a small group of students engaged in intensive study
seminario: grupo pequeño de estudiantes que participan en un estudio intenso

sensory details: words or information that appeal to the five senses
detalles sensoriales: palabras o información que apelan a los cinco sentidos

sequence of events: the order in which events happen
secuencia de los sucesos: orden en que ocurren los sucesos

setting: the time and the place in which a narrative occurs
ambiente: tiempo y lugar en que ocurre un relato

short story: a work of fiction that presents a sequence of events, or plot, that deals with a conflict
cuento corto: obra de ficción que presenta una secuencia de sucesos, o trama, que tratan de un conflicto

simile: a comparison between two unlike things, using the words *like* or *as*
símil: comparación entre dos cosas diferentes usando las palabras como o *tan*

slogan: a catchphrase that evokes a particular feeling about a company and its product
eslogan: frase o consigna publicitaria que evoca un sentimiento en particular acerca de una empresa y su producto

Socratic: adjective formed from the name of the philosopher Socrates, who was famous for his question-and-answer method in his search for truth and wisdom
Socrático: adjetivo derivado del nombre del filósofo Sócrates, que es famoso por su método de preguntas y respuestas en la búsqueda de la verdad y la sabiduría.

speaker: the voice that communicates with the reader of a poem
hablante: la voz que se comunica con el lector de un poema

speaking: the process of sharing information, ideas, and emotions using verbal and nonverbal means communication
hablar: proceso de compartir información, ideas y emociones usando medios de comunicación verbales y no verbales

stanza: a group of lines, usually similar in length and pattern, that form a unit within a poem
estrofa: grupo de versos, normalmente similares en longitud y patrón, que forman una unidad dentro de un poema

stereotype: a fixed, oversimplified image of a person, group, or idea; something conforming to that image
estereotipo: imagen fija y demasiado simplificada de una persona, grupo o idea; algo que cumple esa imagen

subjective: influenced by personal opinions or ideas
subjectivo: influenciado por opiniones o ideas personales

subjective camera view: in film, when the camera seems to show the events through a character's eyes
visión subjetiva de la cámara: en el cine, cuando la cámara parece mostrar los sucesos a través de los ojos de un personaje

subplot: a secondary plot that occurs along with a main plot
trama secundaria: argumento secundario que ocurre conjuntamente con un argumento principal

summarize: to briefly restate the main ideas of a piece of writing
resumir: reformular brevemente las ideas principales de un texto escrito

symbol: an object, a person, or a place that stands for something else
símbolo: objeto, persona o lugar que representa otra cosa

symbolism: the use of symbols
simbolismo: el uso de símbolos

synonyms: words with similar meanings
sinónimos: palabras con significados semejantes

T

talking points: important points or concepts to be included in a presentation
puntos centrales: puntos o conceptos importantes a incluirse en una presentación

tall tale: a highly exaggerated and often humorous story about folk heroes in local settings
cuento increíble: cuento muy exagerado y normalmente humorístico acerca de héroes folclóricos en ambientes locales

target audience: the specific group of people that advertisers aim to persuade to buy
público objetivo: grupo específico de personas a quienes los publicistas desean persuadir de comprar

technique: a way of carrying out a particular task; for example, visual techniques are ways images can be used to convey narration
técnica: una manera de llevar a cabo una tarea en particular; por ejemplo, las técnicas visuales son formas en que las imágenes comunican narración

tempo: the speed or rate of speaking
ritmo: velocidad o rapidez al hablar

textual evidence: quotations, summaries, or paraphrases from text passages to support a position
evidencia textual: citas, resúmenes o paráfrasis de pasajes de texto para apoyar una position

theme: the central idea, message, or purpose of a literary work
tema: idea, mensaje o propósito central de una obra literaria

thesis: a sentence, in the introduction of an essay, that states the writer's position or opinion on the topic of the essay
tesis: una oración, en la introducción de un ensayo, que plantea la afirmación u opinión del escritor acerca del tema del ensayo

tone: a writer's or speaker's attitude toward a subject
tono: actitud de un escritor u orador hacia un tema

topic sentence: a sentence that states the main idea of a paragraph; in an essay, it also makes a point that supports the thesis statement
oración principal: oración que plantea la idea principal de un párrafo; en un ensayo, también plantea un punto que apoya el enunciado de tesis

transitions: words or phrases that connect ideas, details, or events in writing
transiciones: palabras o frases que conectan ideas, detalles o sucesos de un escrito

TV news story: a report on a news program about a specific event
documental de televisión: reportaje en un programa noticioso acerca de un suceso específico

U

universal: characteristic of all or the whole
universal: característico de todo o el entero

utopia: an ideal or perfect place
utopía: lugar ideal o perfecto

V

verse: a unit of poetry, such as a line or a stanza
verso: unidad de la poesía, como un verso o una estrofa

voice: a writer's distinctive use of language
voz: uso distintivo del lenguaje por parte de un escritor

voice-over: the voice of an unseen character in film expressing his or her thoughts
voz en off: voz de un personaje de una película, que no se ve pero que expresa sus pensamientos

volume: the degree of loudness of a speaker's voice or other sound
volumen: grado de intensidad sonora de la voz de un orador o de otro sonido

W

juego de palabras: intercambio verbal ingenioso u ocurrente o un juego con palabras
wordplay: a witty or clever verbal exchange or a play on words

Y

yarn: a long, often involved, story, usually telling of incredible or fantastic events; an entertaining tale; a tall tale
narración: un historia larga, en ocasiones envolvente, que usualmente cuenta sucesos increíbles o fantásticas; un historia entretenida; un cuento fantástico

Index of Skills

Literary Skills

epic, 24
  Hero's Journey, 4, 11
  illustrated, 32, 35
  nonfiction, 106, 179, 181, 196, 199
Narrative Poetry, 24
Narrative techniques, 2, 16, 24, 34, 126, 200
  description, 22, 23, 34, 54, 83, 134, 200, 216
  dialogue, 21, 22, 30, 34, 41, 54, 118, 136, 137, 200, 205, 208, 209, 216, 217, 268, 294
  humor, 264
  pacing, 10, 22, 30, 34, 54, 200
  reflection, 30, 41, 200, 333
Nonfiction, 72, 106
Novel, 35, 123, 124, 126, 130, 134, 136, 138, 297
Nuance, 62
One-liners, 318, 319
Online article, 151, 153, 160
Organization, 91, 135
Panel, 42
Persona, 272
Perspective, 126, 127, 130, 134, 137, 212, 216–219
Plot, 7, 10, 12, 123, 181, 202, 203, 204, 205, 209, 217, 219, 223, 297
  climax, 9, 10
  development of, 10
  drama, 330
  exposition, 8, 22, 23
  falling action, 9, 10
  humorous, 268, 269, 283
  main events, 34, 187, 351
  pacing, 10
  patterns of, 7
  resolution, 9, 10, 124
  rising action, 8, 10
  sequence of events, 10, 32, 181, 268
Plot diagram, 10, 32
Poetry, 7, 64, 77, 78, 81, 188, 189, 306, 309, 311, 314
  epic, 24
  found poem, 220, 221, 222
  hyperbole, 306
  imagery, 13
  narrative, 24
  plot, 312
  structure of, 14, 15, 64, 189
Point of view, 21, 22, 301
  first person, 23, 93, 200
  third-person, 23
Political cartoons, 270, 271
Prose, 220
Puns, 314, 316, 317, 318, 319
Quotations, 4–6, 125, 177, 178, 287, 305
Repetition, 282, 310

Ridicule, 288
Role, 270, 271
Sarcasm, 288
Satire, 285
Science fiction, 104, 123
Sermon, 77
Setting, 10, 11, 21, 22, 23, 123, 130, 181, 196, 202, 203, 204, 209, 217, 219, 223
  social circumstances of, 130–131
Shakespearean comedy, 329, 332
  creating context for, 329
  insulting language in, 332
  performing, 351
Short story, 16, 113, 291
Sound effect, 42
Speaker, 5, 66
Speech, 229, 233, 246
Stanza, 188
Structure, 7, 14, 15, 20, 30, 32, 40, 41, 64, 69, 79, 80, 81, 90, 105, 109, 110, 118, 130, 146, 161, 165, 166, 187, 189, 216, 217, 221, 230, 231, 235, 248, 264, 270, 275, 282, 287, 293, 294, 300, 301, 310, 312, 315, 321, 323, 341
Style, 69, 189, 277, 301
  formal, 84
  informal, 70
Symbol/symbolism, 4, 7, 130, 182, 216
Syntax, 283
Theme (universal truth), 13, 15, 64, 67, 118, 124, 125, 127, 130, 138, 184, 185–190, 189, 190, 193, 196, 202, 204, 205, 209, 212, 217, 219, 223, 258, 277, 280, 283, 303, 317, 320, 321, 324, 325, 351
Theme statement, 15, 66, 67, 223
Thought bubbles, 42
Tone, 62, 63, 181, 205–209, 229, 276, 283, 294, 296, 310, 313
  list of tone words, 63
  shifts in, 21, 64, 66, 209
Topic, 270, 271
Use of language, 32, 40, 54, 66, 69, 81, 109, 118, 187, 269, 283, 332
Utopia, 104, 112, 120, 123
Visual prompt, 1, 101, 155, 173
Wordplay, 314, 317, 318, 319, 337
Yarn (tall tale), 306, 308

Reading Skills

Analyzing the text, 4–6, 16, 24, 32, 53, 64, 77, 184, 188, 190, 232, 238, 270, 296
Annotating the text, 53, 209, 231, 232, 302, 308, 311, 314, 318, 321, 337, 339

Big ideas, 258
Close reading, 4, 112, 318, 332, 336, 343
Compare, 64, 69, 77, 82, 84, 98, 129, 188, 317
Compare and contrast, 105, 130, 189, 270
Connecting to the text, 258, 276, 329, 331
  text-to-self, 181, 223, 236, 276
  text-to text, 181, 193, 223, 276
  text-to-world, 181, 223, 276
Context, 15, 151
Context clues, 7, 13, 24, 35, 64, 67, 73, 77, 81, 89, 106, 129, 130, 145, 153, 159, 163, 165, 185, 187, 190, 205, 212, 220, 229, 234, 238, 243, 246, 259, 264, 274, 280, 285, 291, 293, 294, 297, 300, 306, 308, 311, 312, 314, 321, 334, 339
Contrast, 20
Independent reading, 11, 12
Independent Reading Link, 11, 15, 24, 61, 74, 91, 104, 125, 138, 143, 148, 155, 163, 176, 199, 205, 221, 225, 233, 240, 243, 258, 270, 284, 286, 303, 313, 328, 335, 342, 349
Independent Reading Plan, 11
Inferring, 14, 24, 40, 109, 118, 124, 134, 198, 216, 230, 277
Informational text, 64, 159, 339
  features of, 159, 242
Levels of questions, 123, 127, 181, 283
  develop, 283
  interpretive, 283
  literal, 283
  universal (thematic), 283
Marking the text, 7, 13, 15, 35, 64, 66, 72, 73, 77, 81, 86, 89, 106, 112, 129, 137, 145, 151, 153, 159, 163, 185, 187, 205, 212, 220, 222, 229, 234, 235, 238, 243, 246, 251, 252, 259, 268, 270, 274, 280, 285, 288, 291, 297, 306, 308, 311, 314, 316, 318, 321, 334, 339
Metacognitive markers, 7, 13
Note-taking, 67, 106, 131–132, 138, 190, 191, 196, 232, 236, 268, 275, 281, 287, 288, 290, 293, 300, 303, 308, 310, 315, 323, 327, 329, 330, 335, 341
Observation, 24
Paraphrase, 5, 225, 287, 335, 337
Predicting, 35, 202, 248, 258, 293
Previewing, 7, 11, 16, 35, 64, 77, 89, 106, 112, 124, 129, 145, 151, 177, 179, 180, 185, 190, 205, 212, 220, 229, 234, 238, 243, 246, 258, 259, 274, 285, 291, 297, 306, 314, 334, 339

Writing Skills

Media Skills

Language Skills

Vocabulary Skills

Index of Authors and Titles

Credits

Unit 1

From *Collected Poems*© 1929 by C.P. Cavafy. Translated © 1975 by Edmund Keeley and Philip Sherrard. Reprinted by permission of Princeton University Press.

"The Drummer Boy of Shiloh" from *Bradbury Stories: 100 of the Most Celebrated Tales* by Ray Bradbury. Copyright © 1960 by the Curtis Publishing Company, renewed 1980 by Ray Bradbury. Reprinted by permission of Don Congdon Associates, Inc.

From *The Odyssey* by Homer, translated by A. S. Kline. Reprinted by permission of A. S. Kline.

From "The Happy Medium" from *A Wrinkle in Time* © 1962 by Madeleine L'Engle and Crosswicks, Ltd. Reprinted by permission of Farrar, Straus, and Giroux, LLC and Crosswicks, Ltd. All Rights Reserved.

From A WRINKLE IN TIME: THE GRAPHIC NOVEL© 1962 by Madeleine L'Engle. Adapted and illustrated© 2012 by Hope Larson. Reprinted by permission of Farrar, Straus, and Giroux, LLC. All Rights Reserved.

"A Man" by Nina Cassian, Roy MacGregor-Hastie, translator. Reprinted by permission of Peter Owen Ltd., London.

"Soldier Home After Losing His Leg in Afghanistan," by Gale Fiege, *HeraldNet*, July 9, 2012. Reprinted by permission of The Daily Herald, Everett, WA.

"Where I Find My Heroes" by Oliver Stone as appeared in *McCall's* Magazine, November 1992. Reprinted by permission of Steven R. Pines, CPA.

"Frederick Douglass." Copyright © 1966 by Robert Hayden, from *Collected Poems of Robert Hayden* by Robert Hayden, edited by Frederick Glaysher. Used by permission of Liveright Publishing Corporation.

Unit 2

"Grant and Lee: A Study in Contrasts" by Bruce Catton, *The American Story* by Earl Schenck Miers. Copyright U.S. Capital Historical Society, all rights reserved. Reprinted by permission.

"Harrison Bergeron" from *Welcome to the Monkey House* by Kurt Vonnegut, © 1968 by Kurt Vonnegut Jr. Used by permission of Dell Publishing, an imprint of Random House, a division of Random House LLC. All rights reserved. Any third party use of this material, outside of this publication, is prohibited. Interested parties must apply directly to Random House LLC for permission.

"Banned Books Week: Celebrating the Freedom to Read" from American Library Association. Copyright © 2012.

"Private Eyes" by Brooke Chorlton. Used by permssion.

"Parents Share Son's Fatal Text Message to Warn Against Texting & Driving" by Jason Howerton, The Associated Press, April 11, 2013. Used with permission of The Associated Press. Copyright © 2014. All rights reserved.

"The Science Behind Distracted Driving," KUTV Channel 2, June 28, 2013, http://www.kutv.com/news. Reprinted by permission of KUTV Channel 2.

"How the Brain Reacts" by Marcel Just and Tim Keller as part of "Should Cellphone Use by Drivers be Illegal" by The Editors, *The New York Times*, July 18, 2009, http://roomfordebate.blogs.nytimes.com. Reprinted by permission of Marcel Just.

Brain images from "How the Brain Reacts" by Marcel Just and Tim Keller as part of "Should Cellphone Use by Drivers be Illegal" by The Editors, *The New York Times*, July 18, 2009, http://roomfordebate.blogs.nytimes.com. Reprinted by permission of Marcel Just.

"Cellphones and Driving: As Dangerous As We Think?" by Matthew Walburg, *Chicago Tribune*, www.chicagotribune.com, March 26, 2012. © 2012 Chicago Tribune. All rights reserved. Used by permission and protected by the Copyright Laws of the United States. The printing, copying, redistribution, or retransmission of this content without express written permission is prohibited.

Unit 3

Excerpt from *Night* by Elie Wiesel, translated by Marion Wiesel. Translation copyright © 2006 by Marion Wiesel. Reprinted by permission of Hill and Wang, a division of Farrar, Straus and Giroux, LLC.

From *The Diary of Anne Frank* by Frances Goodrich and Albert Hackett. Copyright © 1956, renewed by Albert Hackett, David Huntoon & Frances Neuwirth in 1986. Used by permission of Flora Roberts, Inc.

From "Chapter Twelve: Shmuel Thinks of an Answer to Bruno's Question" from *The Boy in the Striped Pajamas* by John Boyne, copyright © 2006 by John Boyne. Used by permission of David Fickling Books, an imprint of

Unit 4

Image Credits